THE AUTHOR'S PREFACE.

———●———

THE history of the Jews since their dispersion has been but little investigated even by the literary part of the world, and is almost entirely unknown to the general mass of mankind. The design of this work, including the introduction, is to give a brief sketch of their situation, after their return from the Babylonian captivity, to the nineteenth century. The compiler is sensible, that the subject is not calculated to engage the attention of those readers whose object is merely amusement. [Instead of a narration of new and entertaining events, they will find a tedious succession of oppressions and persecutions, and probably turn with disgust from the gloomy picture of human guilt and wretchedness.]

To the speculative and inquisitive part of mankind, the subject must, however, appear more interesting. The history of the Jews is remarkable above that of all other nations, for the number and cruelty of the persecutions they have endured. They are venerable for the antiquity of their origin. They are discriminated from the rest of mankind by their wonderful destination; peculiar habits, and

religious rites. Since the destruction of Jerusalem,
and their universal dispersion, we contemplate the
singular phenomenon of a nation subsisting for
ages without its civil and religious polity, and thus
surviving its political existence.

But the Jews appear in a far more interesting
and important light when considered as a standing
monument of the truth of the Christian religion;
as the ancient church of God to whom were
committed the sacred oracles; as a people selected
from all nations to make known and preserve the
knowledge of the true God. To them the Gospel
was first preached, and from them the first Christian church in Jerusalem was collected. 'To them
we are indebted for, the scriptures of the New,
as well as of the Old Testament., To them were
given the spirit of prophecy, and power of
working miracles. From them were derived an
illustrious train of prophets and apostles. To
use the language of an inspired writer, "To
them pertaineth the adoption, and the glory, the
service of God, and the promises; and of them,
as concerning the flesh, Christ came."

The history of the Jews by Mr. Basnage, a
learned French refugee, who was pastor of the
Walloon church at the Hague, and died in 1723,
is the principal authority made use of in the first

part of this history; the references are made to
the translation of Mr. Taylor, published in 1708,
which received the approbation of the author.
The compiler is greatly indebted to the writings
of M. Gregoire, formerly bishop of Blois, senator,
member of the National Institute, &c. &c. His
excellent " Essay on the Reformation of the Jews"
has afforded much important information respecting
this extraordinary people. His late valuable work,
entitled " Histoire des Sectes Religieuses," published at Paris, 1810, besides interesting and entertaining accounts of the various denominations
of Christians, contains several curious articles respecting the Jews. The works of David Levi
have furnished materials for what is said of the
religious tenets and ceremonies of his brethren.
Occasional assistance has been given by modern
travellers, whom curiosity has induced to investigate
the present condition of this singular people. The
learned Dr. Buchanan, in his valuable works,
particularly his " Researches in Asia," has furnished authentic documents respecting the state
of the eastern Jews. Some recent intelligence
concerning those in Europe has been collected from
a late work of Mr. Adam, entitled; " The Religious World Displayed, published 1809. The
respectable author observes in his preface, that
" he was indebted for particulars respecting them
to Joshua Van Oven, a learned, distinguished, and

worthy member of the society of German Jews."
Various other authors will be found referred to in
the history ; but the above mentioned have furnished the principal materials for the work.

To the intelligent and well informed the difficulty
of collecting the history of a people so little known,
particularly in this country, during the last and
present century, wholly from desultory and un-
connected materials, will appear obvious. The
compiler can only say, that however deficient and
ill arranged her history may be, she has spared
no exertions in her power to collect authentic documents, and has used them to the best of her
ability. But while she relies on the candour and
indulgence of the public, she cannot forbear to
express the warmest gratitude to those respectable
gentlemen whose generous patronage has enabled
her to devote her time to literary pursuits.

INTRODUCTION.

SECTION I.

Of the state of the Jews under the Persian monarchy; and the change which took place after the Babylonish captivity.

B. C. 536.] THE Jews * having remained in captivity seventy years, according to the prediction of the prophet Jeremiah,† were restored to their native country by Cyrus the Great, king of Persia. For this purpose he issued a decree, in the first year of his reign, by which they were permitted to return to Palestine, and rebuild their city and temple. This opportunity was joyfully embraced by the most zealous of the tribes of Judah, Benja-

---

* So denominated from the name Judah, as this tribe obtained the pre-eminence, and was more numerous than that of Benjamin. All the descendants of Jacob were anciently called Israel, or children of Israel, till the time that ten of the tribes revolted from the house of David: (See 1st. of Kings.) These ten tribes were afterwards called the *house* of *Israel*, and the other two tribes, of Judah and Benjamin, the *house* of *Judah*. From time to time many of the house of Israel joined that of Judah for the enjoyment of religious privileges : (1 Chron. ix. 3.) became incorporated with them, and were with them carried captive to Babylon. Many of these embraced the opportunity of returning to Judea after the captivity ; for the decrees of the Persian kings extended to all the house of Israel. The people of Judah and Israel, after their return, were blended together under the name of *Jews.—Prideaux's Connection*, vol. i. p. 190—210.

† Chap. xxv. 11. "And these nations shall serve the king of "Babylon seventy years."

min; and Levi. A large part of the Jewish captives, who chose to remain in Babylon, made liberal
contributions towards assisting their brethren.*

B. C. 534.] Soon after the return of the Jews,
they began with alacrity and zeal to rebuild their
altar, and laid the foundation of their temple.
While they were engaged in this important undertaking, the Samaritans † expressed an earnest
desire to assist in the completion of the building.
But as they blended the worship of their false
deities with that of the God of Israel, the Jews
rejected their request, alleging that, as the decree
of the Persian monarch extended only to the house
of Israel, they could not admit them to participate
in the work. This refusal gave rise to that implacable enmity which subsisted between the Samaritans and Jews;‡ and induced the former to exert

* Ezra i 6.

† The Samaritans were originally heathen colonies from different
countries. 'After the king of Assyria had taken Samaria, the capital
of the ten tribes, he removed the greatest part of the Israelites into
Babylon and Assyria. And in order to re-people the desolate country,
he brought colonies from Babylon, Cutha, Ava, Hamath, and Se-
pharvaim, and established them in the cities of Samaria instead of
those whom he had carried into captivity. These people being immediately after their settlement much infested with lions, attributed
this calamity to their neglect of the tutelary deity of this country,
and petitioned the king to send one of the captive Jewish priests to
instruct them how to worship the God of Israel. A priest was accordingly sent back, who took up his residence at Bethel, and established the worship of the true God. Yet while Jehovah was feared
because of his supposed influence in that land, the gods of the Baby-
lonians and other countries had divine honours paid to them. This
mixture of idolatry with the Mosaic worship continued till the building of the Samaritan temple on Mount Gerizzim.—*Fleury's Ancient
Israelites*, p. 352.

‡ John iv. 9.

themselves, to obstruct the building of the temple. In consequence of, their malicious attempts, the election of the sacred edifice was suspended, till Darius issued an edict which, not only ratified, the grants of Cyrus, but denounced a severe penalty against all who obstructed the work... When this important decree was communicated to the Jews, they rapidly proceeded in the building, which was finished in the sixth year of Darius, and the dedication performed in the month Adar with all imaginable splendour and solemnity.*,

B. C. 349.] . The history of the Old Testament closes with an account of the restoration of the Jews to Palestine, and the building of their city and temple under Ezra the priest, and Nehemiah the governor. The assiduous labours of these pious and eminent men to reform the abuses of the Jewish state and church, to enforce the observance of the Mosaic law, and restore divine worship to its original purity, are recorded in the books of Ezra and Nehemiah.

It appears from the sacred records, that the Jews, after their return from captivity, were in a feeble state under the first Persian monarchs. They were exposed to the envy and malice of those strangers who resided in the vicinity, in particular to the insults and calumnies of the Samaritans. It is also evident from the cruel edict which Haman obtained against them, from which they were saved by the powerful intercession of queen Esther, that they were in danger of being destroyed upon the least intimation of the king's pleasure. By degrees, how-

---

* Ezra vi. 16, 17.

ever, their affairs were established, and though they
were subjected to an easy tribute, they lived under
their own laws, in the form of a commonwealth,
governed by the high-priest, and the council of
seventy-two elders; and exercised among themselves the power of life and death.* Jerusalem
being at length rebuilt, fortified, and repeopled,
began to resume some appearance of its former
splendour, and the temple was honoured by the
offerings of strangers.†

After the death of Nehemiah, the government of
Judea appears to have been joined to the prefecture
of Syria, from which the high priests received their
authority.‡ This circumstance induced many persons to aspire to that high office merely through
ambition and avarice, who were destitute of zeal

---

* The grand council of the nation called the Sanhedrim, which
assembled in an apartment of the temple at Jerusalem, possessed the
power of life and death. The Jews styled it a hedge to the laws,
because the members of the council had authority to interpret it at
certain times and on certain occasions, as they thought proper. Its
authority extended over all the synagogues in Judea and remote
countries, and no appeal could be made from its sentence. Whether
this consistory of seventy elders was a perpetual, or only a temporary
institution, is a subject of dispute. The Jews, and after them Grotius, Selden, Lightfoot, and several other learned Christians, maintain
that it was first instituted by Moses; that the seventy-two elders
appointed to assist him were its first members; and that the Sanhedrim, so famous in the latter ages of Jewish polity, subsisted after
his time until the destruction of the temple. But Basnage and others
have attempted to prove that the court of the Sanhedrim was first
established in the time of the Maccabees.—*Basnage*, p. 400. *Jennings' Jewish Antiquities*, vol. i. p. 39.

† Fleury's Ancient Israelites.

‡ The candidates purchased this office from the Syrian governor,
and retained it by means of money; hence they oppressed the people
with taxes to enable them to fulfil their pecuniary engagements.

for religion, or love for their country.., For whole
centuries, the office of high priest, being the chief
object of men's ambition, the violent contests for
the sacerdotal dignity, and the arbitrary conduct of
those who obtained it, involved the Jewish nation
in various calamities.

B. C. 373.] A remarkable instance of the truth
of this assertion occurred in the 34th year of Artaxerxes Mnemon; at which period Joiada was
succeeded in the high priesthood by his son Johanan.
Some time after his investiture he received a visit
from his brother Joshua, who asserted that Bagoses,
the governor of Syria, had promised to transfer the
sacred dignity to him. A dispute immediately
ensued, and Joshua was slain in the interior court
of the temple. Bagoses receiving intelligence of
this event, severely upbraided the Jews with defiling
the habitation of their God, and imposed a heavy
fine upon the pontiff, which was not taken off till
the death of Artaxerxes changed the face of affairs.
The Jews were, however, by no means free from,
trouble in the reign of his successor; for Ochus
having subdued the greatest part of Phœnicia, carried his victorious arms into Judea; reduced Jericho, and sent a great number of the inhabitants
into captivity. Ten years after this event Johanan
died, and was succeeded by his son Jaddua.*

After the Babylonish captivity the Jews retained
a constant aversion to idolatry, which they justly
supposed was the principal cause of their expulsion
from their native land.

* Prideaux's Connection, vol. ii. p. 658.

It has been assigned as a reason for this change, that previous to the captivity they had no synagogues * for public instruction, nor places for religious worship, except the temple and the cities of the Levites. In consequence of which the divine laws were neglected, and forgotten, and they were easily allured into the superstitious practices of their idolatrous neighbours. But after their return, they had synagogues erected among them in every city, which were opened, not for ceremonial worship, as sacrificing, for this was confined to the temple; but for praying, preaching, reading the law,† divine worship and social duties. The people repaired to the synagogue morning and evening for prayer, and on sabbaths and festivals the law was read and expounded to them. The custom of reading the scriptures and preaching in the synagogues is supposed to have been introduced by Ezra.‡

* Dr. Prideaux and other learned writers have maintained that there were not any synagogues before the captivity, as there is no mention of them in the Old Testament, but after that period their number was very great. They were places of prayer and religious assemblies for the worship of God. The times of the synagogue service were three days every week besides fasts and festivals. The Jews also attended prayers three times every day, in the morning, afternoon, and at night. At the east end in every synagogue is an ark or chest, in commemoration of the ark of the covenant which was in the temple; and in this ark they lock up the Pentateuch, written upon vellum with a particular ink —See *Prideaux's Connection*, vol. ii. p. 534, 535, and *Picart's Religious Ceremonies of the Jews*.

† The mode of worship adopted in the Jewish synagogues subsequent to the captivity, differed but little from the present worship of Christian assemblies; for it consisted of three parts, reading the scriptures, prayer, and preaching —*Graves's Lectures on the Pentateuch*. Published 1807.

‡ We have a short but beautiful description of Ezra's first preach-

The reformation, begun by Ezra and others, at length degenerated into formality and superstition,; and when the Jews first deviated from the purity of their morals, and the simplicity of their religious worship, their zeal for the rites, and ceremonies of, their law increased. It is supposed the lamentable change became more general after miracles and prophecies ceased,* which had in some measure prevented them from taking the shadow for the substance of religion.†

It is evident, that soon after the termination of the prophetic age,‡ the Jews began to corrupt the law of Moses, by introducing certain precepts and institutions which they professed to have received by oral tradition from the most ancient time. This traditionary law, which chiefly respected religious ceremonies, fastings, and other practices distinct from the moral duties of life, at length obtained with the greater part of the Jewish nation a degree of authority equal to that of the Mosaic law; whilst the minor part, rejecting these innovations, adhered strictly to the institutions of their sacred oracles. These two general classes, which do not appear to have been distinguished by any peculiar appellation, gradually adopted other tenets and customs, and at length formed several distinct sects, of which the principal were the Sadducees, the Caraites, the

---

ing in Nehemiah viii. The Jews had liturgies for their prayers, in which are all the prescribed forms of their synagogue worship.— *Prideaux's Connection*, vol. ii. p 537.

* From the time of Malachi, the Jews had not been favoured with any prophet He flourished about the year 397 before Christ.

† Picart's Ceremonies and Religious Customs of the Jews.

‡ Enfield's Philosophy, vol. ii. p. 171.

Pharisees; and the Essenes.* . These denominations were formed at different periods after the
spirit of prophecy ceased from Israel, and were in
a flourishing state at the time of our Saviour's
appearance upon earth.

SECTION II.

*Sketch of the History of the Jews under Alexander and
his Successors to the Revolt of Mattathias.*

B. C. 330.] A GREAT event, foretold in the prophetic pages † at length arrived, when the mighty
empire of Persia was subdued by Alexander the
Great, 208 years after the overthrow of the Babylonian empire by Cyrus. The Jews gave a striking
proof of their fidelity to Darius Codomanus, the
last Persian monarch; by refusing to assist Alexander in the siege of Tyre. The Macedonian
hero, exasperated at this refusal, after the conquest
of that city led his victorious army against Jerusalem.‡

At this alarming crisis, Jaddua, the high priest,
offered sacrifices and supplications to the God of
Israel, and being, as it is said, directed by a vision
in the night, went forth the following day to meet
the conqueror, dressed in his pontifical robes, attended by the priests in sacerdotal vestments, and
the people in white garments. Alexander, struck
with profound awe at the sight of this solemn procession, bowed himself down before the high priest,

---

* See an account of these sects in Section V.
† Dan. ii. 39.　　　　‡ Josephus's Jewish Antiquities.

and adored the name of Jehovah, inscribed on his mitre. In reply to those who expressed their asto-nishment, that the victorious monarch of so many nations should pay homage to a Jewish priest, he declared, that during his abode in Macedonia, he had seen this pontiff in a vision, encouraging him to pursue the war against the Persians, and promising him complete victory. He was therefore convinced that he had engaged in this expedition under the conduct of God, whom he worshipped in the person of his high priest. The king then entered Jerusalem in the midst of the procession, and of-fered sacrifices in the temple, where Jaddua shewed him the prophecy of Daniel, that a Grecian king should overturn the Persian empire. This predic-tion heightened his confidence of success.[*]

Alexander, after this event, highly favoured the Jewish nation by exempting them from paying the tribute on the seventh, or sabbatical year; permit-ting them to live under their own laws, and enjoy the free exercise of their religion. He transplanted many of them into a new city which he built in Egypt, and called Alexandria, after his own name, granting them privileges and immunities equal to those enjoyed by his Macedonian subjects.[†]

B. C. 333.] Upon the extinction of the Persian monarchy, in consequence of Alexander's[‡] con-

---

[*] Such is the account given by Josephus and some other histo-rians.—*Josephus's History of the Jews*, and *Rollin's Ancient History*.

[†] Prideaux's Connection, p. 696, 697. Fleury's Ancient Israel-ites, p. 235.

[‡] After the conquests of Alexander a distinction is made of the *Hellenist* Jews. This name was given them because they mingled with the Greeks and spoke their language. They read the Scriptures

quests, the Samaritans endeavoured to accomplish. a civil and ecclesiastical union with the Jews. For this purpose Sanballat, governor of Samaria, gave his daughter in marriage to Manasses, the brother of Jaddua the high priest, fully expecting that the succession in the priesthood would devolve upon Manasses, and that by this means a coalition might be effected. Sanballat upon finding that the Jews, particularly the members of the Sanhedrim, highly resented this profane alliance, took his son-in-law under his protection, and having obtained permission from Alexander to build a temple on mount Gerizzim, appointed Manasses its high priest. A powerful body of priests and Israelites, who had been involved in similar connections, joined the Samaritans.* The erection of the temple highly exasperated the Jews; the violent animosity between the parties increased, and gave rise to frequent hostilities.†

B. C. 324.] After the death of Alexander, the Macedonian empire was divided among four of his generals; and Judea being situated between Egypt and Syria, became subject to all the revolutions and wars in which his successors were engaged against each other. It was at first governed by Laomedon, the Mitylenian, one of Alexander's captains, and after he was defeated by Ptolemy Soter, king of

in Greek also, after the Septuagint Version had been prepared, by order of Ptolemy Philadelphus, king of Egypt —*Basnage*, p. 527.

* It is supposed, that when Manasses fled to the Samaritans, he first brought the law of Moses among them; and after they received it they renounced idolatry, and worshipped the true God.—*Prideaux's Connection*, vol. ii. p. 598.

† Josephus, p. 284. Enfield's Philosophy.

Egypt, the Jews refused to violate their engagements to him. Enraged at their resistance, Ptolemy marched to Jerusalem; and being apprized of the religious veneration of the Jews for the Sabbath, fraudulently surprised and took the city on that day, and carried a hundred thousand of the inhabitants captive into Egypt. However, in consideration of the loyalty they had on various occasions evinced to former conquerors, he advanced the most distinguished persons among them to places of trust in the military department; and eventually confirmed all the privileges which Alexander had formerly bestowed upon their nation. Ptolemy settled some of the captives in Lybia and Cyrene; from those who were established in the latter of these countries descended the Cyrenian Jews, mentioned by the writers of the New Testament.* *

Soon after the recovery of Judea by Ptolemy, Simon, the Jewish high priest, died in the ninth year of his pontificate. The character given of him in Ecclesiasticus † evinces his distinguished merit; and the piety and integrity which uniformly marked his conduct, induced his cotemporaries to honour him with the surname of *Just*. He exhibited an ardent love of his country by repairing and fortifying the city and temple; and is said to have rendered the most essential service to religion by completing the canon of the Old Testament. This celebrated pontiff was the last member of the grand synagogue ‡

* Prideaux's Connection, vol. ii. p. 150. Encyclopedia, vol. ix.
† Ecclesiasticus, chap. i.
‡ The grand synagogue consisted of 120 elders who, in a regular

On the decease of Ptolemy Soter, his successor
Philadelphus confirmed and enlarged the privileges
of the Jews. He established many of that nation
in his dominions, ransomed those who had been
carried captive into Egypt, and caused a copy of
their sacred books to be translated into the Greek
language,* and deposited in his famous library at
Alexandria. By means of the translation, which
was styled the Septuagint version,† the Jewish religion was made known among the Gentiles, so that
the temple was enriched with magnificent presents
from the neighbouring monarchs.

The Jews also obtained distinguished favours
from Seleucus Nicator, king of Macedon and Syria,
who admitted them into all the cities which he had
built in Lesser Asia, and allowed them the same
privileges with his Grecian and Macedonian subjects.‡

The Jewish affairs continued to wear a favour-

succession after the expiration of the Babylonish captivity, laboured
assiduously in restoring the Jewish church and state; and exerted
themselves to diffuse an accurate knowledge of the Holy Scriptures
among their brethren.—*Sacred Mirror.*

* This translation is frequently quoted by the sacred writers of the
New Testament.—*Butler's Horæ Biblicæ.*

† A late author observes that, with respect to the history of the
Septuagint, there scarcely is a subject of literature upon which more
has been written, or of which less with any degree of certainty is
known. The popular account of its being made in the reign of
Ptolemy Philadelphus, at the suggestion of Aristeas, and under the
direction of Demetrius Phalerus, by seventy or seventy-two Jews
shut up in cells, appears to be generally exploded. The prevailing
opinion is, that it was made at Alexandria at different times, and by
different interpreters, but that all of them were Jews.—*Butler's
Horæ Biblicæ,* p. 18, and also *Prideaux's Connection,* vol. iii. p. 29—52.

‡ Fleury's Ancient Israelites, p. 235.

able aspect till in the reign of Ptolemy Philopator they were greatly oppressed by the incursion of the Samaritans. At the same time Antiochus the Great, king of Syria, made a vigorous effort to conquer Judea. He was however defeated by the Egyptian monarch, who soon after visited Jerusalem, and offered sacrifices to the God of Israel for his recent victory. Stimulated by an extreme curiosity to view the interior part of the temple, in spite of the remonstrances of the priests and the lamentations of the people, he forced his way through the two outer courts; but it is related, that on his attempting to penetrate into the most holy place he was struck with inexpressible terror, and was obliged to be carried out by his attendants. Instead however of being humbled by this judgment, he was exasperated against the Jews; and on his return to Egypt raised a persecution against those in that kingdom, deprived them of their privileges, ordered them to be enrolled among the lowest order of Egyptians, and sentenced many to slavery and death. He was afterwards however induced to revoke his sanguinary decrees.*

B. C. 212.] After the death of Ptolemy Philopator, Antiochus the Great invaded Cælosyria and

---

* It is said, that the king had resolved to destroy the whole nation, beginning with those who resided in Egypt, whom he ordered to be brought in chains to Alexandria to be killed by his elephants. As this was to be done publicly, a vast concourse of people were collected together to behold the horrid exhibition, when to their great surprise, the elephants having been made drunk with wine and frankincense, turned all their rage upon the spectators, and destroyed great numbers of them, while the Jews remained in perfect safety. The king relented, and restored this persecuted people to their former privileges.—*Prideaux's Connection,* vol. iii. p. 118.

Palestine, and soon made an entire conquest of these provinces. The Jews renounced their allegiance to Egypt, placed themselves under his protection, and offered him their assistance. The Syrian monarch, highly gratified by the fidelity and zeal they exhibited in his service, restored to Jerusalem its ancient privileges ; gave a large sum out of his own treasury for repairing the temple; and maintaining public worship ;' granted an exemption from all taxes for three years to all the dispersed Jews who should return to their capital, and liberated all who had been sold for slaves in any part of his dominions.*

B. C. 176.] Upon the decease of Antiochus, his son and successor Seleucus continued to the Jews the enjoyment of their civil and religious privileges, and the expenses of their sacrifices were defrayed out of the royal treasury. Their prosperity was, however, disturbed by an unhappy altercation between Onias the high priest, and Simon the governor of the temple. The latter, actuated by a principle of revenge, gave such an exaggerated account of the treasures in the temple, that Seleucus determined to appropriate part of them to his own use, and commanded Heliodorus, his treasurer, to convey them to Antioch. Upon his arrival at Jerusalem, Onias endeavoured to dissuade him from his purpose, assuring him that these treasures were appropriated to the use of the widows and orphans in the Jewish community. Heliodorus, however, still persisted to execute his commission.

---

† Prideaux's Connection, vol. ii. p. 128.

But while the priests and people united in ardent
supplication to the God of Israel to preserve the
sanctuary, he was suddenly struck, according to the
book of Maccabees, with inexpressible terror by an
awful vision, and soon after quitted the city, which
he acknowledged was under the protection of a
divine and irresistible power. Simon, enraged at
the defeat of his malicious designs, accused Onias of
having invited the king's treasurer to Jerusalem.
But the high priest justified his conduct to his royal
master; and at length procured the banishment of
the treacherous governor.*

B. C. 173.] Soon after Antiochus Epiphanes
assumed the Syrian diadem, Jason, brother to
Onias, went to Antioch and purchased the high
priesthood for three hundred and sixty talents †. He
also obtained an order that the present pontiff, who
was a man of exemplary piety and justice, should be
sent to that metropolis, and there confined for life.
This impious priest subverted the religion of his
ancestors, by procuring a grant for erecting a *Gym-
nasium*, or place of exercise, at Jerusalem, similar
to those which were built in the Grecian cities; and
encouraged the people by rewards, precepts, and
example, to adopt the superstition of their idolatrous
conquerors. From this time, therefore, a general
apostacy took place, and the service of the temple
was neglected.‡

After Jason had enjoyed his ill-acquired dignity
for a few years, he was supplanted by his brother

* Josephus, p. 303. 2 Maccabees iii. Prideaux's Connection.
† About ninety thousand pounds sterling.
‡ Josephus, p. 304. 2 Maccabees.

Menelaus, whose impiety, if possible, exceeded
that of his predecessor. After he had obtained the
high priesthood by offering the additional price of
three hundred talents, he ordered the sacred vessels
to be sold to pay the stipulated sum, and bribe the
courtiers in his favour. He also caused Onias, who
had reproved him for his impious sacrilege, to be
put to death. He was indefatigable in his exertions to destroy the Jewish religion; engaged that
himself and his party should wholly conform to the
Greeks; drove Jason from Jerusalem, and by his
tyranny and extortion caused an insurrection in that
city.*

B. C. 166.] In the mean time Antiochus was
prosecuting the war in Egypt, and on a false report
of his death, Jason marched to Jerusalem at the
head of a thousand men, and severely chastised the
adherents of Menelaus. But the approach of the
Syrian monarch compelled him to elude his vengeance by flight; and at length he died in exile
universally hated and despised. Antiochus, exasperated at the supposed revolt, and the rejoicings
upon the report of his death, abandoned Jerusalem
for three days to the fury of the Syrian army.
Forty thousand persons were slain, and nearly an
equal number sold for slaves. The impious monarch, conducted by the traitor Menelaus, forced
his way into the temple, and even penetrated into
the most holy place; tore off the golden ornaments,
carried away the sacred treasures and utensils; and
in order to offer the greatest insult to the Jewish

---

* Josephus, p. 303. Prideaux's Connection, vol. ii. p. 175, 176.

religion, sacrificed a large hog on the altar of burnt offering.* After the capital was drained of treasure, and filled with blood, the tyrant appointed a barbarous Phrygian, named Philip, governor of Jerusalem, established the apostate Menelaus† in the high priesthood; and returned in triumph to Antioch.

B. C. 168.] About two years after this terrible event, Antiochus despatched Appollonius, governor of Syria, at the head of twenty-two thousand men; commanding him to destroy Jerusalem, massacre the men, and sell the women and children for slaves. The king's officer concealed his intentions till the first sabbath after his arrival; and while the people were assembled for the solemn worship of God, he executed his horrid commands with unrelenting barbarity. Every part of the city was then plundered, set on fire, and the walls demolished. The temple was indeed permitted to stand, but its service was totally abandoned; for the Syrian troops built a fortress opposite to the sacred edifice, in order to overlook and assault all who came to worship the God of Israel.‡

The impious monarch, not yet satiated with the blood of the Jews, resolved totally to abolish their religion, or extirpate their whole people. He therefore issued a decree, that all the nations within his dominions should forsake their old religion and

---

* Josephus.

† The temporal authority, which was united with the pontifical, made the office of high priest appear of such value to Menelaus and Jason.—*Prideaux*, vol. ii. p. 168.

‡ Rollin's Ancient History, vol. viii. p. 390.

gods, and worship those of the king, under the
severest penalties. To enforce obedience to his
orders, he placed overseers in every province, and
being apprized that the Jews were the only persons
who would presume to disobey his commands, strict
injunctions were given to have them treated with
the utmost severity. Atheneas, an aged and cruel
man, well versed in all the rites of Grecian idolatry,
being sent into Judea, dedicated the temple of
Jehovah to Jupiter Olympus,* and set up his
statue on the altar of burnt-offering. All who
refused to offer their adorations before the idol,
were either massacred, or compelled to endure the
most exquisite tortures. At the same time, altars,
groves, and statues were established not only in
Judea, but in all the parts of the Syrian empire;
and all who professed the religion of Moses, were
obliged to worship them under the same penalties.
The king also promulgated an edict, making it
instant death to offer sacrifices to the God of
Israel, to observe the sabbath, practise circumcision,
or any of the Mosaic institutions. In short, an
energetic attempt was made to destroy every copy of
the law, which the king commanded to be delivered
up under penalty of death, while he strenuously endeavoured to exterminate every faithful worshipper
of God.†

At this distressing period, multitudes quitted their

---

* At this time the Samaritans presented a petition to the king, in
which they declared themselves not to be Jews, and requested that
their temple on Mount Gerizzim might be dedicated to the Grecian
Jupiter, and called after his name.—*Rollin's Ancient History.*

† Prideaux, vol. ii. p 184, 187.

habitations, and retreated to caves among the rocks, where they subsisted on herbs and roots. A large number apostatized; yet the ministers of cruelty were frequently baffled by the intrepid firmness of their victims. The king, exasperated at their boldness in defying his edicts and punishments, resolved to visit Jerusalem in order to enforce the execution of his sanguinary decrees. When the tyrant arrived, he had recourse to the stake and the rack; and commanded and superintended the most horrid executions.* The unshaken constancy of the sufferers filled him with rage and astonishment; while their triumphant deaths strengthened the faith and courage of their brethren.

Though the persecution under Antiochus was the greatest the Jews had ever suffered, they had hitherto endured the horrid cruelties of the tyrant without resistance. But at length men eminently distinguished for valour armed themselves in defence of their religion and laws; and while they fought under the banner of the God of Israel, they were enabled to effect the destruction of their idolatrous enemies, the deliverance of their nation, and the restoration of the true worship.

---

* The venerable Eleazar and the seven brethren, with their pious mother, were at this time put to a most cruel death —2 *Maccabees* vi. vii.

SECTION III.

Sketch of the history of the Jews under the Asmonean family.

MATTATHIAS, an eminent priest of the Asmonean family,* lamented with deep anguish and regret the wretched situation of his country, and had for some time retired to Modin, his native place, in order to avoid the persecution which raged in Jerusalem. Apelles, one of the officers of Antiochus, was sent to that city to establish the heathen worship. After assembling the people, he endeavoured to persuade that venerable priest to set an example of compliance with the king's edict, by insinuating compliments, magnificent promises, and by stating the number who had apostatized. Mattathias boldly replied in the hearing of the multitude, "that though all the Jews, and all the nations on earth, should conform to the king's decree, he and his sons would continue faithful to the law of their God, and that no consideration should ever induce them to abandon the religion of their ancestors." Immediately after, he killed one of his countrymen who offered sacrifices on the altar of Modin. Upon being joined by his sons, and some others, he executed the same summary vengeance on the king's officer and his attendants ;† and hastily passing

* He was the great grandson of Asmoneus, from whom the family derived their name —*Prideaux's Connection*, vol. II. p. 187.

† Mattathias's conduct was conformable to the law of Moses in such cases. See Deuteronomy xiii.

about the city, exhorted all who were zealous for
the law of God to follow him.·

Animated by the example of Mattathias and his
pious family, large numbers of Jews being determined to make vigorous exertions for the recovery
of their civil and religious privileges, followed their
venerable leader into the desarts of Judea.* They
were soon pursued by the royal army ; and being
attacked on the sabbath, many perished without
offering to make the least resistance. Their leaders
were hence induced to pass a decree for defending
themselves for the future on that holy day; which
being ratified by the priests and elders, was privately
communicated to Palestine and the adjacent villages.†

B. C. 167.] The party of Mattathias being strongly
reinforced, furiously attacked the Syrians and apostate
Jews, destroying many, and compelling others to
seek refuge in foreign countries. After having struck
their enemies with terror, the conquerors marched
from city to city, overturning the heathen altars,
demolishing the graven images, opening the Jewish
synagogues, and enforcing the practice of circumcision. They also assiduously employed themselves
in searching for and transcribing the sacred books,
and causing the reading of the scriptures to be
resumed. Their heroic exertions were crowned
with such remarkable success, that in the short
space of one year, a happy reformation had begun
to extend over a large part of Judea, when death arrested Mattathias in his glorious progress. In his

* Whiston's Josephus, vol. iii. p. 46.   † Ibid.

last moments he exhorted his sons, in the most fervent and affectionate 'manner, to emulate their pious ancestors, and hazard their lives in defence of the religion and laws of their country.* .

' B. C. 166.] Judas, surnamed Maccabeus,† his eldest son and successor, is said to have been the greatest uninspired hero of whom the Jews can boast ‡ With his small army, which at first only consisted of six thousand men, he soon made himself master of some of the strongest fortresses in Judea; became terrible to the Syrians and Samaritans; compelled the apostate Jews to retire in confusion, while the pious emigrants returned and enlisted under his banners. The Syrian monarch, and the governors of the provinces, exerted themselves to the utmost to crush this dangerous revolt in its infancy. For this purpose they repeatedly sent formidable armies against Judas, commanded by officers of consummate valour. The Maccabean hero, animated by religious confidence in God, was not alarmed by the vast superiority of numbers on

* 1 Maccabees ii. Josephus, p. 309.

† The motto on the standard of Judas was taken from Exodus xv. "Who is like unto thee among the Gods, O Jehovah!" which being written by an abbreviation formed the initial letters of the words put together, which made the artificial word Maccabees. Such at least is the national tradition concerning the origin of a name applied in its strict sense to persons enlisted under Judas and his brethren; but also more extensively to those who, before Judas raised his standard, had magnanimously braved death in the same religious cause. Particularly to those Jews recently tortured at Jerusalem by the merciless Antiochus Epiphanes, as well as those martyred 30 years before at Alexandria by the cruel Ptolemy Philopater.—*Prideaux's Connection*, vol ii p. 193 *Gillie's History*, vol. iii. p. 183.

‡ Encyclopedia.

the side of his enemies: but continued successfully
to defend, the laws and religion of his countrymen:
and in one year defeated the Syrians in five battles.
In the last of these engagements, the army which
was raised by Lysias the Syrian governor, amounted
to sixty-five thousand men. Judas gained a complete victory, obliged the troops who had escaped
the sword to elude his vengeance by an ignominious
flight, and their commander to abandon the enterprize, and return to Syria.*

: B. C. 165.]: Encouraged by this brilliant success,
the victorious Maccabees marched to Jerusalem,
destroyed the Syrian idols, repaired and purified the
temple, replaced the sacred vessels; and divine worship, which had been interrupted for three years
and an half, was resumed with the greatest splendour
and solemnity. The temple, which was decked with
a profusion of ornaments, was consecrated anew, to
the service of God; and an annual feast appointed
to perpetuate the remembrance of this joyful event.
But notwithstanding the triumphant success of
Judas and his army, they were not able to expel the
Syrians from their fortress on mount Acra, which
was opposite to the temple; in order therefore to
prevent the interruption of divine worship, they
protected the sacred edifice by building high walls
and lofty towers, which were supported by a
powerful and vigilant garrison.†

The surrounding nations, exasperated at the reestablishment of the Jews, united against them, and

* For a particular account of the battles between the Syrians and
Jews, see 1 Maccabees iii. iv.
† 1 Maccabees iv.

attacked them on all sides, being resolved to destroy
every worshipper of Jehovah. But, Judas and his,
valiant brothers repeatedly attacked and vanquished
their forces with prodigious slaughter ; 'reduced
several of their principal places ; and, obtained the
most complete success.* .,. . .-1: i.. !.. . . ‹

' In the mean time Antiochus, being on his return
from an unsuccessful expedition against Persia, received the alarming news, that all the Jews had
revolted, defeated his generals, expelled their armies
from Judea, and restored the primitive worship.
This intelligence filled him with such frantic rage,
that he declared he would utterly extirpate every individual of the Jewish nation. These words were
scarcely uttered,' says the author of the book of
Maccabees; when he was struck with a torturing and
incurable disease, and was compelled to acknowledge, that his sufferings were justly inflicted by the
God of Israel, whose people he had persecuted with
unrelenting cruelty.

After having languished for some time in a miserable condition he expired, and his death freed the
Jews from the most inveterate enemy they had ever
known. Antiochus Eupater, his son and successor,
continued to prosecute the war against the Jewish
nation.†

' Some time after the death of the tyrant, Judas
laid close siege to the tower of Acra, which Appollonius had built to overlook the temple The young
king advanced to the relief of the garrison at the
head of an hundred thousand foot, twenty thousand

---

* Rollin's Ancient History, vol. viii.
† 2 Maccabees ix. Josephus, vol. iii. p. 69.

horse, thirty-two elephants, and three hundred chariots of war. Upon the approach of this formidable army, the Maccabean chief having exhorted his troops to fight valiantly for their liberties, and given for the watchword, " *Victory is of God,*" attacked the enemy in the night, slew four thousand six hundred men, threw the whole army into confusion, and made a regular retreat into Jerusalem.*

Antiochus Eupater, having reduced the fortress of Bethsura, conducted his army to the Jewish metropolis. The garrison defended the city with undaunted courage, till they were reduced to the utmost extremities from want of provisions; but Providence interposed in their behalf, and the report of a rebellion in Syria induced the besiegers to grant them an advantageous peace. The king engaged to leave the fortifications of the temple entire; but upon the cessation of hostilities he caused them to be demolished, in open violation of the treaty which he had just confirmed with the most solemn oath.†

Menelaus the apostate high priest, who had attended the Syrian army in this expedition, was accused by Lysias, the commander, of being the instigator of the war, and condemned to suffer a cruel death. The Syrian government then conferred the pontifical dignity upon Alcimus, a man equally unprincipled and vicious as his predecessor. But the Jews refused to admit him to officiate at their altar, on account of his known impiety, and attachment to the superstitions of the Grecians.‡

* 2 Maccabees ix. Josephus, vol. iii. p. 69.
† 1 Maccabees vi. 62. ‡ 2 Maccabees xiii.

B. C. 162.]   Onias, the son of Onias III. who
was murdered in Antioch, being disappointed in not
obtaining the high priesthood after the death of his
uncle Menelaus, withdrew into Egypt. Indignant at
the promotion of the unworthy Alcimus, he petitioned Ptolemy Philometer and Cleopatra his queen
to permit him to build a temple for the Jews in that
country, alleging that the prophet Isaiah had foretold that " there should be an *altar to the Lord in
Egypt.*"*   The king and queen granted his request,
assigned a portion of land, and an adequate revenue
for the purpose.   The place chosen for erecting the
temple was Heliopolis, or the city of the sun.   It
was built after the model of the temple at Jerusalem ;
but not on so large and magnificent a scale.   Onias
was made high priest ; inferior priests and Levites
were also appointed ; and divine worship conducted
as in the capital of Judea.†

Demetrius, son of Seleucus Philopater, and
lawful heir to the crown, having put Antiochus
Eupator to death, Alcimus, the apostate high priest,
who upon being rejected by the Jews had become
their implacable enemy, petitioned the new king to
support his title.   Demetrius at his instigation sent
large armies under the command of Bacchides the
governor of Mesopotamia, and Nicanor, governor
of Judea.   But the designs of both were frustrated
by the valour and prudence of the Maccabees ; and
Nicanor, who had blasphemed the God of Israel,
and threatened to destroy the temple, was slain in
the engagement, and his army defeated with prodigious slaughter.‡

---

* Isaiah xix. 18, 19.   † Josephus, vol. iii. p. 59.   ‡ Ibid.

Soon after this victory, Judas sent an embassy to
Rome, and obtained an alliance with that powerful
state. But previously to the return of the ambassador, Demetrius despatched Bacchides into Judea
with the flower of his troops, consisting of twenty-
two thousand men, to revenge the death of Nicanor,
and establish Alcimus in the priesthood. At the
approach of this formidable army, 'the soldiers of
Judas, which amounted to only three thousand men,
were intimidated to such a degree, that all left him
except eight hundred. With this small force, which
he exhorted in the most pathetic manner to die valiantly rather than desert, he broke the strongest
wing of the idolatrous army, and chased the fleeing
troops to Mount Azotus. But at length being surrounded on all sides, and overpowered by numbers,
this heroic defender of his country fell, covered
with honourable wounds, on heaps of his expiring
enemies. His death was deeply lamented, and his
heroic exploits deservedly celebrated.*

B. C. 160.] The death of Judas filled his countrymen with the utmost consternation, while their
enemies, inspired with fresh courage, reduced Jerusalem, put many of the adherents of the Maccabees
to death; and reinstated Alcimus in the priesthood,
which sacred office he perverted to the vilest purposes. Josephus observes, " that the calamities the
Jews suffered at this time were equal to any they
had experienced since their return from Babylon."
But at length the impious high priest having presumed to break down one of the walls of the sanctuary, was suddenly cut off in the full career of his

* 1 Maccabees ix.

wickedness, and expired in agonies.* ,. The party of
Judas made the most strenuous exertions against
their enemies, and unanimously chose Jonathan to
succeed his brother as their prince and general.
Under his direction the war was conducted with
such energy and success, that the Syrians, disturbed
by their own intestine divisions, solemnly engaged
to refrain from further hostilities, and a treaty of
peace was concluded.†

Immediately after the Syrian forces left Judea,
Jonathan commenced a regular government, similar
to that of the ancient Israelitish judges ; he repaired
the walls of Jerusalem, fortified the city, and made
several important reformations in the civil and ecclesiastical affairs of his country. The increase of his
reputation and success, induced the competitors for
the Syrian monarchy to court his friendship ; and as
Demetrius had formerly persecuted the Jews, he
joined the party of his rival Alexander Bela. With
the unanimous consent of the people, he accepted the
high priesthood from him ; [B. C. 144.] that place
having been vacant seven years from the death of
Alcimus. Jonathan also formed an alliance with the
Romans and Lacedemonians, and rendered himself
formidable by his military achievements. But after
he had governed the Jewish nation with equal pru-

* By the order of prophets Haggai and Zechariah, a low wall or
inclosure was built round the sanctuary to separate the holy from the
unholy ; and the rule was, that within this no uncircumcised person
was to enter. Alcimus, in order to give the Gentiles equal liberty
with the Jews, to pass into the inner courts of the temple, ordered
this wall of partition to be pulled down.—*Prideaux's Connection*,
vol. ii. p. 264.

† Prideaux's Connection, vol. ii. p 264.

dence and skill for about seventeen years, he and his children were treacherously put to death by Tryphon, a Syrian usurper, in the city of Ptolemais. One thousand persons who attended him as guards were likewise assassinated.* ,

B. C. 143.] After the death of Jonathan, the leaders of the Jewish nation assembled at Jerusalem, and chose Simon, the only surviving son of Mattathias, for their general and high priest ; and settled both the civil and sacerdotal power on his posterity. He imitated the valour and prudence which marked the conduct of his brother ; repaired the fortresses of Judea ; reduced and demolished the tower of Acra ; renewed the treaty with the Romans ; and sent an embassy to Demetrius, lawful heir of Syria, offering to acknowledge his sovereignty, and assist him in depriving the usurper Tryphon of the regal dignity. These proposals were cheerfully accepted by Demetrius ; and a letter was returned, which constituted Simon sovereign prince and high priest of the Jewish nation ; ordered all public acts to be made in his name, and released his territories from all foreign dominion. After the independent reign of Simon had commenced, he bravely defended his country ; took Gaza and Joppa ; restored peace to Jerusalem ; beautified the sanctuary, and enforced obedience to the divine law. At length, however, [B. C. 135.] a period was put to his life and usefulness at the castle of his son-in-law, by whom he and two of his sons were treacherously murdered after he had governed the Jews eight years.†

* Whiston's Josephus, vol. v. p. 13. 1 Maccab. x—xiv.
† 1 Maccabees xvi.

Immediately after Simon's death, Antiochus Sidetes, the then reigning king of Syria, marched to Palestine with a powerful army, and compelled the Jews to deliver their arms, demolish the fortifications of Jerusalem, and pay him an annual tribute. Not long after, this monarch was slain in an expedition against the Parthians ; and the intestine commotions which distracted the kingdom after his death afforded Hyrcanus, the son and successor of Simon, an opportunity to enlarge his dominions, and deliver his country from the yoke of foreign power. His exertions were crowned with such complete success, that neither he nor his descendants were ever after subjected to the kings of Syria.*

He was also successful in his wars with the Idumeans, whom he compelled to renounce their idolatrous rites, or abandon their country ; in consequence of which they lost their political existence, and became incorporated with the Jewish nation. The conqueror next turned his arms against the Samaritans ; demolished their capital city, and the temple which was erected on Mount Gerizzim.†

Hyrcanus renewed the alliance which his predecessors made with the Romans, who were now rapidly advancing to the meridian of their power. And having subdued his enemies, and amassed prodigious treasure by his conquests, enjoyed his authority without disturbance, made Judea flourish under his wise administration, and raised his nation to a greater degree of splendour than it had ever enjoyed since the Babylonish captivity His last days

* Whiston's Josephus, vol. v. p. 14. Prid. Conn. vol. ii. p. 325.
† Rollin's Ancient History.

were however embittered by a contest with the Pharisees,* who, at this time had acquired great power and popularity ; and had incensed the king by calling in question his title to the high priesthood. Hyrcanus, however, after having enjoyed the royal authority twenty-nine years, died in peace, greatly beloved and lamented by the generality of the Jewish nation.†

Aristobulus, his eldest son, succeeded him both in the regal and sacerdotal dignities. He was the first after the Babylonian captivity who assumed a diadem, and the title of king. The commencement of his reign was marked with several acts of de-spotic cruelty. He even put his own mother to death, because she aspired to the government ; and imprisoned his brothers, one of whom he also caused to be slain upon an unjust suspicion. During his government the Itureans, who inhabited the north easterly parts of Galilee, were attacked and van-

---

* Learned men differ respecting the origin of the Pharisees. Some suppose that they arose about an hundred and fifty years before the appearance of our Saviour. Josephus, who was himself of this sect, speaks of it as flourishing in the time of Jonathan the high priest The dissensions between the schools of Hillel and Shammai, a little before the Christian era, increased the number and power of the Pharisees. Hillel, having acquired a profound knowledge of the most difficult points of the Jewish law, became master of the chief school in Jerusalem, and laid the foundation of the Talmud. Sham-mai, one of his disciples, deserted his school, and formed a college, in which he taught doctrines contrary to his master. He rejected the oral law, and followed the moral only in its literal sense. These dif-ferent schools long disturbed the Jewish church by violent com-motions. However, the party of Hillel was at last victorious.— *Enfield's Philosophy.* See also Section V. for a further account of this denomination.

† Josephus, vol. v. p 19.

quished. After a short reign the tyrant expired, filled with the utmost horror and remorse of conscience.*

B. C. 105.] Alexander Janneus, brother of Aristobulus, being liberated from prison, ascended the throne. This martial prince defeated the Philistines, and compelled them to receive circumcision.† He also achieved other brilliant conquests in Arabia, Gilead, and Moabitis. During his reign, however, the Jews were in a very miserable condition, being not only involved in foreign wars, but distracted by intestine commotions. The powerful party of the Pharisees, who detested him for enforcing his father's decrees against their constitutions, exerted themselves to the utmost to vilify his government, and exasperate the people against him. Their malicious attempts gave rise to a civil war which lasted six years, involved both parties in innumerable calamities, and occasioned the death of more than fifty thousand persons. At length Alexander having in vain endeavoured to effect a reconciliation, gained the victory in a decisive battle, and punished his enemies with the utmost severity. The king died in the 27th year of his reign, after he had bequeathed the government to his wife Alexandria, whom he appointed guardian to the young princes.

When the queen ascended the throne, in compliance with the advice which she received from her

---

* Josephus, vol. v. p. 19.

† The practice of obliging the nations, who were conquered by the Jews, to quit their country, or embrace the Mosaic religion, was invariably followed by the Asmonean princes.—*Rollin's Ancient History*, vol. ix. p. 221.

husband just before his death, she sent for the principal leaders among the Pharisees, to whom she
entirely committed the management of her affairs.
By this measure she acquired popularity, and established herself on the throne. But this turbulent
sect having compelled the queen to grant their
exorbitant demands, commenced a violent persecution against the Sadducees,* and exercised their
authority in the most arbitrary and oppressive
manner. Alexandria died in the ninth year of her
reign, having appointed her eldest son Hyrcanus,
who had been made high priest, to succeed her in
the regal dignity.†

Immediately after Hyrcanus II. ascended the
throne, his brother Aristobulus raised a powerful
army against him, which soon compelled him to sue
for peace, on condition of resigning all title to the
regal and pontifical dignity. But the ambition of
Antipater, governor of Idumea and father of Herod,
involved the Jews in a new war. He used all his
address to replace the late king on the throne, in
order that he might govern under him. By his assistance, and that of Aretas, king of Arabia, Hyrcanus
assembled a body of troops, which defeated Aris-

---

* The Sadducees derived their origin and name from one Sadoc,
who flourished about two hundred and sixty years before Christ.
Sadoc was a pupil of Antigonus Sochæus, president of the sanhedrim,
who having inculcated in his lectures, that men ought to serve God
out of pure love to him, and not in a servile manner, either for fear
of punishment or hope of reward, Sadoc, not understanding this
spiritual doctrine, concluded that there was no future state of
rewards and punishments. His adherents were denominated Sadducees.—*Jennings' Lectures*, vol. i. p. 456. See part v. for a farther
account of this sect.

† Josephus, vol. v. p. 26.

tobulus, and kept him closely besieged in Jerusalem.*

B. C. 65.] ' In this situation of affairs, Aristobulus implored the protection of the Romans; and his petition being accompanied with large presents, effectually answered his purpose, and induced the republic to write to Aretas, commanding him to raise the siege, and leave the country.' The Arabian prince obeyed the injunction, and Aristobulus escaped from his confinement, and gratified his vindictive rage by the destruction of his enemies.†.

Some time after this event, the two brothers sent embassadors to Pompey, at that time commander in chief of all the Roman forces in the east, and chose him the arbitrator of their mutual differences.

The Roman general heard each party with apparent impartiality, and dismissed them with a promise, that he would embrace an early opportunity of deciding the controversy. Aristobulus, offended at the delay, and suspecting Pompey favoured his brother, made formidable preparations for war. Exasperated at this, and other parts of his conduct, the Roman commander caused him to be imprisoned, and marched with his whole army against Jerusalem.‡

Though the gates of the city were readily opened by Hyrcanus's party, yet the faction of Aristobulus took shelter in the temple, and resolved to defend themselves to the last extremity. Pompey therefore closely besieged them ; and the superstitious rigour, with which the Jews observed the sabbath, facilitated

* Josephus, vol. i p. 28.   † Ibid.   ‡ Ibid. vol. v. p. 30.

the conquest of their metropolis. For though, since the commencement of the Maccabean war, they had agreed to defend themselves on that holy day, when actually attacked, they still thought it unlawful to prevent the works of the enemy. The Romans therefore were unmolested, while they employed themselves in preparations for an attack, on the sabbath, and made themselves masters of the city after a siege of three months. A terrible slaughter ensued, in which more than twelve thousand persons were killed, and many perished by suicide. During these horrid transactions, the priests, who were offering sacrifices, continued their devotions with great composure, and suffered themselves to be murdered before the altar without any resistance. Their constancy excited the astonishment and admiration of the conqueror.*

Jerusalem was reduced on that very day, which the Jews observe as a solemn fast for the taking of the city and temple by Nebuchadnezzar. After Pompey had completed the conquest of Jerusalem, his curiosity induced him to examine every part of the temple. Accompanied with some of his superior officers, he even penetrated into the holy of holies. But he left the treasures of the sacred edifice untouched, and ordered the priests to make a solemn purification, and offer sacrifices according to the Mosaic institutions.†

* Rollin's Ancient History, vol. iv. p. 293.
† Josephus, vol. v. p. 31—33.

D 2

SECTION IV.

*Sketch of the history of the Jews, from the conquest of
Pompey to the birth of our Lord Jesus Christ.*

B. C. 63.] JOSEPHUS and Tacitus date the loss
of the liberty of the Jews, and the translation of
the sovereign authority to the Romans, from the
reduction of Jerusalem by Pompey. For though
Hyrcanus was restored to the pontifical dignity with
the title of prince, he was deprived of the ensigns
of royalty, and condemned to pay a disgraceful
tribute. His dominions were also reduced to nar-
rower limits; for Pompey restored to Cœlo Syria
all the towns taken by the Jews, gave liberty to
Samaria and other maritime towns, and strictly prohibited him from attempting any new conquests.
To prevent future revolts, the Roman general commanded the walls of Jerusalem to be demolished;
and, after regulating the government of Judea
according to his pleasure, returned to Rome, Aristobulus and his sons Alexander and Antigonus being
sent prisoners to that city to adorn his future
triumph.*

B. C. 57.] From this period, for many years, civil
dissensions and desolating wars raged in Judea.
Alexander, the son of Aristobulus, found means to
escape from Rome, and appeared in that country at
the head of a formidable army. Hyrcanus had left
the management of affairs to Antipater, who, having
used every artifice to ingratiate himself with the
Romans, was enabled, by their assistance, to suppress

* Josephus, vol. v. p. 34.

the rebellion. Some time after, Aristobulus obtained
his liberty, and joined the discontented party in Palestine. . But his attempts were frustrated ;. and he
was again committed to prison.. A few years after,
Julius Cæsar set him at liberty, in order to gain his
assistance against Pompey.; and both he and his son
Alexander were put to death by the partizans of that
famous general.*, : ,l , , · · , · ·' , j' l.

'B. C. 52.] About this time Crassus, the Roman
governor of Syria, invaded the Parthians ;. and
on his march against that nation stopped at Jerusalem, and stimulated by his insatiable avarice,
seized the sacred treasures in the temple. The
wealth he acquired by this sacrilegious pillage is said
to have been upwards of two millions sterling. But
the vengeance of heaven overtook him ; for he was
soon after defeated and slain by the Parthians.† ·';

. B. C. 48.] Meantime the power and influence
of Antipater rapidly increased. Julius Cæsar, who
after the death of Pompey usurped the supreme
authority at Rome, rewarded the services he had
rendered him in the Egyptian war, by making him
lieutenant of Judea, and honouring him with the
title of a Roman citizen. He also confirmed Hyrcanus in the priesthood, gave liberty to fortify the
city and repair the walls of Jerusalem, which
Pompey had demolished, and bestowed such signal
favours upon the Jews, that during his life, they
could scarcely be said to feel the Roman yoke.

At this time Antipater procured the government
of Jerusalem for his eldest son Phasael, and that of
Galilee for his second son Herod.‡

---

* Josephus, vol. v. p. 37—40.   † Ibid.   ‡ Ibid. p. 43.

During the domestic calamities, which engaged
the attention of the Romans upon the assassination
of Julius Cæsar, Hyrcanus was deprived of his
authority by his nephew Antigonus, who, after
making vigorous efforts, in which he was assisted
by the Parthians, recovered the kingdom. Hyrcanus and Phasael were thrown into a dungeon ; but
Herod escaped destruction by a precipitate flight.
He first took refuge in Egypt, from whence he
repaired to Rome for assistance, and by the powerful patronage of Mark Anthony, who was then in
the zenith of his power, was inaugurated king of
Judea. Soon after he entered Palestine with a
numerous army, and subdued Galilee. He was
however repulsed at Jerusalem with great slaughter ;
but being reinforced by Sosias, governor of Syria,
he made himself master of the city, after an obstinate
siege of six months. The immediate consequence
was a cruel pillage and massacre, which was followed
by the death of Antigonus the son of Aristobulus.
Thus ended the reign of the Asmonean family, after
a duration of an hundred and twenty nine years
from the beginning of the government of Judas
Maccabeus.*

Upon the entire reduction of the holy city, Herod,
a stranger and Idumean, ascended the throne of
Judea.

Herod, who proved one of the greatest tyrants
ever recorded in history, commenced his reign with
a cruel persecution of the adherents of Antigonus :
the most affluent among them he caused to be put to
death, and confiscated their estates in order to re-

* Josephus, vol. v. p. 43.

plenish his empty coffers: The tyrant decoyed
Hyrcanus from Parthia, where he had, fled for
shelter; and, contrary to the most solemn engagements, caused him to be assassinated. Aristobulus,
the grandson of Hyrcanus, who was appointed high
priest, was drowned in a bath by his contrivance.
Mariamne, his queen, who descended from the illustrious Asmonean family, and was distinguished for
her beauty, virtue, and accomplishments, fell the
next victim to his resentment and jealousy. Three
of his sons, in the course of his tyrannical reign,
were condemned to suffer death. He sacrificed his
friends as well as foes to his ungovernable fury,
oppressed the people in the most cruel and arbitrary
manner, and exhausted the treasures of the nation
by his boundless extravagance.*

After Herod had destroyed the greatest part of his
supposed enemies, he began to exhibit a marked
contempt for the Jewish religion and laws. From
the beginning of his reign to the final destruction of
the temple, the high priests had no hereditary right;
but were set up and removed at his pleasure, and
that of his successors. He also destroyed the authority of the grand sanhedrim,† and burnt the Jewish
records, that he might be thought originally an Israelite. He built temples in the Grecian taste, erected
statues for idolatrous worship, consecrated a superb
theatre and amphitheatre, to celebrate games, in
honour of Augustus, adopted in his ordinary habits

* Josephus.

† Herod had been obliged to appear before the grand sanhedrim,
in order to answer for his conduct, previously to his obtaining the
regal dignity; and from a principle of revenge he attacked the
assembly, which by degrees lost its power.

Roman manners and usages, and in his public capacity was absolutely devoted and subservient to the Romans.

Under the administration, and through the influence of this tyrant, the Roman luxury was introduced into Palestine, accompanied with all the vices of that licentious people. In a word, Judea, governed by Herod, groaned under all the corruption, which might be expected from the authority and example of a prince, who though a Jew in outward profession, was, in point of morals and practice, a contemner of all laws human and divine.*

B. C. 23.] After Herod had amassed a prodigious treasure by his cruel extortions and confiscations, he proposed to regain the favour of the Jewish nation by repairing the temple ; and for eight or nine years employed upon it eighteen thousand workmen, who at last completed the stupendous design. The magnificent structure, which he erected, is said, in some respects, to have even exceeded the first temple, which was built by Solomon.† Rising in all its grandeur from the summit of a mountain, it commanded an extensive prospect ; its appearance, says Josephus, exhibited every thing, that could strike the mind and astonish the sight. It was on every side covered with solid plates of gold, and, when the sun arose upon it,

---

* Mosheim's Eccl. Hist. vol. i. p. 31. Horæ Biblicæ.

† It was built of hard white stones of prodigious magnitude. Hence, the disciples expressed their admiration of its grandeur, and of the large and magnificent stones, of which it was erected, Mark xiii. 1.—See *Harwood's Introduction to the New Testament*, vol. ii. p. 158.

reflected such a dazzling effulgence, that the eye was unable to sustain its radiance. The temple was encompassed with august porticoes, on which immense riches were profusely expended; and every ornament bestowed, that human art and genius could devise. This superb structure was continually receiving additions to the time of the ministry of our Saviour.* Herod set up a golden eagle of exquisite workmanship, the arms of the Roman empire, over the gates of the temple.

About this period there was a general expectation through the eastern world of the advent of some illustrious prophet and deliverer, who should change the aspect of human affairs.† The Jews in particular eagerly anticipated the coming of the promised Messiah, as the time predicted by Daniel for his manifestation was arrived. Devout persons waited day and night for the consolation of Israel ; and the whole nation, groaning under the Roman yoke, and stimulated by the desire of liberty or of vengeance, expected their deliverer with the most anxious impatience.

At length, that most interesting and important epoch arrived, when the Saviour Jesus Christ made his appearance on earth. When the sun of righteousness arose on a benighted world, Polytheism was in

---

* Hence the Jews might with literal propriety assert, as they ostentatiously did, " Forty and six years was this temple in building," John ii. 20. As the whole was executed under the idea of repairs, it continued to be called the second temple.

† Josephus, Suetonius, and Tacitus, mention this general expectation ; and hence Virgil, the Roman poet, in his fourth eclogue, describes the blessings of the government of some great personage who was, or should be born about this time.

every country, except Judea; the predominant, and almost universal religion. The Roman empire under Augustus had attained the zenith of its power: while the pagan nations, who composed this vast monarchy, exhibited the most glaring picture of human depravity; and the Jewish state, and true religion, were almost at the lowest ebb. Just before our Saviour was born, the temple of Janus was shut, to intimate that the nations of the earth were at peace. This remarkable peace, after so many ages of tumult and war, was a fit prelude to the introduction of the glorious prince of peace into the world.*

The malicious attempt of Herod to involve the Saviour of the world in the slaughter of the babes of Bethlehem is recorded by the sacred history.† The tyrant died the following year in exquisite tortures. During his illness he sent for the heads of the most eminent families in Judea, confined them, and left orders, that, as soon as he had breathed his last they should all be put to the sword, to oblige the nation to go in mourning at his death. He expired soon after, in the thirty-seventh year of his reign; the sentence was not executed; and the nation rejoiced at their deliverance.‡

After the death of Herod, the Roman emperor divided the kingdom of Judea between his sons. The brothers, for some years, governed Palestine without any open rebellion or disturbance. But Archelaus, who obtained half the kingdom, under the title of exarch, proved so corrupt and wicked a prince, that both Jews and Samaritans sent ambas-

* Mosheim's Ecclesiastical History, vol. i. p. 16.   † Matthew xi.
‡ Josephus, vol. v. p. 154

sadors to accuse him to Augustus. The emperor deposed and banished him for his tyrannical conduct; and reduced Judea to the form of a Roman province, to be ruled by procurators, who were to be appointed and recalled at the pleasure of the reigning monarch. The power of life and death was taken from the Jews; their taxes were regularly gathered by the publicans; and justice was from that time administered in the name, and by the laws of Rome.*

SECTION V.

Of the different denominations among the Jews at the time of Christ's appearance upon earth.

. Though the Jewish nation, at the time of our Saviour's appearance, retained the worship of the true God, they had grossly perverted their religion, by exalting the traditions of their ancestors above the clear and positive injunctions of their law ; and while they presumed to infringe the strongest moral obligations, they were scrupulously exact in performing the most minute and trifling ceremonies, which were enjoined by their rabbies. The ultimate object of many, was to obtain popular applause; hence, they publicly displayed all the parade of ostentatious charity, and were privately guilty of the

* The precise year, when this event took place, it may be difficult to ascertain ; but the judicial forms which were observed on the trial and condemnation of our Saviour, and the acclamation of the Jews, "We have no king but Cæsar," irrefragably shew that it had arrived. Horæ Biblicæ, p 42. This event illustrates the celebrated prophecy of Jacob, Genesis xlix 10. The generality of interpreters, Jewish as well as Christian, have by Shiloh understood the Messiah.

greatest extortion and cruelty. Yet, elated with spiritual pride, they considered themselves as the only favourites of heaven, and excluded all other nations from the hopes of eternal life.* .

During Christ's ministry on earth the temple was used as a place of merchandize, and the most sacred offices, even the high priesthood, were sold. The chief priests, who purchased their places by bribes, maintained their ill acquired authority by the most abominable crimes. The inferior priests, and those who possessed any degree of authority, had become dissolute and abandoned in the highest degree: while the multitude, excited by their corrupt example, ran headlong into every kind of iniquity, and, by their seditions, robberies, and extortions, armed against themselves both the justice of God and vengeance of man.

The Jewish nation, at the time of our Saviour's appearance, were divided into a great variety of sects. The principal points in dispute among them respected the law of Moses, the immortality of the soul, the resurrection of the body, future rewards and punishments, and the nature of virtue. All admitted the divine authority of the Mosaic law. All agreed in thinking, that their religious tenets and observances were the only objects worthy of their attention.†

The rabbies, or the teachers of each sect, defended their tenets with the greatest zeal and pertinacity. The Jews and Samaritans were, in particular, violently opposed to each other. The latter, at first,

---

* Harwood's Introduction, vol. i. p. 108, 109. Mosheim.
† Prideaux's Connection, vol. i. p. 353. Horæ Biblicæ.

were heathens, who worshipped the God of Israel, in conjunction with other deities, till Menasses, who was made their high priest, with other fugitive Jews, coming to them from Jerusalem, brought with them the book of the law, and taught them to worship the true God only, according to the Mosaic institution. From this period they are considered a sect of the Jewish religion. They looked upon the temple of Gerizzim, as the only place where God was pleased to be worshipped, and the centre of true religion. They received no scriptures except the books of Moses, Joshua, and Judges, which two latter, however, they did not allow to be of divine authority like the Pentateuch.*

The Pharisees were the most distinguished, flourishing, and popular sect among the Jews. They assumed this name on account of their separating themselves for superior strictness in ritual observances. Their separation consisted chiefly in certain distinctions respecting religious ceremonies, and does not appear to have interrupted the uniformity of religious worship, in which the Jews of every sect always seem to have been united.†

It appears, from the frequent mention which is made by the evangelists of the scribes and pharisees in conjunction, that the greatest number of Jewish teachers, or doctors of the law, were at that time of the pharisaical sect. The ecclesiastical scribes were the learned of the Jewish nation, who expounded the law, and taught it to the people.‡

The Pharisees were principally distinguished by

---

* Basnage, p. 115. † Jennings' Jewish Antiquities, vol. i. p. 437.
‡ Jennings' Jewish Antiquities, p. 392.

their zeal for the traditions of the elders, which
they not only maintained to be of equal authority
with the written law, but in many cases explained
the latter by the former, entirely contrary to its true
intent and meaning ; and thus made the *commandments of God of no effect by their traditions.* They
pretended that those traditions, which they called
the oral law, were delivered by God to Moses, on
Mount Sinai, and preserved through successive generations. They were charged with maintaining,
that by observing both, the written and oral law,
man may not only obtain justification before God,
but perform meritorious works of supererogation ;
that fasting, alms, ablutions, and confessions, are
sufficient atonement for sin ; that thoughts and
desires are not sinful, unless they produce evil actions.
They acknowledged the immortality of the soul,
future rewards and punishments, and the resurrection
of the body.* According to Josephus, they maintained the doctrine of predestination ; but supposed,
that the divine decrees did not interfere with the
freedom of the human will.†

---

* Dr. Prideaux supposes that the Pharisees maintained only a Pythagorean resurrection, that is, the transmigration of the soul into
another body.   David Levi, on the other hand, asserts, that the
Pharisees knew and taught the true resurrection of the body and soul
together.   For proof of this, he quotes Ezekiel xxxvii, and other
passages in the Old Testament. Whence he asserts, that " the doctrine
of the resurrection, and consequently that of a future state of rewards
and punishments, was well known and established in the Jewish nation,
(and that in the most clear, explicit, and unequivocal manner) for
almost a thousand years before Christ."—*David Levi's Ceremonies of
the Jews,* pp. 255—261.

† They maintained, that " before a man is born, it is predes-
tinated, whether he shall be wise or foolish, weak or strong, rich or

This denomination, by their apparent sanctity of manners, had rendered themselves extremely popular. It appears both from the scripture, and the testimony of Josephus, that the common people were entirely at their disposal, and gave their suffrage to every religious prescription and judicial sentence, that had obtained their sanction. The great; who feared their artifice, were frequently obliged to court their favour. Hence they obtained the highest offices both in the state and priesthood; and assumed the chief direction both of public and private affairs.*

The peculiar manners of this sect are strongly marked in the writings of the evangelists ; particularly their exactness, in performing the rites and ceremonies of the law, both written and traditionary ; the rigour of their discipline in washings, fastings, and ablutions ; their scrupulous care to avoid every kind of ritual impurity : their long and frequent prayers, made not only in the synagogues and temples, but in the public streets ; their phylacteries on the borders of their garments, on which were written sentences of the law ; their assiduity in making proselytes ; their ostentatious charities ; and, under all this specious mark of zeal and purity, their abominable and atrocious vices. According to our Saviour's representation of them, they were a race of the most demure hypocrites that ever disgraced human nature, resembling whited sepulchres, which

poor. But whether he is to be wicked or righteous, vicious or virtuous, is entirely in his own free will."—*David Levi's Ceremonies of the Jews,* p. 267.

* Josephus.

outwardly appear beautiful, but inwardly are full of putrefaction.*

The above account is confirmed by the testimony of the Jewish writers themselves. The Talmudic books mention several distinct classes of Pharisees, under characters, which show them to have been deeply immersed in superstition. Among these were the truncated Pharisee, who, that he might appear in profound meditation, as if destitute of feet, scarcely lifted them from the ground; the mortar Pharisee, who, that his contemplations might not be disturbed, wore a deep cap in shape of a mortar, which would only permit him to look upon the ground at his feet; and the striking Pharisee, who, shutting his eyes, as he walked, to avoid the sight of women, often struck his head against the wall. They practised many painful austerities and mortifications, frequently observed severe fasts, covered their features with gloom and solemnity, and used every artifice to captivate the admiration of the populace.†

The sect of the Sadducees was inconsiderable in number; but some of those who professed its tenets, were of illustrious families, and others distinguished for their opulence. We find that Caiaphas, an high priest, was of this denomination, and Josephus mentions several other Sadducees, who were exalted to the supreme power in church and state. The chief heads of the doctrine of this sect are as follow.

All laws and traditions not comprehended in the written law, are to be rejected as merely human

* Harwood's Introduction.
† Godwin's Jewish Antiq. p. 45. Enfield's Philos. vol. ii. p. 181.

inventions.' Neither angels nor spirits have a distinct existence, separate from this corporeal vestment. The soul of man therefore does not remain after this life, but expires with the body. There will be no resurrection of the dead, nor any rewards and punishments after this life. Man is not subject to irresistible fate, but has the framing of his condition chiefly in his own power. Polygamy ought not to be practised.*

The sect of the Caraites, though its history be exceedingly obscure, is not to be confounded with that of the Sadducees. The name denotes a scripturist, and seems intended to distinguish those, who adhere to the scriptures as the whole and only rule of their faith and practice. This denomination was given them about thirty years before Christ, when, upon the dissension betwixt Hillel the president of the Sanhedrim, and Shammai the vice-president, by which their respective pupils were divided into two parties, betwixt whom there were perpetual contests, those, that were of the opinion of the Caraites, sided with the school of Shammai, and those, who were zealous for traditions, with that of Hillel. According to Dr. Prideaux they did not absolutely reject all traditions, but only refused them the same authority with the written oracles of God. They were distinguished from the Sadducees, by maintaining the doctrines of the immortality of the soul, and future rewards and punishments.†

The Essenes differed from all the above mentioned sects, as they secluded themselves not only

* Josephus. Enfield's Philosophy.
† Prid. Con. vol. ii. p. 388. Jennings' Lectures, vol. i. p. 433.

from politics and public affairs, but, as much as
the nature of man and constitution of society will
admit, from the common concerns and intercourse of
private life. Some suppose they took their rise,
from the dispersion of their nation, after the Babylonish captivity; others, that they began when
the persecution of Antiochus compelled the Jews to
retire to the woods and mountains. They maintained, that rewards and punishments extended to
the soul alone, and regarded the body as a mass
of malignant matter, and the prison of the immortal
spirit. The greatest part of this sect considered the
laws of Moses as an allegorical system of spiritual
and mysterious truth, and renounced all regard
to the outward letter in its explanation. The
leading traits in the character of this sect were, that
they were sober, abstemious, peaceable, lovers of
retirement, and had a perfect community of goods.
They paid the highest regard to the moral precepts
of the law ; but neglected the ceremonial, excepting
what regarded personal cleanliness, the observation
of the sabbath, and making an annual present to the
temple at Jerusalem. They commonly lived in
a state of celibacy, and adopted the children of
others, to educate them in their own principles and
customs. Though they were, in general, averse to
swearing, or to requiring an oath, they bound all,
whom they initiated, by the most sacred vows, to
observe the duties of piety, justice, fidelity, and
modesty : to conceal the secrets of the fraternity ;
to preserve the books of their institutions; and with
great care to commemorate the names of the angels.*

* Enfield, vol. ii. p. 186. Jennings' Lectures, vol. i. p. 170.

Philo mentions two classes of Essenes; one of which followed a practical institution, the other professed a theoretical system. The latter, who were called Therapeutæ, placed their whole felicity in the contemplation of the divine nature. Detaching themselves entirely from secular affairs, they transferred their property to their relations and friends, and retired to solitary places, where they devoted themselves to an holy life. The principal society of this kind was formed near Alexandria, where they lived not far from each other, in separate cottages, each of which had its own sacred apartments, to which the inhabitants retired for the purposes of devotion.*

Besides these eminent Jewish sects, there were several of inferior note, at the time of Christ's appearance; the Herodians, mentioned by the sacred writers, and the Gaulonites, by Josephus.

The Herodians derived their name from Herod the Great, and were distinguished by their coinciding with the plan of that monarch to subject himself and his dominions to the Romans; and also by complying with many of the heathen usages. Their distinguished tenet appeared to be, that it is lawful, when constrained by superiors, to comply with idolatry, and with false religion. Herod seems to have formed this sect, in order to justify himself in his practice of studying every artifice to ingratiate himself with the emperor, and to secure the favour of the principal personages in the court of Rome. We find the Sadducees readily embraced the tenets of this party; for the same persons, who, in one of

* Enfield, vol. ii. p. 186.

the gospels, are called Herodians, are in another styled Sadducees. The Herodians were not so much a religious, as a political sect, attached to Herod during his life, and to his sons after his decease.* ,

The Gaulonites were Galileans, who derived this name from one Judas Theudas, a native of Gaulon, in Upper Galilee, who, in the tenth year of Jesus Christ, excited his countrymen, the Galileans, and many other Jews, to take arms, and venture upon all extremities, rather than ' pay tribute to the Romans. The principles he instilled into his party were, not only that they were a free nation, and ought not to be in subjection to any other ; but, that they were the elect of God, that he alone was their governor, and, that therefore they ought not to submit to any ordinance of man. Though Theudas was unsuccessful, and his party, in their very first attempt, entirely routed and dispersed ; yet so deeply had he infused his own enthusiasm into their hearts, that they never rested, till they involved the city and temple in their own destruction.† ,

Many of the Jews were attached to the oriental philosophy concerning the origin of the world. From this source the doctrine of the Cabala is supposed to be derived. That considerable numbers of the Jews had imbibed this system, appears evident, both from the books of the New Testament, and from the ancient history of the christian church. It is also certain, that many of the Gnostic sects were founded by Jews.‡

* Josephus. Prideaux's Connection.   † Josephus.
‡ Mosheim's Eccles. Hist. vol. i. p. 38.

At the time when our Lord Jesus Christ appeared upon earth, the great body of the Jewish nation were waiting with great anxiety for their promised Messiah. Yet they formed erroneous ideas of his character. They expected not a spiritual, but a temporal sovereign. They supposed he would manifest himself as a mighty conqueror, free them from subjection to the Romans, aggrandize their nation, render Jerusalem the metropolis of the world; and, after subduing all their enemies, commence a glorious reign of prosperity and peace. Hence they were disgusted with the humble appearance of the divine Redeemer; while the Pharisees and great men were exasperated at the boldness and severity of his rebukes. For though he united in himself the accomplishment of every ancient prophecy, he was ignominiously rejected and put to death by the Jewish nation. The tremendous calamities which befell them after perpetrating this horrid crime; the fulfilment of our Saviour's predictions, respecting the destruction of their city and temple, and their consequent dispersion and sufferings, will be related in the following pages.

HISTORY OF THE JEWS.

CHAPTER I.

Tyranny of the Roman government in Judea.—Herod Agrippa made king.—The emperor Caligula attempts to have his statue placed in the temple of Jerusalem.—Resistance of the Jews.—Death of Herod Agrippa—Arbitrary conduct of the Roman governors.—Many Jews depart for foreign countries—Number of Jews in Jerusalem at the Passover.—The prodigies which preceded the war.—Of the contest respecting the city of Cesarea.—Jews and Syrians take up arms.—Vast numbers destroyed on both sides.—The Jews take several important fortresses.—Cestius Gallus marches against them and besieges Jerusalem.—The Christians retire to Pella.—Jews make great preparations for war.—Vespasian is sent against them with a powerful army.—He reduces the cities of Galilee.—Of the parties among the Jews.—Of the civil war in Jerusalem; and the cruelty of the Zealots.—Vespasian is proclaimed emperor, and sends his son Titus to terminate the war by the reduction of Jerusalem.

THE ministry of our blessed Saviour, while he remained on earth, was principally confined to the Jews; and notwithstanding the obstinate incredulity of the majority of the nation, who, impatient under the tyrannical government of the Romans, eagerly expected a temporal deliverer, a large number acknowledged him as the true Messiah. The apostles also, in obedience to the command of their divine Master, began to preach the Gospel to this distinguished people. Under their ministry

many were converted, and the first Christian church
was founded at Jerusalem. But the unbelieving
Jews, who had rejected and crucified the *Prince of
Life*, exhibited the same enmity against his apostles
and followers, and, in the infancy of the Christian
Church, they were its most cruel persecutors.* The
most signal marks of divine vengeance, however,
soon pursued this infatuated people; and the predictions of the Divine Redeemer, respecting the
tremendous destruction of Jerusalem, began to be
accomplished.

The governors of Judea, appointed by the Romans, constantly insulted the feelings of the Jews,
by exhibiting a marked contempt for their religion
and law. Pontius Pilate, during his administration,
took every occasion of introducing his standards,
with images, pictures, consecrated shields, &c. into
their city; and at length attempted to drain the
treasury of the temple, under pretence of bringing
an aqueduct to Jerusalem. Seven years after the
crucifixion of Jesus Christ, complaint being made
of the tyranny and rapine of Pilate, he was superseded, and, in extreme poverty and misery, perished by suicide at Vienne in France.†

Soon after, Herod Agrippa, grandson to Herod
the Great, was promoted to the regal dignity; and,
during his reign, the Jews were involved in new
difficulties. The Roman emperor, Caligula, intoxi-

---

* The early ecclesiastical historians, as well as the New Testament writers, attest the enmity of the Jews against the Christians,
and, that they were more particular y exasperated against those be
lievers, who were of their own nation.

† Josephus, vol. v.

cated with mad ambition, claimed divine honours ;
and, being determined to have his statue placed in
the sanctuary of the temple, ordered Petronius, the
governor, to raise an army to enforce obedience to
his impious injunction. At this alarming period,
the Jews went in a large body to the governor,
beseeching him in the most pathetic terms not to
defile their temple with images ; and, falling pros-
trate on the ground, offered to die rather than
disobey their law.* Their moving entreaties excited the compassion of Petronius, and he engaged
to interest himself in their behalf. At length
Agrippa, who was in high favour at court, undertook their cause ; and, upon the emperor's solemnly
engaging to grant whatever he should ask, he,
generously preferring the welfare of his people to
his own emolument, requested the monarch to
relinquish the design of having his statue erected in
the temple. Caligula reluctantly granted his suit ;
and the death of the tyrant, which took place soon
after, prevented his renewing the impious attempt.†

According to the sacred historian,‡ Agrippa, who,
from an ambitious desire of popularity among his
countrymen, raised a persecution against the Christians, and blasphemously suffered himself to be
styled a God by some deputies from Tyre and Sidon,
was miraculously struck with a terrible disease, which
soon put an end to his life. After his death Judea
was again reduced to a Roman province, and the
new governors appointed over it were continually

* Josephus, vol. v. p. 172, 173.   † Ibid.
‡ Acts v.

irritating the minds of the people by the most glaring infringements upon their privileges.*

Felix, who had advanced from obscurity and servitude to rank and power, with the true spirit of a slave, exercised the tyranny of an eastern prince.† His oppression, rapine, and cruelty, excited a spirit of revolt; while the false prophets (who were so numerous under his government, that some of them were apprehended and killed every day) were continually blowing the flames of sedition. The people were massacred by the troops of Felix for following these deceivers, who, according to our Saviour's prediction, drew multitudes into the desart to shew them signs and wonders. In particular, a certain Egyptian Jew, entered Judea with a numerous banditti, and, having collected about thirty thousand men, led them to Mount Olivet, and promised to deliver them from the Romans. Felix, with his legions, met him at the foot of the mountain, slew many of his followers, and took others prisoners. The impostor, with a remnant of his adherents, made their escape.‡

Judea, during the government of Felix, was infested with robbers, and clandestine assassins, named Sicarii, who, with poiniards concealed under their garments, used to mingle in the crowd, and stab their supposed enemies.§ By the just judgment of heaven, the Jews, who had crucified their Messiah, and desired a robber and murderer to be granted to them, had their country overrun with robbers and

* Josephus's Wars of the Jews, vol. v. p. 184.   † Tacitus.
‡ This is supposed to have happened in the year of Christ 55.
§ Josephus, vol. v. p. 184, 185.

murderers; and the frequency of the horrid assassinations among them, excited universal consternation.

Porcius Festus, who succeeded Felix upon his removal from the government, supported a better character than his predecessor. At the commencement of his administration, the assassins were spreading terror throughout Jerusalem. He punished these wretches with exemplary severity, and exerted himself to the utmost to suppress the civil discords, which, in consequence of the extravagant claims, and frequent depositions of the Jewish pontiffs, raged among the priests, and filled the country, the city, and sometimes the temple, with blood.*

Festus died in his government, and the Roman emperor Nero sent Albinus in his room. Insatiable avarice being his ruling passion, he burdened the nation with extraordinary tributes; and became the encourager of all kinds of villany, by yielding to bribery and corruption.†

Gessius Florius, who succeeded Albinus, far surpassed him in wickedness; and gloried in his greater violence. He even robbed the sacred treasury, pillaged whole provinces, oppressed the Jews by all kinds of rapine and extortion, encouraged the robbery and plunder of the banditti, for a share of their booty; fomented the public divisions; and even used his utmost exertions to excite an open rebellion, in hopes, that the public confusion might prevent complaint against his iniquitous conduct. In a word, he was one of the vilest wretches, that ever disgraced

---

* Josephus, vol. v. p. 186. Mavor's Univ. Hist. vol. ii. p. 347.
† Josephus, vol. v. p. 186.

human nature; and a distinguished instrument of divine vengeance upon the subjects of his capricious tyranny.*

In consequence of the distracted state of Judea, many of its inhabitants sought an asylum in foreign countries; while those who remained, applied to Cestius Gallus, governor of Syria, who was at Jerusalem, at the passover, earnestly beseeching him to deliver them from the tyranny of their cruel governor. Cestius, instead of making a strict inquiry into the conduct of Florus, dismissed the Jews, with a general promise, that he should behave better for the future. In the meantime directions were given to compute the number of Jews then at Jerusalem, by that of the lambs offered at the festival, which were found to amount to 2,556,000.†

A. D. 65.] While the arbitrary conduct of the governor, and the irritated state of the Jewish people, threatened them with the horrors of war; famines, earthquakes, and terrific sights in the heavens, appeared to fulfil the awful predictions of our Saviour. Josephus, among many other fearful prodigies, relates, that before the rebellion, when a great multitude were assembled in Jerusalem, at the Passover, at the ninth hour of the night, so great a light shone round the altar, and the temple, that it seemed to be bright day; that a few days after the festival, before sun-set, chariots and troops of soldiers in armour were seen passing through the clouds, and surrounding cities; and that the priests, going into the inner temple, felt the place move

* Josephus, vol. v. p. 187.   † Ibid.

and tremble, and heard a voice, more than human, crying, " Let us depart hence."*

This account is confirmed by Tacitus, the Roman historian, who says, " Portents and prodigies announced the ruin of Jerusalem; swords were seen glittering in the air; embattled armies appeared; and the temple was illuminated by a stream of light, that issued from the heavens, the portal flew open, and a voice more than human announced the immediate departure of the gods; there was heard at the same time a terrific sound, as if superior beings were actually rushing forth."†

A contest had long subsisted between the Jews and Syrians concerning Cesarea, which was situated in the confines of Syria and Judea. The Jews maintained, that the city belonged to them, because it was built by Herod their king; while the Syrians pretended, that it had always been considered as a Grecian city, since even that monarch had erected in it temples and statues. During the administration of Felix, the contest rose to such a height, that both parties armed against each other. That governor allayed the ferment for a time, by sending some of the chiefs of both nations to Rome to plead their

---

* Josephus, vol. v. See Archbishop Newcome's Observations on the character of our Lord, for an admirable detail of these events.

† Murphy's Tacitus. Dr. Jortin remarks, that " if Christ had not expressly foretold, that there *should be fearful sights, and great signs from heaven*, many, who give little heed to portents, and know that historians have been too credulous in this point, would have suspected that Josephus had exaggerated, and that Tacitus was misinformed: but, as the testimonies of Josephus and Tacitus confirm the predictions of Christ, so the predictions of Christ confirm the wonders related by these historians."—*Jortin's Remarks on Ecclesiastical History*

cause before the emperor. The affair hung in sus-
pense till this period, when Nero decided it against
the Jews. This event was the immediate cause of
the fatal war with the Romans, which proved the
most desperate of any recorded in history; and terminated in the destruction of Jerusalem.*

A. D. 66.] The decree of the emperor was no
sooner published, than the Jews, in all parts of the
country, took up arms; Agrippa,† who happened
to be at Jerusalem at the commencement of the war,
attempted to appease the fury of the multitude by an
elaborate speech, in which he painted, in glowing
colours, the vast extent and grandeur of the Roman
empire; the mighty nations who had been subdued
by its all-conquering arms; the folly and infatuation
of the Jews in opposing the masters of the world;
and concluded by a pathetic exhortation to his
country-men, to lay down the weapons of their
rebellion. But his entreaties and remonstrances
were alike disregarded; and he was compelled to
provide for his personal safety by quitting the city.‡

The flames of intestine war now raged with irresistible fury in every part of the unhappy province,
and its progress was marked by acts of cruelty and

---

* Josephus, vol. v. p. 188.

† He was the son of Agrippa, great grand son to Herod, and king
of Chalcis. He resided chiefly at Jerusalem, and obtained the administration of the temple, and a right to appoint or depose the high
priests. When the high priest Ananus, had condemned St. James to
death, some Jews who disapproved of this cruelty, complained to
Agrippa, and this prince deprived him of the high priesthood. He,
with his sister Bernice, heard St. Paul's defence before Festus, the
Roman governor, and he owned himself almost convinced by it.
See Acts xxv. 26. *Basnage's History of the Jews*, p. 23.

‡ Josephus, vol. v. p. 215

desperation. Twenty thousand Jews were massacred at Cesarea, fifty-two thousand at Alexandria, two thousand at Ptolemais, and three thousand five hundred were cut off at Jerusalem by the troops of Florus in one day. The Jews, to the utmost of their power, exercised similar cruelties on the Syrians and Romans, and slaughtered immense numbers of people.*

The rebellious Jews being joined in Jerusalem by numerous assassins, with their assistance beat the Romans out of the fortresses of Antonia and Massada, possessed themselves of the towers of Phasael and Mariamne, and reduced the palaces of Agrippa, Bernice, and the high priest to ashes. . They even carried their fury to such a height, as to massacre those Romans, who had capitulated on condition of having their lives preserved. Their treachery was, however, soon revenged on the Jews in Sythopolis, who had offered to assist in reducing their factious brethren. For their sincerity being suspected, above thirteen thousand of their number were inhumanly massacred. The rebels, in the mean time, crossed the Jordan, and took the fortresses of Machærus and Cyprus; the latter of which, after putting all the Romans to the sword, was razed to the ground.†

Upon the general revolt of the Jews, Cestius Gallus, president of Syria, marched at the head of a powerful army into Judea and Galilee, burning all the towns and villages in his way, and slaughtering the inhabitants. He was met at Gibeon, a city about six miles from Jerusalem, by large numbers of Jews, who attacked him with such fury, that his whole

* Josephus, vol. v. p. 215.   † Ibid.

army was in danger. Agrippa, who joined him with a body of troops, endeavoured once more to appease his rebellious countrymen by sending two of his officers to them with proposals of peace. But after they had killed one of his officers and wounded the other, Cestius advanced with his whole army, repulsed the rebels, and made himself master of the lower parts of Jerusalem.* Josephus says, "If Cestius had continued the siege a little longer, he would have taken the city; but God being angry with the wicked, would not suffer the war to be terminated at that time." But Cestius suddenly and unexpectedly raised the siege at the instigation of some of his officers, who, it is said, were bribed by Florus. Emboldened by this impolitic step, the insurgents pursued Cestius to his camp at Gibeon, from whence he escaped by night, with the loss of upwards of five thousand of his army.†

It is recorded by an ancient historian,‡ that the Christians abandoned Jerusalem at this awful period. Having called to mind the warning of their divine Master, that, when they should see Jerusalem encompassed about with armies, and the abomination of desolation (the Roman army with their idolatrous images §) standing in the holy place, they should

* About A. D. 67.　　　† Josephus.
‡ Eusebius's Ecclesiastical History, Book iii. chap. 5.
§ "The Roman armies are styled, *the abomination of desolation,* because they not only spread desolation before them, but were held in the utmost abhorrence by the Jews, on account of the images of their gods and emperors, which they carried in their standards, by which they swore, and to which they sacrificed The usual ornaments of these standards gave such offence to the Jews, that, in peaceable times, the Romans entered Jerusalem without them: and Vitellius, at the request of some eminent Jews, humanely avoided

flee unto the mountains. In obedience to this sacred injunction, they removed to Pella, a city beyond the river Jordan, about an hundred miles from Jerusalem, belonging to Agrippa, and inhabited by Gentiles. Here they obtained a safe asylum; and we do not find, that even a single individual of them perished in the ruin of the Jewish metropolis.*

The defeat of Cestius heightened the obstinacy of the Jews, who, elated with their success, made formidable preparations for the prosecution of the war. Ananus, the high priest, and Joseph, the son of Gorion, were appointed to govern Jerusalem, and repair the walls; while persons of approved valour and resolution were sent to command the troops in the provinces. Josephus,† a priest of considerable

marching his forces through Judea on account of these ensigns. When therefore they were planted within sight of the city and temple, when they stood within the holy precincts of Jerusalem, rivalling, as it were, the God of Israel, this was a hostile contempt of the Jews, and is justly placed among the presages of their utter destruction."— *Newcome's Observations on our Lord*, p. 240.

* Newton on the Prophecies, part ii. p. 19.

† Josephus was born at Jerusalem, 37, and descended from the illustrious Asmonean family. He soon discovered great acuteness and penetration; and made so rapid a progress in the learning of the Jews, that he was occasionally consulted by the chief priests and rulers of the city at the age of sixteen. He adopted the opinions of the Pharisees, and engaged in civil affairs. In the early part of the Jewish war, he was a famous general; and after he was taken prisoner admitted to share the confidence of Vespasian, and his son Titus, the latter of whom he accompanied to the siege of Jerusalem. After the city was taken, he attended Titus to Rome, where Vespasian gave him the freedom of the city, and settled a pension upon him. At Rome he applied himself to study the Greek language, and composed his history of the wars of the Jews. He lived till the thirteenth year of Domitian; and died in 93, aged fifty-six years —*General Biographical Dictionary*, vol. ix. p. 28.

rank, and the celebrated writer of the antiquities and wars of the Jews, was appointed governor of the two Galilees.

Nero, the Roman emperor, who had received intelligence of the defeat of Cestius, and was alarmed at the energetic measures which were taken by the Jews, commanded Vespasian, an officer of distinguished prudence and bravery, to march with all possible expedition into Judea. Accordingly, that commander employed himself in raising forces; and his son Titus was despatched to fetch two of the Roman legions from Alexandria. But the Jews, previous to the arrival of the army in their country, had twice attempted to take the city of Ascalon, and were each time repulsed, with the loss of ten thousand of their number in the first, and eight thousand in the second engagement.

Early in the following spring, the imperial army, which amounted to sixty thousand men, completely armed, and fully disciplined, entered Galilee. Soon after their arrival, Gadara was taken on the first assault; all the adults were put to the sword, and fire set to the adjacent towns and villages. The conquerors next closely besieged Jotaphata. Josephus, being apprized of their design, supplied the city with ample stores, and defended it with heroic valour for forty-seven days. The Romans, however, finally surprised and took the place, and all the inhabitants were either slain, or made prisoners. The captives amounted to one thousand two hundred; and forty thousand lost their lives on this occasion.*

* Josephus, vol. v. p. 285.

Josephus was among the prisoners. He had escaped the general massacre, by flying from the midst of his enemies, and with forty of his bravest men, concealed himself in a deep cavern. His retreat was discovered to Vespasian, and that famous general sent to offer him life, upon honourable conditions. Upon his preparing to accept the terms, his companions upbraided him in the severest manner, and even offered to murder him. At this critical moment, he appeased their fury, by advising them, if they were determined upon death, to draw lots, who should kill his companion, in order to avoid the crime of suicide. This dreadful proposal was accepted; and Providence so ordered it, that the two last survivors were Josephus, and a person whom he easily persuaded to live. The Jewish commander, upon his arrival in the Roman camp, assured Vespasian; that he should soon be chosen emperor; and, in consequence of this prediction, the conqueror treated him with great respect and generosity.*

While the Roman forces were besieging Jotaphata, the inhabitants of Japha, a neighbouring city, rebelled. The general sent a powerful army against them, and they were reduced, after an obstinate siege. All the men, amounting to 15,000, were massacred; and the women and children made prisoners. About a week after, the Samaritans, who had assembled in a riotous manner on Mount Gerizzim, were almost all put to the sword, or perished. Joppa, which had been formerly laid waste by Cestius, being now re-peopled and fortified

* Josephus, vol. v. p. 293.

by some seditious Jews, who infested the country, fell the next victim to the Roman vengeance. When the imperial army invaded that city, large numbers of the wretched inhabitants betook themselves to their ships. But they were driven back by a violent tempest, which dashed the vessels against the rocks. In this extreme distress many perished by suicide; others were swallowed up by the waves, or crushed by the broken ships; and such as were enabled to reach the shore were killed by the merciless Romans. The sea was for a long space discoloured with blood; four thousand two hundred dead bodies strewed the coast, and not a messenger remained to report this great calamity at Jerusalem.*

After Vespasian had refreshed his troops, he marched to Tiberias; the city yielded; and the inhabitants were spared at the moving intercession of king Agrippa. Tarichæ, on the sea of Galilee, was next attacked; and, after an obstinate resistance, reduced by the victorious Romans. Multitudes of Jews were destroyed, and upwards of thirty thousand sold for slaves. Vespasian proceeded to invest Gamala, a city placed on a rocky isthmus. The assailants were driven back with prodigious slaughter. Their last attack, however, was successful, the flight of their darts being favoured by a violent storm, which obstructed those of the enemy. After the city was taken, the exasperated victors slew four thousand of the inhabitants; and a large number fell victims to their own impatience and ungovernable fury. The Romans also obtained a decisive

---

* Josephus, vol. v. p. 291. Newcome's Observations on our Lord, p. 228.

victory over the Jews, who had retired to a strong
hold on Mount Itabys.*

Titus, who was sent to besiege Gischala, earnestly
exhorted the inhabitants to save themselves from
destruction, by a timely surrender. The citizens
were inclined to accede to his advice ; but a seditious
Jew, named John, the son of Levi, head of his
faction, vehemently opposed it ; and, having the
mob at his command, overawed the whole city. On
the sabbath he entreated Titus to forbear hostilities
till the following day, engaging, on that condition,
to accede to his proposal. But, after his request
was granted, he with a number of his followers,
withdrew to Jerusalem. The citizens then surrendered, and, having apprized Titus of John's
flight, earnestly besought him not to punish the
innocent with the guilty. The conqueror, after
yielding to their entreaties, pursued and killed six
thousand of the followers of John, and brought back
three thousand women and children prisoners. The
traitor himself eluded their pursuit, and exasperated
the inhabitants of Jerusalem against the Romans.†

After the conquest of Galilee was completed, by
the reduction of Gischala, Titus joined his father, at
Cesarea, where his troops were permitted to enjoy
an interval of repose; during the remainder of this,
and in the following year, the revolutions in the
Roman empire prevented Vespasian from pursuing
the war with vigour. He the more readily deferred
commencing the siege of Jerusalem, from being

* Josephus.
† Hence Josephus says, " God saved John for the destruction of
Jerusalem," p. 294.

apprized, that the Jews were wasting their strength
by internal divisions, and facilitating the conquest of
their devoted city.*

The Jewish nation at this time were divided
into two very opposite parties. The more rational
part, who clearly saw that the war, if continued,
would end in the total ruin of their country, strongly
urged the necessity of immediate submission to the
Romans. Another party, called Zealots, from their
boasted zeal for the law of God, and the religious
customs of their ancestors, vehemently opposed all
pacific measures. This faction, which was far the
most numerous and powerful, consisted of men of
the vilest and most abandoned characters ever recorded in history. They were the remains of the
sect of the Gaulonites, which was headed by Judas
Theudas, and like him affirmed, that it would be
offering the greatest dishonour to God to submit
to any earthly potentate, much less to Romans and
heathens. Under the mask of religion, these
wretches committed the most horrid and unnatural
crimes.†

John, who had fled from Gischala, put himself
at the head of these incendiaries; and, being joined
in that city by a band of robbers and assassins,
seized upon the temple for a fortress, and that holy
place was made a theatre of civil war. The opposite
party, under the conduct of Ananus, a wise and
venerable man, among the chief priests, armed in
their own defence; and, after an obstinate contest,
forced the Zealots into the inner cincture of the
temple, where they were closely invested. John,

* Josephus, vol. v. p. 355.   † Ibid, p. 334.

who·had pretended to agree with·those, who desired
peace, was sent to the Zealots with terms of. accommodation ; but he··betrayed his trust, and earnestly
exhorted· them to persevere with unshaken firmness.
He; intimated to them the ;necessity, of foreign
assistance ;، and, persuaded them to، enter into، a
treaty· with· the Idumeans. But Ananus shut، the
gates of Jerusalem, and . precluded، the new allies
from entering the city.*

. ؛ On the ؛night؛,the، Idumeans، were excluded, there
was a tremendous storm, accompanied with thunder,
lightning, and، a violent؛ earthquake. ؛The، Zealots
took . advantage ؛of· the prevailing terror and ,con-
fusion, sawed، the bolts and hinges، of ,the temple
gates، without، being heard, forced the guards, sallied
into the city, and introduced twenty thousand of، their
allies:،؛ After being thus strengthened and assisted,
they perpetrated the most horrid cruelties. Twelve
thousand persons of noble birth, and in the prime
of life, upon their refusal to, join , them, were inhumanly murdered.· ، Ananus and Joshua, the chief
priests, ،were next put to death; and ،their . dead·
bodies left without burial. .After massacreing many
persons of distinction, they turned their sanguinary
cruelty upon the citizens and lower classes, and the
capital was filled ,with blood and carnage. At this
dreadful period, none dared . publicly to lament the
loss of his nearest·friends or relations; or even afford
them the last ·melancholy rites of interment. This
cruel despotism compelled many to forsake Jerusalem, and take refuge with the Romans, though the
·attempt was extremely hazardous, as the avenues of

* Josephus, vol. v. p. 378.

the city were strictly guarded; and all, who were
detected in attempting to escape, were immediately
put to death. The Idumeans, who were of John's
party, at length complained of the vast numbers,
who were massacred; repented of having joined
the tyrant, and returned to their native country.*

The Zealots, after they had massacred or driven
away all, who were capable of opposing them,
turned their murderous weapons against each other.
A new faction was formed against John by Simon,
a man of an abandoned character, and daring spirit,
who had his head quarters in the fortress of Masada.
To increase his party, he published a proclamation,
in which he promised liberty to the slaves, and
suitable encouragement to all freemen, who would
enlist under his banners. After he had, by this
stratagem, collected many followers, he invaded
Idumea, perpetrated all kinds of cruelty, corrupted
the general of that country, and having gained
possession of their military forces, advanced towards
Jerusalem, and encamped before the city. This
army destroyed the Jews without the walls, and
were more dreaded than the Romans; while the
Zealots within excited still greater terror than
either.*

The inhabitants of Jerusalem, in order to oppose
the tyranny of John, who, they apprehended,
would burn the city, formed the fatal resolution of
admitting Simon and his troops. Accordingly, they
entered the metropolis, and increased the calamities
of the miserable people, who were exposed alternately to the rage of both factions. Another party

* Josephus, vol. v. p. 347.   † Ibid.

also arose in the city, under Eleazar, formerly a commander of the Zealots, seized upon the court of the priests, and kept John confined within that of the Israelites. He, being enclosed by Simon, who had possession of the city, and by Eleazar, who occupied the inner temple, defended himself with great resolution against both his powerful enemies; killed and wounded many of each party; and the temple and altar were frequently polluted with blood.*

A. D. 69] During the internal contest in the city, Vespasian had marched from Cesarea, and conquered the yet unsubdued part of the country; he stormed Hebron near Jerusalem, slew all the adults, and burned the city. He had also gained possession of Gadara, the metropolis of Perea, and reduced all the Idumean towns to ashes, except such as were deemed serviceable to the troops, whom he appointed to overawe the country. As every place was now reduced, but Herodium, Masada, and Machærus, which the robbers had occupied, Jerusalem became the grand object of the Romans. Vespasian, therefore, being elected emperor, previously to his taking possession of his dominions, sent his son Titus to reduce this metropolis. An account of the tremendous calamities of the Jews, during the destruction of their city and temple, will be related in the following chapter.

In the meantime, while, with the most painful sensations, we read an account of calamities, which no other description of men ever experienced in any age or country, let us recollect, that the Jews had

* Josephus, vol v. p. 369.

called down the divine wrath, by crucifying the
Lord of glory, and blasphemously exclaiming, "His
blood be upon us and our children." This dreadful
imprecation was fulfilled ; and the vengeance of
heaven, of which they had been mercifully fore-
warned by the prophets, and by Christ himself,
was discharged upon them by that very nation,
whom they had instigated to condemn the Messiah.

CHAPTER II.

Strength of Jerusalem.—The Jews are assembled from all parts to keep
the passover.—The city is invested by Titus.—They make great
preparations for an attack.—They gain the first and second wall.—
A famine raged in Jerusalem.—Inhuman practices of the Zealots.—
Jerusalem is surrounded by a wall.—Terrible situation of the city.
—The temple is plundered, and daily sacrifice ceaseth.—The temple
set on fire.—Horrid massacre of the Jews.—All Jerusalem conquered by the Romans.—The temple and city demolished.—The
remaining castles in Judea are taken.

JERUSALEM was built on two mountains, and
surrounded by three walls on every side, except
where it was enclosed with deep vallies, which were
deemed inaccessible.   Each wall was fortified by
high towers.   The celebrated temple, and the
strong castle of Antonia, were on the east side of
the city, and directly opposite to the Mount of
Olives. But notwithstanding the prodigious strength
of this famed metropolis, the infatuated Jews brought
on their own destruction by their intestine contests.
At a time, when a formidable army was rapidly
advancing, and the Jews were assembling from all
parts, to keep the passover,* the contending factions
were continually inventing new methods of mutual
destruction, and in their ungoverned fury they wasted

---

* " The day on which Titus encompassed Jerusalem was," says
a late author, " the feast of the passover; and it is deserving of
particular attention, that this was the anniversary of that memorable
period, in which the Jews crucified their Messiah." See a pamphlet
entitled, " The destruction of Jerusalem an absolute and irresistible
proof of the divine authority of Christianity." London, published 1805.

and destroyed such vast quantities of provisions as
might have preserved the city many years.*

A. D. 70.] Such was the miserable situation of
Jerusalem, when Titus began his march towards it
with a formidable army ; and, having laid waste the
country in his progress, and slaughtered the inhabitants, arrived before its walls. The sight of the
Romans produced a temporary reconciliation among
the contending factions, and they unanimously resolved to oppose the common enemy. Their first
sally was accordingly made with such fury and
resolution, that, though Titus displayed uncommon
valour on this occasion, the besiegers were obliged
to abandon their camps, and flee to the mountains.
No sooner had the Jews a short interval of quiet†
from their foreign enemies, than their civil disorders
were renewed. John, by an impious stratagem,
found means to cut off or force Eleazar's men to
submit to him ; and the factions were again reduced
to two, who opposed each other with implacable
animosity.‡

The Romans, in the mean time, exerted all their
energy in making preparations for a powerful attack
upon Jerusalem. Trees were cut down, houses
levelled, rocks cleft asunder, and vallies filled up ;
towers were raised, and battering rams erected, with
other engines of destruction, against the devoted city.

---

* Josephus.

† Bishop Newcome remarks, that at this period the Christians had
an opportunity of escaping from Jerusalem, according to our Lord's
solemn exhortation. For some time before this flight was precluded,
as it bore the appearance of a revolt to the Romans.—*Newcome's
Observations*, p. 242.

‡ Josephus, vol. vi. p. 127.

After the offers of peace, which Titus had repeatedly sent by Josephus, were rejected with indignation, the Romans began to play their engines with all their might. The strenuous attacks of the enemy again united the contending parties within the walls, who had also engines, which they plied with uncommon fury. They had taken them lately from Cestius, but were so ignorant of their use they did little execution, while the Roman legions made terrible havock. The rebels were soon compelled to retire from the ponderous stones, which they threw incessantly from the towers they had erected, and the battering rams were at full liberty to play against the walls. A breach was soon made in it, at which the Romans entered, and encamped in the city, while the Jews retreated behind the second enclosure.*

The victors immediately advanced to the second wall, and plied their engines and battering rams so furiously, that one of the towers they had erected began to shake, and the Jews, who occupied it, perceiving their impending ruin, set it on fire, and precipitated themselves into the flames. The fall of this structure gave the Romans an entrance into the second enclosure. They were, however, repulsed by the besieged; but at length regained the place entirely, and prepared for attacking the third and inner wall.†

The vast number of people, which were enclosed in Jerusalem, occasioned a famine, which raged in a terrible manner; and, as their calamities increased,

* Josephus, vol. vi. p. 38.
† Ibid, p. 49—50. Mavor's Universal History.

the fury of the Zealots, if possible, rose to a greater height. They forced open the houses of their fellow citizens in search of provisions; if they found any, they inflicted the most exquisite tortures upon them,· under pretence that they had food concealed. The nearest relations, in the extremity of hunger, snatched the food from each other.

Josephus, who was an eye witness of ·the un-. paralleled sufferings the Jews experienced ·during the siege of their metropolis, remarks, that "all the calamities that ever befel any nation ' since ' the beginning of the world, were inferior to the miseries of his countrymen at this awful period." * .Thus we see the exact fulfilment of the emphatic words of our Saviour respecting the great tribulation in Jerusalem.† .

Titus, who was apprized of their wretched condition, relaxed the siege four days; and, being still desirous of saving the city, caused provisions to be distributed to his army in sight of the Jews, who flocked upon the walls to behold it. Josephus was next sent to his countrymen to attempt to persuade them not to plunge themselves in inevitable ruin by persisting in defence of a place, which could hold out but little longer, and which the Romans looked upon as already their own. He exhorted them in the most pathetic terms, to save themselves, their temple, and their country; and painted in strong colours the fatal effects, which would result from their obstinacy. But the people, after many bitter invectives, began to dart their arrows at him; yet he continued to address them with greater vehe-

* Josephus, vol. \i. p. 63.　　† Matthew xxiv. 21.

mence, and many were induced by his eloquence, to run the utmost risk in order to escape to the Romans; while others became more desperate, and resolved to hold out to the last extremity. *

. The Jews, who were forcibly seized by the Romans without the walls, and who made the utmost resistance for fear of punishment, were scourged and crucified near the city. Famine made them so daring in these excursions, that five hundred, and sometimes more, suffered this dreadful death every day; and, on account of the number, Josephus observes, that " space, was wanted for the crosses, and crosses for the captives." And yet, contrary to Titus's intention, the seditious Jews were not disposed to a surrender by these horrid spectacles. In order to check desertion, they represented the sufferers as suppliants, and not as men taken by resistance. Yet even some, who deemed capital punishment inevitable, escaped to the Romans, considering death, by the hands of their enemies, a desirable refuge, when compared with the complicated distress which they endured. And though Titus mutilated many, and sent them to assure the people, that voluntary deserters were well treated by him, and earnestly to recommend a surrender of the city, the Jews reviled Titus from the walls, defied his menaces, and continued to defend the city by every method, which stratagem, courage, and despair could suggest.†

In order to accelerate the destined ruin of Jerusalem, Titus, discouraged and exasperated by the re-

* Josephus, vol. vi. p. 50.

† Ibid, p. 51—65. Newcome's Observations, &c. p. 245.

peated destruction of his engines and towers, undertook the arduous task of enclosing the city with a strong
wall, in order to prevent the inhabitants from receiving
any succour from the adjacent country, or eluding
his vengeance by flight.   Such was the persevering
spirit of the soldiers, that in three days they enclosed
the city by a wall nearly five miles in circuit. , Thus -
was the prophecy of our Saviour accomplished :*
" *The days shall come upon thee, when thine enemies
shall cast a trench about thee, and compass thee
round, and keep thee in on every side.*"   Upon.this,
the famine raged with .augmented violence, and
destroyed whole families ; while Jerusalem exhibited
a horrid spectacle of emaciated invalids and putre-
scent bodies.†   The dead were too numerous to be
interred ; .and many expired in the performance of
this office.   The public calamity was too great for
lamentation, and the silence of unutterable woe over-
spread the city.   The Zealots, at this awful period,
endeavoured to encourage the obstinacy of the people,

---

* Luke xix. 43.

† The vast number of people shut up by the war, occasioned pestilential diseases, and afterwards famine of course advanced more
rapidly. Dr. Lardner observes, that "it might have been expected,
that the bad food, which the Jews were forced to make use of, the
strictness of the siege, and the noisome smell of so many dead bodies
lying in heaps in the city itself, and in the vallies and ditches without
the walls, should have produced a plague. But nothing of this kind
appears in the history; which must have been owing to the special
interposition of divine providence. Josephus, in some of the places,
where he speaks of the putrefaction of the dead bodies, may use
expressions equivalent to pestilential ; but he never shews, that there
was an infection: if there had been, it would have equally affected
the Romans and the Jews, and the siege of the city must have been
broken up, and the Romans would have gone off as fast as they
could '—*Watson's Tracts*, vol. v. p 170.

by hiring a set of wretches, pretenders to prophecy, to go about the city, and declare the near approach of a speedy and miraculous deliverance. This impious stratagem for a while afforded delusive hopes to the miserable remains of the Jewish nation. But at length an affair took place in Jerusalem, which filled the inhabitants with consternation and despair; and the Romans with horror and indignation. A Jewess, eminent for birth and opulence, rendered frantic with her sufferings, was reduced to the dreadful extremity of killing and feeding upon her infant. Titus, being apprized of this inhuman deed, swore the total extirpation of the accursed city and people; and called heaven to witness, that he was not the author of their calamity.*

The Romans, having pursued the attack with the utmost rigour, advanced their last engines against the walls; after having converted into a desert, for wood to construct them, a country well planted, and interspersed with gardens, for more than eleven miles round the city. They scaled the inner wall; and after a sanguinary encounter, made themselves masters of the fortress of Antonia. Still, however, not only the Zealots, but many of the people, were yet so blinded, that, though nothing was now left but the temple, and the Romans were making formidable preparation to batter it down, they could not persuade themselves, that God would suffer that holy place to be taken by heathens; but still expected a miraculous deliverance. And though the war was advancing towards the temple, they themselves burnt the portico, which joined it to Antonia;

* Josephus, vol. vi. p. 73—82. 108.

G

which occasioned Titus to remark, that they began to destroy with their own hands, that magnificent edifice, which he had preserved. When Josephus was sent for the last time to John, who commanded in the temple, to upbraid him for obstinately exposing that sacred building, and the miserable remains of God's people to inevitable destruction, he answered with the bitterest invectives, adding, that " he was defending the Lord's vineyard, which he was sure could not be taken by any human force;" yet this monster had not scrupled to plunder the temple of a large quantity of its golden utensils, and the magnificent gifts of kings, which he converted to his own use. He also seized the sacred oil, which was to maintain the lamps; and even used to intoxicate himself and his party with the wine, which was intended for sacrifice.*

On the 17th of July, the daily sacrifice ceased for the first time since its restoration by the brave Judas Maccabeus, there being no proper person left to make the offering. Titus upbraided the Zealots for neglecting their worship; and challenged them to leave the temple, and fight on more proper ground, in order to preserve that sacred edifice from the fury of his troops. But, as they persisted in their inflexible obstinacy, Titus, after several bloody engagements, took possession of the outward court of the Gentiles, and forced the besieged into that of the priests. The Roman commander had determined in council not to burn the temple, considering the existence of so proud a structure an honour to himself. He, therefore, attempted to

* Josephus. vol. vi. p. 79. Mavor's Universal Hist. vol. ii. p. 313.

batter down one of the galleries of the precinct; but as the strength of the wall eluded the force of all his engines, his troops next endeavoured to scale it, but were repulsed with considerable loss. When Titus found, that his desire of saving the sacred building, was likely to cost many lives, he set fire to the gates of the outer temple; which, being plaited with silver, burnt all night, and the flame rapidly communicated to the adjacent galleries and porticoes. Titus, who was still desirous of preserving the temple, caused the flames to be extinguished; and appeased the clamours of his troops, who vehemently insisted on the necessity of razing it to the ground. The following day was, therefore, fixed upon for a general assault upon that magnificent structure.[*]

The utmost exertions of Titus to save the temple were, however, ineffectual. Our Saviour had foretold its total destruction, and his awful prediction was about to be accomplished.[†] And now, says Josephus, " the fatal day approached in the revolution of ages, the 10th of August, emphatically called, *the day of vengeance,* in which the first temple had been destroyed by the king of Babylon." While Titus was reposing himself in his pavilion, a Roman soldier, without receiving any command, seized some of the blazing materials, and, with the assistance of another soldier, who raised him from the ground, threw them through a window into one of the apartments, that surrounded the sanctuary. The whole north side, up to the third story, was immediately enveloped in flames. The Jews, who now began to suppose Heaven had for-

---

* Josephus, vol. vi. p. 93, 94.   † Matthew xxiv. 2.

saken them, rushed in with violent lamentations, and spared no effort, not even life itself, to preserve tho sacred edifice on which they had rested their security.

Titus, being awakened by the outcry, hastened to the spot, and commanded his soldiers to exert themselves to the utmost to extinguish the fire. He called, urged, and threatened his men. But so great was the clamour and tumult, that his entreaties and menaces were alike disregarded. The exas-perated Romans, who resorted thither from the camp, were engaged either in increasing the confla-gration, or killing the Jews; the dead were heaped about the altar, and a stream of blood flowed at its steps.*

Still, as the flames had not reached the inner part of the temple, Titus, with some of his chief officers, entered the sanctuary and most holy place, which excited his astonishment and admiration. After having in vain repeated his attempts to prevent its destruction, he saved the golden candlestick, the table of shew bread, the altar of perfumes, which were all of pure gold; and the volume of the law, wrapped up in a rich golden tissue. Upon his leaving the sacred place, some other soldiers set fire to it, after tearing off the golden plaiting from the gates and timber work.†

A horrid massacre soon followed, in which pro-digious multitudes perished; while others rushed in a kind of phrensy into the midst of the flames, and precipitated themselves from the battlements of their falling temple. Six thousand persons, who, de-luded by a false prophet, with hopes of a mira-

* Josephus. vol. vi p 117.   † Ibid. p. 115.

culous deliverance, had fled to a gallery yet standing without the temple, perished at once by the relentless barbarity of the soldiers, who set it on fire, and suffered none to escape. The conquerors carried their fury to such an height, as to massacre all they met, without distinction of age, sex, or quality. They also burnt all the treasure houses, containing vast quantities of money, plate, and the richest furniture. In a word, they continued to mark their progress with fire and sword, till they had destroyed all, except two of the temple gates, and that part of the court which was destined for the women.*

In the meantime, many of the Zealots, by making the most vigorous exertions, effected their escape from the temple, and retired into the city. But the avenues were so strictly guarded, that it was impossible for them to escape. They therefore fortified themselves, as well as they were able, on the south side of it; from whence John and Simon sent to desire a conference with Titus. They were answered, that though they had caused all this ruin and effusion of blood, yet their lives should be spared if they would surrender themselves. They replied, that " they had engaged by the most solemn oaths, not to deliver up their persons to him on any conditions; and requested permission to retire to the mountains with their wives and children." The Roman general, enraged at this insolence, ordered proclamation to be made, that not one of them should be spared, since they persisted in rejecting his last offers of pardon.†

The daughter of Zion, or the lower city, was

* Josephus, vol. vi. p. 116, 117.　　† Josephus, vol. vi. p. 127.

next abandoned to the fury of the Roman soldiers,
who plundered, burnt, and massacred with insatiable rage. The Zealots next betook themselves to
the royal palace in the upper and stronger part
of Jerusalem, styled also, the city of David, on
Mount Zion. As many of the Jews had deposited
their possessions in the palace for security, they
attacked it, killed eight thousand four hundred of
their countrymen, and plundered their property.*

The Roman army spent nearly twenty days in
making great preparations for attacking the upper
city, especially the royal palace; during which
time, many came and made their submission to
Titus. The warlike engines then played so furiously upon the Zealots, that they were seized with
a sudden panic, quitted the towers, which were
deemed impregnable, and ran like mad men towards
Shiloah, intending to have attacked the wall of
circumvallation, and escaped out of the city. But
being vigorously repulsed, they endeavoured to
conceal themselves in subterraneous passages; and,
as many as were discovered, were put to death.

The conquest of Jerusalem being now completed,
the Romans placed their ensigns upon the walls
with triumphant joy. They next walked the streets,
with swords in their hands, and killed all they met.
Amidst the darkness of that awful night, fire was set
to the remaining divisions of the city, and Jerusalem, wrapt in flames, and bleeding on every side,
sunk in utter ruin and destruction. During the
siege, which lasted nearly five months, upwards of
eleven hundred thousand Jews perished. John and

* Josephus, vol. vi. p. 127.

Simon, the two grand rebels, with seven hundred of
the most beautiful and vigorous of the Jewish youth,
were reserved to attend the victor's triumphal
chariot. After which, Simon was put to death;
and John, who had stooped to beg his life, condemned to perpetual imprisonment.*.

The number, who were taken captive during the
fatal contest with the Romans, amounted to ninety
seven thousand; many of whom were sent into
Syria, and other provinces, to be exposed on the
public theatres, to fight like gladiators, or to be
devoured by wild beasts. The number of those
destroyed during the war, which lasted seven years,
is computed to have been one million four hundred
and sixty two thousand.+

When the sword had returned to its scabbard for
want of objects whereon to exercise its fury, and
the troops were satisfied with plunder, Titus commanded the whole city and temple to be demolished.
Upon viewing the strength of the works, he exclaimed, " We have fought with the assistance of
God; it was God who drove the Jews out of these
fortifications; for what can the hands of men, or the
force of machines effect against these towers." In
order to give posterity an idea of the strength of the
city, and the astonishing valour of its conquerors,
he preserved the highest towers, Phasælus, Hip-
picus, and Mariamne, and a part of the wall which
surrounded Jerusalem to the west. All the other
circuit of the city was so levelled, as not to leave
those, who approached it, any proof that it ever had
been inhabited.‡ It is recorded in the Talmud,

* Josephus, vol. vi. p. 139.   + Ibid.   ‡ Ibid. p. 142, 143.

and by Maimonides, that Terentius Rufus ploughed up the foundations of the temple ; thus were our Saviour's prophecies fulfilled : " *Thine enemies shall lay thee even with the ground ; and there shall not be left one stone upon another.*"*

On the reduction of Jerusalem, Titus returned in triumph to Rome, where the senate decreed him a triumph with Vespasian, his father ; and all things, that were esteemed the most valuable and beautiful, were exhibited to grace this great occasion. Among the rich spoils, those, which were saved from the temple of Jerusalem, were the most remarkable ; and the volume of the law was the most venerable of all the trophies of the conqueror.

Three strong castles still remained untaken in the almost desolated land of Judea. Lucillius Bassus was sent by Vespasian, as lieutenant general ; and soon reduced Herodium and Machærus. But the castle of Masada, being very strong both by nature and art ; and defended by Eleazar, a man of un-daunted courage, baffled the attacks of the Romans. At length, however, they caused it to be surrounded by an high wall, set fire to the gates, and prepared to storm it the following day. When the Jews found no way of saving themselves, or their fortress, from the hands of the enemy, Eleazar instigated the garrison to burn the valuable stores of the castle, destroy first their women and children, and then themselves. Ten men who were chosen by lot exe-cuted this horrid purpose. The last survivor among these executioners, set fire to the place, and de-stroyed himself. [A. D. 73.] When the Romans

* Luke xix. 44. Newcome's Observations, p. 258.

on the morrow were preparing to scale the walls, two women, who had escaped by concealing themselves, while the rest were intent on slaughter, related to them the whole transaction.*

After this terrible event, the opposition on the part of the Jews ceased. It was, however, the submission of despair. Every where ruin and desolation presented itself to the solitary passenger, and a melancholy and deathlike silence pervaded the whole region:

"The ruin of the Jews," says a late historian, "is, in itself, a very interesting event; but infinitely more so, when considered as connected with religion. A bloody war, in which party rage conspires with foreign arms to destroy the nation; an ancient and famous people, who from their country, as from a centre, had spread themselves into every part of the known world, smitten with the most dreadful calamities ever recorded in history; a great and lofty city devoured by flames, and eleven hundred thousand inhabitants buried under its ruins; a temple, the wonder of the world, and the object of the veneration of those, who followed a different worship, so entirely demolished, that not *one stone was left upon another,* are surely such events, as, if they were merely human, could not but highly interest every one. How much more regard ought we to pay to them, when we reflect, that they were foretold by Jesus Christ forty years before they happened, at a time when nothing seemed to portend such an event;† that the dispersion of the Jewish people,

* Josephus, vol. vi. p. 188, 189.

† It ought to be remembered, that the prediction of our Saviour

and the ruin of their temple, form a part of the gospel system, by means of which, a knowledge of the
true God was no longer to be confined to one nation
only, or his worship attached to one particular place.
In short, that these disasters, the greatest that can
be conceived, are the vengeance, which God took
for the greatest crime which ever was perpetrated
upon the face of the earth, the cruel and ignominious
death of his Son.''*

It has pleased Providence, that this important part
of history should be transmitted to us by Josephus,
one of the Jewish nation, who was an eyewitness,
and had himself a great share in the principal events.
He has, unintentionally, given us a striking demon-
stration of the truth of the christian religion, by
exhibiting, in the most lively manner, how the
prophecies of our blessed Lord, concerning the
destruction of Jerusalem, were literally fulfilled in
their fullest extent.

was given at a time, when Judea was at peace, under the sway of a
nation, which never, till the destruction of Jerusalem, treated their
enemies with utter excision, and unsparing desolation.—*Watson's
Tracts.*

* Crevior's Roman History.

CHAPTER III.

Wretched state of the Jews after the destruction of Jerusalem.—Titus commands their lands to be sold, and confiscates the tribute which was paid annually to the temple.—His successor, Domitian, treats them with still greater severity.—Sedition at Alexandria.—The temple built by Onias is shut up.—The Jews seek an asylum in various countries.—Institution of the patriarchs in the west.—State of literature among the Jews.—Of the Cabbalistic philosophy.—Account of the celebrated cabbalistic book.—Of the rabbi Akibha.

THE condition of the Jews was extremely miserable after the destruction of their capital. The multitude of the dead, the prisoners who were sold, and the fugitives who had fled into various parts of the world, had left the country almost depopulated. The once flourishing plains of Palestine were covered with dead bodies; and of the celebrated cities, which existed formerly on their coasts, such as Capernaum, Bethsaida, and Chorazin, nothing was left but shapeless ruins. Some women and old men were permitted to remain in Jerusalem; but all, who were able to bear arms, were removed. A strong attachment to their native residence probably induced a number to return, and dwell among the ruins of their devoted city.*

After the war was terminated, the emperor ordered all the lands in Judea to be sold; strictly prohibited building any cities therein, and commanded the Jews, on condition of preserving their religion, to pay to Jupiter Capitolinus the capitation tax, which devotion had destined annually for the service of the temple. Although the sum assessed on the head of

* Basnage, p. 508.

each individual was inconsiderable, the use for which it was assigned, and the severity with which it was exacted, was considered as an intolerable grievance.*

Domitian, brother to Titus, who succeeded in the Roman empire, increased the calamities of this wretched people. They were involved in the persecution, which the Christians endured during his tyrannical reign; and many of them were condemned to suffer death.* This emperor intended to extirpate all the lineage of David, but when the grandsons of St. Jude the apostle, kinsmen of our Lord, were brought before him, their poverty induced him to retract his sanguinary purpose.

A. D. 72.] Notwithstanding their late calamities, some of the seditious Jews, who had retired to Alexandria in Egypt, began to excite fresh insurrections. But their countrymen who resided in the city, apprehending the consequences that might ensue, prudently interfered, and delivered them up to the Romans, who put six hundred of them to death. They maintained their inflexible obstinacy to the last; and even their children would suffer the most exquisite tortures, rather than acknowledge Cæsar for their lord. The emperor, being apprized of their rebellious disposition, ordered the temple,

* Though, after the conquest of Pompey, Judea was made tributary to the Romans, they were permitted to collect the taxes by their own receivers, and were exempted from tribute during the sabbatical year. The annual tribute to the temple, they supposed to be an offering to God, as his subjects. But after the destruction of Jerusalem, the emperor usurped the place of God, and appropriated the tribute to himself. This was the more afflicting and disgraceful, because it obliged them to purchase the liberty of exercising their religion.—*Basnage*, p. 509.

† Basnage, p. 509.

which Onias had built in Egypt, to be shut up, lest
it should afford them a pretence for assembling themselves, and thus give them an opportunity of exciting
some new sedition.*

Multitudes of Jews, who had survived the sad
catastrophe of the destruction of their city and temple, sought an asylum in various parts of the world.
Many retired to Egypt, where a Jewish colony had
resided from the time of Alexander; others fled to
Cyrene; a large number removed to Babylon, and
joined their brethren, who had remained in that
country ever since the captivity; some took refuge
in Persia, and other eastern countries. By degrees,
they formed themselves into a regular system of
government, or rather subordination, connected with
the various bodies of their brethren dispersed
throughout the world. They were divided into the
eastern and western Jews; the western included
Egypt,† Judea, Italy, and other parts of the Roman
empire. The eastern were settled in Babylon,
Chaldea, Assyria, and Persia. In process of time
both these parties chose a distinguished personage
to preside over each of their respective divisions.
The heads of the eastern Jews were styled princes
of the captivity; and those of the western Jews
were known by the title of patriarch. Mr. Basnage
and other learned men have supposed, that the
patriarchal‡ dignity was first instituted in the reign

* Basnage, p. 492.

† Some refugees passed from Egypt to Ethiopia.—*Basnage*, p. 494.

‡ According to the Jewish writers, this office originated at a
much earlier era. The first patriarch was Hillel, surnamed the
Babylonian. He came to Jerusalem about thirty years before the
birth of Christ, and lived to an advanced age. The Jews regarded

of Nerva, who succeeded Domitian.   This emperor
favoured the Jews; recalled those who had been
banished on account of their religion ; relieved them
from the heavy taxes which had been imposed upon
them by his predecessor; and forbade their being
molested in future on account of their religion.
They are supposed to be of the Levitical race, since
the least attempt in the tribe of Judah to recover any
of their former power, would have excited the
jealousy of the Romans.* But the priests and Levites
were permitted to assume the power of teaching
the people, to set up schools, to appoint preceptors
over them, and at length install one above the rest,
with the title of patriarch; because neither their
tribe, which was excluded the regal authority, nor
their office, which was confined to religious concerns,
could give umbrage to the Romans. The celebrated
city of Tiberias, situated on the banks of a lake
which bears its name, and was rebuilt by Herod,
tetrarch of Galilee, was chosen for the patriarchal
seat.   The dignity of their chiefs was hereditary. †

The authority which the patriarchs acquired over
the people committed to their charge, owed its rise
and gradual increase to their great reputation for

him as a second Moses, who was little inferior to their lawgiver:
and asserted, that the patriarchal dignity continued in his family till
the fifth century.—*Modern Universal History*, vol. xiii. p. 141.

* The house of David was now almost extinct; and the few who
remained reduced to poverty, and obliged to labour for their daily
subsistence. If there was any shadow of authority among this people,
after the destruction of their city and temple, it fell into the hands of
the priests of the race of Levi and Aaron. Their understanding and
science raised them above the vulgar; and as the people became
more numerous, their authority increased.

† Basnage, p. 146.

learning and piety. They decided cases of con-. science, and religious controversies; presided over synagogues; were empowered to appoint subordinate ministers and missionaries to execute their orders; and to receive an annual contribution from their dispersed brethren, in order to support their dignity. They obtained, by degrees, a great authority over the western Jews, who were pleased to depend upon them in order to maintain some shadow of union. The power, which these chiefs obtained, has, however, been much exaggerated by the Jews, to enable them to repel a powerful argument urged by the Christians, viz. that the sceptre, or regal authority, was departed from them.*

The learned Dr. Lightfoot has imagined, that the Jewish sanhedrim was not immediately destroyed, but only removed to Jafna, and thence to Tiberias, where it subsisted till the death of Judah, the saint. Other learned men, particularly Mr. Basnage, suppose this tribunal did not exist after the destruction of Jerusalem, for the following reasons.† If Titus had made any such concession, Josephus would have mentioned it for the honour of his nation. Domitian, who hated and oppressed the Jews, would never have allowed them such a signal privilege : besides, it has been the prevailing idea of the Jews, as well as of the Christians, that this tribunal had not power to sit in any other place but in Jerusalem. Our

* Basnage, p. 146.

† After the Sanhedrim was abolished, the Jews substituted in its room some particular tribunals for the decision of religious disputes. These tribunals, which were afterwards called houses of judgment, were a very imperfect image of the sanhedrim.—*Picart's Religious Ceremonies*, p. 195.

Saviour, it appears, alluded to this, when he said,
(Luke xviii. 33) that it could not be, that a prophet
should perish or be condemned to death out of Jerusalem, since the sanhedrim alone had the power
of passing that sentence on him.*

The Jews, though a considerable part of their
religion was involved in the destruction of their
country, still adhered with inflexible obstinacy to
those customs and religious rites, which remained in
their power to practise. After their national polity
was dissolved, they appear to have been confirmed
in their attachment to the oral traditions and unau-
thorized decisions of the rabbies. As they agreed
in thinking, that their religious rites and observances
were the only objects worthy their attention, it followed, that their literary controversies, instead of
embracing, like those of the philosophical sects of
the Pagans, the wide field of general literature, were
directed and confined to their religious and ritual
institutions, and were exhausted in questions or discussions immediately referrible to these subjects.†

After the devastation and ruin of their country, a
small number of learned men only were left among
them to transmit their ancient doctrines and institutions to posterity. Of these, part escaped into
Egypt, and part withdrew into Babylon ; in both
which countries the refugees were humanely received. Those, who remained in Palestine, collected
the scattered fragments of Jewish learning from the
general wreck into the academy of Jafna (frequently
called by the Greek writers, Jamnia) where they

---

* Basnage. Modern Universal History, vol. xiii. p. 136.
† Butler's Horæ Biblicæ, p. 40.

also revived their forms of worship. The rabbi
Jochanan,* was the founder of this school, and the
design which he begun was completed, as far as the
state of the times would permit, by the rabbi Gamaliel,
who is from this circumstance called Gamaliel
Jafniensis. The success, which attended this school,
induced many of the dispersed Jews to return to
Palestine ; and another academy was formed at
Tiberias, which soon became the chief seat of Jewish
learning in its native country. This school obtained
immunities and privileges from the emperor Antoninus Pius; and it produced that curious record of
Jewish wisdom, the Jerusalem Talmud. Other
schools, after the examples of Jafna and Tiberias,
were erected at Bitterah near Jerusalem, at Lydda
or Diospolis, at Cesarea, and (which became more
celebrated than the rest) at Zippora, or Sephora, in
Galilee.†

From this time, there was not wanting a succession
of Jewish doctors to transmit their religion and philosophy to posterity. These doctors flourished, not
only in Palestine, but in the Babylonish schools,
which, in process of time, were established at Sora,
Pundebita, and other places on the Euphrates.‡

Two methods of instruction were in use among the

* The Jewish writers assert, that the academy which Jochanan
erected at Jafna, consisted of three hundred schools, or classes of
pupils. They extol the extraordinary merit of this rabbi in the
most extravagant terms. According to them, "If the whole heavens
were paper, all the trees in the world pens, and all the men writers,
they would not be able to record all his merits." *Modern Universal
History*, vol. xiii. p. 141.

† Enfield's Philosophy, vol. ii. p. 198.

‡ According to Basnage, these schools were not founded till the
beginning of the third century.

H

Jews ; the one public, the other secret.   The public
doctrine was that, which was openly taught the
people from the law of Moses, and the traditions of
the fathers.   It comprehended the popular articles
of faith, and rules of manners.*

The secret doctrine of the Jews was that, which
treated of the mysteries of the divine, nature and
other sublime subjects, and was called cabbala, from
a Hebrew word, which signifies to receive, because
it was received by tradition.   After the manner of
the Pythagorean and Egyptian mysteries, it was
taught only to certain persons, who were bound,
under the most solemn anathema, not to divulge it.

The cabbala is divided into three sorts.   By the
first, the Jews extract from the words of scripture
recondite meanings, which are sometimes ingenious,
but always fanciful.   The second is a kind of magic,
in employing the words and letters of the scriptures
in certain combinations, which they suppose have
power to make the good and evil spirits of the
invisible world familiar with them.   The third,
which is properly the cabbala, is an art, by which
they profess to raise mysterious expositions of scripture, upon the letters of the sentences to which they
apply them.†

The Jews assert, that the mysteries of the cabbala
contain the profoundest truths of religion, which, to
be fully comprehended by finite beings, are revealed
through the medium of allegory and similitude, in
the same manner as angels can only render themselves visible upon earth ‡ by assuming a subtle body

* Enfield.   † Butler's Horæ Biblicæ. Basnage, p. 202.
‡ Maurice's Indian Antiquities, vol. iv. p. 588.

of refined matter. According to their account, while Adam was in paradise, the angel Rasael brought him a book from heaven, which contained the doctrines of heavenly wisdom. And when Adam received this book, angels came down to him to learn its contents ; but he refused to admit them to the knowledge of sacred things, entrusted to him alone. They assert, that, after the fall, this book was taken back into heaven ; after many prayers and tears, God restored it to Adam, and it passed from Adam to Seth. The Jewish fables proceed to relate, that the book, being lost,..and the mysteries it contained almost forgotten in the degenerate age before the flood, they were restored by special revelation to Abraham, who committed them to writing in the book Jezirah ; that the revelation was renewed to Moses,* who received a traditional and mystical, as well as a written and preceptive law, from God ; that, being again lost amidst the calamities of the Babylonish captivity, it was once more revealed to Esdras ; that it was preserved in Egypt, and has been transmitted to posterity, through the hands of Simeon-ben-Setach, Elkanah, Akibha, Simeon-ben-Jochai, and others.

Dr. Enfield,† from whom the above account is

* According to the Jewish accounts, all the patriarchs of the ancient world had their separate angels to instruct them in these mysterious arcana; and Moses himself was initiated in them by the illustrious spirit Metatron.—*Basnage,* p. 185.

† The chief heads of the cabbalistic doctrine, are thus delineated by the abovementioned author.

" From nothing, nothing can be produced, since the distance between existence and non-entity is infinite. Matter is too imperfect in its nature, and approaches too near to non-entity to be self-existent. The Being from whom all things proceed is a spirit, un-

chiefly selected, supposes, that the mystical or cabbalistic philosophy of the Jews, arose in the time created, eternal, intelligent, percipient, having within itself the principles of life and motion, existing by the necessity of its nature, and filling the immensity of space. This spirit is *En soph*, the infinite Deity. This Eternal Fountain of existence sends forth from himself natures of various orders, which, nevertheless, are still united to their source The world is a permanent emanation from the Deity, in which his attributes and properties are unfolded, and variously modified. The nearer any emanation is to the First Fountain, the more perfect and divine is its nature; and the reverse.

" Before the creation of the world, all space was filled with the *Or Haen Soph*, or infinite intellectual light. But, when the volition for the production of nature was formed in the divine mind, the eternal light, hitherto equally diffused through the infinite expanse, withdrew itself to an equal distance in every direction, from a certain point, and thus left about this centre, a spherical portion of empty space, as a field for the operation of emanation, by which all things were to be produced · In the space from which the divine light was thus withdrawn, there was still, however, some portions or traces left of the divine essence, which were to become the receptacle of rays, sent forth from the Eternal Fountain, or the basis of future worlds. From a certain part of the concavity of infinite light, which surrounded the opaque sphere, the energy of emanation was first exerted, and rays were sent forth in right lines, into the dark abyss. ' The beam of light, thus produced, formed a channel, through which streams were to flow for the production of worlds. This beam was united to the concave of light, and was directed towards the centre of the opaque sphere. From this luminous channel, streams of light flowed, at different distances from the centre, in a circular path, and formed distinct circles of light, separated from the concave of light, or from each other, by portions of dark or empty space. Of these circles of light, ten were produced, which may be called *Sephiræ*, or *Splendours*.

The rectilineal beam of light, which is the first emanation from the eternal fountain, and is itself the source of all other emanations, may be distinguished by the name of *Adam Kadman*, the first man, the first production of divine energy, or, the *Son of God*. The Sephiræ are fountains of emanations, subordinate to Adam Kadman, which send forth rays of divine light or communicate essence and life to inferior beings The ten Sephiræ are known, according to the order of emanation, by the names Intelligence, or the Crown. Knowledge,

of the first Ptolemies, and originated in Egypt, where they learned, by the help of allegory, to mix

Wisdom, Strength, Beauty, Greatness, Glory, Stability, Victory, Dominion.

"These are not the instruments of the divine operations, but media, through which the Deity diffuses himself through the sphere of the universe, and produces whatever exists. They are not beings detached from the Deity, but substantial virtues or powers, distinctly, but dependently, sent forth from the eternal source of existence through the mediation of Adam Kadman, the first emanating power, and becoming the immediate source of existence to subordinate emanations. They are dependent upon the First Fountain, as rays upon a luminary, which is conceived to have sent them forth with a power of drawing them back, at pleasure, into itself.

"The first infinite source of being is the *Ensophic* world, or world of infinity, within which, after the manner above described, four worlds are produced by the law of emanation, according to which the superior is the immediate source of the inferior; these are *Aziluth*, or the world of emanation, including the Sephiræ; *Briah*, or the world of creation, containing certain spiritual natures, which derive their essence from the Sephiræ; *Jezirah*, or the world of forms, composed of substantial natures, derived from the superior spiritual substances, and placed within etherial vehicles, which they inform; and *Asiah*, or the material and visible world, comprehending all those substances which are capable of motion, composition, division, and dissolution.

"These derived worlds are different evolutions, or expansions of the divine essence, or distinct classes of beings, in which the infinite light of the divine nature is exhibited with continually decreasing splendour, as they recede from the First Fountain. The last and most distant production of the divine energy of emanation is matter; which is produced when the divine light, by its recession from the Fountain, becomes so attenuated as to be lost in darkness, leaving nothing but an opaque substance, which is only one degree above non-entity. Matter has no separate and independent existence, but is merely a modification and permanent effect of the emanative energy of the divine nature.

"The Sephiræ, or first order of emanative being, existing in *Aziluth*, are superior to spirits, and are called *Parzuphim*, *Persons*, to denote that they have a substantial existence. The inhabitants of the second world are called Thrones, on account of the dominion, which they possess over the various orders of Angels, which inhabit the

Oriental, Pythagorean, and Platonic dogmas with
Hebrew wisdom. The cabbala having, according
to this author, obtained early credit among the
Jews, as part of their sacred tradition, was trans-

third world. The fourth, or material world, is the region of evil
spirits, called *Klippoth*, the dregs of emanation. These are the
authors of the evil, which is found in the material world; but they
are continually aspiring towards the sephiræ, and will, in the great
revolution of nature, return into the inexhaustible fountain of deity.
Spirits of all orders have a material vehicle, less pure and subtile in
proportion to their distance from *En Soph*; and this vehicle is of the
nature of the world next below that to which they belong *Metatron*
is the prince of *Jezirah*, or the angelic world, in which there are ten
distinct orders; *Sandalphon* of *Asiah*, or the material world: these,
together with the hosts over which they preside, animate aerial
vehicles, capable of impression from corporeal objects, and in different ways requiring renovation

" The human soul, proceeding by emanation from the Deity, is an
incorporeal substance of the same nature with the divine intellect.
Being united to the body, one complex nature is produced, endued
with reason, and capable of action. The human soul consists of four
parts : *Nephesh*, or the principle of vitality ; *Ruach*, or the principle
of motion; *Neschamah*, or the power of intelligence; and *Jechidah*,
a divine principle, by means of which it contemplates superior natures,
and even ascends to the *Ensophic* world. All souls were produced at
once, and pre-existed in Adam. Every human soul has two guardian
angels, produced by emanation at the time of the production of souls.

" The mind of man is united to the divine mind, as the radius of
a circle to its centre. The souls of good men ascend above the
mansion of the angels, and are delighted with the vision of the first
light, which illuminates all the worlds.

" The universe continues to exist by the divine energy of emanation. Whilst this energy is exerted, different forms and orders of
beings remain; when it is withheld, all the streams of existence
return into their fountain. The *Ensoph*, or Deity, contains all things
within himself; and there is always the same quantity of existence,
either in a created or uncreated state. When it is in an uncreated
state, God is all, when worlds are created, the Deity is unfolded, or
evolved, by various degrees of emanation, which constitute the
several forms and orders of created nature."—*Enfield's Philosophy*,
vol ii p 217—221.

mitted under this notion by the Jews in Egypt to their brethren in Palestine.

Simeon ben-Jochai, a celebrated rabbi, was the first who committed these mysteries to paper ; and, as the Jews affirm, by divine assistance, he composed the Zohar, or brightness.* He is said to have lived some years before the destruction of Jerusalem. Titus condemned him to death.; but he and his son escaped the persecution, by secreting themselves in a cave, where he had leisure to compose the abovementioned book., He perfected the work with the assistance of the prophet Elias, whom God sent from heaven, from time to time, to explain to Simeon such mysteries as were above his comprehension †

The *Sepher Jetzirah,* or book of the creation, is the next in cabbalistic fame to the Zohar : and is quoted by the Jews, as of divine authority. Some ascribe this work to the patriarch Abraham ; others suppose it was written by the rabbi Akibha, who lived in the second century.

He was president of the academies of Lydda and Jafna ; and a disciple and successor of the rabbi Gamaliel. Until he was forty years of age, he was a shepherd in the service of a rich citizen of Jerusalem ; but his master's daughter having promised to marry him, if he became a learned man, he assiduously applied himself to study. So successful was his application, that he became one of the most famous teachers in the schools of Jewish learning.

* David Levi calls the Zohar a cabbalistical commentary on the Pentateuch.

† Basnage, p. 185.

He was considered by his nation, as the oracle
of the times; and one of the greatest preservers of
the traditional law.*   The Jews in Palestine did
not scruple to say, that God revealed to him, what
he concealed from Moses; and, if their accounts
are to be credited, he had twenty four thousand disciples. This rabbi is mentioned with veneration,
through the whole Talmud; not only on account of
his great attainments in the cabbalistical learning,
but for his extraordinary abilities, and wisdom in
solving important questions in the law.†   Towards
the close of his life, he followed the standard of the
impostor Barchocheba, who appeared under the character of the Messiah, to deliver his countrymen
from the power of the emperor Adrian.   An account
of this revolt, and the new and dreadful calamities,
which the Jews suffered, in consequence of the
insurrection, will be related in the following
chapter.

* De Rossi's Hebrew Biography.
† David Levi's Ceremonies of the Jews.

CHAPTER IV.

The Jews rebel in the reign of the emperor Trajan.—They are subdued
. and banished from the Isle of Cyprus.—The emperor Adrian begins
to rebuild Jerusalem, and plants a Roman colony in the new city.
—Rebellion of the Jews.—Barchocheba declares himself the Messiah, and is made leader of the insurgents. He chooses the famous
. rabbi Akibha for his precursor.—The rebels raise a formidable army.
—Adrian sends forces against them, and besieges them in Bither.
—This city surrenders to the Romans.—The false Messiah is slain.
—Horrid carnage of the Jews.—Multitudes of them are sold, and
transported to Egypt.—Adrian completes the building of Jerusalem;
and prohibits the Jews from entering the city.

NOTWITHSTANDING the complicated afflictions, which the Jews suffered in Palestine during
the destruction of their city and temple, the measure
of their calamities was not completed. They had
scarcely begun to breathe after the ruin of their
country, when their impatience under a foreign yoke
broke out in an open revolt during the reign of the
emperor Trajan, who had interdicted them from
reading their law, and treated them with great severity.*

A. D. 115.] The rebellion was commenced by the
Jews in Cyrene, where they had been settled for many
years, and become powerful. At first they gained
considerable advantages over the enemy, who fled to
Alexandria, and massacred all the Jews in the city.
Those of Cyrene, exasperated at this dreadful re-
prisal, having chosen one Andrew for their commander, murdered two hundred and twenty thousand
of the Lybians, and depopulated the country. The
emperor Trajan sent Martius Turbo with a power-

* Basnage, p. 511.

ful army against them, and the rebels were reduced after several desperate battles, which were attended with great slaughter.*

A. D. 116] The following year, the Jews in Mesopotamia, alarmed at the fate of their brethren in Egypt, appeared in arms, and with such force, that the inhabitants of the whole country were filled with consternation. This induced Trajan to send Lucius Quietus, the greatest general in the empire, against them, who slew great numbers of the insurgents, and subjected the rest to the Roman power. To prevent their again assembling and rebelling, the emperor appointed him governor in Palestine, to watch their motions and keep them in awe.†

Soon after, the Jews, who were numerous in the island of Cyprus, made a more dreadful insurrection, and massacred two hundred and forty thousand of the inhabitants. Trajan sent Adrian, a famous general, against them, with a powerful army. After an obstinate conflict, the rebels were reduced, and the emperor published an edict, banishing them from the island, and forbidding them to return, under the severest penalties ‡

A. D. 130.] Notwithstanding the miseries, which the Jews suffered by their revolt, their rebellious spirit was still unsubdued. Adrian, the successor of Trajan, had prohibited them from circumcising their children; and sent a colony to rebuild Jerusalem, near the place where the ancient city stood. He designed to adorn it after the Roman style, and call it Œlia Capitolina, from the name of his family.

* Basnage, p. 511.　　† Ibid.　　‡ Ibid. p. 512.

This exasperated the minds of the Jews, and stimulated them to commence an open rebellion.*.

A. D. 132.] . Coziba, one of the banditti, who
infested Judea, and committed all kinds of violence
against the Romans, was the leader of the insurgents. To facilitate the success of his bold
enterprize, he assumed the name of Barchocheba,
which signifies the son of a star; and pretended he
was the person prophesied of by Balaam in the
words, " There shall come a star out of Jacob, and
a sceptre shall rise out of Israel." This barbarian,
so well calculated by his courage and enterprising
spirit to be the Messiah, according to the perverted
conceptions of the Jews, was acknowledged in that
character by his infatuated countrymen.† He engaged to deliver his nation from the power of the
emperor Adrian, and restore its ancient liberty and
glory. The famous rabbi Akibha, being chosen by
him for his precursor, espoused his cause, afforded
him the protection of his name, and not only publicly anointed him as the Messiah, and king of the
Jews, but placed a diadem on his head, caused
money to be coined in his name, and followed him
to the field, at the head of twenty thousand of his
disciples, and acted in the capacity of master of his
horse. By calling on all the descendants of Abraham
to assist the hope of Israel, an army of two hundred
thousand men was soon raised, who repaired to

---

* Basnage, p 512.

† Several impostors had appeared before him; some under the
title of the Messiah; others under that of his precursors; most
of whom were the disciples of Judas the Gaulonite. But Barchocheba was the first who obtained great celebrity.

Bither, a city near Jerusalem, chosen by the famous
impostor for the capital of his new kingdom.*

Adrian at first neglected to take measures against
the revolt, supposing the Jews had been too effectually humbled by his predecessor to be able so soon
to raise a formidable insurrection. But being apprized, that numbers had flocked to the standard of
Barchocheba, he sent Tinius Rufus, governor of the
province, with a powerful military force against
them. The rebels, however, gained great advantages over the imperial army, and destroyed vast
numbers of Romans and converted Jews. Their
rapid success and sanguinary devastations, filled
Rome with astonishment and consternation. At
length, Julius Severus, one of the greatest generals
of his age, was despatched to crush this dangerous
revolt. This able commander, not thinking it
prudent to oppose at once so formidable an army,
attacked and defeated the insurgents in parties ; and,
at length, cut off the supplies of the enemy, and
besieged them in Bither.†

The rebels defended themselves with obstinate
resolution; and, even put Tryphon, a famous rabbi,
to death, because he proposed their surrendering to
the Romans. However, they were not able long to
withstand the repeated and vigorous attacks, which
were made upon the city. In one of these assaults,
the pretended Messiah was killed, and Bither obliged
to surrender. The Jewish history, bloody as it is
in almost every page, records no fact; excepting the
destruction of Jerusalem, more horrid, than the
undistinguished and promiscuous slaughter which

* Basnage, p 515.   † Ibid. p. 518.

ensued. Akibha* and his son were put to a most cruel death. Five hundred and eighty thousand fell by the sword in battle, besides a vast number; who perished by famine, sickness, fire, and other calamities. The Jewish historians affirm, that a greater number were destroyed in this war, than the whole amount of their nation, when they emigrated from Egypt ; and, that their sufferings, under Nebuchadnezzar and Titus, were not so great as those they endured under Adrian. Of these unhappy people, who survived the second ruin of their nation, vast numbers were exposed for sale at the fair of Terebinth,† at the price of horses,. and dispersed over the face of the earth. Those who could not find purchasers at this place, were removed to another fair, which was kept at Gaza ; others were transported to Egypt.‡

A. D. 136.] After the war was terminated, Adrian completed his design of rebuilding Jerusalem. In order to prevent new revolts among the Jews, he caused the ancient monuments of their religion to be destroyed, and studiously profaned all the places which they revered. He erected a theatre with the stones, which had been used for the temple, and dedicated a temple to Jupiter Capitolinus, where that of Jehovah formerly stood. He placed a hog of marble upon the gates of the city, on the side of

* With him, say the Jews, perished the glory of their law. After his death, his tomb, which they suppose to have been at Tiberias, was visited with great solemnity.—*Enfield's Philosophy*, vol. ii. p 201.

† The fair of Terebinth was annually kept on the plain of Mamre, sacred for having been the place where Abraham pitched his tent, and where he received the heavenly guests Gen. xvii. 17.

‡ Basnage, p. 519.

Bethlehem ; and, as he hated the Christians as well
as the Jews, he erected a statue of Venus in the
·place where Christ was crucified ; and in that where
he arose from the dead, one of Jupiter. In the
grotto of Bethlehem, where our Saviour was born,
he established the worship of Adonis.*

The emperor, by a severe edict, prohibited the
Jews, upon pain of death, from entering Jerusalem,†
and fixed a vigilant garrison of the Roman cohorts
to enforce the execution of his orders. He even
forbade them to view their once beloved city at a
distance. " Before this period," says a late author;
"they were seen covered with rags, traversing,
midst sighs, and lamentations, the Mount of Olives,
and the remains of their temple. They were
reduced to the necessity of being economists in their
misery to purchase this favour from the avarice of
the soldiery. At this price they obtained, as a
singular indulgence, permission to go thither and
weep on the anniversary of the sacking of their city ;
and the Jews were obliged to pay for the right of
shedding tears, in those places where they purchased
and shed the blood of Jesus Christ !" ‡

In the calamities of the Jews, we contemplate the
fulfilment of the prophecies, which foretold them

* Basnage, p. 519.

† Though Adrian interdicted the Jews from entering Jerusalem,
they were not banished from Judea ; the patriarchs still resided in
that country, and the famous school of Tiberias still existed. The
condition of those, who remained in Palestine, was, however, extremely wretched. According to Juvenal, some of the Jews in Rome
and Egypt, after the revolt, were obliged to turn fortune-tellers for
their subsistence —Basnage, p 519

‡ Gregoire, in his Essay on the Reformation of the Jews, quotes
as an authority for this fact, St. Jerome in Sophonian. chap. x.

long before they took place. Moses had predicted, that they should be carried into Egypt, and sold at a very low price. " *And the Lord,*" said he, " *shall bring thee into Egypt again with ships, and ye shall be sold unto your enemies, and no man shall buy you.*" * When Jerusalem was taken by Titus, the captives, with their wives and children, were sold at the lowest price ; and we learn from St. Jerome, " that after their last overthrow by Adrian, many thousands of them were sold ; and those, who could not find purchasers, were transported into Egypt, and perished by shipwreck or famine, or were massacred by the inhabitants."†

---

* Deut. xxviii, 68.   † See Newton on the Prophecies, p. 70.

CHAPTER V.

State of the Jews in the East.—Of the princes of the captivity.—Judah
the saint compiles the Misna.—History of that work.—Jews rebel
under Marcus Antoninus —Marcus Aurelius renews Adrian's edict
against them.—They are treated. with kindness by Septimius
Severus.—Of their state under Heliogabalus.—They are favoured
by Alexander Severus, and the subsequent Roman Emperors.

WHILE the Western Jews were exposed to the
terrible calamities, which have been related in the
preceding chapter, a milder destiny attended their
brethren in the east. Trajan, indeed, had carried
his arms against them as far as Mesopotamia; but
Adrian, after his accession to the throne, consented,
that the Euphrates should be the boundary of the
Roman empire. Those, therefore, who resided
beyond that river, were not concerned in that
prince's war against their nation. Many, however,
who panted after liberty in the most remote provinces of the empire, passed into Judea to assist
their brethren. Yet they answered no other purpose, but to augment the number of the slain,* and
increase the triumph of the conquerors †

A. D. 122.] · The history of the eastern is more
obscure than that of the western Jews, the former
having but an imperfect knowledge of the events
which took place among their brethren in those
remote countries. Previous to the destruction of

---

* The number of the slain, according to Basnage, amounted to
above six hundred thousand, which number could not have been
found in Judea, after the sufferings of that country under Trajan.

† Basnage, p. 162.

the temple, those of that nation, who resided in the
eastern countries, sent presents to Jerusalem; repaired thither from time to time, to pay their
devotions ; and acknowledged the supreme authority
of the high priests. But after the ruin of their
country, having no longer the band of unity, which
was formed by the temple and high priests, they
imitated their brethren in Palestine, and elevated
chiefs to preside over their synagogues, whom they
styled princes of the captivity.*

The origin of these chiefs is not known ; it is
only evident, that they did not exist till the second
century. They were installed with great pomp and
solemnity. Babylon or Bagdat was chosen for the
place of their residence, where they presided over
ten courts of justice. There were twenty-eight
synagogues, among which was that of the prince,
supported with pillars of marble of various colours.
His office was to confer ordination on all the heads
of the synagogues in the east, from whom he received
contributions to enable him to support his dignity,
and pay the tribute which was exacted by the kings
of Persia. It is believed that Huna, who was
cotemporary with Judah the Saint, was the first
prince of the captivity at Babylon. These princes
exercised the same authority in the eastern, that the
patriarchs of Tiberias maintained in the western
countries.†

The Jews, however, pretend, that these chiefs
were superior in power and dignity to the patriarchs
of Judea, and affirm, that all, who remained of the

* Modern Universal History, vol. xiii. p. 156.
† Basnage, p. 162. Lewis's Hebrew Antiquities

I

race of David, abandoned that province, and retired
to Babylon, where they conclude the sceptre mentioned by Jacob is to be found. But men of learning
among the Christians have proved, that they have
greatly exaggerated the grandeur and authority of
these princes, who were subjected to the Persian
monarchs. And, if we consider the low condition
of the Jews, and the oppressions, which they endured
from the Parthians, Romans, and other nations, it
will appear evident, that the princes of the captivity
could possess only a small share of authority.*

In order to raise the glory of their nation, the
Jews bestow the highest encomiums on the learned
men, who flourished among them during the second
century. In particular, they extol the famous rabbi
Judah,† the third Jewish patriarch, who obtained
the appellation of Saint. He was born in the city of
Sephora, and having acquired great celebrity for his
piety and profound learning, presided over the
academy of Tiberias with uncontrolled authority,
and decided the most abstruse controversies. His
memory was so highly revered among the Jews,
that they compare him with the Messiah; they
relate many extraordinary accounts of this rabbi;
among the rest, they assert, that he made the emperor, Marcus Antoninus, a proselyte to Judaism,
and, that it was by his order, that Judah compiled
the Misna.‡

---

* Modern Universal History, vol. xiii. p. 180
† Judah was born on the same day that Akibha died, and the Jews
imagine this event was predicted by Solomon, when he says, *The sun
riseth, and the sun goeth down.* Akibha dying was the sun that set,
and Judah the Saint the rising sun.—*Basnage,* p. 156.
‡ Enfield's Philosophy, vol. ii. p. 198.

This celebrated book is a code of the Jewish canon and civil law. It was held in such profound veneration by the Jews, that they called it the second law, (which the name Misna signifies in Hebrew) importing, that it has the same authority with their Pentateuch or first law. Judah was induced to undertake this work from a just apprehension, that his nation, in their various dispersions and migrations through so many provinces, and during the interruption of their public schools, would neglect to practise the rites of their religion ; and the traditions of their fathers would be obliterated from their memory.*

" The history of the Misna," says Enfield,† " is briefly this : The sect of the Pharisees, after the destruction of Jerusalem, prevailing over the rest, the study of traditions became the chief object of attention in all the Jewish schools. The number of these traditions had, in a long course of time, so greatly increased, that the doctors, whose principal employment it was to illustrate them by new explanations, and to confirm their authority, found it necessary to assist their recollections by committing them under distinct heads to writing. At the same time, their disciples took minutes of the explanations of their preceptors, many of which were preserved, and grew up into voluminous commentaries. The confusion, which arose from these causes, was now become so troublesome, that, notwithstanding what Hillel‡ had before done in arranging the traditions,

* Basnage. Maurice's Indian Antiquities.
† Enfield's Philosophy, vol. ii. p. 198.
‡ The name of Hillel is held in the highest esteem among the

Judah found it necessary to attempt a new digest of the oral law, and of the commentaries of the most famous doctors. This arduous undertaking is said to have employed him forty years. It was completed, according to the unanimous testimony of the Jews, about the close of the second century. This Misna, or first Talmud, comprehends all the laws, institutions, and modes of life, which, beside the Hebrew scriptures, the Jews supposed themselves bound to observe." *

This work was soon respected by the Jews as a sacred book. It consists of a variety of traditions, and explanations of several passages of scripture, and serves as a supplement to their written law. According to their account, these traditions were delivered to Moses, during his abode on mount Sinai, and he afterwards communicated them to Aaron, Eleazar, and his servant Joshua. They transmitted them to the elders, who delivered them to the prophets; and they passed from Jeremiah to Baruch, and from him to Ezra, who delivered them to the grand synagogue, the last of whom was Simon the Just. Thus these traditions were handed down from generation to generation, in regular succession, till they were transmitted to Judah the Saint, who committed them to writing, and thus formed the voluminous compilation styled Misna; † this work

Jews, for his exertions to perpetuate the knowledge of the traditionary law. He arranged its precepts under six general classes, and thus laid the foundation for that digest of Jewish law, called the Talmud.—*Enfield's Philosophy.*

* Enfield.

† See a particular account of all the receivers of oral tradition, in David Levi's Ceremonies of the Jews, p. 276—286.

was taught in all the schools, both in Palestine and Babylon. Such is the account of David Levi,* and the creed of every rabbi.

Dr. Prideaux, rejecting the Jewish fiction, observes, that, " after the death of Simon the Just, about two hundred ninety nine years before Christ, the Mischnical doctors arose ; who, by their comments and conclusions, added to the number of those traditions, which had been received and allowed by Ezra, and the men of the great synagogue ; so, that towards the middle of the second century, under the empire of Antoninus Pius, it was found necessary to commit these traditions to writing, more especially, as the country had greatly suffered under Adrian; many of the schools had been dissolved, and their learned men cut off; and, therefore, the usual method of preserving these traditions had failed.†

The Misna of Judah did not, however, resolve all the doubtful cases and questions, which were agitated by the Jews ; and it was thought to need some larger explanation to render it more intelligible. This induced Jochanan, a celebrated doctor of the Jewish law, with the assistance of two disciples of Judah, to write a commentary on the Misna. This work was called the Talmud of Jerusalem, because it was composed in Judea, for the use of the Jews, who remained in that country.

In the second century, several new sects were formed among the Jews, while those remained, which had figured in the time of our Saviour. The Gaulonites still retained their seditious spirit against

* David Levi's Ceremonies of the Jews.
† Prideaux's Connection.

all foreign government. But the Pharisees had, since the destruction of Jerusalem, formed the bulk of the nation. The Hemero-Baptists were a branch of this denomination, only distinguished by their more frequent washings. The Masbotheans, were a branch of the Sadducees, for they denied the immortality of the soul, and attributed all events to chance. The Hellenists were the Jews, who spoke Greek, and read the Septuagint in the synagogues. Though there was at first some jealousy between them and their brethren, who performed public worship in the Hebrew language, they were allowed to use the Greek translation in their religious assemblies. But, after they found, that the Christians, in disputing against Judaism, derived advantage from the Septuagint version, their prejudice against it was heightened, and those who vindicated it were regarded by the other party, as sectarians and schismatics.*

The edict of Adrian, which prohibited the Jews from circumcising their children, being still in force, their impatience under this restriction stimulated them, notwithstanding their late calamities, again to have recourse to arms. The emperor Antoninus, however, soon suppressed the revolt ; and afterwards restored to them the privilege for which they contended, and treated them with great moderation and kindness. He, however, forbade their attempting to make proselytes to their religion.

In the commencement of the reign of Marcus Aurelius, the eastern Jews, who were subjects of the king of Parthia, joined that monarch in a war

* Basnage, p. 528.

against the Romans. The emperor, incensed at
this conduct, after he had reduced the rebels, renewed Adrian's severe edict against them. But
those laws were not executed in the remote provinces.*

A. D. 197.] The emperor Septimius Severus, in
the commencement of his reign, declared war against
the Samaritans and Jews. They had settlements
in Galilee; but the prohibition, which excluded
them from entering the precincts of Jerusalem, was
still in force. This unhappy people, though so
often humbled and subdued, attempted once more to
repel their enemies, and invaded Samaria and Judea.
After the emperor had reduced them to obedience,
he relaxed his severity against them. In order to
reward their fidelity to him, when Pescennius Niger
was competitor for the throne, he allowed them the
privileges of Roman citizens, and rendered them
eligible to offices of trust and honour.†

A. D. 200.] The chiefs and doctors of the
eastern Jews obtained celebrity in the commencement
of the third century, and established academies in
various parts. After the Persian monarchy was
restored, and the Parthian overthrown, the rabbies
were for some time treated with great respect. At
this prosperous period, Samuel Jarchi, who was
famed for his literary acquirements, particularly for
his skill in astronomy, came from Judea, was constituted chief of an academy at Nahardea ; and among
other dignities obtained that of prince of the captivity.‡

The tranquillity, which the Jews enjoyed in the

* Basnage, p. 523.   † Ibid. p. 531.   ‡ Ibid.

east proved, however, only a prelude to a violent persecution, which Sapor, king of Persia, commenced against them. According to the Jewish historians, he was instigated by his subjects, who, being jealous of the influence of their nation, endeavoured to effect their destruction.

The scene was reversed, and their affairs assumed a favourable aspect under Zenobia, queen of Palmyra. During the reign of this celebrated princess, they flourished in every part of her dominions; erected superb synagogues, and were exalted to the highest dignities. But, after this heroine was subdued by Aurelian, they retired from her dominions to Persia.*

A. D. 218.] Heliogabalus, who at this time ascended the throne, had been circumcised, and abstained from swine's flesh. He, however, erected a superb temple in honour of the sun, the idol he worshipped. He ordered the palladium, the vestal fire, the mother of the gods, and whatever the Romans held in the highest veneration, to be conveyed to this temple. Being well acquainted with the tenets of the Samaritans and Jews, he intended to blend their religious rites with the adoration of his deity. The unexpected death of this emperor, who was assassinated by his soldiers, delivered the Jews, who never would have consented to adopt his religion, from the fiery trial which awaited them.†

Alexander Severus, who succeeded Heliogabalus, highly favoured the Jews, corresponded with them, and was instructed in their religion. This emperor had a domestic chapel, where he placed the statues

* Basnage, p. 533.   † Ibid.

of Abraham, of Orpheus, and of Christ. He was desirous of erecting a temple to Christ, and, receiving him into the number of gods. His object was, by the aid of the Eclectic philosophy, to blend the Pagan, Jewish, and Christian religions.*

The subsequent Pagan Roman emperors continued the tranquillity which the Jews enjoyed. In particular Philip, who was born in Arabia, where they carried on commercial pursuits, treated them with the greatest indulgence. And it does not appear, that they were involved in any of the violent persecutions which the Christians suffered during the reigns of Decius, Valerian, and Dioclesian.†

It seems from the preceding account, that the Jews enjoyed intervals of tranquillity, and were treated with kindness and indulgence by several of the Pagan emperors of Rome. The numerous remains of this people, though they were still excluded from the precincts of Jerusalem, were permitted to form and maintain considerable establishments, both in Italy, and in the provinces; to acquire the freedom of Rome, to enjoy municipal honours, and to obtain at the same time, an exemption from the hard and burdensome offices of society. The moderation of the Romans gave a legal sanction to the forms of ecclesiastical police which were instituted by the vanquished sect. New synagogues were erected in the principal cities in the empire, and the institutions and rites of the Mosaic law were celebrated in the most public and solemn manner.‡

---

* Basnage, p. 532. Gibbon's Roman Empire, vol. ii. p. 305.
† Basnage, p 533   ‡ Gibbon, vol. ii. p. 337.

Alexander Severus and his successors in particular treated the Jews with great clemency. But, as it will appear in the following parts of this history, when the Christian princes were at the head of the Roman empire, they did not show so much indulgence to a nation, whom they considered as the inveterate enemies of Jesus Christ.

CHAPTER VI.

State of the Jews under Constantine and his successors.—The emperor Julian highly favoured this people, and proposed to assist them in rebuilding the temple of Jerusalem.—Of the vast preparations which were made for this purpose, and the miracle which caused his design to be abandoned.

IN the fourth century, one of the most important revolutions took place, that ever was known in the annals of mankind. The splendid edifice of pagan superstition was subverted, and Christianity established under Constantine the Great and his successors. During the reign of this monarch, the city of Jerusalem, which Adrian called Elia, resumed its ancient name. The emperor enlarged and beautified it with many superb buildings and churches; and his pious munificence extended to every spot which had been consecrated by the footsteps of the apostles and prophets, and of the Son of God.*

This important change in the religion of the Roman empire did not prove advantageous to the Jews. Constantine, in the commencement of his reign, enacted some severe laws, which abridged their privileges. Their increasing numbers and prosperity having rendered them insolent, they insulted and abused those who deserted the synagogue and embraced Christianity. The emperor charged them with stoning and burning those who renounced their religion; and condemned them and all their accomplices to suffer the same punishment. He also forbade them to make proselytes under the

* Gibbon, vol. iv.

severest penalties ; and gave liberty to all the slaves, who accused their masters of having circumcised them, or who professed the Christian religion. He further ordered, that they should be obliged to serve at all public offices, like the other subjects of the empire, from which, however, he exempted the pa- triarchs, priests, and others, who officiated at the synagogues, schools, &c.*

The council of Elvira in Spain, which is com- monly placed in the reign of Constantine, prohibited the Christians, who had been in habits of social inter- course with the Jews, from eating with them in future. Though the penalty fell only on the Chris- tians, who were made liable to excommunication, it subjected the unhappy Israelites to insults and con- tempt. By another decree this council prohibited the possessors of land from permitting Jews to bless the fruits of the earth,† because their benedictions would render those of the Christians useless. The council threatened to expel from the church those, who refused to obey these orders.‡

During the reign of Constantine, the Jews were numerous in Persia, and having experienced great kindness and liberality from many of the sovereigns in that kingdom, had acquired great influence at court. Emboldened by their prosperity, and stimu- lated by a desire of revenging the insults and indig- nities they suffered in the Roman empire, they, in

---

* Basnage, p. 354.

† The Jews in this country appear to have been tenants to the Christians. They had public prayers in their synagogues for divine blessings on their grounds.—*Jortin's Remarks on Ecclesiastical History*, vol. ii. p 294.

‡ Basnage, p. 544.

conjunction with the Magi, raised a bloody persecution against the eastern Christians. Many were
slaughtered at their instigation, their churches
demolished, their sacred books burnt, and, as the
persecution was long as well as bloody, every trace
of Christianity was nearly obliterated.*.
- "A. D. 341.] The cruelty of the Jews did not long
remain unpunished. Constantius, who succeeded
his father, and hated this people on account of their
religion, treated them with the utmost rigour. During
his reign they raised an insurrection in Diocæsarea
in Palestine, in order to co-operate with the Persians,
who at the same time invaded the Roman empire,
and laid siege to Nisibis. The emperor sent an
army, who took Judea in their way to Persia,
defeated the rebels, and destroyed the city.†
. Soon 'after, Constantius, incensed against the
Jewish nation, not only revived the laws which had
been enacted against them in the former reigns, but
added new ones still more severe. Every Jew that
married a Christian, circumcised a slave, or retained
any who were Christians, was punished with death.
The Jewish patriarch, who was still permitted to
exercise a precarious jurisdiction, held his residence
at Palestine; and the neighbouring cities were filled
with a people who fondly adhered to the promised
land. But the edict of Adrian, which exiled them
from Jerusalem, was renewed and enforced; and
they viewed from afar the walls of the holy city,
which was profaned in their eyes by the triumph
of the cross, and the devotion of the Christians.‡

* Basnage, p 544.   † Ibid.   ‡ Ibid.
‡ Basnage. Gibbon's Roman History, vol iv. p. 99.

The death of Constantius delivered the Jews from the evils they endured. Their affairs assumed a more favourable aspect, when Julian, styled the apostate, was elevated to the imperial dignity. As it was his determined purpose to subvert the Christian, and restore the Pagan worship, his aversion to the Christians induced him to treat the Jews with distinguished kindness and liberality. He allowed them the free exercise of their religion; and exempted them from the heavy taxes which were imposed upon them by his predecessors. Emboldened by such powerful protection, they assembled in several cities in Syria and Judea; demolished the churches, and committed other outrages. Their example was followed by their brethren in Egypt, who destroyed the finest churches in Alexandria.*

Julian established the Pagan religion by law; disqualified the Christians from bearing offices in the state; fined and banished their clergy; forbade them to teach the sciences in the public schools; imposed a tax on all who refused to sacrifice to idols; and in short used every method that human ingenuity could invent, to destroy the Christian religion. But finding his attempts baffled by the inflexible firmness of the Christians, he formed the famous design of rebuilding the temple of Jerusalem. Its final destruction had been foretold by Christ and the prophets; and it was, as he imagined, reserved for him to falsify their predictions; and he meant to have converted the success of his undertaking into a specious argument against the faith of prophecy and truth of revelation.†

* Basnage, p. 546.   † Ibid.

In pursuance of his general design of opposing revelation to itself by setting one sect against another; the emperor addressed a public epistle to the nation or community of the Jews, dispersed throughout the provinces. In this letter he honours the patriarch with the title of brother. He compassionates their misfortunes, praises their constancy, declares himself their gracious protector, and concludes with a promise, that, if he should return victorious from the Persian war, he would rebuild Jerusalem, and pay his grateful vows to the deity in that holy place.*

The prospect of an immediate and important advantage would not suffer the impatient monarch to await the remote and uncertain event of a Persian war. He resolved to erect a stately temple on the commanding summit of Moriah; to establish an order of priests, whose interested zeal would detect the arts, and resist the ambition of their Christian rivals; and to invite a numerous colony of Jews, whose stern fanaticism would be always prepared to second, and even anticipate, the hostile measures of the Pagan government.†

For this purpose, the emperor assigned immense sums out of the public revenue; and committed the superintendency of the plan to Alypus, his intimate friend, whose aversion to Christianity was congenial to his own. This minister, having obtained the strenuous support of the governor of Palestine, provided immense quantities of materials, and large numbers of workmen. To use the words of a

---

* Warburton's Julian.

† Gibbon, vol. iv. p. 105. Warburton's Julian.

celebrated author, "At the call of their great deliverer, the Jews from all the provinces of the empire assembled on the holy mountain of their fathers ; and their insolent triumph alarmed and exasperated the Christian inhabitants of Jerusalem. The desire of rebuilding the temple has in every age been the ruling passion of the children of Israel. In this propitious moment, the men forgot their avarice, and the women their delicacy; spades and pickaxes of silver were provided by the vanity of the rich, and the rubbish transported in mantles of silk and purple. Every purse was opened in liberal contributions; every hand claimed a share in the pious labour, and the commands of a great monarch were executed by the enthusiasm of a whole people." *

A. D. 363.] On this occasion, however, the power of Julian, who had all the resources of the empire at his command, and the enthusiasm of the Jews, were unsuccessful; it is attested by several respectable writers, that while the workmen were digging up the foundations of the temple; terrible earthquakes and balls of fire broke forth, which obliged them to desist, and caused a total suppression of the work.†

The most unexceptionable testimony to this extraordinary fact is that of Ammianus Marcellinus, a celebrated Pagan historian, who was a friend and admirer of Julian. This writer, in his history of his own times, has thus recorded the obstacles which interposed to interrupt the restoration of the temple of Jerusalem: " Whilst Alypus, assisted by the governor of the province, urged with vigour and

---

* Gibbon, vol. iv. p. 106.   † Basnage, p. 546.

diligence the execution of the work, horrible balls of fire, breaking out near the foundations with frequent and reiterated attacks, rendered the place from time to time inaccessible to the scorched and blasted workmen ; and the victorious element continuing in this manner obstinately and resolutely bent, as it were, to drive them to a distance, the undertaking was relinquished." *

This wonderful event is also attested with some variations † by Ambrose, Chrysostom, and Gregory Nazianzen, cotemporary Christian writers, the last of whom published his account of the miracle before the expiration of the same year, and has boldly declared, that this preternatural event was not disputed by the infidels. The subsequent writers, who relate this extraordinary fact, are the historians Socrates, Sozomen, and Theodoret.‡

In latter times the truth of this miracle has been maintained by some writers of high reputation 'in the republic of letters; particularly the learned bishop Warburton, who has published an ingenious treatise in order to prove the miraculous interposition of Providence in defeating the attempt to rebuild the temple of Jerusalem.

In defence of the truth of this miraculous interposition, it has been alleged, that it differs from the pretended miracles of those days, that it was not wrought to serve a party. No sect could claim any honour or credit from it; but it was performed by Providence for the credit of Christianity, and

---

* Ammianus Marcellinus, Lib. XXIII. chap. i. p. 380.
† All, however, agree in the principal points.
‡ See Warburton's Julian, and Jortin's Remarks.

K

to serve the common cause against Judaism and Paganism.*

Others, particularly Mr. Basnage and Dr. Lardner, have expressed their doubts respecting the truth of this miracle.† The latter of these writers judiciously observes, "Julian's intention (or desire at least) to rebuild the city of Jerusalem and the Jewish temple, was never accomplished, but was frustrated and defeated. Whether it was owing to miraculous interposition, or to his expensive preparations for the Persian war, and other circumstances of his affairs, and to his defeat and death in that war, the overruling providence of God ought to be acknowledged in the event; and the argument for the truth of the Christian religion, taken from the fulfilment of our Saviour's prediction in the destruction of Jerusalem, and the overthrow of the Jewish people by Vespasian and Titus, and their continued dispersion, remains in all its force." ‡

* Jortin's Remarks, vol. ii. p. 327.

† The reader is referred to Basnage's History of the Jews, and to vol. viii. of Lardner's Jewish and Heathen Testimonies, for the reasons on which they ground their disbelief of this miracle.

‡ Lardner's Jewish and Heathen Testimonies, vol. viii. p. 393.

CHAPTER VII.

State of the Jews under Valentinian and Valens.—During the reign of Theodosius they insult the Christians at the feast of Purim.—Edicts of Theodosius II.—A false Messiah appears in Candia.—Tumult in Alexandria.—Violent behaviour of Cyril, bishop of that city.—Jews in the west favoured by Honorius.—Reputed conversion of those in Minorca.—Suppression of the Jewish patriarchs.—State of the Jews after the irruption of the barbarous nations into the Roman empire.

A. D. 387.] THE reign of Jovian, who succeeded Julian, was too short to affect any material alteration in the condition of the Jews. Valentinian, who, under the reign of an apostate, had signalized his zeal for the honour of Christianity, granted a general toleration to his subjects. The Pagans, the Jews, and all the various sects which acknowledged the divine authority of Christ, were protected by the laws from arbitrary power and popular insult. He prohibited the Jewish synagogues from being profaned, plundered, and demolished. Under his reign, and that of Valens, the Jewish patriarchs were restored to the enjoyment of all their privileges. However, Valens deprived this people of one great advantage, by revoking the decree which had exempted them from public offices.*

The Jews enjoyed a peaceable interval during the reigns of Gratian, Theodosius, and Arcadius. Theodosius I. granted them particular jurisdiction; and besides their civil and public judge, they had the power of electing officers and magistrates of their own persuasion. They possessed also authority to

* Basnage, p. 547.

K 2

execute the decrees, which were passed respecting
the religion and discipline of their brethren.   The
tranquillity which they enjoyed under Theodosius
was, however, disturbed by some bigotted Christians, who caused one of their synagogues to be
burnt; but upon complaint being made to the emperor, he ordered it to be rebuilt.   St. Ambrose, it
is said, justified the outrage, and was highly offended
with the emperor for protecting an unbelieving
nation.*

During the reign of Theodosius II. the liberal
treatment which the Jews had long experienced,
emboldened them to offer an insult to the established
religion.   Being assembled to celebrate the feast of
Purim, instead of hanging a figure of Haman on a
high gibbet, as had been their common custom, they
presumed to fix it on a cross, and with their usual
execrations burnt the cross and the figure.   The
emperor being apprized of their insolent behaviour,
prohibited their erecting and burning such gibbets,
under the penalty of being deprived of all their
privileges.   The Jews generally obeyed; but those
of Macedon and Dacia continued their insults of this
kind; which the Christian magistrates retaliated by
burning their houses and synagogues, and putting
their leaders to death.†

A. D. 408.] In order to suppress these disorders,
the emperor issued an edict, forbidding the Christians
to burn the synagogues, and the Jews to offer insults
to the established religion.   About three years after,
those of Inmestar, a city in Chalcis, being inflamed

* Basnage, p. 547.   Jortin's Remarks on Ecclesiastical History.
† Basnage, p. 550.

with wine at the feast of Purim,* fastened a young
Christian to a gibbet, who died in consequence of
their cruel treatment. The Christians, exasperated
at this conduct, took arms, and the Jews being
numerous in that country, a bloody engagement
ensued, in which many of both parties were killed.
At length the governor of the province was ordered
by the emperor to punish the instigators of these
disorders, and an end was put to the tumult.†

The Christians, however, still continued to plunder
and burn their synagogues, and appropriate their
goods to the use of the church, particularly at
Antioch, where the Jews were numerous and
affluent. Upon complaint being made to Theodosius, he ordered the people to restore what they
had taken, and erect new synagogues. But he was
induced to repeal this equitable act at the instigation
of the famed saint in the air, Simon Stylites,‡ who
was in high esteem with the clergy, and exerted all
the influence he had acquired by the fame of his
sanctity, to prevent restitution being made. After
Theodosius had revoked his orders, the Christians
of Antioch and the neighbouring provinces were
emboldened to commit new acts of violence against

* The Jews celebrate the feast of Purim by drinking much wine,
because they say by means of a wine banquet Esther made the king
so good humoured, that he was induced to grant her request.—
Prideaux's Connection.

† Basnage, p 151.

‡ Simon was a Syrian, who derived his appellation from his living
on the top of a pillar, where he is said to have continued thirty-seven
years. This fanatic had thus acquired a most shining reputation,
and attracted the veneration of all about him. It has been said, that
the emperor wrote a polite letter to him, in which he styles him the
holy martyr in the air.—*Basnage,* p. 551.

the Jews. The emperor was obliged, in 425, to publish an explanation of his former edicts, in order to suppress the cruelty, and injustice, which the revocation of his late decree caused the bigotted people to inflict upon this unhappy nation.

A. D. 432.] The Jews were numerous in the island of Candia, and had acquired wealth. About this time an impostor appeared, who pretended to be a second Moses, sent to deliver his people. He promised to divide the sea, and afford them a safe, passage through it to their own land. During one year he passed through every town and village in the island, and persuaded his countrymen to meet him on the day, and at the place appointed. They collected as much of their effects as they were able to carry, and having assembled with their wives and children, he led them to the top of a rock, and commanded them to cast themselves into the sea. The men, with unshaken faith, instantly obeyed, and the women and children followed with equal ardour. Many were drowned; others were saved by Christian fishermen. They became sensible of their infatuation, and endeavoured to seize the impostor; but he had the address to elude the search, which led them to suspect that he was the devil. Ashamed of their blind credulity, many were induced to embrace the profession of Christianity.*

A. D. 415] The city of Alexandria was computed to contain about one hundred thousand Jews, who had early distinguished themselves by their dexterity in trade, and like the other Egyptians were mutinous and seditious. At this time they

* Basnage, p. 551.

appear to have been greatly relaxed in the strictness
of their religious habits; and a number of them,
instead of attending the synagogues on the sabbath,
chose to be present at the public diversions, which
were exhibited on that day. On these occasions
frequent dissensions took place between them and
the Christians, which seldom terminated without
bloodshed. Cyril, the bishop of the city, was ardent
in the prosecution of heresy, and entertained, in
particular, an extreme aversion against the Jews,
whom he threatened with ecclesiastical execution.
But confiding in the protection of Orestes, the
governor of Alexandria, who was their friend
and patron, they despised the menaces of the
bishop.

An altercation having taken place with the
Christians, the Jews resolved to attack them in the
middle of the night. For this purpose they despatched several persons through the streets of the
city, who exclaimed, that the principal church was
in flames. Alarmed at this outcry, the Christians
came hastily out unarmed; and the Jews, who
distinguished them by some peculiar marks, immediately attacked them, and many were slain in this
tumult.* Exasperated at this outrage, Cyril, without waiting for a legal sentence, led a seditious
multitude to the attack of the synagogues, which
they levelled with the ground. They then entered
the houses, and, without making any distinction
between the guilty and the innocent, plundered them
of all their goods, which were appropriated to the
use of the church. They next compelled the rem-

* Basnage, p. 551.

nant of the unbelieving nation to abandon the city almost naked, and Alexandria was impoverished by the loss of an industrious and wealthy colony.*

Orestes was enraged at this infringement upon his authority. The people also declared against the proceedings of the bishop, and endeavoured to persuade him to submit to the governor: But he resolutely refused, and, taking the gospel in his hand, endeavoured to intimidate him to a reconciliation. Upon finding Orestes inflexible, he commanded a regiment of monks,† amounting to fifteen hundred, to descend from the mountains, and attack him in his chariot. Accordingly, having first reviled, they assaulted and dangerously wounded him. His life, however, was preserved by the people, who repaired to his assistance, rescued him out of the hands of the monks, and compelled them to provide for their safety by flight. After the tumult was appeased, Orestes caused Ammonius, the principal offender, to be put to death, and sent an account of the whole transaction to his court. Cyril, also wrote to the emperor to justify his conduct; and in his next sermon declared Ammonius a martyr in the cause of Christianity.‡

The indiscreet zeal of Cyril produced a new commotion, in which many persons lost their lives; and an atrocious murder gave additional horrors to this sedition. Hypatia, daughter of Theon, a cele-

* Basnage, p. 532.

† Cyril kept a standing army of dragoons, namely, the Egyptian monks and Alexandrian ecclesiastics, who were always ready to fight his battles.—*Jortin's Remarks on Eccles. Hist.* vol. viii. p. 106.

‡ Basnage, p. 556.   Jortin's Remarks on Ecclesiastical History, vol. iii. p. 106.

brated astronomer, publicly taught philosophy in
the Platonic school at Alexandria, where her
father had presided. This lady, who was eminently
distinguished for her talents and learning, had
obtained great celebrity, and attracted a crowded
audience. Orestes was in the habit of consulting
her in all difficult cases, and paid great deference to
her judgment. She was, however, a Pagan, and
being suspected of hindering a reconciliation between the governor and Cyril, was assaulted by the
fanatical populace, and barbarously assassinated
before one of the Christian churches. It is even
said, that Cyril, who detested her religion, who was
jealous of her reputation, and suspected her of
taking an active part against him, instigated his
followers to put her to death.*

A. D. 412.] While the bishop of Alexandria
exhibited this intolerant spirit, a Roman monarch
displayed the liberality of a more enlightened period.
The Jews in the west, under the protection of
Honorius, enjoyed the full exercise of their religion.
This emperor enacted a law, which exhibited his
generous and extensive views, importing that the
real glory of a prince consisted in allowing all his
subjects of different religious sentiments, the full and

* Basnage, p. 553. Dupin and some other ecclesiastical writers
endeavour to vindicate Cyril, and clear him from being concerned
in the murder. But a learned writer observes, "if there be not
sufficient evidence to condemn him as author of the murder, neither
is there room to acquit him. If he was innocent he should at least
have excommunicated those who were concerned in this vile assassination; but it does not appear that this was done; and neither
Socrates nor Valerius have said one word in his vindication."—*Jortin's
Remarks*, vol iii. p. 155.

peaceable enjoyment of all their rights and privileges. Agreeably to this decree, he expressly prohibited the destruction of synagogues, and the appropriation of them to any other purposes. He also gave orders, that they should not be compelled to violate the sabbath on account of their public services, alleging that the rest of the week was sufficient for secular purposes. ·He disapproved of the unjust calumnies which were raised against this people; and commanded the governors of provinces to do them justice, by resisting all the encroachments which had been, and should in future be made upon their privileges. He·also allowed them to retain Christians in their service, provided they left them at entire liberty to fulfil the duties of their religion.* On the other hand, to prevent the Jews from abusing their liberty, the emperor prohibited their building new synagogues, and making proselytes; and deprived them of some offices † which they formerly enjoyed in the empire.

A. D. 428.] The celebrated but disputed conversion of the Jews in Minorca, is said to have taken place in the fifth century. There were two considerable towns in this island; and the Hebrews were interdicted from that, in which the Christian bishop resided. It is even related, that those who presumed to enter it were generally punished with sudden and miraculous death. The other was chiefly inhabited by the Jews who, under Honorius,

---

* Basnage, p. 557.

† The Jews were admitted into the Roman troops for four centuries; they continued on the same footing till the emperor Honorius thought proper to declare them incapable of military service.— *Gregoire's Essay on the Reformation of the Jews.*

, enjoyed very considerable and lucrative offices. Theodosius, president of the synagogue, and doctor of the law, was the principal person in the island. Severus, the bishop, was persuaded by Orosius, who had lately returned from Jerusalem, loaded with miraculous relics, to attempt their conversion. They began with private, and proceeded to public conference in the synagogue. The Christians, being apprized that the Jewish women intended to assault them, provided for their defence. A tumult ensued, in which the synagogue was destroyed. It is said, however, that the bishop exhibited such a number of miracles, that their principal men were induced to relent, and in the course of eight days the greatest part of the Jews were converted to the Christian faith, and their synagogue to a church. But some, who continued obstinate and intractable, concealed themselves in caverns, till hunger compelled them to quit their retreats; others, leaving their property behind them, sought an asylum in foreign countries. These facts clearly demonstrate that compulsory means had been used to effect a conversion.*

A.D. 429.] The Jews sustained a severe affliction in the fifth century, by the office of patriarch, which had kept up a centre of unity among them, being abolished by the imperial law. Those chiefs were supported by taxes levied upon the Jewish people, which, at length, became so exorbitant, that they applied to the civil power for relief. Instead, however, of obtaining redress, they had the mortification of seeing the tribute converted to the emperor's use; and, as there was no income to support the dignity,

* Basnage, p. 558. Modern Universal History, vol. xiii.

it became extinct. After this period the western
Jews were solely under the direction of the chiefs
of the synagogues, whom they called Primates.*.

The fifth century was remarkable for the eruption
of the barbarous nations upon the western empire.
Yet the Jews only participated in the calamities
which usually attend great revolutions. Under the
Vandals they were allowed the free exercise of their
religion, and on the payment of tribute were permitted the freedom of commerce. One of the effects
of the invasion was the destruction of trade, which
those barbarians, who delighted in war, held in little
estimation. Commerce was therefore transferred to
a people, who were generally treated with ignominy
and contempt, and precluded from enjoying titular
dignities, and civil and military offices.†

After the Goths obtained possession of Italy, the
Jews continued to be protected by those barbarous
kings. Theodoret, in particular, deserves high
commendation for the liberality of his conduct.
During his reign, the Jews had formed establishments
at Naples, Rome, Milan, and Genoa, for the benefit
of trade, and under the sanction of the laws. Yet
their persons were insulted; their effects pillaged by
the populace of Ravenna and Rome, upon the most
frivolous, or extravagant pretensions. Theodoret
endeavoured to rectify these abuses; he defended
them against the Christian zealots, and forbade any

---

* Theodosius and Valentinian deprived the patriarchs of their
office, and applied the taxes which were levied for their support to
the imperial treasury. Honorius also published, at the end of the
fourth century, a law upon the same subject.—*Basnage*, p. 556.

† Basnage, p. 560 Anderson on Commerce.

compulsory measures to be employed for their conversion. He reproved the senate for suffering one
of their synagogues to be burnt at Rome; and the
clergy of Milan for attempting to seize upon
another.* When the citizens of Genoa deprived
them of the privileges which they had for a long
time enjoyed among them, they sought redress from
Theodoret, who permitted them to rebuild their
synagogues, and restored to them the free exercise
of their civil and religious rights. Thus the Jews
concluded the fifth century in the Roman empire;
though they had frequently suffered from the violent
tumults and animosities of the people; yet the
authority of their sovereigns enabled them to preserve some of their most important privileges.†

* Basnage, p. 561. Gibbon, vol. v. p. 29.   † Ibid.

CHAPTER VIII.

Of the Jewish academies in the east.—Rabbi Asce begins to compile
the Talmud of Babylon.—An account of the Masora.—Persecution
of the Jews in Persia during the fifth and sixth centuries —Of the
Sebureans and Gaons.—State of the Jews under the Persian monarchs.—Their attempt upon Tyre.—Of their state in the west.—
Justinian's edicts against them.—Appearance of a false Messiah.—
Revolt in Cesarea.—The Jews assist the Goths against Justinian.—
They raise an insurrection in Antioch.—Conversion of those in the
island of Cyprus.

THE Jewish academies in the east were towards
the close of the fifth century in a flourishing condition, under the direction of rabbi Asce, who was
eminently distinguished for his talents and learning.
He was born at Sora in Babylon, and at the early
age of fourteen was chosen president of the celebrated academy in that city, which office he enjoyed
sixty years. He died in 427.

After having taught with the highest reputation
forty years, he began a collection of the sayings,
debates, and decisions of the rabbies, from the time
of Judah the Saint to the period in which he lived.
He arranged thirty-five books ; but his death prevented his completing the work. However, it was
at length finished by his disciples, and styled the
Talmud of Babylon.* This collection, like the

---

* It is so called from its being the production of the Babylonian
schools, as the Talmud of Jerusalem derives its name from its being
compiled for the Jews in Palestine. This consists of the Misna of
Judah the Saint, and the Gemara of Jochanan. The Talmud of
Babylon consists of the same Misna, with the Gemara of rabbi Asce.
On the subject of these Gemaras, a distinguished Jew has remarked,
that " being nothing more than a collection of sentiments, parables,

Talmud 'of Jerusalem, comprises the Misna, which is the text, and is common to both ; and the Gemara or commentary, which is called the completion. The Jews entertain the highest veneration for this work ;* a learned writer of their nation styles it, "a complete system of all their learning, and a comprehensive rule of all the practical parts of their laws and religion."†

Rabbi Asce left a son called Huna, and two celebrated disciples, who were to have finished the Babylonian Talmud. But the work was retarded by a violent persecution which raged in Persia against the Jewish nation, and which is said to have continued seventy-three years. The synagogues were shut, the observation of the sabbath prohibited, and the schools and chapels given to the Magi. Huna, who was then the Jewish chief, and his two disciples were imprisoned, and suffered death with astonishing constancy. But the youthful part of the community, being more attached to the pleasures of life, were easily induced to apostatize from their religion ; and their example was followed by a general defection in Israel.‡

and legal determinations of the several great men of their schools at different times, the two Gemaras may be considered as one, and the Babylonish only a continuation of the Jerusalem. It is true, however, says he, the former is that intended to be designated by the generic expression of Talmud; but only because, as being later and more complete than that of Jerusalem, it comprises the last."—*Adams' Religious World displayed,* vol i. p. 33.

* It has even been said, that though they affirm the Scripture, the Misna, and Gemara, to be equally of divine authority, they compare the Scripture to water, the Misna to wine, and the Gemara to the choicest wine.—*Basnage,* p. 168.

† Levi's Ceremonies of the Jews, p. 310.   ‡ Basnage, p. 562.

The compilation of the Talmud was, however, resumed by the learned men of the nation, and it is generally supposed, that it was completed in the sixth century. This work was received with high applause by the Jews, who agreed that no addition or diminution should be made to it for the future. But a new order of doctors arose, called Sebureans or Sceptics, who professed to doubt of every thing, and opposed the infallibility which their brethren attributed to the Talmud.*

After the Jews had lost their existence as a nation, they were solicitous to preserve the purity and integrity of their sacred books. For this purpose a number of learned rabbies compiled a work, styled the Masora, in which they first fixed the true reading of the Hebrew text by vowels and accents; and, secondly, numbered not only the chapters and sections, but even the verses, words, and letters of the Old Testament   A late learned writer has styled this work "the most stupendous monument in the whole history of literature, of minute and persevering labour."† The Jews call the Masora "the hedge, or fence of the law," because the enumeration of the verses, &c. is a mean of preserving it from being altered or corrupted.

They assert that when God gave the law to Moses on mount Sinai, he taught him the true reading, which was handed down by oral tradition from age to age, till it was committed to writing. Elias Levita, a celebrated rabbi, who bestowed twenty years' labour on explaining the Masora, makes the first compilers of it the Jewish doctors of the famous

* Basnage, p. 562.   † Butler's Horæ Biblicæ, p. 57.

school of Tiberias, about five hundred years after Christ.*

The age in which the Masorites arose has, however, been much disputed. Some writers placed their origin in the sixth century; and others maintained, that they did not appear till the tenth. Basnage asserts, that they were not a society, but a succession of men; and that the Masora was the work of many grammarians, who, without associating and communicating their notions, composed this collection of criticisms on the Hebrew text.†

The sixth century commenced with a violent persecution of the Jews in the east, under Cavades, a prince of a cruel disposition, who attempted to compel all his subjects to embrace the Persian religion. The celebrated Meir, a learned rabbi, lived at this time, and, exasperated at the severe treatment of his brethren, declared war against the king of Persia. At length, however, he was defeated and put to death. The Persians then entered the city in which Zeutra, the prince of the captivity, resided, and having pillaged it, caused him and the president of the council to be executed. [A. D. 522.] The family of the prince escaped destruction by a precipitate flight. Zeutra, his son, retired into Judea, and was raised to an office of trust and honour by his brethren in that country.‡

Chosroes the Great, who succeeded Cavades, treated the Jews with greater severity than his predecessor. They endeavoured to obtain the favour of this prince, by persuading him to break off his

---

* Jennings' Lect. vol. i. p. 401.   † Basnage, p. 182.
‡ Ibid. p. 504.

negotiations for peace with the emperor Justinian;
which were then in great forwardness. For this
purpose they promised Chosroes, that, if he would
consent to continue the war, they would furnish him
with fifty thousand men, by whose assistance the
might be enabled to conquer Jerusalem, one of the
richest cities in the world. The king, duped by
their flattering promises, broke off his treaty with
the emperor, and prepared to carry the project into
execution. He was, however, soon informed, that
the persons who were employed in the treacherous
design had been seized by order of government ; and
after making a full discovery of their plan and
abettors, had been put to death. But this intelligence did not deter Chosroes from prosecuting the
war, which was conducted with great energy, and
many successful inroads were made into Syria and
Palestine. The Jews, however, participated in the
common calamities, and were treated with equal
severity with the other inhabitants of the conquered
countries. Their academies were shut ; their love
of learning became extinguished ; the prince of the
captivity was obliged to remove into Judea, and the
eastern Jews were destitute of chiefs to preside over
them.*

A. D. 589.]   When Hormisdas the Third ascended the throne, he restored their former privileges,
which they continued to enjoy during the reign of
this prince. The academy of Pundebita was opened
under the direction of the celebrated rabbi Chanan
Mehischa. A new order of doctors appeared, who
were called Gaons, (sublime, or excellent,) and de-

* Basnage, p. 565.

stroyed the Sebureans, or Sceptics. These doctors were constituted chiefs of the academies, were consulted upon all difficult questions, and their decisions were regarded as oracles by their brethren, who considered them the ablest interpreters of the law.[*]

After Chosroes II. had murdered his father Hormisdas in order to obtain the throne, his son Varanes rebelled against him, and had the address to engage the Jews in his interest. They, however, paid dear for their presumption; and Varanes being reduced to subjection, they were regarded as a faithless and implacable people, that excited the subjects against their princes, and fomented sedition. Those of Antioch were the first victims of Chosroes' resentment; many of whom perished by the sword; others, were put to death by the most cruel torments; and those, who survived, subjected to the most abject slavery.[†]

A. D. 613.] Chosroes, however, was afterwards reconciled to the Jews, who appear to have rendered him many signal and important services. They acted in concert with this monarch during his invasion of Palestine, and even furnished him with an army of twenty thousand men. When, after the reduction of Galilee, the Persian monarch made himself master of Jerusalem,[‡] they, with furious bigotry, pillaged and destroyed the Christian churches; and the king having delivered the Christian prisoners into their hands, they satiated their implacable hatred against

---

[*] Basnage, p 565. Modern Universal Hist. vol. xiii. p. 208.

[†] Basnage, p. 566. Mavor's Universal Hist. vol. xiii. p. 18.

[‡] Jerusalem was recovered from the Persians by the Greek emperor Heraclius, and soon after taken by the Arabians. See the following chapter.

them, by putting ninety thousand of this unhappy
people to a cruel death.*

While Chosroes was besieging Constantinople,
and all the forces of Syria and Judea were employed
in defence of that city, the Jews conspired with
their brethren in Palestine to make an attempt to
conquer Tyre, and destroy its inhabitants. But
the Tyrians having obtained timely intelligence of
their design were prepared for the attack, and repulsed them with great bravery. After this disap-
pointment, they dispersed themselves through the
country, and assaulted and burned many of the
Christian churches. They were, at length, vanquished by the Tyrians, who sallied out of the city,
and made a terrible slaughter.†

Whilst the eastern Jews, in the sixth century,
sustained a series of persecutions in Persia, their
brethren in the west were cruelly oppressed, and
gradually stripped of their immunities and privileges.
The emperor Justinian, who assumed the preroga-
tive of deciding on all religious controversies, issued
an edict which prohibited their celebrating the
passover according to their own calculation, and
obliged them to observe it at the same time with the
Christian church. Soon after he forbade the magistrates to admit them to give evidence against the
Christians ; and deprived them of the privilege of
making wills, and bequeathing legacies. These
decrees were followed by another, still more oppressive, which interdicted them from educating their
children in their own faith. Justinian also, at the
request of the council of Carthage, deprived those of

* Basnage, p. 566   † Basnage. Modern Univer. Hist.

Africa of the exercise of their religion, and commanded the prefect to convert their synagogues into churches.*

A. D. 530.] The Jews were exasperated by these severe edicts, and the general discontent and indignation soon ripened into an open rebellion. One Julian, who pretended to be the Messiah, had the address to attract many of his brethren in Palestine to his standard. After assuming the title of conqueror, he armed his followers; led them against the Christians; and they, being wholly unprepared for an attack, were slaughtered in great numbers. At length, however, Justinian sent troops against the insurgents; and, though they fought with desperation, they were soon entirely routed. The false Messiah was taken, and immediately put to death; and thus the revolt was terminated.†

A. D. 555.] Twenty-five years after, the Jews in Cesarea rebelled against the Roman government; and, notwithstanding the inveterate hatred which subsisted between them and the Samaritans, they united their forces against the Christians. The insurgents attacked and demolished many of the churches, and massacred large numbers of the people, particularly the governor in his own palace. Justinian, upon being apprised of the revolt, and the cruelties which were perpetrated, confiscated the property of the most affluent; and the others, who engaged in the rebellion, were beheaded or banished.‡

---

* Basnage, p. 576. Modern Univer. Hist. vol. xiii. p. 215.
† Ibid.   ‡ Basnage, p. 577.

The Jews joined the Goths* in Italy against Justinian and his general Belisarius. While this celebrated officer was engaged in the siege of Naples, they defended the city with the most obstinate resolution. When the citizens were about to capitulate, they encouraged and persuaded them to hold out to the last extremity. In consequence of their exertions the siege was protracted, which occasioned the destruction of many of the Roman soldiers. When the city was taken, though Belisarius endeavoured to inspire his troops with sentiments of clemency and pity, the Jews, without any distinction of age, sex, or rank, were cruelly put to death. Intimidated by this dreadful severity, they remained peaceable during the two subsequent reigns.

A. D. 602.] At length, under the reign of Phocas, the Jews at Antioch, where they had become populous and affluent, raised an insurrection against the Christians, who defended themselves with great resolution ; but not being sufficiently powerful to repel their enemies, they became the victims of their cruelty. Many were burnt in their houses ; and bishop Anastasius, and several others, after having endured the greatest indignities, were put to death. The rebellion, however, after an arduous conflict, was suppressed by a powerful body of forces, which Phocas sent against them ; and the barbarous conduct of the insurgents severely punished.†

* The fidelity of the Jews to the Gothic kings cannot justly be alleged against them, since they were then their subjects.— *Basnage*, p. 579.

† Basnage, p. 578

A. D. 606.] The Jews, at this period, notwithstanding the edict of Adrian, had become numerous in Cyprus. About four years after the insurrection at Antioch, bishop Leontius, fearing that the island would suffer similar calamities, resolved to use every possible method to effect their conversion. His endeavours proved so successful, if we may depend upon his apology to be genuine, that the greater part of them renounced Judaism, and were baptized.* Many of their brethren, in other parts, were about this time induced to profess the Christian religion. A learned ecclesiastical historian, however, remarks, that "it must be acknowledged, that of these conversions the greater part were owing to the liberality of Christian princes, rather than to the force of argument, or love of truth."†

* Basnage, p. 579.   † Mosheim's Ecclesiastical Hist. vol. ii. p. 98.

CHAPTER IX.

Appearance of Mahomet.—His behaviour to the Jews.—They take
arms against him, are reduced, and compelled to become tributary.
—Rapid conquests of the caliph Omar; he besieges and takes Jerusalem.—The Jews rejoice at his success in Persia.—They are favoured by the first caliphs.—Those in Italy are protected by pope
Gregory the Great.—They are severely treated by the emperor
Heraclius, who instigates other monarchs to persecute them.

A. D. 609.] MAHOMET, the famous Arabian
impostor, appeared in the early part of the seventh
century, and established a new religion, which, by
force of arms, made a rapid progress in the world.
Many of the Jews, after the destruction of their
country, had fled to Arabia; and the industrious
exiles, who aspired to liberty and power, obtained
possession of several towns and fortresses, and had
armies, and princes to command them. Their
number and respectability induced Mahomet at first
to treat them with great attention. He ordered his
followers when they prayed, to turn towards the
temple of Jerusalem; and adopted many of their
opinions and customs, in order to engage them
in his interest.*

The Jews, dazzled by the splendour of his victories, began to regard him as the expected Messiah,
and some persons of distinction among them embraced his religion. However, they were, soon
after, much offended at his eating camel's flesh, which
is forbidden by the Mosaic law. But the fear of
appearing inconstant, or the hope of deriving advantage from the impostor, induced them to aid him

* Basnage p 566. Gibbon, vol. vi.

in his design. The Arabian writers assert, that this nation sent twelve of their doctors to assist him in compiling the Koran.* But they afterwards became his inveterate enemies; and their behaviour gave rise to the most implacable hatred on his part. His aversion to this unhappy people continued till the last moment of his life; and, in "the double character of an apostle and a conqueror, his persecution extended to both worlds."† In his Koran, he reproaches them with betraying and murdering the prophets, and styles them, "a people justly cursed of God for their violation of his sabbath and laws; for their treatment of Jesus Christ, whom he acknowledges to be a great prophet; and for having filled up the measure of their iniquity by rejecting his own mission."‡

The Jewish tribe at Kainoka dwelt at Medina under the protection of the city. Mahomet seized the occasion of an accidental tumult, and summoned them to embrace his religion, or contend with him in battle. " Alas!" replied the trembling Jews, " we are ignorant of the use of arms; but we persevere in the faith and worship of our fathers; why wilt thou reduce us to the necessity of a just defence." But as war was inevitable, Cajah, one of the most distinguished persons of the Jewish nation, who had uniformly opposed all the measures of the impostor, appeared at the head of his country-men.§

In the third year of the Hegira,‖ Mahomet be-

* Basnage, p. 566   † Gibbon, vol. vi.
‡ Sale's Koran, vol i p. 35.   § Basnage, p. 568.
‖ Hegira, is a term signifying the epocha, used by the Arabians

sieged the Jews in Hegiasa, and having. obliged
them to surrender. at discretion,.,drove them into
exile. Their wealth was confiscated, and.distributed
among.his followers. After several. engagements,
in which the impostor was victorious, Cajah attacked
him near Kaibar; and though this place was the seat
of the Jewish power in Arabia, this miserable people
were defeated with great slaughter. Their leader,
who with difficulty escaped, being resolved to try
the event of another engagement, was again completely routed; and suffered death with that constancy which characterizes his nation. After the
termination of the unequal conflict, the Jews were
compelled to submit to the power of the conqueror,
and become tributary: Some time after the death
of the impostor, they were transplanted to Syria,
he having left it as his dying injunction, that one
and the true religion should alone be professed in
his native land of Arabia.*

In the caliphs, who succeeded Mahomet, were
united both the temporal and the spiritual power;
and their valour, being animated by the violent spirit
of fanaticism, was altogether. irresistible. Omar,
the second caliph, was one of the most rapid conquerors, who ever spread desolation over the face
of the earth. During the ten years of his reign,
he subdued Arabia, Syria, Mesopotamia, Persia,
and Egypt. With the Saracens under his command,
he invested Jerusalem, and after an obstinate siege,

and Turks, who begin their computation from the day that Mahomet
was compelled to make his escape from the city of Mecca, which took
place, July 16, A. D. 622, under the reign of the emperor Heraclius.

* Gibbon, vol. vi.

which lasted four months, the Christians, having obtained an honourable capitulation, surrendered the city. The conqueror would not allow them to be deprived of their churches. But by his command, the ground where Solomon's temple stood, was prepared for the foundation of a mosque, which was the first Mahometan place of worship erected in Jerusalem.*

When Persia submitted to the victorious Saracens, the Jews, who hoped for a favourable change in their affairs, rejoiced in their success. Isdesgerdi the Third, the last Persian monarch, had, according to their annals, either begun, or carried on a bloody persecution against them; giving their synagogues to the Magi, and causing their academies to be shut. The rapid conquests of the enemies of their cruel oppressors, who were either Pagans or Christians, and the frequent destruction of the churches of the latter, highly gratified their inclinations. They are even accused of having ingratiated themselves with the Saracens, by instigating them against the Christians. Those enthusiastic conquerors for some time used their prosperity with moderation; and though the Jews often changed masters by the swift succession of monarchs, they only participated in the

* Basnage, p. 572. Jerusalem was transferred from the possession of the Greek Christians, to the dominion of the Arabian Musselmans, and continued in subjection to the caliphs, about four hundred years. When Omar took the city, the inhabitants were allowed the exercise of their religion; but they were prohibited from building any new churches, either in the metropolis, or the adjacent country; from riding upon saddles, or bearing any kind of arms. They were obliged to dress in a different manner from the Mahometans, and subjected to pay tribute to their conquerors' *Ockley's Saracen's Conquests.* p 258.

common calamities which attend great revolutions
in governments. They highly extol the humanity
of the first caliphs, who restored them to the free
exercise of their religion ; allowed the princes of the
captivity to enjoy great authority, and permitted
their academies to be opened, and placed in a
flourishing condition.*

A. D. 606.] A number of the Roman pontiffs
have been equally indulgent to the Jewish nation
with the first caliphs. In Italy, where this people
were numerous in the seventh century, they were
treated with moderation and kindness by pope
Gregory the Great. Their general conversion was
the object of his ardent desires, and earnest endeavours. In order to effect this benevolent design, he
wrote to his receiver in Sicily, to abate those who
professed the Christian religion a third part of the
revenues they were indebted to him. He also
warmly exhorted his clergy and flock to use the Jews
with candour and tenderness, alleging, that they
were one day to be recalled, and become a large
part of Christ's fold ; and that the proper method to
conduct them to the unity of the faith, was kind and
friendly treatment. " Violence," said he, " will disgust those who might be allured by gentleness and
charity." He strongly expressed his abhorrence of
the persecution they suffered in different countries,
and condemned the zeal of some of the bishops
against them He even reprehended the conduct of
a converted Jew, who, in order to ingratiate himself
with the Christians, set up a cross, and image of the
virgin, in a synagogue. Gregory ordered the cross

* Basnage. p. 573.

and image to be removed, alleging, that since the laws did not permit the Jews to build new synagogues, they ought to be allowed the free enjoyment of those they already possessed.* With the same liberal spirit he condemned the conduct of the bishop of Terracina, who had deprived them of a synagogue in his diocese, which was permitted by the laws; and had expelled them from another place, where they had retired in order to perform their devotional exercises.†

This pontiff, however, who was frequently consulted respecting the domestic affairs of the Jews, disapproved of their purchasing Christian slaves, and revived the laws which had been enacted against this traffic. He also ordered, that all their Jewish domestics, who professed the Christian religion, and received baptism, should obtain their liberty.‡

The cruel treatment which the Jews soon after experienced from Heraclius, the Greek emperor, formed a striking contrast to the clemency of the Roman pontiff. This monarch hated the Hebrew race on account of their religion, and his animosity against them was increased by finding at Tiberias one of the nation so rich as to be able to supply his army and court with provisions. This man, elated with his affluence, molested the Christians with troublesome law suits, and malicious prosecutions. But, being sensible that he had exposed himself to the resentment of the emperor, he endeavoured to elude

* It appears that the former edicts of the emperor Theodosius were still in force against the Jews, notwithstanding the clemency of pope Gregory towards this people.—*Modern Univer. Hist.* vol. xiii. p. 220.

† Basnage, p. 579.   ‡ Ibid.

his vengeance by professing the Christian religion. This expedient, however, did not lessen the monarch's aversion to the Jewish nation.*

Heraclius was still more exasperated against the Jews, when, upon his consulting the diviners concerning the fate of the empire, he received for answer, that a circumcised nation would prove its ruin. Considering how powerful and numerous the Hebrews were in most parts of his dominions, and that they still cherished the hope of being restored to their native country, he believed them to be the people intended by the prediction. The great and frequent efforts they had made to recover their liberty, and their cruel and sanguinary proceedings against the Christians at different times, and in various places, confirmed him in this belief; and induced him to persecute them with the utmost severity. He banished them from Jerusalem, to which they had once more gained access ;† and issued an edict, prohibiting them from approaching within three miles of the city. The emperor was not satisfied with persecuting this unhappy people in his own dominions ; but instigated other monarchs to follow his example.‡ The calamities which they suffered in Spain, Gaul, and other kingdoms, will be related in the following chapter.

* Basnage, p. 580. According to the account of Mosheim, " the emperor Heraclius, being incensed against this miserable people, by the insinuations of the Christian doctors, persecuted them in a most cruel manner, and ordered multitudes of them to be inhumanly dragged into the Christian churches, in order to be baptized, by violence and compulsion."—*Mosheim's Ecclesiastical History*, vol. ii. p. 152.

† Previous to the conquest of Jerusalem by the Saracens, which has been mentioned in the preceding part of this chapter.

‡ Basnage, p. 581.

CHAPTER X.

The Jews in Spain are cruelly persecuted by Sisebut, the Gothic king of that country.—Decrees of the councils of Toledo.—Frequent apostasy of the Jewish converts.—The archbishop of Toledo writes in order to convert them.—They form a conspiracy against the Spanish government.—Severe laws are enacted against them.—Of the Jews in Gaul.—They are expelled by king Dagobert, and by Wamba, king of the Goths.—They found an academy in Lunel.

THE Jews, who were transplanted to Spain by the policy of Adrian, had become numerous in that kingdom, and acquired wealth by their dexterity in trade. Their affluence excited the avarice of their masters; and, as they had lost the use of arms, they might be oppressed with impunity. The emperor Heraclius, who had been engaged in war with Sisebut, the Spanish monarch, made it one of the principal articles of the peace, that the king should compel them to receive baptism, or abandon the kingdom. The religious bigotry of Sisebut induced him readily to accede to this article; and without consulting any of his bishops, and even contrary to their remonstrances, he imprisoned the most distinguished personages among this unhappy people.*

After having remained some time in confinement, large numbers of Jews, in order to preserve their wealth and lives, consented to be baptized. The estates of the more obstinate were confiscated, and their bodies tortured. Some found means to retire into Gaul, where similar miseries awaited them. They assert, however, that during the life of Sisebut, they were not even allowed the privilege of

* Mariana's History of Spain.

preferring their religion to their country, and endeavouring to escape by a voluntary exile from the evils they endured.*　.ᵗ ⸴ .ᵎ ⸴ ,

A. D. 633.] The conduct, of the, king was highly censured by Isidore, bishop of Seville, and condemned by the clergy in Spain. In the fourth council of Toledo,† in which Isidore presided, it was declared unchristian and unlawful to use compulsory measures in religion. The reasons assigned were, that God hardens, and has compassion on whom he pleases ; and that none can be saved without their own free consent. This council, however, ordained, that those whom persecution had induced to receive baptism, should be compelled, for the honour of the church, to persevere in conforming to the external rites of the Christian religion. This decree, which derogates from the liberal spirit exhibited in the former, was enacted, because the pretended converts relapsed into Judaism, whenever the immediate influence of terror was withdrawn.‡

A. D. 638.] Chintila, who succeeded Sisenand, treated the Jews with the greatest rigour ; and appeared to be totally regardless of the sacred rights of conscience. The decree of this monarch, which commanded all his subjects to profess the Christian faith, was the signal of persecution and exile ; and an edict was passed for their total expulsion. It

---

* Basnage, p. 581. History of Spain.

† This council was assembled by Sisenand, who having dethroned the son of Sisebut, endeavoured to reconcile the minds of the people to his government, by prevailing upon the clergy to give a religious sanction to his proceedings. The council conformed to his views, and instructed the Goths to unite under his government.—*Basnage*, p. 581.

‡ Basnage, p. 582. History of Spain.

appears probable, that the usurious advantage, which they might derive from their wealth, augmented the public hatred against them. Yet the Goths were unwilling to deprive themselves of industrious men over whom they might exercise lucrative oppression; and the Jews continued in Spain under the weight of the civil and ecclesiastical laws.*

In order to engage the Spanish clergy to forward his views, Chintila convened the fifth council of Toledo. This assembly passed several decrees in his favour, which the king caused to be confirmed by another council, convoked the same year, and at the same place. The divines, who composed this assembly, highly commended his zeal against the Jews; and blessed God for having given them such a wise and pious prince. They solemnly ratified the edict he had enacted for the banishment of this miserable people; and declared, that no prince, for the future should ascend the Spanish throne, till he had taken an oath to observe all the laws against them; and he who violated this sacred engagement was to be anathematized.†

These severe laws were punctually observed by the succeeding monarchs. The Visigothic kings enacted a law which completely authorized persecution; and alleged in their vindication, that "since the violent take the kingdom of heaven by force, men ought to be stimulated to obtain this blessing."

---

* Basnage, p. 582. History of Spain.

† Basnage observes, that the different decrees enacted in this, and the preceding council, were owing to the death of Isidore of Seville. This benevolent prelate, who was a strong advocate for mild treatment, presided in the fourth council of Toledo, but died before the sixth. *Basnage*, p. 582.

M

By this law it was ordained, that every Jew, who refused to receive baptism, should suffer a severe corporal punishment, be exiled from the kingdom, and have all his goods confiscated.*) (; ‾ ,, .''

A. D. 653] Multitudes of this persecuted people, intimidated by the gloomy prospects before them, were induced to conform externally to the national faith. But as their conformity was only extorted by terror, many were soon observed to apostatize. To remedy this evil, a new council was convened. The Jews, apprehending that the decrees of the assembly would be the prelude of a violent persecution against them, resolved to shelter themselves from the impending calamity. For this purpose, the most distinguished personages of their nation met, and wrote to the king in the name of their brethren in Spain, declaring that, though they had till then dissembled, they were now firmly resolved to become sincere converts, and wholly conform to the laws of the gospel. They assured his majesty, that they would no longer observe their sabbath, circumcise their children, or form any connexions by marriage with those who were unbaptized; and promised to persecute any of their brethren, who should presume to violate these engagements. They even consented; provided their lives might be spared, to be doomed to perpetual slavery, and have all their effects confiscated.† ' ' ' ' (, : ' !' ,'' '

The ample promises contained in this letter, rendered their sincerity more suspected, and their conduct more strictly observed. It was accordingly

---

* Modern Universal History, vol. xiii. History of Spain.
† Basnage, p. 582. Modern Universal History, vol. xiii p. 223.

discovered, that they still performed the Jewish rites, and even ventured to attack the Christian religion. The king, finding the difficulty of effecting his purpose by coercive measures, ordered Julian, archbishop of Toledo, to write against them; and this prelate, in 686, published a learned treatise, in which he proves from the prophetic writings, that *Jesus of Nazareth is the Messiah.*

The Gothic kings and bishops at length discovered, that injuries would produce hatred, and that hatred would find an opportunity of revenge. The Jews exulted in the victories of the Mahometans, and commenced a dangerous and hostile correspondence with their brethren, who, under the administration of Chintila, had sheltered themselves from persecution in Africa. On receiving from them assurance of support, and with the secret hope of more effectual succour from the Saracens, they fixed a day to erect the standard of revolt.*

Before the appointed time arrived, their preparations had alarmed, and their intentions been betrayed to king Egica. This monarch complained of the conspiracy to the council of Toledo, and demanded the assistance and advice of the divines, who composed the assembly. Upon deliberation they resolved, that all the circumcised should be declared perpetual slaves, that their estates should be confiscated, and their children taken from them, and educated in the Christian faith.†

If from Spain we turn to a neighbouring country, we find the Jews still oppressed and persecuted.

---

* Basnage, p. 583. History of Spain. † Basnage.

As soon as the Romans* were driven out of Gaul, and the Visigoths suppressed, several directions and decrees were made respecting them, and one in particular, under Childebert, [A. D. 540.] who forbade them to appear in the streets of Paris from Tuesday in the holy week to Easter Sunday. The council of Orleans about the same time enacted a similar decree, which renders it evident, that they were dispersed in several parts of France.† They were still more numerous in Languedoc. Ferreol, bishop of Uzes, was expelled from his diocese, for having treated them with too great familiarity and kindness. His motive was, an ardent desire to effect their conversion. After he had continued in exile many years, and the king had restored him to his bishopric, he fell into the other extreme, and banished the Jews.‡

Avitus, bishop of Clermont, was distinguished by his zeal for the conversion of this people, and induced several persons among them to profess their belief in Christianity. One of the new converts entered the city in his white garment, which being observed by a Jew, he threw a pot of oil of very offensive odour upon him. This outrage irritated the Christians to such a degree, that had not the bishop interposed, the offender would have been

---

* Gaul was shared by the Visigoths and Burgundians, when Clovis, king of the Franks, defeated Syagrius, a Roman usurper in that province, and established a new kingdom, to which he gave the name of France, or the land of freemen.—*Russell's Modern Europe.*

† The Jews who settled in Gaul at an early period, made but little figure, and are only known by some edicts of Constantine, which mention them in Belgic Gaul. They began to be noticed in the histories of the country in the sixth century.

‡ Basnage, p. 589.

immediately put to death. The humanity of Avitus, however, only delayed the effects of their resentment till the succeeding festival. The people at that time demolished their synagogue, and the Jews were reduced to the alternative of professing Christianity, or being exiled. The greater part of them chose to conform to the established worship, and were baptized.*

King Chilperic, who observed, that the Jews in Paris were numerous and affluent, resolved to use compulsory measures to induce them to abjure their religion. As he led an immoral life he hoped, by his zeal in attempting the conversion of an unbelieving people, to make an atonement for his sins, and secure the favour of heaven. He therefore commanded, that all who refused to receive baptism, should be punished with the utmost rigour.†

A. D. 692.] They were treated with still greater severity by king Dagobert, who was notorious for the scandalous irregularity of his conduct. In order to avoid public odium, to ingratiate himself with his clergy and people, and gratify the emperor Heraclius.‡ he banished from his kingdom upon pain of death, all the Jews, who refused to profess the Christian religion. Many who had fled from Spain to escape persecution suffered a second exile. But still more of them preferred dissimulation, and consented to be baptized.§

* Basnage, p. 584.   † Ibid.

‡ The emperor Heraclius, who had expelled the Jews from his dominions, and caused them to be banished from Spain, sent ambassadors to Dagobert to oblige him to imitate these examples.— *Basnage*, p. 584.

§ Modern Univer. Hist. vol. xiii. p. 226.

A. D. 673.] Wamba, king of the Goths in
Languedoc, also exhibited a violent enmity against
this people ; and issued an edict which expelled them
from his dominions. But he experienced the most
determined opposition from the abbot Raymirus; and
the court of Toulouse; who united to protect this
persecuted race; and opposed the king's edict by
force of arms. The king entrusted count Paul, his
favourite; with the command of an army; which was
destined to act against the rebels. But, instead of
suppressing, he united with them, took Narbonne,
and caused himself to be crowned king. At length,
however, he was defeated, and condemned by
Wamba ; and his accomplices, especially the Jews,
felt the effects of this monarch's resentment, and
were expelled from the kingdom.*

Notwithstanding the sufferings of the Jewish
nation in the seventh century, the academy which
they had founded at Lunel, a city in Languedoc,
began to flourish. In process of time it acquired
great celebrity, and was the place where some of
the most learned Jewish rabbies received their
education.

* Basnage, p. 584.

CHAPTER XI.

Of the pretended conversion of the king of Chozar to Judaism.—
State of the eastern Jews in the eighth and ninth centuries.—They
are favoured by several of the caliphs, who were attached to literary
men.—Edict of Iman Jaaffar against them.—Al-Walhek obliges
them to pay heavy taxes—Motavel condemns them to wear a
disgraceful badge of distinction.—State of the Jews under the
Grecian emperors.—A false Messiah appears in Spain.—Of their
state in France.—Punishment inflicted upon them by the emperor
Charlemagne.—They are highly favoured by Lewis, surnamed Debonair; but their condition is less agreeable under Charles the Bald.

THE eighth century is celebrated by Jewish
writers for the conversion of Chozar, a Pagan prince,
to their belief. According to their accounts, he
became dissatisfied with the religion of his people
and progenitors ; and conversed on this subject with
philosophers, Christians, Mahometans, and Jews.
At length, a learned rabbi convinced him, that
Judaism was the only true religion, to which all
others were but as the shadow to the substance,
or the picture to the living original. Chozar therefore abjured his former tenets, and, after he was
initiated in the belief and ceremonies of the Jews,
employed himself in converting his subjects. He
sent for the most learned men of this nation from all
countries to instruct his people ; and from that time
the original Jews were held in high estimation. A
tabernacle was erected, similar to that of Moses in
the wilderness ; to which they and the Chozrean
converts repaired to the Jewish worship. The king
became prosperous , triumphed over his enemies,

and enlarged his dominions by new and considerable
conquests. Such is the account of Jewish writers;
but notwithstanding the degree of credit which they
have endeavoured to attach to the conversion of
Chozar, and of his subjects, the real existence of
that prince, and of his kingdom, has always been
much disputed.*

During the eighth, and part of the ninth century,
the eastern Jews under the dominion of the caliphs,
sustained their share in the calamities which resulted
from the civil wars among their conquerors. They,
however, enjoyed entire liberty of conscience under
the caliph Abdalmelech, and his two successors
Alwalid and Solyman. Their academies flourished,
and their doctors possessed all their ancient privileges.

In the reign of Zeyd they suffered some oppressions, which were caused more from the rapacious-
ness of his ministers, than the cruelty of the
monarch. But upon the dissolution of the government of the Ommiades under Mervan, their condition was ameliorated by the princes of the dynasty
of the Abbassides.†

A. D. 740.] The caliph Almansor, who was a
learned prince, patronised and encouraged literary
men, and invited a large number of them to his
court, without any regard to their particular religious opinions. Many Jews accepted the invitation
of this monarch, and took advantage of his liberality
to place their academies in a more flourishing condi-

---

* Basnage, p 587. Modern Universal Hist. vol. xiii. p. 228.

† The fall of the Ommiades, and the establishment of the dynasty
of the Abbassides, took place about 750.—*Gibbon.*

tion than ever. They boast of the many famous men who appeared among their nation at this period; among whom Rabbi Acha was distinguished for his profound learning, and his voluminous treatise on the precepts of the law, under the title of Shealtoth, or Questions. About this time rabbi Annanus revived the sect of the Sadducees, which had been almost extinct after the destruction of Jerusalem; but under him the denomination acquired new vigour, and became formidable to that of the Pharisees.*.

A. D. 760.] The Jews of Arabia and Persia experienced the mortification of having an edict issued against them by Iman Jaaffar, surnamed the Just. Stimulated by zeal for his religion, he ordained, that those who embraced the Mahometan faith should be sole heirs of the property of the whole family. This decree, which was punctually executed, induced many Jewish, and other children to apostatize in order to obtain estates, to which they were unable to claim any just title.

Almansor was succeeded by Mohadi, who obliged the Jews either to embrace the Mahometan religion, or wear a disgraceful badge of distinction. In the reign of this prince, Hakem, an impostor, appeared, and by pretended miracles gained many disciples. This man, who is said to have been of Jewish origin, asserted, that the divinity, which in former times appeared in a human shape, now made his abode in him, and that he was the visible image of the

* Some writers have styled Annanus the founder of the Caraites but according to Basnage, and the authors of the Modern Universal History, this denomination were of much earlier date; and Annanus only revived the sect of the Sadducees.

most high God. Mohadi sent forces against the impostor, who besieged him in one of his fortresses. Upon which he first poisoned his followers, and then destroyed himself.*

A. D. 786] Aaron, the successor of Mohadi, was distinguished for his love of literature, and encouraged and patronized learned men of all religions, and of every profession. In particular he highly favoured the Jews, who were dispersed in his dominions, and chose one of their nation to send on an embassy to Charlemagne, the emperor of the west. He succeeded in his commission, and enjoyed a distinguished reputation at the court of Aaron. This caliph placed the academies of the eastern Jews in a flourishing condition ; and they enjoyed profound tranquillity during his reign.†

A. D. 831.] Mamoun, the brother of Aaron, was also attached to literature, and caused the most valuable Jewish works to be translated into Arabic: And though this instance of his liberality exasperated his subjects, he continued to distinguish learned men of all nations and religions. Mashalla, a celebrated Jewish astronomer, was so highly esteemed at his court, that he was styled the Phœnix of the age. During the reign of Mamoun, the famous impostor Moses appeared, who pretended that he was the great lawgiver of the Jews, whom God had recently raised from the dead.‡

A. D. 841.] Al-Wathek, instead of imitating the conduct of the most enlightened caliphs who preceded him, became an implacable enemy to the

* Basnage, p. 591. Gibbon, vol. vii. p. 180.
† Basnage. p. 592. ‡ Ibid. p. 594.

Jews. , He hated this people, because they refused to receive the Koran as an authentic revelation ; and the fraudulent practices of which they had been guilty in the management of the finances, during the reign of his predecessor, increased his enmity against them. During his reign they were loaded with heavy taxes; and obliged to pay large sums into the treasury.*

A. D. 849.] Motarakel the successor of Al-Wathek, treated the Jews with still greater severity. He compelled them to wear a cord or sash round their waists, as an invidious mark of distinction ; and excluded them from all offices in the Divan, which it appears, they had till then enjoyed. He forbade their riding on horses, and only permitted them to use asses or mules with iron stirrups.

The edicts of this monarch not only extended through his empire, but spread into the neighbouring kingdoms ; and these marks of infamy, in a greater or less degree, have subsisted ever since in those countries which are subjected to the Turks ; and also in other parts of Europe under Christian kings. Many of Motarakel's successors treated this degraded people with equal contempt. In the reign of Mahomed, the last of the princes who succeeded him, Achmet, the governor of Egypt, revolted, and formed a new dynasty.†

If we turn from the Mahometan to the Christian monarchs, we find the Jews exposed to equal, if not greater, vexations and persecutions. The empire in

* Basnage, p. 594.

† Egypt was dismembered from the caliphate about the end of the ninth century.

the west, in the eighth century, was greatly agitated
by the civil dissensions between the Iconoclasts and
the worshippers of images ; and the Jews were unjustly accused of fomenting these dissensions. Leo
Isauricus, the Grecian emperor, commenced his
reign with the persecution of this people ; and commanded them to abjure their tenets, and embrace
Christianity under the severest penalties. They
saved their lives by dissimulation, and consented to
be baptized, and receive the communion ; but at the
same time expressed their internal aversion to the
religion they had recently professed, by washing
themselves in common water, and eating common
bread immediately after receiving the sacraments.
The patrons of images, notwithstanding the strenuous exertions of the emperor, at length prevailed.
The Jews, who had pretended obedience to the
mandates of Leo, being suspected of insincerity,
were obliged to subscribe a new formulary, in which
they acknowledged themselves worshippers of the
cross, and holy images ; and prayed to God that he
would inflict upon them the leprosy of Gehazi, and
the fear of Cain, if they did not willingly conform
to the established religion.*

Nicephorus, who succeeded Leo about the commencement of the ninth century, protected the Jews,
and permitted them to live quietly under his government. They were still more favoured by his successor Michael, who tolerated all religions ; is said
to have imbibed something from each denomination ;
and entertained a peculiar regard for the Jews.†

* Fleury's Ecclesiastical History, vol. v. p. 43. Basnage, p. 569.
† Modern Universal History. vol. xiii. p. 230.

But little is known respecting the situation of this people in Italy and Spain during the eighth and ninth centuries. About the year 724, those who resided in Spain involved themselves in a new calamity by listening to the delusive promises of one of their countrymen, named Serenus. This man, taking advantage of the dissensions between France and Spain, proclaimed himself the Messiah, and induced multitudes to follow his standard towards Palestine, where he engaged to establish his empire. The wealth which this infatuated people left behind them was seized by the government. Those, who did not perish by the way, returned to Spain to lament their blind credulity, and the losses they had sustained.*

A. D. 763.] Languedoc, being at this time in the possession of the Visigoths, (as well as part of Spain,†) was infested with frequent incursions of the Arabs. It is said they were in alliance with, and even invited by the Jews, who engaged to assist them in destroying the Christians. They are also accused of requesting the aid of the Saracens to emancipate themselves from the tyranny and oppression of the bishop of Toulouse. These Mahometan invaders, after traversing Narbonne, penetrated as far as Lyons, and laid waste the country with fire and sword. Charlemagne, having afterwards completely defeated the Saracens and retaken Toulouse, resolved to destroy the treacherous Jews, who had encouraged the invasion, and occasioned so much

* Basnage, p. 597.

† The Saracens, or Moors, had invaded Spain, and reduced a large part of that kingdom.

bloodshed. He was, however, prevailed upon to
commute their punishment, and only the principal
and most guilty suffered death. The others, who
inhabited the city, were condemned to receive a box
on the ear thrice a year at the gates of one of the
churches, which should be named by the bishop;
and to pay a perpetual fine of thirteen pounds of
wax.*

Charlemagne, however, in some instances, treated
the Jews with gentleness and moderation. They
boasted of having the liberty of purchasing the
sacred utensils and rich furniture of the churches,
which the bishops and abbots, induced by luxury
and avarice, had exposed to sale. And though this
monarch enacted a severe law, prohibiting the clergy
from carrying on this scandalous traffick, he did not
exact any restitution from those of Hebrew origin,
or lay any restrictions upon their commerce.†

They were highly favoured by Lewis, surnamed
Debonair, whose chief physician, named Sedecias,
was one of the Jewish nation. This man had
acquired such an ascendancy over the monarch,
that the courtiers endeavoured to conciliate his
and his countrymen's friendship with the richest
presents. They had an easy access to the person
of their sovereign, who allowed them the liberty of

* This event, though related by many historians, is disputed by
Basnage, who admits only the truth of two facts, viz. that Toulouse
was besieged by the Saracens, and that the Jews in the city were ill
used and buffetted in the person of their syndic. "This," says he,
" was done out of hatred to the Jews, without their being guilty of
the imputed crime of betraying the city; and the story of their
treachery was invented, in order to authorize the punishment and the
infamy."—*Basnage*, p. 598.

† Basnage, p 598.

erecting new synagogues, and granted them other
extensive privileges. Such powerful protection rendered them haughty and insolent, and excited the
jealousy of the Christians.
Agobard, bishop of Lyons, not only prohibited them
from purchasing Christian slaves, but forbade them
to observe the sabbath, and carry on any commerce
with the Christians during Lent. They complained
of these edicts to the king, who sent three commis-
saries to Lyons to make inquiries into the bishop's
conduct; and, upon their report, the Jews were
immediately restored to their ancient privileges.
Agobard, being mortified and disappointed, formed
new accusations against them; but they were rejected at court, as false and groundless.*

After the bishop found all his attempts frustrated,
he resolved to take a journey to court, to solicit
Lewis more effectually against the Jews. But the
king, surrounded by courtiers who hated the prelate,
and were attached to this people, absolutely resisted
all his solicitations, and only granted him an audience
when he was about to depart. The protection the
outcasts of Israel found at the court of Lewis against
one of the most learned bishops of the age, rendered
them so popular, that it was said openly at court,
that the descendants of Abraham were entitled to
respect. Even some Christians observed Saturday
for the sabbath, and preferred attending the sermons
of the rabbies to those of the curates and monks,
who at this time were extremely ignorant. It is
even said, that a deacon named Paudo, quitted his
office in the church, and went over to the synagogue.†

* Basnage, p. 599. Mod. Univ. Hist. vol. xiii. p. 241.   † Ibid.

The Jews under Charles the Bald, were less flourishing and popular, than they had been during the
reign of his predecessor. One of the French bishops,
named Remisius, ordered the clergy in his diocese,
to preach every Saturday in the synagogues. This
induced a number of Jewish parents to send their
children to other parts of the kingdom in order to
prevent their conversion. Remisius complained of
their conduct to the king, and persuaded him to
command the bishop of Arles, and other prelates, to
follow his example. The consequence was, that
many of the Jewish children were voluntarily baptized. Soon after Charles was poisoned by Sedecias,
the Jewish physician, who was so famous in the
preceding reign; and it was supposed he was instigated to commit this crime by his countrymen,
who hated the king, because he favoured these
conversions. It was, however, discovered, that
many of the nobility corrupted Sedecias, and engaged him to destroy the life of his sovereign.[*]

The Jews were also accused of favouring the
incursions of the Normans, which took place during
the reign of Charles; and of treacherously betraying
Bourdeaux and other cities into the hands of these
invaders. They were still exposed to the ignominious sentence of being buffetted three times every
year at the church door. But this indignity, which
originated from a decree of Charlemagne, was not
executed on all the Jews, but confined to the syndic,
or head magistrate, who received this punishment
in the name of the rest. In remote cities they were
also liable to many insults from the populace. At

* Basnage, p. 599. Modern Universal History, vol. xiii. p. 243.

Beziers, in Languedoc, it was the custom to throw stones upon them from Palm Sunday to the Tuesday in Easter week. This indignity, however, was at length redeemed by a tribute which they paid to the bishop in this place.*

* Basnage, p. 692. Gregoire, p. 224.

CHAPTER XII.

Flourishing state of learning among the eastern Jews at the commencement of the tenth century.—Their tranquillity is interrupted by internal divisions.—Of their learned rabbies.—The Jews in Egypt are persecuted by the caliph Hakem, who introduces a new religion.—They are expelled from the east.—Some of the most learned among them pass into Spain, and cultivate literature under the Saracens.—The Talmud is translated into the Arabic language.—They attempt to convert the Mahometans; and are persecuted by the king of Grenada.—King Ferdinand I. resolves to destroy them; but is prevented by the pope and bishops.—The revolution caused by the Moors in Africa extricates them from persecution.—They are favoured by Alphonso, and his grandson Peter.—The Crusaders massacre the Jews.—Disputes arise among them respecting the study of the sciences.—Of the learned rabbies in Spain and France.

A. D. 927.] WHILE Christendom was involved in darkness and ignorance, the Saracens became the patrons of philosophy in the east. The Jews, under their dominion, imitated their example, and applied. to learning with assiduity and success.* New academies were erected in consequence of the rapid increase of professors and pupils; and those which had subsisted for ages were placed in a flourishing condition, under able preceptors. The Jews boast, that the famous men who appeared among them at this time, were superior to those of any preceding age, since their dispersion.†

Their tranquillity was, however, soon interrupted

---

* In the ninth century the Jews began to make themselves acquainted with the sciences of the Arabs. In particular they excelled in the study of medicine. From the beginning of the ninth to the end of the thirteenth century, eminent schools of philosophy flourished in the Saracen empire.—*Enfield's Philosophy*, vol. ii. p. 234.

† Basnage, p. 601.

by internal divisions. David, prince of the captivity, a haughty and ambitious man, had, according to the Jewish accounts, found means to deliver his nation from the tribute which till then they were compelled to pay to the caliphs. After having thus augmented his authority; he reigned as absolutely as an eastern monarch. In consequence of his arrogant behaviour, frequent altercations took place between him and the heads of the academies,* which produced fatal divisions, and involved the Jews in fresh difficulties.

A. D. 1037.] The nation at this time were numerous and powerful, especially in the city of Pheruty Shiboour. A new academy was founded in this city, at the head of which was the famous rabbi Sherira, under whom it flourished about thirty years. He was a man of great learning, but a violent enemy to the Christians, particularly to the monks; and on that account more highly respected by his brethren. When arrived at an advanced age, he was succeeded by his son Hay,† who obtained such a distinguished reputation, that the Jews resorted from all parts to attend his instructions; and

* The power of the heads of the academies was almost equal to that of the princes. For the latter could not enact any laws except they were sanctioned by the former. These chiefs have had frequent insurrections against each other. The princes of the captivity and heads of the academies were both elected by a majority of votes; and sometimes both these dignities were vested in the same person.— *Basnage*, p. 602.

† The Jews pretend that he was lineally descended from king David; hence he bore the lion on his arms, as did all the kings of Judah, agreeably to Jacob's prophecy concerning that tribe. But he acquired still greater celebrity by various writings, particularly the famous cabbalistical work, styled, "The voice of God in power."—*Modern Universal History*, vol. xiii. p. 247.

styled him, " the most excellent of all the excellent."
He was placed at the head of two academies, and
elected prince of the captivity.   He died in 1037,
aged sixty-nine years.*

The Jews, in the reign of the caliph Hakem,
suffered persecution for a short time in Egypt. The
object of this monarch was to abolish Islamism, and
establish a new religion, of which he should be the
head.†   The large number of Pagans, who acceded
to his novel dogmas and pretensions, flattered his
vanity, and induced him to persecute the Christians
and Jews, who opposed and contemned his doctrines.
He obliged the latter to wear a disgraceful mark of
distinction ; commanded their synagogues to be shut;
and compelled them to embrace his tenets. But
he soon changed his opinions, and permitted them
to return to their former religion.‡

A. D. 1039.]   The caliphs of the house of the
Abbassides, who had always favoured the Jews,
having lost their authority, the sultan Gela Doullat,
who reigned by the name of Cajem, resolved to
extirpate this unhappy people. For this purpose he
shut up their academies ; banished their professors ;
and killed the prince of the captivity, with his family.
This persecution dispersed some of the nation into
the deserts of Arabia, while others sought an asylum
in the west. From the period in which the Jews
were expelled from the east, most authors date the
total extinction of the princes of the captivity ; but,

---

* Basnage, p. 602.

† He blended the religion of the Druses, with other tenets, which
he pretended to receive from the deity.—*Basnage,* p. 605.

‡ Basnage, p. 603.

if we may believe the Jewish travellers, Benjamin de Tudela and rabbi Petachiah, who visited their brethren in the twelfth century, they still found one of these chiefs among the Israelites in Persia, who boasted that he was lineally descended from the prophet Samuel. If this account is true, it proves that these princes were not all of the lineage of David, as the Jews pretend. It is evident, however, that they were seldom seen after the eleventh century; and preserved only an empty name without authority. *

When the Jews were expelled from the east, multitudes of the nation passed into Africa, and from thence joined their brethren in Spain, who were favoured by the caliphs. They had assisted the Saracens in the conquest of this kingdom; and gratitude, as well as policy, induced the victors to reward those to whose open or secret aid they were so much indebted. An intimate connexion, therefore, took place between the disciples of Moses and those of Mahomet, which was cemented by their reciprocal hatred of the Christians; and subsisted till their common expulsion.†

Some of the most learned men among the Jews, after their banishment from the east, found an asylum in Spain, and were patronized by the Saracen monarchs. This period, therefore, was one of the most brilliant epochas of Jewish literature from the time of the destruction of Jerusalem. Even in the darkest ages of their history they cultivated their language with assiduity, and were never destitute of grammarians, or subtle interpreters of the scripture.

* Basnage, p. 605.   † History of Spain.

But, generally speaking, it was only during their
union with the Saracens in Spain,* or in the flourishing ages of the caliphs of Bagdat, that they
ventured into general literature, and used in their
writings a foreign, and consequently (in their view)
a profane language.†

While the attention of the Christians and Mahometans in Spain was occupied by their mutual
hostilities, the Jews enjoyed an interval of tranquillity. Their academies were in a flourishing state
under the Saracen monarchs; and they became
numerous and affluent. During this prosperous
era many learned doctors appeared among them,
whose erudition has been celebrated by Jewish
writers. The Talmud, however, was so little
known in Spain, that they were obliged to send
deputies to the Babylonian academies, to decide the
disputes which arose among them. Even the prayers
which they offered up on the grand expiation day,
and other national fasts, were composed by one of
the Babylonish rabbics. Hasheym II. the Saracen
monarch of Cordova, who was a friend and patron
to the Israelites, commanded this celebrated work to
be translated into the Arabic language, in order
either to gratify his curiosity, or prevent their
frequent excursions to Bagdat, or Jerusalem, from
which it is said he apprehended fatal consequences.‡

The wars in Spain, which raged with violence
during the eleventh century,§ and the revolutions to

---

* The Saracens subdued Spain in the eighth century.
† Butler's Horæ Biblicæ.   ‡ Basnage, p. 606.
§ About the beginning of the eleventh century, Toledo, Valentia,

which they gave rise, were in their commencement beneficial to the Jews. Rabbi Samuel Levi, being secretary and prime minister to the king of Grenada, was by him appointed chief of their nation, and exerted himself to the utmost to promote their interest and honour. For this purpose he sent for some of the most learned Jewish rabbies from Babylon and Egypt, to whom he was a liberal benefactor. His countrymen had the satisfaction of seeing his son succeed him in all his dignities. [A. D. 1055.] Their joy, however, was damped by his arrogant behaviour, which was very different from that of his father, who in the zenith of his prosperity was distinguished for humility and moderation.*

The interval of tranquillity which the Jews enjoyed, was, about the middle of the eleventh century, disturbed by an unfortunate event. Joseph Hallevi, a learned and zealous rabbi, assisted by the Arabic version of the Talmud, endeavoured to convert the Mahometans to the Jewish faith. The king of Grenada, highly exasperated at this attempt against the established religion, caused the principal offender to be apprehended and executed. A violent persecution of his nation immediately followed, and one hundred thousand families experienced its destructive effects. The severity of this monarch was more sensibly felt after a series of prosperity, which had rendered them affluent and powerful. They were apprehensive that the other sovereigns would follow his

---

Seville, and almost all the great cities in Spain, had their independent kingdoms.—*Russel's Modern Europe*, vol. i. p. 180.

* Basnage, p. 607.

example. But the persecution was quickly suppressed, and did not extend beyond the kingdom of Grenada.*

The Jews were exposed to suffer still more severe and cruel treatment under king Ferdinand. This monarch, having declared war against the Saracens, resolved to consecrate his enterprise by previously extirpating all the Israelites in his kingdom. But the Spanish prelates openly condemned and opposed this measure ; and pope Alexander II, wrote a letter to them, in which he highly commended their opposition to Ferdinand's bloody design ; severely reproved this monarch for his furious and unchristian zeal ; and reminded him of the example of pope Gregory the Great, who had strenuously opposed similar persecution, and the demolishing of the synagogues. The united remonstrances of the pope and bishops delivered the Jews from the impending evil.†

A. D. 1080.] The revolution, caused by the Moors in Africa, more effectually extricated them at this period from persecution. Alphonso, the successor of Ferdinand, being extremely distressed by the increasing power of the Saracens, found himself obliged to befriend and caress the Jews, in order to obtain from them personal and pecuniary assistance. Accordingly he promoted them to great and lucrative offices ; and even allowed them to be judges over the Christians. Pope Gregory highly disapproved of this last instance of the king's indulgence ; and upbraided him with having " exalted the synagogue of Satan above the church of Christ." The remon-

* Basnage, p 607   † Ibid.

strances of the Roman pontiff could not induce the monarch to diminish those privileges, which he had granted merely from interested motives.*

A. D. 1096.] Peter I. the grandson of Alphonso, was equally regardless of the remonstrances of Nicolas de Valentia, who endeavoured to prejudice the king against the Jews, by painting in strong colours their hatred to the Christians ; and assuring him, that they were his most dangerous and inve‑ terate enemies. But this monarch was averse to persecution ; and maintained that violence would have no lasting, or beneficial effect. The moderation of Peter could not, however, preserve this unhappy people in several other parts of Spain from the fury of the crusaders,† who massacred vast numbers of

---

* Basnage, p. 607.

† The crusades, or expeditions to recover the holy land from the hands of the Mahometans, commenced about the year 1095. The foundation of these expeditions was a superstitious veneration for those places where our Saviour performed his miracles, and finished the work of redemption. Peter the Hermit, a native of Amiens in Picardy, had made the pilgrimage to Jerusalem, and being deeply affected with the dangers to which the pilgrims were exposed, as well as the oppressions which the eastern Christians endured, formed the bold design of leading into Asia, from the furthest extremities of the west, armies sufficient to subdue that warlike nation, which then pos‑ sessed the holy land. This fanatical monk ran from province to province, with a crucifix, exciting princes and people to the holy war ; and wherever he came kindled the same enthusiastic ardour with which he himself was animated. People of all ranks caught the contagion ; not only the gallant nobles of the age with their martial followers, but men in the more humble and pacific stations in life ; ecclesiastics of every order, and even women and children engaged with emulation in an undertaking which was deemed sacred and meri‑ torious. If we may believe the concurring testimony of contemporary authors, six millions of persons assumed the cross, which was the badge that distinguished such as devoted themselves to this holy warfare. Nor did the fumes of this enthusiastic zeal evaporate at

them. Under the idea of procuring a blessing on their expedition, they destroyed the descendants of those, who crucified our Saviour.*

Notwithstanding all the persecutions the Jews suffered in Spain during the eleventh century; many rabbies appeared, who were distinguished for ability and learning. Samuel Cophni, a native of Cordova, published a commentary on the Pentateuch, the manuscript of which is still extant in the Vatican library. Soon after him flourished the five Isaacs at nearly the same period; one of whom, called Isaac Alphesi, came from Africa to Spain. He was esteemed the most learned man of his age; and was chosen chief of the captivity in this kingdom. The second of the Isaacs was the son of Baruch, who derived his origin from the ancient Baruch, and pretended, that his family came to Spain as early as the reign of Titus, and had subsisted there till this time. He understood Latin, Greek, and Arabic; and was so profoundly versed in mathematics, that the king of Grenada, who was a passionate admirer of this science, sent for him to court in order to receive his instructions. This monarch treated him with such flattering distinction, that he continued to reside at his court till his death, which took place 1007. The other three Isaacs were also men of distinguished ability and learning.†

once; the phrensy was as lasting as it was extravagant. During two centuries Europe seems to have had no object but to recover, or keep possession of the holy land; and during this period vast armies continued to march to Palestine —*Robertson's History of Charles V.* vol. i. p. 22.

* Basnage, p. 608.
† Basnage, p. 609. Modern Univer. Hist. vol. xiii. p. 256.

The number of famous rabbies, who appeared in Spain during the eleventh and twelfth centuries, gave rise to disputes respecting the utility of studying the sciences. Those who had acquired a taste for literature ardently wished to make farther improvements. According to Enfield,* " the attention, which was paid to the writings of Aristotle,† both by Arabians and Christians, excited the emulation of the Jews, who addicted themselves to the study of the Peripatetic philosophy. This innovation, so inconsistent with the reverence which they professed to entertain for the law and traditions of their fathers, was exceedingly displeasing to the zealous advocates for Talmudic learning, who easily perceived, that as the one gained ground, the other would decline." The ancient curse denounced upon the Jew who should instruct his son in Grecian learning was revived. But rabbi Solomon-ben-Abraham, who taught at Barcelona, mitigated the severity of this decree, which he had not sufficient courage to abolish; and pronounced an anathema and sentence of excommunication against all, who began to study Greek before they were twenty years old. Rabbi Mar, however, restored the Jewish students to the entire liberty of learning the languages, as well as the arts and sciences.‡

In France, during the tenth and eleventh cen-

* Enfield's Philosophy, vol. ii. p. 204.

† To facilitate the study of Aristotle among the Jews, his writings were translated from the Arabic to the Hebrew tongue. Several other ancient works, particularly the Elements of Euclid, and the medical writings of the Greeks, towards the close of the thirteenth century, appeared in a Hebrew dress.

‡ Basnage, p. 610.

turies, only a few rabbies appeared, who were distinguished for ability and learning. The most celebrated among them was rabbi Gersion, who flourished in the eleventh century. Some suppose he was a native of Germany; however, he published his book of constitutions in this kingdom. Though a long time elapsed before this work met with the approbation of the other Jewish doctors; yet it was received as a code of excellent laws about the year 1204, and its author dignified with the title of the " Light of the French Captivity."*

Jacob, the son of Jekar, one of Gersion's pupils, was a great musician and casuist; and the succeeding Jewish doctors followed his decisions with implicit reverence. Rabbi Judah, another of his disciples, also held a distinguished rank among the learned men of his nation. He composed a treatise on the rights of women; and a work on the Jewish calculations of time. According to his account their first epocha was from their departure from Egypt; they began another date from the period in which they were first governed by kings; and a third from the time Alexander the Great first entered Jerusalem, which was observed till the tenth century, during which period rabbi Sherira flourished, and obliged his nation to date from the creation of the world. He also published a number of sermons. Another of Gersion's pupils, rabbi Moses Hardarsian, or the preacher, acquired a distinguished reputation. He, and rabbi Judah, introduced the custom of preaching in the synagogues, which had been much neglected. The former was the author of a commentary on

* Basnage, p. 610.

Genesis, which has often been quoted by Christians against the Jews.*

Joseph-Ben-Gorian, known to his nation by the name of Josippon, is supposed, by Basnage and others, to have been a French rabbi of the eleventh century. He endeavoured, in his History of the Jews, written in Hebrew, to pass for the famous historian Josephus, and has succeeded with his nation.† But the most learned Christian writers reject this performance as spurious, on account of the many interpolations, modern names, and contradictions, which are found in this history.

* Basnage, p. 609.
† Priestley's Letters to the Jews, p. 4. David Levi asserts, that the work called Josephoen Ben Gorian was written by Josephus to the Jews in Hebrew; and that the other history, to which his name is prefixed, was written to the Romans in Greek.—*Levi's Letters to Priestley*, p. 67.

CHAPTER XIII.

Of the Jews in Hungary during the eleventh century.—Persecution of this people in Germany and Bohemia.—The Crusaders massacre vast multitudes of them in their march through the cities of Germany to the Holy Land.—They arrive at Jerusalem, besiege and take the city, and put all the Jews to death.—Of the second crusade. —The Jews are massacred in most parts of Europe.·

A. D. 1092.] DURING the latter part of the eleventh century, St. Ladislaus, king of Hungary, convened a synod, which prohibited the Jews from marrying Christian women,ᵟ or purchasing slaves who had embraced this religion. Coloman, his son and successor, also forbade their making use of Christian slaves ; but he permitted them to buy and cultivate lands within the jurisdiction of a bishop. These laws clearly demonstrate, that they were numerous and powerful in this kingdom.*

The number and power of the Jews had also become great in Germany ;. and they had erected superb synagogues in most of the principal cities, particularly at Treves, Cologne, Metz and Francfort. They had passed from Franconia into Bohemia ; and having in the eleventh century assisted the Christians against the irruptions of the barbarians, were allowed the privilege of a synagogue. They-suffered indeed severe persecutions in several parts of these kingdoms ; and the fanaticism of the populace frequently exposed them to destruction. A priest named Gotescal, at the head of fifteen thousand banditti, declared war against them ; and being supported and encouraged by several monarchs, passed

* Basnage, p. 616.

into Hungary, and committed the, most horrid outrages upon this unhappy people. But at length it
being discovered, that he pillaged the Christians as
well as the Jews, he was surprised and slain with
the greatest part of his army.

Not long after, the landgrave of Lininghen
declared himself the persecutor of the Jews, and
committed several acts of violence against them. But
on his attempting to penetrate into Hungary, he
was surprised and defeated. The emperor Henry IV.
exerted himself in defence of this oppressed people;
and ordered them to be reinstated in their abodes
and property. This occasioned fresh complaints
against them: and they were accused of having
exaggerated their losses, in order to enrich themselves by a more plentiful restitution.[*]

A. D. 1096.] Soon after, the Crusaders involved them in the most terrible calamities they had
ever experienced since the reign of Adrian. These
expeditions awakened all the rage of their enemies
against them; and "their population seemed to have
increased only to furnish new-victims." The champions of the cross, in their march through Germany
to the holy land, massacred all who refused to profess
the Christian religion. Fifteen hundred were burnt
at Strasburgh, thirteen hundred at Mayence; and
the flames being communicated to the city, it was in
great danger of being reduced to ashes.[†] This
massacre was continued from the month of April till
July. According to the Jewish[‡] historians, five

* Basnage, p 616
† Gregoire on the Reformation of the Jews, p. 5.
‡ A modern Jewish author has thus described the miseries his

thousand of their nation were either slaughtered or
drowned; and the number of those, who preserved
their lives by dissimulation, was much more considerable.   They were so far from exaggerating, that
the Christian writers make the amount of those who
were destroyed vastly greater.   The Batavian an-
nalists assert, that upwards of twelve thousand were
·slain in their country; and all agree, that the .
number of those who' perished in other parts of
Germany* was almost incredible.   Many, in the
phrensy of despair, put a period to their own lives.
Even some women at Treves, seeing the Crusaders
approaching, killed their children, telling them,
" that it was much better to send them into Abraham's
bosom, than to abandon them to the Christian's."
Some of the men barricaded their houses, and preci-
pitating themselves, their families, and wealth into

nation endured from the fury of the Crusaders: " When from his solitary retreat an enthusiastic hermit preached the crusades to the
nations of Europe, and a part of its inhabitants left their country to
moisten with their blood the plains of Palestine, the knell of promiscuous massacre tolled before the alarm-bell of war. Millions of Jews
were then murdered to glut the pious rage of the Crusaders. It was
by tearing the entrails of their brethren that these warriors sought to
deserve the protection of Heaven. Skulls of men and bleeding hearts
were offered as holocausts on the altars of that God who has no
pleasure even in the blood of the innocent lamb; and ministers
of peace were thrown into a holy enthusiasm by these bloody
sacrifices. It is thus that Basil, Treves, Coblentz, and Cologne,
became human shambles."—*Appeal to the Justice of Kings and
Nations, by M. Michael Berr.*

* Metz is, perhaps, the only city in Germany where the Crusaders
did not imbrue their hands in the blood of the Jews. Lewis the
Young, on his departure for Palestine, assembled his army in this
place; and yet it is not said, that the Jews received any insult   The
silence of history in this respect amounts to a positive proof, if we
consider, that Metz then had historians.—*Gregoire,* p. 242.

the rivers, or the flames, disappointed the malice, or at least the avarice, of their implacable enemies. Others, who were less obstinate, fled for refuge to the palace of Egibert the bishop. This prelate preached to them a sermon, by which they pretended to be converted. But as soon as the influence of terror was withdrawn, all except one resumed their former religion.

During this period of darkness and fanaticism, while the public outcry denounced vengeance against an unbelieving race, it must gratify every benevolent heart to catch a feeble voice in history whispering consolation to the sufferers in Israel. Our pleasure is increased when we discover this humanity among the clergy, who have been often accused of instigating the persecutions against them. At Mayence and Spires we find prelates sheltering them from the fury of the Crusaders, receiving the fugitives to their houses, and even causing some of their persecutors to be executed. The bishop of Spires, in particular, has been celebrated for his active interference in their behalf.*

A. D. 1099.] After murdering the Jews in the cities through which they passed, the champions of the cross advanced in order to invest Jerusalem, which they regarded as the consummation of all their labours. They took the city† by assault, after

---

* Gregoire on the Reformation of the Jews, p. 5, 6.

† This great event took place on the fifth of July, in the last year of the eleventh century. The Christian princes and nobles, after choosing Godfrey of Bouillon king of Jerusalem, began to settle themselves in their newly conquered countries. Some of them, however, returned to Europe, in order to enjoy at home the glory which

O

a siege of five weeks; and impelled by a mixture of military and religious rage, destroyed the inhabitants without distinction of sex or age. Their fury rose to such a height, that all the Jews, being the successors of those who had crucified our Saviour, were most inhumanly put to death.*

A. D. 1147.] The persecutions which the Jews suffered from the Crusaders were not terminated after the conquest of Jerusalem. Other expeditions were undertaken in order to secure to the Christians the possession of the holy land, to enlarge their conquests, and to recover the city after it was retaken by the Mahometans.† The second crusade was promoted by the exhortations of St. Bernard, and supported by the emperor Conrad, and the French king Lewis VII. The hermit Rodolphus, who was commissioned to proclaim the holy war along the banks of the Rhine, earnestly inculcated upon the German princes the necessity of exterminating the enemies of Christ within their own territories. Other preachers followed his example; and the Jews, seized with consternation, retired to Nuremburg, and other cities, in which the emperor kindly received and protected them. Many of the Christian bishops highly condemned the hermit's persecuting doctrine. St. Bernard in particular severely

they had acquired by this popular enterprize.—*Hume's History of England*, vol. i p 232.

* Guthrie's History of the World, vol. vii., p. 66.   Gibbon, vol. xi. p. 85.

† From the time that Jerusalem was taken by the western Christians, that is, from July 5, 1099, to the end of the year 1162, the city was governed by five Latin kings, and the church by eight patriarchs.—*Maritie's Travels.*

censured it; and, in a letter to the archbishop of Metz, advised to have the fiery zealot banished to his solitude. Not contented, however, with writing pathetic letters upon the subject, he repaired to Germany, where he afforded an efficacious protection to the Jews by the influence he derived from his talents, learning, and virtues.*

The persecution kindled by the Crusaders was not confined to Germany, but extended through the greatest part of Europe. The public outcry was, "Let us exterminate the descendants of those, who crucified Jesus Christ; and let the name of Israel be no more remembered." But though vast multitudes fell a sacrifice to the bigotry of the princes and people, a still greater number, driven to despair by the miseries they suffered, perished by suicide.†

While our attention is engaged, and our feelings agitated in reviewing the terrible calamities which the Jews were compelled to endure, we may be led to inquire, What are the causes of the reciprocal hatred which has subsisted between them and other nations? A celebrated author, who has deeply interested himself to ameliorate the condition of this persecuted nation, has given the following answer to this query.

"The resistance of the Jews in their last war against the Romans greatly incensed the latter, who took every opportunity of inspiring all the people of the empire with their prejudices. The Jews, driven from their country, but continually elevated by the imposture of false Messiahs, who added fuel to their fanaticism, could not tamely submit to a foreign

* Basnage, p. 617. Gregoire, p. 6. † Basnage, p. 616.

o 2

yoke; and they preserved, even to the seventh
century, a spirit of sedition, which excited hatred
against them.

 " Besides, people pardon each other least for
thinking differently in respect to religion; and if
there be any religion capable of offending the vanity
of those, who are not followers of it, without doubt
it is that of the Jews.   Its divine author gave it this
spirit with a view to raise a barrier between his
people and the corruption of those idolatrous nations,
by whom they were surrounded.   Judaism is an
exclusive worship; and though it imposes the obligation of universal philanthropy; its singularity
tends to make other men be considered as odious and
profane.   As it professes that there is only one God,
the Gentiles revolted against a dogma which sapped
the very foundation of Paganism; besides they
never spoke of circumcision, the most ancient of all
rites, but with a smile of derision; and, the passage
from ridicule to contempt is immediate.   It is a principle in morals, that people do not hate what they
despise : but the misfortunes of the Jews have rendered them an exception. Contempt consigned them
to disgrace, and fury to torture. The Christians,
beholding in them the authors of a Deicide, sometimes forgot the example of their Founder, who,
when upon the cross, implored forgiveness for his
executioners.   Mahomet at first shewed a great
respect for the Jews; but this sentiment soon gave
place to fury. His Koran was filled with violent
declamation against men, enemies to his doctrine;
and the Mussulmans, who argued with the sabre,
included the Jews in the proscription of all religions

different from Islamism. Length of time gave strength to this animosity, which became hereditary, because fathers took care to inspire it into their children. Soon after, it was supposed that the Jews, irritated, but too weak to oppose striking vengeance to barbarous oppression, privately occasioned public misfortunes; and the vulgar adopting this idea without examination, massacred them in the most brutal manner. 'The Jews, forced to follow usurious practices, when they became rich excited envy by their opulence, which rendered them still more odious. Such are the sources of the hatred which the whole world have sworn against the Jewish people, and of the persecution that has every where followed them.

"The result of these events exhibits action and re-action. The Jews of the same sect have always been united together, because there was little disproportion among them of rank and fortune, and very little luxury. Their years of jubilee brought them very near to the primitive equality, which civil institutions continually destroy; and their misfortunes have made this union closer, and strengthened its ties. But, being banished, proscribed, and every where abused, can they entertain any affection for their tyrants? They must indeed conceive an aversion to all those who are leagued against them; and particularly to the Christians, whom they consider as guilty intruders, for having eclipsed their religious splendour."*

* The above extract is made from the English translation of Gregoire's Essay on the Physical, Moral, and Political Reformation of the Jews, p. 30—32.

CHAPTER XIV.

State of the Jews in various parts of the east in the twelfth century.
—Of the princes of the captivity.—The Israelites were numerous
in Egypt, but only a small number was found in Palestine.—Of
those in the Turkish dominions, and in Italy, Germany, and
France.—St. Bernard exerts his influence in their behalf.—They are
favoured by pope Innocent II. and Alexander III.—They become
powerful in Spain during the reign of Alphonso VIII.

A. D. 1172.] BENJAMIN of Tudela, a city
in Navarre, affirms that he visited many regions
both in the east and west, in the twelfth century, for
the purpose of ascertaining the situation of the
Jewish people. He published an account of his
travels,* and gave a minute relation of whatever
was honourable and interesting to his nation. He
even invented new countries, and mentioned kingdoms and cities, which did not then exist. A learned
modern author, speaking of this work, and that of
rabbi Petachiah, who travelled about the same
period, observes, that "a wish to magnify the importance of their brethren is discernible in the
writings of both; and, for their extreme credulity,
both are justly censured. But, after every reason-
able deduction is made on these accounts from the
credibility of their narrative, much will still remain
to interest an intelligent and cautious reader.†

Benjamin informs us, that the Jews in the east, in
the twelfth century, enjoyed the peaceable exercise
of their religion, and possessed several considerable

* This work has been translated from the Hebrew into the French,
by J. P. Barratier.
† Butler's Horæ Biblicæ.

synagogues. . Four thousand of his brethren inhabited Bassorah, an island on the Tigris.. Seven
thousand resided at Almozal, answering to the ancient Nineveh. In this city our traveller found
Zaccheus, a prince descended from the house of
David, and a Jewish astronomer named Beren al
Pherec, who officiated as a chaplain to Zin Aldin,*
a Mahometan king. Passing through Rehoboth, in
his way to Bagdat, he discovered three thousand
Jews; and five hundred at Karchemish, famed for
the defeat of Pharaoh Necho, and situate on the
banks of the Euphrates.†

The celebrated academy of Pundebita had lost
much of its original grandeur, and contained only a
few learned rabbies, who superintended about two
thousand of their brethren, part of whom applied
themselves to the study of the law. The academy
of Sora was also in a decayed condition; and that
of Nahardea was only famed for a synagogue, which
its superstitious inhabitants had built of materials
conveyed from Jerusalem. The great men, who
formerly resided in the eastern countries, had fled
to the west; and the Jewish academies declined in
consequence of their departure. But, though there
were but few learned rabbies in the east, the Jews,
according to our author's account, were still numerous; he informs us he found ten thousand of them
at Obkeray, which city he pretends was built by
king Jechoniah during the Babylonian captivity.‡

* It may appear surprising, that a Jewish astronomer should be
chaplain to a Mahometan prince; but many of the Jews were induced
to temporize, either through fear, or interested motives.—*Modern
Universal History*, vol. xiii. p. 262.

† Basnage, p 6 19.   ‡ Ibid. p. 620.

Benjamin arrived at Bagdat during the reign of the caliph Mostanged, who highly favoured his nation, and retained a number of Jews in his service. This prince was well versed in the Hebrew language, and had acquired some knowledge of the Mosaic law. The city of Bagdat contained about one thousand Jews, who possessed twenty-eight synagogues. They were also allowed ten tribunals, under the direction of ten eminent men of their nation, who were chosen to transact their affairs. These chiefs were, however, subordinate to the prince of the captivity. Benjamin asserts, that the person who then enjoyed this dignity was styled Lord by the Jews, and by the Mahometans the son of David, he being, according to our author, lineally descended from that monarch. His authority extended over all his brethren in the dominions of the caliph ; and from Syria to Hindostan. Our traveller also affirmed, that this chief received regal honours ; had an hundred guards to escort him when he visited the caliph ; and that a herald marched before him, crying, Prepare the way for the Lord, the son of David. The Jewish people in the most remote parts were, he says, obliged to receive their teachers from him by the imposition of hands ; and he was enabled to support his dignity by the large presents and tribute which he received from his nation.*

The existence of a succession of these imaginary potentates has been strenuously maintained by Jewish authors. Their views were to aggrandize the glory of their nation, and deprive Christians of the force of the argument furnished by the prophecy

* Basnage, p. 620.

of Jacob, concerning the termination of the Jewish
polity and independence speedily after the coming
of the Messiah.* ⸱ ⸱

Some of the most learned of the Jewish rabbies,
however, acknowledge, that the regal and judicial
power has been abolished. David Kimchi lamented
the calamities of his nation, foretold by the prophet
Hosea, and exclaimed, that " he saw in his time the
accomplishment of the oracle; and those days of
exile, in which there was neither prince or king of
the house of David; but on the contrary, they were
subjected to other nations." Abarbanel also observes
that " Isaiah speaks of a new calamity the Jews
were to suffer, viz. that they should have neither
kingdom, sovereignty, nor judicial sceptre." The
testimony of these eminent men clearly evinces,
that the Israelites, deprived of jurisdiction in their
native country, possessed only the shadow of authority in the east. Even Benjamin confesses, that
his nation was tributary, that the synagogues were
maintained by means of a patent given by the caliph,
when he was promoted to the regal dignity ; that
the prince of the captivity purchased his privileges
and grandeur ; and that he received his power from
this monarch by the imposition of hands.†

Leaving the province of Bagdat, our traveller
passed through Resen, where he found five thousand

---

* Gisborne on the Christian Religion.

† The persecution, which the Jews in the east suffered in the preceding century, renders it probable, that our author's account of the
grandeur of the prince of the captivity is greatly exaggerated. Yet
still he acknowledges, that his dignity was purchased by a tribute to
the caliph, and by large presents to his officers.—*Basnage*, p. 20.
Modern Universal History, vol. xiii. p. 264.

of his brethren, who possessed a spacious synagogue.
In Hila, about five miles from ancient Babylon, he
discovered four synagogues, and ten thousand Jews.
Passing eastward, he arrived at the banks of the
river Chebar, where he found sixty synagogues.
He asserted, that the prophet Ezekiel was buried
on the banks of this river; that his tomb was preserved; and that both Jews and Persians resorted
to it as a place of devotion.   In Cufa, once the metropolis of the caliphs, he discovered nearly seven
thousand of his nation, who possessed only one synagogue.*

Our traveller found the Jews numerous in Egypt,
and computed thirty thousand of them in one city
upon the frontiers of Ethiopia.   There were about
two thousand Israelites and two synagogues at Mis-
raim, at present Grand Cairo.   The chief of all
the synagogues in Egypt resided in this city; appointed the Jewish doctors; and supported the interest of his nation.   Several parts of the land of
Goshen were inhabited by Jews; two hundred were
found in one place, in another five hundred; and
nearly three thousand in the city of Goshen.   About
the same number resided at Alexandria, and but
a few at Damietta.†

Our author found at Tyre about four hundred of
his nation, most of whom were employed in the
glass manufacture.   There were, however, a few
learned men among them, who were well versed in
the Talmud.   The Samaritans having abandoned
their ancient capital, some of them retired to Cæsarea,
where he found about two hundred, and one hundred

* Basnage, p. 620.   † Ibid.

at Sichem, which had become the seat of their religion. They were extremely strict in solemnizing their festivals, and offering their sacrifices on Mount Gerizzim.*

In Jerusalem, the ancient capital of the Jewish religion, Benjamin found only two hundred of his nation, who all resided together, and made but a mean figure in the metropolis. They were not numerous in other cities of Judea; in one of which he found only two, in another twenty. Shunan contained about three hundred. At Ascalon there were five hundred and fifty three, Jews and Samaritans. Upper Galilee contained a larger number; many of the Israelites retired into this province after the destruction of Jerusalem, and founded the famous academy of Tiberias. Yet he discovered only one synagogue in this part of Judea.†

From Palestine our author passed into Greece, and found two hundred Jews, who resided in and about Mount Parnassus, and obtained a subsistence by cultivating vegetables. There were three hundred of this nation at Corinth, and two thousand at Thebes, who were either dyers, or silk weavers. There were a small number at Lepanto, Patras, and other parts of the Turkish empire; but they were neither numerous nor affluent. When Benjamin arrived at Constantinople, he discovered about two thousand of his nation, who resided in the suburb called Galata, or Pera, where they had formerly been settled by the emperor Theodosius. They were all silk weavers, or merchants. There were besides five hundred Caraites, who were sepa-

* Basnage, p. 622. † Ibid.

rated by a wall from the other Jews, in order to prevent all intercourse between them. The remnants of the nation in the Ottoman empire were forbidden to ride on horses throughout the streets of the cities; and were hated and insulted both by Turks and Greeks.*

From Constantinople our traveller passed into Italy: and relates the dissensions, which then reigned between the inhabitants of Genoa, Pisa, and other republican cities. He observes, that the Jews were few in these parts; and that whatever party gained the ascendancy, they were sure to be oppressed. When he repaired to Rome, he found his brethren more numerous; among whom were several learned doctors, particularly rabbi Jechiel, who was superintendant of the pope's finances. Capua was no less famed for the number and learning of her doctors, though the city contained only three hundred Jews. Benjamin reckoned five hundred at Naples, two hundred at Salerno. There were others settled at Benevento, Ascoli, and Trani. The islands of Sicily and Corsica also contained a considerable number of Jews; particularly the former, where he discovered about two hundred at Messina, and five hundred at Palermo.†

Our traveller passed from Italy into Germany, where he asserts, that he found his nation not only more numerous and affluent,‡ but also more learned, devout, and hospitable to strangers. They lamented

---

* Basnage, p 624   † Modern Univer. Hist. vol. xiii. p. 274.

‡ Benjamin wrote an account of his travels about 1170; in seventy years, the Jews had recovered from the massacres of the Crusaders, mentioned in the preceding chapter.—*Gibbon*, vol. ii. p. 26.

the desolation of their city and temple; and earnestly expected a glorious recall to their once happy country. Those, however, who dwelt upon the banks of the Rhine, were uneasy on account of the long delay of the Messiah's appearance; and Benjamin confesses he was not able to console them by what he related respecting the state of their nation in the east.*

He concluded his tour with visiting the synagogues in France, in some of which he found but few Jews. Three hundred of his brethren resided at Narbonne, under the direction of the famous rabbi Calonymo, who had acquired great power and wealth, and was said to have been lineally descended from king David. In Montpelier there were many Jews, as well as Turks and Greeks, who resorted thither from foreign parts.

Lunel, a city in Languedoc, contained an academy, in which the Jews studied the divine law with intense application. Our author also discovered an assembly at Paris, who were devoted to the study of the law, and received those of their nation who repaired to the city from foreign parts as brethren.†

It appears from the above account, and that of rabbi Petachiah,‡ a native of Ratisbon, who visited his nation at nearly the same period, that the Jews were in a declining state in many countries. In particular, their number was greatly diminished on

---

* Basnage, p. 624.   † Ibid.

‡ Rabbi Petachiah gives an account of some Jews he found in Tartary, who did not observe the traditions of the fathers. Upon his inquiring why they neglected the observance of these traditions, they answered they had never heard of them.—*Modern Universal History.*

the banks of the Euphrates ; and in the ancient
cities where they were formerly computed to have
amounted to nine hundred thousand.

A. D. 1147.] St. Bernard, whose humanity to
the Jews has been noticed in the preceding chapter,
continued to repress the violence of their enemies.
He alleged, that it was necessary to tolerate them at
present, in order to effect their future conversion ;
and made use of his influence over pope Innocent
the Second, to inspire him with the same sentiments
of gentleness and forbearance. When this pontiff
made his grand entrance into Paris, they approached
him with profound respect, and presented him the
roll, or volume of their law. Upon receiving it
from their hands, he returned this answer, " I reverence the law given by God to Moses, but condemn
your exposition of it, because you still expect the
Messiah, whom the catholic church believes to be
Christ, who liveth and reigneth with the Father, and
the Holy Ghost." His successor, Alexander III.
also favoured and protected the Jews, and prohibited
the people from insulting them on their sabbaths,
festivals, or any other occasion. Under such powerful patronage, they became flourishing, affluent,
and learned in Rome, and several other cities in
Italy.*

A. D. 1170.] The Jews were no less powerful
in Spain during part of the twelfth century. One
of them, named Joseph, was prime minister to Alphonso VIII. and had a coach of state, and guards
to attend him. At length, however, he was expelled
from his office, by the treachery and intrigues of

* Basnage, p. 634.

Gonzales, one of his dependents, who, having incurred the displeasure of his benefactor by his criminal conduct, resolved to escape the punishment he deserved, by effecting his ruin. Under pretence of filling the monarch's coffers, this wretch prevailed upon Alphonso to grant him eight of the principal Jews. These he caused to be put to death, and confiscated their effects. He next offered a much larger sum for twenty more. But the king thought it more honourable to seize their estates for defraying his expences, than to deprive them both of their lives and property. This unhappy people, who rejoiced to be able to purchase their lives and liberty upon any terms, voluntarily poured immense sums into the treasury. Gonzales was soon after imprisoned by the king, and his fall established their tranquillity.*

Alphonso was afterwards induced to treat the Jews with great indulgence, in consequence of his passion for a beautiful young Jewess, named Rachel, to whom he sacrificed his honour and interest. Her countrymen, seizing the advantage, grew extremely powerful and insolent, and the court and clergy were offended at the haughtiness of their behaviour. At length, the fury of their enemies rose to such an height, that they caused the young Jewess to be murdered. The nation, however, derived essential benefit from this prosperous epoch, and became numerous and affluent. Rabbi Eliakim, who was highly esteemed in Spain, and composed his ritual of all the ceremonies used in every synagogue, commonly styled, " The Ritual of the Universe," has

* Basnage, p 635.

computed that there were twelve thousand Jews in
the city of Toledo. They were also in a flourishing
state at Andalusia, where great numbers applied to
the study of theology and the sciences. At length,
they divided themselves into three different sects, of
which Maimonides, who lived at this time, has given
an account. This division was regarded by him as
one of the fatal consequences of the abolition of the
Sanhedrin.*

* Basnage, p. 635.

CHAPTER XV.

Of the learned men who flourished among the Jews during the twelfth century.—An account of the impostors who pretended to be the Messiah, and of the calamities in which they involved their nation during this period.

DURING the twelfth century many celebrated Jewish rabbies appeared, whose abilities and learning did honour to their nation; and whose writings have furnished assistance towards understanding the Old Testament. They often, however, instead of explaining the literal sense, eagerly searched after mystical and allegorical interpretations; and gave a tedious and minute detail of the ceremonies, which had caused them to relinquish the spirit of their law.[*]

Nathan Ben Jéchiel is ranked among the great men, who appeared in the twelfth century. He was the author of a work called Harak, in which he explained all the terms in the Talmud in so copious a manner, that he has exhausted the subject. He was chief of the Jewish academy at Rome; and died in that city in the year 1106.[†]

Abraham Ben Ezra, one of the greatest men of his age and nation, was born at Toledo in Spain, and styled by the Jews, the wise, great and admirable doctor. He travelled for the purpose of acquiring knowledge; and far excelled his brethren in sacred and profane literature. A learned Italian writer[‡] asserts, that " he was an able philosopher,

[*] Basnage, p. 625.   [†] Ibid.
[‡] De Rossie's Hebrew Biography. Enfield's Philosophy.

P

physician, astronomer, mathematician, grammarian, and poet; and, that he was so well versed in Hebrew, Chaldaic, Arabic, and other languages, that he composed in them all with great facility."— His method of explaining the scriptures differed from the other rabbies; for instead of seeking after mystic interpretations, he generally adhered to the literal meaning; and gave such proofs of his genius and good sense, that the Christians prefer him to the other Jewish expositors. His most celebrated work is, "Commentaries on the Old Testament."* He died at Rhodes, 1174, in the seventy-fifth year of his age.†

Moses Maimonides, who was eminently distinguished among the learned men of this age, was born of an illustrious family at Cordova in Spain, in the year 1131. He boasted of being descended from the house of David, as did many of the Spanish Jews. He made such a rapid progress in science and literature, that his countrymen styled him the " eagle of doctors ;" and asserted that "of all their nation none ever so nearly approached to the wisdom and learning of their great founder and lawgiver as Moses the son of Maimon." At length, however, the superiority of his genius, and the vast fund of knowledge which he acquired, excited the envy and jealousy of the Jews. Perhaps also his connexion with Averroes, a celebrated Arabian philosopher, who was one of his preceptors, might

---

* He also wrote various theological, grammatical, mathematical, and astrological works, many of which remain in ancient libraries, not yet edited.

† Basnage, p. 626.

have led him to adopt obnoxious opinions. His writings, particularly his Moreh Nevochim, or resolution of doubtful questions, soon raised him many opponents. The design of this work was to explain the meaning of several difficult and obscure words, phrases, metaphors, parables, allegories, &c. in scripture. It was written for the benefit of those who were in doubt whether they should interpret such passages according to the letter, or rather figuratively and metaphorically. It was asserted by many at this time, that the Mosaic rites and statutes had no foundation in reason; but were ordained by God upon a principle purely arbitrary.* On the other side, Maimonides argued, that the Mosaic dispensation in general was instituted with a wisdom worthy of its divine author, and explained the causes and reasons of each particular branch of it. But he exhibited less respect for the decisions of the Talmud, than the other Jewish doctors who preceded him. Those of his nation who were most attached to these fables were highly offended. Rabbi Solomon, then chief of the synagogues at Montpelier, persuaded the doctors who studied under him to engage in defence of the Talmud. Accordingly they not only opposed the doctrine of Maimonides, but endeavoured to blast his reputation. They burnt his works, and excommunicated those who read them, and addicted themselves to the study of philosophy.†

The rabbies of Narbonne, with the great David Kimchi at their head, exerted all their eloquence in

* Basnage, p. 627. Biographical Dictionary.
† Basnage, p. 627. Modern Universal Hist. vol. xiii. p. 287.

defence of Maimonides, and excommunicated their.
brethren at Montpelier. This contention, lasted
forty years, and called forth the abilities of the
learned men on both sides of the question. The
schism to which this dispute gave rise was abolished
in 1232.

Maimonides, finding his residence in Spain troublesome and hazardous, removed to Egypt, and
settled at Cairo. His knowledge of the healing art
induced the sultan of Egypt to choose him for his
physician ; and he employed his credit at court in
protecting his nation. He also founded an academy
at Alexandria for their benefit, and gained many
pupils from various countries. They were, however,
soon dispersed by persecution. Some assert, that
this great man died in Egypt 1201 ; others, that
his death took place in Palestine 1205.*

This learned Jew was not only master of many
eastern languages, which was a singular accomplishment in his time, but was well versed in the Greek
tongue, and had read the works of the Grecian philosophers, whom he frequently quotes. He was
celebrated for his knowledge of the arts and sciences,
as well as languages ; was eminently distinguished as
a physician ; and in Talmudic learning excelled all
his cotemporaries.† His writings are too numerous
to be particularly mentioned.‡

Solomon Ben Isaac Jarchi is ranked among the
illustrious rabbies of the twelfth century. He was

---

* Basnage, p 637.   † Enfield's Philosophy, vol. ii. p. 205.
‡ He was the author of twenty-five noted works, besides some
others of less importance.—*Modern Universal History*, vol. xiii.
p. 2⁻1

born 1104, at Troyes in Champagne, in France:
Having acquired a large fund of Jewish learning, he
travelled through Germany; Italy, Greece, Jerusalem; Palestine and Egypt; where he had an inter-
view with Maimonides. From Egypt he passed to
Persia, and thence to Tartary and Muscovy. After
his return to Europe, he visited all the academies,
and disputed against the professors; upon any questions proposed by them. He was well versed in
physic and astronomy, and master of several languages besides' the Hebrew. He wrote Commentaries on the Pentateuch, and some of the Prophets;
also on the Gemara; which procured him the title of
Prince of Commentators. He died at Troyes,
1180.*

The family of the Kimchis has been eminently
distinguished in the annals of Jewish literature:
Joseph Kimchi was a man of great learning; but a
violent enemy to the Christians; whom he inveighed
against in his writings. David Kimchi, his son;
one of the most zealous defenders of Maimonides,
flourished in Spain at the end of the twelfth, and at
the commencement of the thirteenth century. This
celebrated rabbi far excelled his father in ability and
learning, and had not imbibed such strong prejudices against the Christians. His writings have been
held in such high estimation by his nation, that they
supposed it impossible to attain to any eminence in
letters and theology without studying them. He
composed a grammar and dictionary of the Hebrew
language, by which he acquired the reputation of
excelling all the Jews who preceded him in gram-

* Basnage, p. 657. General Biographical Dictionary.

matical knowledge. He also was the authór of a
Commentary on, the Psalms, and other books of the
Old Testament. Part of this work has been
translated into Latin, and inserted in the Bibles of
Venice and Basil. Moses Kimchi, his brother, was
also distinguished for his learning ; and has written
a treatise, styled the Garden of Delight, the
manuscript of which was preserved in the Vatican
library.*

Three celebrated rabbies, named Levi, or Halevi,
appeared during the twelfth century. Abraham
Halevi was a learned cabbalistical Jew, who, having
placed himself at the head of the traditional party,
violently attacked the Caraites ; but being inferior to
them in point of argument, he had resource to
Alphonso VII. for whom he had performed signal
services, and who rewarded him by commanding his
opponents to be silent.†

Juda Levi was the author of the Cosri, a pole-
mical treatise on religion, especially the Jewish ; and
a pathetic elegy, in which he deplored the destruction of Jerusalem.‡

Another learned rabbi, named Judas Halevi, was
born at Cologne ; and after many conferences with
the Christians became a convert, and was baptized
by the name of Herman. After he embraced Christianity, he entered among the regular canons of
St. Augustine.§

Some learned Jewish women appeared during the

* Basnage, p. 630.   † Ibid.
‡ This elegy has been translated by Mr. Bing, and inserted in a note
of Gregoire's work on the Reformation of the Jews, p. 280.
§ Basnage, p. 630.

twelfth century. The rabbi Petachiah, who visited the synagogues of his nation at that period, has asserted, that the daughter of the prince of the captivity was so well versed in the law and Talmud, that many resorted to her for instruction; and that she read lectures through the lattice of her window, in order to be heard without being seen by her pupils.

It appears from the Jewish annals, that some of the nation have been raised to the highest offices in the courts of princes. Others have acquired applause at the head of armies ; in particular, the celebrated don Solomon, a Portuguese Jew, who was as much distinguished for his knowledge in philosophy, as for his skill in the military department. His merit raised him, in 1190, to the dignity of field-master-general ; and he discharged the duties of his office with such fidelity, that he soon obtained the command of the whole army. The envy and jealousy of the grandees was at length excited by his valour and success. But he subdued their enmity by his remarkable humility and moderation.* ;

In the twelfth century several learned Jews renounced their religion. For instance, Samuel Ben Jehudah, or, as he is commonly called, Asmouil, deserted the synagogue, and professed the Mahometan faith. In order to prove the sincerity of his conversion; in 1174 he wrote a book against his nation, in which he charges them with having altered the law of Moses. This accusation was received with such applause by the Mahometans, that they forbade the quoting or translating any part of

* Basnage, p. 630.

the Pentateuch according to the Jewish or Christian copies.*

, One of the Christian converts received the name of ·Peter Alphonso at his baptism.· After he deserted the synagogue, he wrote dialogues against the Jews, and ,was appointed physician to Alphonso VII. king of Castile and Leon. ` He died in the year 1108.†

It is indeed surprising, that the learned rabbies of the twelfth century. did not sufficiently enlighten their nation as to prevent their being frequently duped by impostors. But the number of those who appeared in this age was greater than in any preceding or subsequent century. In 1137, a false Christ arose in France, and engaged his followers to hold unlawful assemblies. In consequence of the impostor's crimes, the government caused many of the synagogues to be demolished. But at length he and a large number of his followers were apprehended and put to death.‡

The following year the Persians were disturbed by a Jew, who called himself the Messiah; and collected a formidable army of his nation. The Persian monarch hired him to disband his soldiers; but when the stipulated sum was paid, the king finding himself out of danger, compelled the disarmed Jews to reimburse him the money, and caused the impostor to be beheaded.§

In 1157, another false Messiah appeared in Spain. He was a native of Cordova, and was supported in his imposture by one of the greatest rabbies in that city, who had previously written a

* Basnage, p. 630.   † Modern Univer. Hist. vol. xliii. p. 291.
‡ Jortin's Remarks, vol. ii. p. 304.   § Basnage, p. 632.

book to prove the near approach of his manifestation by the stars. The majority of the most intelligent Jews regarded him as insane; but the great body of this infatuated people believed in him, and many were ruined by their blind credulity.[*]

Ten years after, another impostor declared that the Messiah would manifest himself in the course of a year. This person appeared in the kingdom of Fez, and involved the Jews, who were dispersed through the country, in a new persecution.

The same year an Arabian Jew assumed the title of the Messiah, and pretended to work miracles, and gained many followers. But at length he was apprehended, and brought before the Arabian king. When he was questioned by the monarch, what had induced him to act this imposture, he boldly replied, that he was indeed a prophet sent from God. The king then asked him, what miracle he could perform to confirm his mission? Cut off my head, said he, and I will return to life again.[†] The monarch took him at his word, promising to believe in him, if his prediction was fulfilled. After his death his deluded followers cherished the expectation, that though he did not immediately rise from the dead, he would at length reanimate their hopes by his appearance. But they were compelled to give up the idea, and were severely fined and punished for their blind credulity.[‡]

[*] Basnage, p. 632. Jortin's Remarks, vol. ii. p. 304.

[†] This is supposed to have been an artifice of the impostor, who preferred a speedy death to the cruel and lingering torture to which he would otherwise have been exposed.

[‡] Basnage, p. 632.

Some time after, a Jew who dwelt beyond the
Euphrates, called himself the Messiah, and drew
vast multitudes after him. He founded his pretensions on his having been a leper, and being wonderfully healed in one night of this obstinate disease.
The Jewish doctors soon persuaded him and his
followers, that this supposed miracle was not a sufficient evidence of his mission. The populace
became ashamed of their blind credulity ; but, as
they had taken arms in his cause, a fresh persecution
was raised against them. One of their writers
informs us, that, exhausted with their sufferings on
his account, ten thousand of this miserable people
renounced their religion ; which has rendered the
memory of this impostor odious to the whole
nation.*

In the year 1174, another pretended Messiah
arose in Persia. This impostor seduced multitudes
of the common people, and involved his nation in
a new and severe persecution.

A Jew, named David Almusser, appeared in
Moravia, in the year 1196, who set up for the
Messiah, and boasted that he possessed the power of
rendering himself invisible whenever he pleased.
Vast multitudes followed him, and were deceived by
his artifice. In order to prevent the ill consequences
of his popularity, the king promised him his
life on condition that he would surrender himself.
He complied ; but the prince caused him to be imprisoned. He had the address, however, to escape ;
and for some time eluded all pursuit. At length the
king summoned the Jews to deliver him up ; and, in

* Basnage, p 632.

order to avoid a fresh persecution; they complied. He was put to death, and a heavy fine imposed upon his nation.* , , , , , , , , , , , , , , , , , ,

·· David·Alroi, or El-David, was' the most famous impostor, who appeared during the twelfth century. He was a native of Almaria, which city contained about one thousand Jews, who paid tribute to the king of·Persia. In the year 1199 he assumed the title of the Messiah; and being a man of learning, and well versed in all the arts of deception, he attracted many followers. After he had deluded the populace by his pretended miracles, he prevailed upon them to arm themselves in his cause. The Persian king, alarmed at the rapid progress of the insurgents, commanded the impostor to repair to court, promising, that if he proved himself the Messiah, he would acknowledge him as a king, sent from heaven. El-David, contrary to expectation, obeyed the summons, and assured the king that he was really the Messiah. Upon which he was ordered to be imprisoned till he could prove his mission by extricating himself by a miracle. He had the address to escape, and though the king despatched messengers in search of the impostor, they were unable to find and apprehend him. But at length, upon a promise of receiving ten thousand crowns, his father-in-law consented to betray and put him to death. Vast numbers who had been deluded by him were cruelly slaughtered. †

After giving an account of the false Messiahs who appeared among the Jews, Dr. Jortin remarks, " It

* Basnage. p. 632. Jortin's Remarks, vol. ii. p. 304.
† Basnage, p. 633.

may seem strange that they should have rejected
Christ, who gave them so many proofs of his mission,
and yet should follow every impostor who pretended
to be the Messiah, without offering any sufficient or
even plausible evidence of it. The reason is plain ;
our Saviour, by not setting up a temporal kingdom,
dashed all their worldly views at once ; but the
claimers of the title of Messiah began with promises
of delivering them from their enemies, and restoring
to them their country, and their lost liberties."*

* Jortin's Remarks, vol. ii. p. 319.

CHAPTER XVI.

Of the Jews in England.—William the Conqueror brings a colony of them into the kingdom.—They are favoured by William Rufus.—Henry II. grants them new cemeteries in London.—They are massacred at the coronation of Richard I.—Their sufferings from the Crusaders.—Five hundred perish by suicide in York Castle.—Of the cruel oppression they suffered under king John.—They are also oppressed by Henry III.—They are accused of adulterating the coin; two hundred and eighty are executed for that crime in London.—They are expelled from England by Edward I.

IT is difficult to ascertain at what period the Jews first settled in England. But it appears that there were considerable numbers established in the kingdom before the conquest.* William the Conqueror brought a large colony of this nation from Rouen in Normandy for a stipulated sum of money, which they presented him. After he had introduced them, he assigned them a place to inhabit, and carry on commerce. It appears by an ancient law, mentioned by Sir Henry Spelman, that they were mere vassals to the king, and could not dispose of their persons or property without his consent.

During the feudal ages, the Jews appear to have been the most opulent, polished, and literary

* Basnage asserts, that the English Jews were banished from the kingdom in the beginning of the eleventh century. But does not mention on what account, or under what monarch the expulsion took place.

Dr. Tovey, the author of a work called Anglia Judaica, who has taken great pains to search after the antiquities of the Hebrew nation in England, contends that the existence of Jews in the kingdom, was coeval with Julius Cæsar, and says nothing of any banishment of them prior to that of Edward I.—*Adams' Religious World Displayed,* vol. i. p 11.

portion of the laity. They were the only bankers, or, as the vulgar termed them, the usurers of the times. They conducted what then existed of foreign trade ; and often visited the civilized south of Europe. They wrought most of the gold and silver ornaments for churches.

William Rufus, who was an irreligious prince, highly favoured this singular people ; and not only permitted, but encouraged them to enter into solemn contests with his bishops concerning the true faith. It is said, that he sent for some learned Christian divines and rabbies, and ordered them fairly to dispute the question of their religion in his presence; assuring them, he was perfectly indifferent between them, and that he would embrace that doctrine which upon comparison, appeared to be supported by the most solid arguments. Accordingly, it is related, that there was a public meeting of the chief leaders on both sides in London, where the Jews opposed the Christians with so much energy, that the bishops and clergy were not without some solicitude how the dispute might terminate. No other class of men were at this time sufficiently enlightened to engage with the priesthood. Some young Jews were even so imprudent as to value themselves upon their infidelity. It has been asserted, that they became so powerful and opulent towards the conclusion of the reign of William Rufus, that they not only held public disputes, but endeavoured by pecuniary bribes and other allurements to induce the poor to embrace their religion.*

* Hume's History of England, vol. i. p. 189.   Molloy De Jure Maritimo, p 400.

A. D. 1177.] Henry II. has been highly censured by monkish writers for tolerating and protecting the Jews. They were so numerous in his reign, that, possessing only one burying-ground in the city of London, they petitioned the king to allow them some new cemeteries. This request was granted; and places to inter their dead were assigned them on the outside of every city where they dwelt. In this reign one Joshua, a Jew, furnished the rebels in Ireland with large sums of money; and their opulence had rendered them so presumptuous as to ridicule the higher dignitaries of the church. We may in part attribute to them the spirit which dictated the constitutions of Clarendon.* In 1188, the parliament at Northampton proposed to assess them at £60,000, and the Christians at £70,000, towards the projected war. The Jews must, therefore, have been vastly rich, or the parliament extremely tyrannical. But this nation, from their first residence in England, were always considered as vassals to the crown, who might be pillaged according to the caprice of the reigning sovereign.†

A. D. 1189.] When Richard I. ascended the throne, this people brought large presents in order to secure the royal protection. Many having hastened from remote parts of England to Westminster, the court and populace imagined they had

---

* Decrees enacted by the council of Clarendon, which Henry II. convened in order to check the usurpations of the pope and clergy. *Hume*, vol. i.

† Monthly Magazine and British Register, 1796. Molloy de Jure Maritimo.

conspired to bewitch the king,* and an edict was issued to prevent their presence at the coronation. But considerable numbers, whose curiosity was greater than their prudence, fancied they might pass unobserved among the crowd, and ventured to insinuate themselves into the abbey. Upon being discovered, they fled in great consternation; but the people pursued them and murdered several.†

A rumour spread rapidly through the city, that the king, in honour of the festival, had given orders for the massacre of the Jews: a command so agreeable was instantly executed on all who fell into the hands of the populace. Those who remained at home were exposed to equal danger; the people moved by rapacity and zeal broke into their houses, which they plundered, after having murdered the owners. Where the Jews barricaded their doors and defended themselves with vigour, the rabble set fire to the houses, and made way through the flames to exercise their pillage and violence. The usual licentiousness of London, which the sovereign power with difficulty restrained, broke out with fury, and continued these outrages. The inhabitants of the other cities of England, hearing of the slaughter of this unhappy people in the metropolis, imitated the example; and, though the government published a proclamation the day after the coronation, in order to suppress the fury of the populace, the persecution was continued the greater part of the year.‡

---

* A superstitious idea that the Jews were most of them conjurors was prevalent during the dark ages.—*Basnage*, p. 638.

† Hume's History of England. Smollet's History of England.

‡ Hume's History of England

This miserable race suffered a still more severe persecution, when Richard I. impelled. more by the love of glory than by superstition, engaged in the crusades.* They had furnished him with vast sums towards the expedition; but this did not satisfy the people, whose zeal against an unbelieving race was heightened by the holy war; and who complained of the conduct as well as the faith of the Jews. The prejudices of the age had made the lending of money on interest pass by the invidious name of usury; yet the necessity of the practice had still continued it, and the greater part of this dealing fell every where into the hands of the Jews, who, being already infamous on account of their religion, had no honour to lose. They were therefore apt to exercise a profession odious in itself, by every kind of rigour, and even sometimes by rapine and extortion. The industry and frugality of this nation had put them in possession of all the ready money which the idleness and profusion, common to the English and other European nations, enabled them to lend at an exorbitant and unequal interest.†

Those who were preparing for the holy war, felt indignant that the enemies of Christ should abound

---

* This was the third crusade. Saladin, the sultan of Egypt and Syria, had taken the city of Jerusalem from the Christians, and placed on its walls the banners of Mahomet. This incident rekindled with fresh fury, the zeal of the military adventurers among the Christians.

† Hume, vol. i. p. 135. The Jews took this extravagant interest with the dreadful prospect of murder before their eyes, and a certainty of paying a large portion of it to the king. It is, therefore, natural to suppose, that a people who were exposed to such cruelties and insults, and had so uncertain an enjoyment of their riches, would carry usury to the utmost extremity.—*Macpherson on Commerce.*

in wealth, while they, who supposed themselves his peculiar friends and favourites, should be obliged to deprive their families of necessaries in order to defray the expenses of the crusades. Hence they persuaded themselves it would be a meritorious act to destroy the descendants of those, who crucified our Saviour, and apply their wealth to this holy enterprize. Though the king at his departure had left orders that they should not be molested; yet as soon as he quitted the kingdom their fury broke out anew. They destroyed many of these wretched people at Norwich, Stamford, and other places, and seized upon their property. The murderers took shipping as soon as possible, and fled to Jerusalem; not so much as one of them being detained by the magistrates, or any further inquiry made respecting their injustice and cruelty.*

A still more horrid transaction took place at York, where the Jews were great usurers; and where, as they lived in a splendid manner, their opulence excited envy, and increased the hatred against them. The populace in this city assembled to inflict the same barbarities upon them, which their countrymen had suffered in London, and other places. Upon which, the principal persons among this people applied to the governor of York Castle, and prevailed upon him to grant them an asylum. The place was sufficiently strong for their defence. But a suspicion arising, that the governor, who frequently went out into the city, had combined with their enemies to destroy them, they one day refused him entrance. He complained to the sheriff, and to the

* Monthly Magazine and British Register, 1796.

heads of the violent party who were deeply in debt to the Jews, and was ordered to attack the castle. The sheriff, however, repented of; and revoked the order, and the superior citizens refused their aid. But, as the fury of the populace could be appeased only by murder and robbery, an attack was made.* When the Jews found that they could not hold out any longer, and their offers of purchasing their lives with money were rejected, they took the horrid resolution of destroying themselves, one of the most desperate among them exclaiming in despair, that "it was better to die courageously for the law, than to fall into the hands of the Christians." Accordingly, after setting fire to the towers of the castle, and destroying their wives and children, they put a period to their own lives. Five hundred perished at this time. A few who surrendered in hopes of mercy, were murdered by the populace.† .

Immediately after this dreadful catastrophe, those who were indebted to the Jews, repaired to the cathedral where the bonds were deposited, compelled the officer to deliver the obligations, and discharged their debts by burning them in the

* A late writer asserts, that the leader of the rabble who attacked the castle was a canon regular, whose zeal was so fervent, that he stood by them in his surplice, which he considered as a coat of mail, and reiteratedly exclaimed, "Destroy the enemies of Jesus." This spiritual laconism invigorated the arm of men, who perhaps wanted no other stimulative than the hopes of obtaining the immense property of the besieged. The same author also asserts, that a venerable rabbi, who was highly esteemed among his brethren, first proposed to them to perish by suicide, in order to elude the tortures which they expected would be inflicted upon them if they fell into the hands of their enemies.—*Curiosities of Literature*, vol. ii. p. 427.

† Basnage, p. 638. Anderson, vol. i. p. 224. Macpherson, vol i. p. 83.

church, with great solemnity. They also entered
and plundered the desolate houses which belonged
to the Jews.' The king, incensed at this insult to
his authority, ordered the bishop of Ely, at that
time chief justice of the realm, to make severe examples of the guilty. But before he arrived in York-
shire, the principal offenders had fled into Scotland,
and the city of London. Imputing what had happened to the ungoverned fury of the multitude, the
prelate contented himself with depriving the high
sheriff and governor of their offices, and levying fines
upon the most opulent of the inhabitants.*

A. D. 1199.] The cruel persecutions which the
Jews suffered during the reign of Richard, had induced many of the wealthiest among them to leave
the kingdom. The consequent diminution of the
revenue was so sensibly felt, that John, upon his
accession to the throne, used various arts to allure
them to return. He granted them, upon receiving
a large sum of money, a charter which confirmed
all their ancient privileges; and allowed them to hold
land, to build synagogues, and name a high priest
by the title of Presbyter Judæorum.† Many of
this oppressed people returned, and were afterwards
more cruelly plundered than ever. Their exorbitant

* Basnage, p 688 Smollet's History of England, vol. ii. p. 227.
When the king employed Granville the justiciary to inquire into
the authors of these crimes, the guilt was found to involve so many
of the most considerable citizens, that it was deemed more prudent
to drop the prosecution, and very few suffered the punishment due to
this enormity.—*Hume's History of England*, vol. i. p. 351.

† By the canon law no Jews could erect a synagogue; for if they
attempted to build these places of worship they might be seized by
the crown.—*Matthew Paris's History of England. Macpherson on
Commerce.*

usury, united with the religious prejudices of the
age, had rendered them so odious to the people, that
they were continually demanding their expulsion,
or rather extermination. But the English kings
found a more advantageous way of punishing them
by heavy fines. This procedure proved to the Jews
that their extortions would not only be tolerated, but
encouraged, if they were well paid for. This compelled them to rise in their demands upon those who
applied to them for the use of money. And thus
a system of usurious oppression was at the same time
prohibited by law, and sanctioned by the practice
of the sovereigns, who used them as their instruments to fleece the people in order to fill their own
coffers.*

A. D. 1210.] King John, regardless of the privileges which the Jews had purchased from him in
the beginning of his reign, ordered the whole of
them, women as well as men, to be imprisoned and
tormented till they should pay 66,000 marks. The
ransom required from a wealthy Jew of Bristol,
was 10,000 marks of silver; and, on his refusing to
pay that ruinous fine, he ordered one of his teeth
to be extracted every day, to which the unhappy

---

* The kings even went so far as to claim the whole property of the
Jews. They were to reside only in such places as they assigned them,
so that their officers might on all occasions find them and their families They were not suffered to remove without special license. They
were banished, executed, and subjected to fines and ransoms whenever
the kings thought proper, and were sold or mortgaged to those who
would advance money on their assignment. They were always obliged
to wear a disgraceful mark of distinction on their garments. The
revenue arising from their wealth was so great, that there was a particular office established for the management of it, called the Ex-
chequer of the Jews.—*Molloy de Jure Maritimo*, p. 407, 408.

man submitted seven days, and on the eighth agreed to satisfy the king's rapacity. Isaac, a Jew of Norwich, became bound to pay 10,000 marks. It is asserted by some historians,* that the king, not satisfied with the vast sums extorted from this miserable people, confiscated all their property, and expelled them from the kingdom. It appears, however, that they soon returned.

A. D. 1216.] Henry III. liberated such Jews as were in prison, and ordered them to be protected against the cruelty of the Crusaders.† In 1233, this monarch founded a seminary, where Jewish converts might be supported without labour or usury. This induced many of the nation to profess Christianity; and the house continued till after their expulsion from England.‡

Upon a petition of the inhabitants of Newcastle, the king granted them the inhospitable privilege, that no Jew should reside among them. During this reign, the archbishop of Canterbury, and the bishops of Lincoln and Norwich, in order to expel the Jews for want of sustenance, published injunctions through their respective dioceses, that no Christian should presume to sell them any provisions under pain of excommunication. The prior of Dunstable, however, about the same period, granted to several Jews liberty to reside within his domains,

---

* Matthew Paris. Macpherson, vol. i. p. 376.

† The Jews were so deeply alarmed at the persecution which their brethren in France, Spain, and Germany, suffered at this time from the Crusaders, that they purchased an edict from the king to preserve them from similar outrages. *Basnage*, p. 678.

‡ Basnage, p. 679.

in consideration of the annual payment of two silver spoons.*

A. D. 1235.] The Jews of Norwich were accused of having stolen a Christian child and kept him a year, that they might circumcise and crucify him at the ensuing passover; but being detected previously to that period, they suffered a severe punishment. In London they were also accused of murder,† and, after enduring various vexations and torments, were deprived of a third part of all their estates. This, however, did not satisfy the insatiable king, who soon after renewed his extortions. This wretched people were accused of coining false money, and counterfeiting the prince's seal; and under these pretences were loaded with enormous taxes. In 1241, 20,000 marks were exacted from them. Two years after, a Jew, named Aaron, of York, was compelled to pay four gold and four thousand silver marks. Seven years after, the same man was accused of forgery, and condemned to pay four thousand marks of gold and fourteen thousand of silver. The high penalty imposed upon him, which it seems he was thought able to pay, may be deemed by some rather a presumption of his innocence than of his guilt.‡

A. D. 1254.] New supplies were demanded

---

* Monthly Magazine, 1796.

† It appears probable, that most, if not all the accusations of this kind were made against the Jews, to give a better pretence for extorting their money; for, according to Basnage, those of London were accused of murder, on their refusal to pay the great sums the king demanded. The least surmise, made upon the slightest foundation, obtained credit among their enemies, who sought their destruction.

‡ Hume's History of England.

from the Jews for carrying on the Spanish war.
Irritated to the highest degree by this oppression,
they requested permission to depart from England
for some more propitious and friendly country.*
But this they were refused, and compelled to pay
part of the contribution. The following year the
king renewed these extortions. He represented,
that notwithstanding the taxes he had raised, he still
continued poor and involved in debt ; and declared,
that " he must have money from any hand, from any
quarter, or by any means." He then demanded
eight thousand marks of the Jews, and, upon
their pleading insolvency, sold them to his brother
Richard for that sum. It was expected he would
demand a rigorous payment of the debt ; but he
compassionated their situation, and was convinced
of their poverty and inability.

, A. D. 1262.] The hatred of the people against
the Hebrew nation had, during the reign of Henry,
arrived at such a height, that, when the barons
appeared in arms against the king, they endeavoured
to attach the citizens of London to their interest by
massacreing seven hundred of this devoted race.
An attempt, which was made by one of the nation
to oblige a Christian to pay an enormous interest for
a loan of money, is said to have afforded a pretence

---

* Elias, a London Jew, undertook to plead for his brethren before
the council ; and made a pathetic speech, representing the impossibility of their paying the sum demanded. Several instances are related by Basnage of the Jews bribing their judges to be favourable to
them. In particular, John Lunel, though in the ecclesiastical line,
was accused of receiving large sums from many Jews for his protecting them at the bar, and diminishing their taxes. Page 679.

for this barbarous act.* They first plundered their houses, and burnt their new synagogue to the ground.† It was however rebuilt; but in 1270 taken from them by the king and given to the friars penitents, who had complained that "they were not able to make the body of Christ in quiet for the great howlings the Jews made during their worship."‡

A. D. 1276.] In the third year of the reign of Edward I. a law passed the commons concerning Judaism, which seemed to promise this unhappy people a qualified security. The apparent design of it was to introduce a regularity in the revenue exacted from them, which had hitherto consisted of arbitrary taxes levied upon them by the king. This statute prohibited the usury of the Jews; but allowed them to purchase houses and lands.§ No Christian was, however, permitted to lodge in their dwellings; and every Jew above seven years of age was obliged to wear a peculiar mark of two cables joined upon his upper garment.

---

* Macpherson on Commerce.

† This synagogue was built during the time the Jews were most favoured by king Henry; and surpassed in magnificence the Christian churches. After this synagogue was seized by the king, it was dedicated to the blessed virgin.—*M. Paris's Hist. of England,* p. 393.

‡ The learned author of Anglia Judaica observes, " that the friars were situated in Old Jewry, and having but a small dark chapel belonging to their friary, thought the Jews' fine synagogue which stood next to it, more convenient for them, and therefore begged it of the king, and furnished him with that reason for it."—*David Levi's Letters to Priestley,* p. 6.

§ Among other curious particulars contained in this statute, with regard to the terms on which the Jews were tolerated in England, by the second section, " the good Christians were not to take above half their substance."—*Observations on the Statutes,* p 180.

A. D. 1287.] King Edward, however, whose prejudices against this unhappy people were increased by his expedition into the holy land, treated them with great rigour. He forbade their selling or assigning their debts without his license. He ordered all their repositories throughout the kingdom to be searched, and established an inquisition to take cognizance of those who neglected to wear the distinguishing badges. The oppression and misery under which they continually groaned appear to have rendered them regardless of character; and the frequent extortion of vast sums from them* seems to have made them imagine every method justifiable, which they could take to indemnify themselves. They were accused of adulterating the coin, circulating counterfeit money, and making fraudulent exchanges. In consequence of their guilt, and the outcry raised against them, all the Jews in England were imprisoned on one day, and two hundred and eighty executed in London, besides vast numbers in other parts of the kingdom. Their houses and lands, as well as the goods of multitudes, were sold and confiscated. The king, lest it should be suspected that the riches of the sufferers were the chief part of their guilt, ordered a moiety of the money raised by these confiscations to be set apart, and bestowed upon such as were willing to be converted to Christianity. But resentment was more prevalent with them than any temptation from their

---

* It was computed, that the Jews paid the crown in the space of seven years, viz. from the fiftieth year of Henry III. to the second year of Edward I. no less than four hundred and twenty thousand pounds, or two hundred and sixty thousand pounds of our modern money.—*Anderson on Commerce*, vol. i. p. 322.

poverty; and very few could be induced by interest to embrace the religion of their persecutors.[*]

A. D. 1290.] About this time king Edward, prompted by his zeal and rapacity, ordered the Jews to be banished from the kingdom, and never to return, upon pain of death. He seized at once their whole property, and allowed them only money sufficient to bear their expences into foreign countries, where new persecutions and extortions awaited them.[†] But the seamen of the cinque ports despoiled most of them of this small pittance, and even threw some hundreds of this miserable people into the sea. The king inflicted a capital punishment upon the perpetrators of this crime. The number of those who were expelled amounted to sixteen thousand five hundred and eleven. Edward had previously banished them from his territories in France. After this expulsion, the Jews never appeared again in a body in England during three hundred and fifty years.[‡]

[*] Basnage, p. 680. Macpherson, vol. i. p. 432. Hume, vol. ii. p. 4.

[†] The clergy were so well pleased with the banishment of the Jews, that they granted a tenth of their benefices to the king; and afterwards joined with the nobility in obliging him with a fifteenth of their temporalities, to make some amends for the loss he sustained by the expulsion of a people, from whom his predecessors had exacted considerable subsidies in the emergency of affairs.—*Smollet,* vol. i. p. 140.

[‡] Anderson on Commerce, vol. i. p. 322. Macpherson, vol. i, p. 450. Henry's History of Britain, vol. iv. p. 46.

CHAPTER XVII.

State of the Jews in France.—They are expelled the kingdom by Philip Augustus.—They are severely persecuted under the reign of Lewis IX. who at length banishes them from his dominions.—Severe laws enacted against them by the duke of, Brittany, and the councils of Lyons and Vienne.—The Jews are recalled by Philip the Bold.—They are banished by Philip the Fair, and recalled by Lewis XI.—Irruption of the shepherds, and their cruelty.—The Jews are accused of causing the rivers, wells, &c. to be poisoned.—The terrible punishment they suffered for this supposed crime.—They are banished by Philip the Tall.—They invent bills of exchange.—They are recalled by John II.—They are accused of various crimes, and cruelly treated during the reign of Charles VI. —They are finally expelled the French dominions.

WHILE the Jews in England were enduring all kinds of oppression and misery, their brethren in France were subjected to similar sufferings and persecution. About the year 1182, King Philip, surnamed the August, under pretence of piety and zeal for the honour of God, banished them from his dominions,* and confiscated their estates. They were permitted to retain only what could be collected from the sale of their furniture ; for which they found it difficult to obtain purchasers. It is even said, that they were robbed of the small sums they were enabled to raise, and reduced to the greatest misery, and that many fell victims to these tyrannical proceedings. Soon after, however, the king ordered them to be recalled ; and upon finding that this measure excited the resentment of the Zealots, he

---

* The murder of a youth named Richard, was laid to their charge, and served as a pretence for expelling them from France.—*Picart*, p 173.

excused himself by alleging, that his object was to extort money from them to defray the expences of the crusade.*

A. D. 1218.] After the Jews were resettled in the kingdom, they resumed their former usurious practices, and accumulated wealth, with which they purchased lands.† The king at first connived at their extortions, because they had bought his protection; but, upon the remonstrance of his people, new laws were enacted to remedy this evil.

A. D. 1230.] Lewis IX. surnamed the Saint, in the beginning of his reign called a council at Melun; in which a new law was enacted, expressly prohibiting all his subjects from borrowing any money of the Jews. It appears from various edicts, that the effects of all this unhappy people who were settled in the kingdom belonged to the barons, within whose territories they had fixed their residence. They were forbidden by the law to change their abode without the permission of their lord, who was empowered to follow and claim them as fugitive slaves even in the royal domain. It also appears that they were regarded as an object of traffic, and transferred with the land from one proprietor to another, and sometimes sold separately, their value being estimated according to their talents

* Basnage, p. 636.

† During the reign of Philip Augustus, the Jews were in some measure the property of the lord in whose territories they resided; but servitude did not always prevent them from becoming the possessors of land. We even find that in France they were the owners of vast domains; yet it may be readily perceived that it was a matter of no great difficulty to deprive these of their wealth, who were not masters of their own persons.—*Gregoire*, p. 10.

and industry. If a Jew became a convert to Christianity, the whole of his property, was confiscated to
the use of his lord.* The passion for extorting
wealth from this miserable race was so vehement,
" that a conversion was considered as a bankruptcy,
and even paradise did not possess the right of
asylum."†

Saint Lewis not only sanctioned and confirmed,
but even extended these oppressive laws. He ordered the Jews to be severely fined if they neglected
to wear a distinguishing and disgraceful badge on
their garments, and prohibited them from having
any intercourse with the Christians. During his
reign, when a Jew appeared in evidence against a
Christian, he was compelled to swear by the ten
names of God; and his oath was accompanied with
a thousand imprecations upon his own head, if he
deviated from the truth. The person who administered the oath thus addressed him, " May the
Lord God send you a continual fever or ague, if
you are guilty of perjury; may he destroy you
in his anger, you, and your family, and your
effects; may the sword and death, fear and inqui-

---

* This singular custom of confiscating all the goods of the Jews
who embraced Christianity, was first introduced into France; and is
known only by the law which suppressed it, given at Basville, 1392.
Thus by a strange and impious inconsistency, this wretched people at
one time incurred a severe penalty by renouncing Judaism; at
another epoch, those in the same country, who refused to profess
Christianity, were ordered to be burnt The practice of confiscating
the property of those Jews who professed Christianity began under
the feudal government, and was continued in most parts of Europe
till the end of the fourteenth century.—*Montesquieu's Works. French
Encyclopedia.*

† Essay on Public Happiness, vol. ii. p. 427.

etude, pursue you on all sides ; may 'the earth
swallow you up like Dathan and Abiram ; may
all the sins of your parents, and all the male-
dictions contained in the law of Moses fall on your
head." To this dreadful imprecation the Jews were
to answer three times, "So be it."*

A. D. 1238.] The most signal calamity which
the Jews suffered during the reign of St. Lewis was
a persecution raised against them by the Parisians,
on acount, as was pretended, of their sacrificing
some Christian children on Good Friday, and of
using their blood at the solemnity of the passover.
For this imputed act of murder and impiety, they
were cruelly slaughtered in the metropolis. The
persecution was also extended to Brie, Touraine,
Anjou, Poitou, and Maine ; in which places upwards of two thousand five hundred Jews, who
refused to embrace Christianity, were put to death
by the most cruel tortures. Their sufferings would
probably have been prolonged, had not pope Gregory IX. interposed, and written to St. Lewis,
requesting him to allow them liberty of conscience.

During the king's imprisonment in the holy land†
a crusade was formed in his kingdom of simple shepherds, whose professed object was to march thither
and release him. They grounded their chimerical
design upon revelations, and pretended they had the
gift of working miracles. The enthusiastic fury
spread till their army amounted to an hundred thousand men, who marched to Bourges, plundered the

* Gifford's History of France, vol. i. p. 436, 437—450.
† St. Lewis was at the head of the sixth and seventh crusades in
1248 and 1270.

Jews, and seized all their books in order to commit them to the flames:. At length, however, they were subdued, and many of them put to death.*

The following year a conference was held in the presence of Blanche, the queen regent, during St. Lewis's absence, between rabbi Jechiel, a learned cabbalist, and Nicholas Donim, a celebrated Jewish convert. The French authors assert, that Jechiel, baffled and mortified by the powerful arguments of his opponent, retired in disgust to Jerusalem. While the king was under confinement in the holy land, he sent an edict to France to expel the Jews from his dominions, which was punctually executed by the queen regent.

A. D. 1239.] The Israelites being numerous and great usurers in Brittany, the nobility and merchants united in a complaint against them to John le Roux, the duke. An act was passed which declared, that at the request of the bishops, abbots, barons, and vassals in Brittany, all the Jews should be for ever banished from that province. By this law all their debtors were exonerated, and their effects ordered to be retained; and those who had recently killed a Jew were forbidden to be disturbed. The king of France was to be requested to expel this hated race, and confiscate their property. The duke engaged for himself and his successors, for the present and future to support this law; and, if he violated it, he authorized the bishops to excommunicate him, and confiscate his lands in their dioceses without regard to any privileges †

* Basnage, p. 672.　　† Ibid. p. 671.　Gregoire, p. 243.

A. D. 1240.] The celebrated council of Lyons passed also a decree enjoining all Christian princes who had Jews in their dominions, under penalty of excommunication, to compel them to refund to the Crusaders all the money they had obtained by usury. This oppressed people were also prohibited from demanding any debts due to them from the Crusaders till their death or return.

The council of Vienna, held in the same century, defended the Christians against the exorbitant usury of the Jewish nation. This people, however, notwithstanding these decrees and precautions, in some provinces of France, particularly in Languedoc, were raised to the magistracy,* and in most parts of the kingdom kept Christian slaves.

A. D. 1275.] Philip the Bold, the successor of St. Lewis, was induced to recal the Jews in order to promote commerce, effect the circulation of money, and improve his exhausted finances. They became powerful and affluent under the reign of this prince. In 1290, Edward king of England, banished this people from Gascony, and his other dominions in France.†

A. D. 1300.] The example of the English monarch was followed by Philip the Fair, who published an edict by which all the Jews who refused to profess Christianity were expelled the kingdom, never to return upon pain of death. It is allowed, that this

---

* The city of Montpelier in particular had been frequently in danger of seeing a Jew at the head of the magistracy; upon which account, William IV. lord of it, found himself obliged to forbid it by his last will, as his grandfather had done about fifty years before. —*Modern Universal History*, vol. xiii. p. 317.

† Hume's History of England.

unhappy people were sacrificed to the king's extreme avarice,* for he seized upon all their wealth, and only allowed them money to defray their expenses to the frontiers. Many perished by the way with fatigue and want, and those who survived retired into Germany. Hence the Jews of that country supposed themselves of French extraction. Among those who escaped exile by receiving baptism, many relapsed and returned to Judaism.

The conversion of the celebrated Nicolas de Lyra, however, appears to have been sincere. He wrote a learned treatise against his nation, and spent the remainder of his life in the explanation of the scriptures. Most of the proselytes think themselves obliged to give a testimony of their faith by writing against their deserted brethren; but he is said to have adduced more cogent arguments against them than any Jewish convert before him. He studied some time in the university of Paris, and then entered into the Franciscan order. He died at his convent at Verneuil in the year 1340.†

A. D. 1314.] The same avarice which caused Philip to expel the Jews from France, induced Lewis the Tenth, the succeeding monarch, to recal them. He expected by this measure to recruit his finances, and thus be enabled to reduce the Flemings to subjection. The condition of their return was paying a very heavy tax; and the time of their remaining in the kingdom limited to twelve years. During this period they were at liberty to engage in trade, or support themselves by labour. They were allowed

* Basnage, p. 674.
† Modern Universal History, vol. xiii. p. 321.

to collect their old debts, two thirds of which the
king claimed for himself. They were also permitted
to purchase synagogues, burying-places, and their
books, except the Talmud. But they were now
obliged, as before, to wear a particular mark of
distinction. They were prohibited from lending
money on usurious interest, written obligation, or,
in short, any thing but pledges. They were likewise forbidden to dispute on religion either in public,
or private.*

A. D. 1320.] In the reign of Philip V. surnamed
the Tall, the shepherds and other inhabitants of the
country left their flocks and farms, and asserted, that
they were going to Jerusalem for the relief of the
holy land. With no other weapons than a pilgrim's
staff they marched in great bodies, which were increased by the junction of the populace, which they
met on their way. Their leaders were two profligate
priests, who pretended to work miracles, and thus
imposed upon the credulity of the people. They
ravaged several of the southern provinces, broke
open the prison doors, and enlisted all the criminals
they found into their society. By these means they
made themselves masters of several cities, and committed the vilest outrages and cruelties; but more
particularly against the Jews. This miserable race,
left to the choice of death or baptism, collected their
most valuable effects; and fled before this tumultuous
rabble. A considerable number of them having
taken refuge in the royal castle of Verdun, in the
diocese of Toulouse, were there besieged by the
shepherds. They defended themselves with vigour

* Basnage, p. 674.

R 2

and desperation ; and, finding their arms fail, began
to throw their children over the walls in hopes to
excite the compassion of their enemies ; but in
vain.*

The shepherds set fire to the fortress, and expected
to satiate their rage with the slaughter of the besieged. But the Jews perceiving there was no
means of escape, to avoid falling into the hands of
the enemy, requested one of their brethren, a young
man of great strength, to put them all to death.
The wretch accepted the fatal commission, and after
he had massacred five hundred he presented himself
to the besiegers with a few children, whose lives he
had spared, and demanded baptism. His request,
however, was rejected, and he received the punishment due to his barbarity. At length a great
number of the shepherds were apprehended and
executed at different places, particularly at Toulouse, where they had massacred all the Jews in the
city.†

A. D. 1330.] This miserable people were ten
years after involved in another calamity, pretended
to have been occasioned by their having suffered
themselves to be bribed by the Saracen king of Grenada, to procure the poisoning of all the rivers,
wells, and reservoirs of water. A leper having deposed, that he was hired by a certain rich Jew to
effect this purpose, the people in several provinces,
without waiting for the necessary formality, attacked
the Jews, and put them to the most cruel death.
Some, driven to despair, perished by suicide. At

* Basnage, p. 675. Gifford.
† Basnage. p 664. Gifford, vol. i. p. 550

Paris, however, none but those who were supposed guilty were destroyed. The rich were imprisoned till they would discover their treasures, the greatest part of which the king seized for his own use, and expelled this devoted race from his dominions.*

After the Jews were banished the kingdom by Philip the Tall, they took refuge in Lombardy, and gave to the foreign merchants bills of exchange, drawn upon those to whom they entrusted their effects at parting, and those bills were accepted. Thus " commerce was seen to arise from the bosom of vexation and despair."† It was reserved for an oppressed people to invent a method, by which merchants in regions the most remote from each other could procure the value of their commodities without the inconvenience of transporting gold or silver. In this way the Jews often eluded the violence and rapacity of their enemies; the richest among them frequently having none but invisible effects, which they could convey imperceptibly wherever they pleased. Thus they accelerated their return; for though the princes were willing to banish their persons, they wished to retain their wealth.‡

A. D. 1360.] In the reign of John II. the Jews endeavoured to procure their recall. During the king's captivity§ they had made several proposals

---

* Basnage, p. 675. Gifford, vol. i. p. 139, vol. ii. p. 206.

† Montesquieu's Works, vol. ii. p. 60.

‡ French Encyclo. Gregoire's Observations nouvelles sur les Juifs.

§ King John was taken prisoner in 1356 by the celebrated prince of Wales, surnamed the Black Prince, son of Edward III. of England. The French king had agreed to pay three millions of gold crowns for his ransom. The first payment was to be 600,000 crowns; and as France could not then furnish the money, they were obliged to recall

to the regent, who evinced a disposition to grant
them a favour which they offered to purchase at a
very high price. Soon after his release John published a declaration, by which he permitted them to
return and remain in the kingdom twenty years.
Besides the sum which they advanced for this privilege, every master of a family paid twelve florins of
gold on his entrance into, and six florins yearly for
the liberty of residing in France. A general poll
tax was also levied upon them of one florin per
head. The king strictly prohibited their exorbitant
usury, and permitted them only to take moderate
interest.*

During the reign of Charles VI. the Jews were
accused of murdering a new convert, and other
crimes;† for which some were executed, others
scourged, and fines levied upon the synagogues.
These severities induced many to assume the mask
of Christianity.‡ The people, however, in 1380,
insisted upon their expulsion, and assembled as it is
said at the instigation of certain noblemen, who had
borrowed large sums of this persecuted race, who
though generally considered as the outcasts of society, exerted their industry with success in the
acquisition of wealth. The houses of the public
receivers, most of whom were Jews in Lombardy,
were broke open, the chests in which the money

---

the Jews, and sell them the liberty of trading in France.—*Anderson*,
vol. i. p. 452

* Gifford, vol. ii. p. 269. Basnage, p. 676.

† Charles VI. during his reign, becoming deranged in his intellect,
it was suspected that the Jews deprived him of his reason.—*Gregoire*,
p. 22.

‡ Basnage p. 676.

was deposited were seized, and their contents emp-
tied into the streets ; while the registers, bonds, and
all other securities for money lent, were destroyed.
In one street alone thirty houses were pillaged, and
all the furniture, clothes, plate, and jewels, became
the prey of the populace. The Jews endeavoured
to preserve their lives by flight, but most of them
were intercepted and massacred ; while the few who
escaped; took refuge iu the dungeons of the Chatelet.
The women in despair attempted to follow their
husbands with their children in their arms ; but the
mob forced their children from them, and carried
them to be baptized.*

The government was too weak to inflict on the
insurgents the punishment which their crimes
deserved. The Jews, however, were re-established
in their habitations ; and an order was issued by the
council for every one to restore, under pain of
death, whatever he had taken from them ; but the
order was treated with contempt. These miserable
objects of oppression, after being despoiled of their
property, were exposed to prosecutions from those
who had left pledges in their hands ; but an ordinance was passed to exempt them from the consequences, on taking an oath, that the property which
was the object of the action had been taken from
them during the tumult.†

A. D. 1394.] In the reign of Charles VI. a
council, which was held on the 17th of September,
passed an act for the final expulsion of the Jews
from France. The provost was ordered to super-
intend the execution of the edict, and take an inven-

* Gifford, vol. ii p. 269.   † Ibid

tory of all the effects which could be found in their
houses at the time of their departure. They were
obliged to leave the kingdom in November ; and
from this last exile they begin the date of their
years. The greater part of this persecuted people
retired into Germany. In the city of Metz in Lor-
raine they preserved their ancient privileges,* the
city being at the time of their expulsion a free town
in the imperial territories. After it was annexed to
the French dominions, the king of France continued
to tolerate the Jews who were settled there, and for
a long period it was the only place in the kingdom
where they enjoyed a privileged abode.†

Respecting the repeated accusations brought
against the Jews, of crucifying Christian children,
poisoning the rivers, &c. a late author observes, " In
the dark periods of the middle ages‡ the Jews,
punished but in the most dreadful manner for real
crimes, suffered oftener for crimes merely chimerical.
The relations of their sacrificing Christian children
are given by Christian historians. But even granting, that rage, madness, or a desire of revenge, may

* The Jews were established at Metz as early as the year 888,
since at that epoch Gombert the dean brought some complaints
against them. Sigebert de Gemblours taught in this city in the
twelfth century with such success, that they eagerly resorted to hear
his instructions.—*Gregoire on the Reformation of the Jews*, p. 283.

† Basnage, p. 676. Gifford, vol. ii. p. 344.

‡ The middle age, as it is called, is considered as terminating at
the taking of Constantinople in the fifteenth century. Its commencement is not so well fixed by historians, some carrying it back even to
the reign of Constantine, and some only to the division of the empire
under Theodosius. The middle age contains a period of about one
thousand years. The term dark age is sometimes used to express the
ninth, tenth, and eleventh centuries, which were the most barbarous
portions of this dark period.

have induced some fanatics to commit these excesses, are we to consider the whole nation as culpable ?

" The poisoning of fountains, by bundles of herbs, or noxious mixtures, forms an accusation much more absurd ; for in order to commit crimes, people must be actuated by some motives, and the hopes of success. . But what success could the Jews expect in poisoning the springs, which were constantly renewed, and from which they themselves daily drew water. Ask the physicians, if, at a time when chemistry was only in its infancy, a poison was known sufficiently active to produce that effect. Can we allow ourselves to be persuaded, that the Jews, who were so much interested in living upon good terms with other nations, should attempt crimes, the execution of which was evidently impossible ; and which they must naturally expect would provoke new persecutions ?"*

It ought, however, to be remembered, that the cruelty of professed Christians to the Jews in the dark ages is no argument against the truth of that sacred religion, the genuine spirit of which breathes " peace on earth and good will to men." This spirit was exemplified in the primitive Christians, the apostles, and martyrs, and more especially in their Lord and Saviour Jesus Christ, who prayed for his persecutors, saying, " Father, forgive them, for they know not what they do."†

* Gregoire on the Reformation of the Jews, p. 26.—According to Basnage most of these accusations against the Jews were the reports of their inveterate enemies, who continually sought their destruction, p. 644.

† See Letters of certain Jews to Voltaire.

CHAPTER XVIII.

The Jews in Spain are persecuted by the bishop of Toledo.—They are
massacred by the Crusaders.—Raymond de Penneforte attempts to
convert them.—They are favoured by Alphonso X. and James I.
king of Arragon.—They are deluded by an impostor, who predicted
the appearance of the Messiah.—Irruption of the shepherds.—The
pestilence spreads from their army.—The Jews are accused of poisoning the rivers.—They are favoured by Alphonso XI.—Their
enemies conspire to destroy them.—Fresh insurrections at Toledo.
—Many Jews perish by suicide.—Of the persecutions they suffered
at Castile and Arragon in the latter part of the fourteenth century.
—Pope Benedict appoints a conference between them and the Christians.—A large number of Jews profess Christianity.—Of the pretended conversions by Vincent Ferrier.—Cruelty of the inquisition.
—They are banished from Spain.—Terrible distress of the refugees.
—They are received into, and soon after expelled from Portugal.

A. D. 1209.]   THE sufferings of the Jews in
Spain, were equally severe with those of their brethren in England and France.   At the commencement of the thirteenth century, the bishop of Toledo
perceiving them to increase in number and wealth
excited the populace against them, and, putting
himself at their head, entered and plundered their
houses and synagogues.   He endeavoured to vindicate his conduct by accusing the Hebrews of having
betrayed the city when it was besieged by the Moors;
but the silence of impartial historians exculpated
them from the charge.*

A. D 1212.]   The Crusaders, who soon after
assembled near Toledo, completed the work of destruction which the bigoted prelate had begun.   They
prescribed no limits to their cruelty, but made such

* Basnage, p. 659.

havock and carnage 'among this miserable people, that Abarbanel, a celebrated Jewish writer, considered this as one of the most severe and bloody persecutions which his nation ever suffered, and that it caused a greater number to abandon Spain than Moses conducted out of Egypt. The Spanish nobles endeavoured to interpose their authority, and to suppress these cruelties. But Ferdinand, who then possessed the sovereign power, and wished to ingratiate himself with the populace by the extirpation of the Albigenses and other sects, encouraged and promoted the persecution.*

A. D. 1250.] During the reign of James I. king of Arragon, who was distinguished for his zeal for Christianity, great efforts were made to convert the Jews. Raymond de Penneforte,† general of the Dominicans, confessor to the king and minister to the pope, used energetic measures to effect this purpose. He had already, by his reputation and address, suppressed the violence of the populace against this unhappy people; and persuaded the king that mildness and instruction were the most effectual means to induce them to embrace Christianity. Agreeably to his benevolent plan, several of the Dominican friars were chosen to learn the Hebrew and Arabic languages, and directed to apply themselves assiduously to the study of the scriptures, that they might be enabled to dispute with the Jewish rabbies in order to convince them of their errors. The attempts made to convert the Jews were, however, in general unsuccessful; though they highly

* Basnage, p. 670.
† Raymond was canonized by pope Clement VIII.

esteemed Raymond for his singular humanity and
moderation.*

A. D. 1255.] Alphonso X. king of Castile, and
a celebrated astronomer, encouraged and promoted
learned men of all religious denominations. By his
order Judah de Toledo translated and improved the
astronomical works of Avicenna, a learned Arabic
writer. Isaac, the son of Cid, and other rabbies,
assisted him in compiling certain astronomical tables,
which bear the name of the king, and do honour to
his memory.†

Alphonso rewarded them with royal munificence,
and became so generous a patron to the nation, that
the jealousy of the Zealots was excited, and they
formed new plots and accusations against them. Three
villains of the city of Orsana, in Andalusia, threw the
dead body of a man into the house of a Jew, and
accused him of the murder. This improbable assertion gained credit, and awakened the popular
fury and hatred against them. A great number of
Jews were inhumanly put to death, and others fled
for refuge to the houses of their Christian acquaintance. The inhabitants of Palma also rose, and
destroyed many of this unhappy people. Upon this

* Raymond Martin, another Dominican, wrote a treatise against
the Jews, called " Pugio Fidei," or the " Poniard of Faith." This
work is considered as a learned and powerful defence of the Christian
religion against the arguments of the Jews. Another monk, named
Paul, of the same order, held a conference in the palace of the king
with Moses Nachmanides, a famous cabbalistical Jew. Both sides
claimed the victory. Paul obtained an edict from king Ferdinand,
enjoining the Jews to open their houses and synagogues to him,
and to furnish him with all their Hebrew books whenever he came to
dispute with them.—*Basnage*, p. 660.

† Modern Universal History, vol. xiii. p. 304.

they sent a deputation to court to obtain the suppression of a massacre which was so likely to prove general. Their enemies also sent deputies on their part, who arrived first at court, and accused them. Joseph, however, who was at the head of the deputation, and chief of the Jewish council, was so eloquent in pleading his cause before the Spanish monarch, that his countrymen were acquitted of the pretended murder.*

Many learned men appeared among the Jews during the time that they enjoyed the favour of the king Alphonso. In this number, Meir Mithridos, a native of Toledo, was eminently distinguished. He was the author of a famous cabbalistical work, and a volume of letters against Nachmanides and Maimonides, and educated many pupils who became the boast of the Jewish nation.

Nor was it only at the court of Castile that learned rabbies appeared and were respected. James I. king of Arragon, was so far from adopting the prejudices against them, that he applied to them for moral and religious instruction.† For, though the Jewish people were hated and despised by the populace, and by the ignorant among the clergy, they were at this time admired and encouraged by the great and learned.

A. D. 1258.] Their happiness was, however, soon after disturbed by a celebrated impostor named Zechariah, who formed the design of deceiving all the

* Basnage, p. 663.

† The king, it is said, expressed an approbation of some parts of the Jewish prayer books. The clergy in this age applied themselves rather to controversy than devotion. *Modern Universal History*, vol. xiii. p. 307.

synagogues in Spain. He pretended, that by his knowledge of the prophecies he had discovered the exact time of the appearance of the Messiah, which he predicted to be just at hand. This impostor even foretold the very day on which this mighty deliverer was to appear, who should gather together his elect people; subdue their enemies, and replace them in their ancient inheritance. Deceived by this prophecy and expectation of the Messiah, the Jews prepared themselves for the event by fasting and prayer, and at the time appointed repaired to the synagogues clothed in white. But discovering the imposture, they became ashamed of their blind credulity, and were exposed to the insults and derision of their enemies.*

A. D. 1320.] But the most terrible calamity which they suffered during this period was by the body of shepherds who had committed such fatal ravages in France. Having become numerous and powerful they entered Spain, and carried fire and sword into several provinces. The Jews, in particular, were the victims of their rapacity and cruelty. Many preserved their lives by surrendering their property and renouncing their religion. Those who could not be induced to make these sacrifices were instantly and inhumanly put to death.†

The pestilence which arose in the army of the shepherds, and extended through the neighbouring countries, was productive of new evils to this unhappy people. The desolation occasioned by this destructive scourge, was attributed to their malice

---

* Basnage, p. 664. Modern Universal History, vol. xiii.
† Basnage, p. 664.

against the Christians., They were accused of having bribed the peasants of Mesura to poison the rivers, and of having furnished them with poison for that purpose. This absurd allegation* gained credit, and caused great numbers of Jews to be imprisoned and tried. After a long confinement, however, they acquitted themselves of the crimes laid to their charge. But the king, who was unwilling to confess and condemn the injustice of his conduct, pretended that he detained them in prison in order to effect their conversion; and caused fifteen thousand who refused to receive baptism to be put to a cruel death.

A. D. 1333.] Alphonso XI. king of Castile, was the friend and protector of the Jews, being principally directed in his affairs by Joseph, one of the nation, whom he had appointed intendant of his finances. This monarch was, however, prevailed upon by his mutinous and discontented subjects to pass a decree against them, on account of a pretended indignity offered to the sacrament by a Jewish boy. The clamour of the populace was so violent, that a council was convened to deliberate whether they should be put to death or banished. The latter measure being preferred, they were commanded to abandon the kingdom in three months. Happily for them, the prince royal obtained a revisal of the process, by which it appeared, that a young Christian had inadvertently committed the supposed crime. On this deposition, the king

* The inventors of this palpable calumny were those who owed money to the Jews, and who wished to be delivered from their embarrassment without paying it.—*Gregoire*, p. 23.

recalled his edict. The acquittal of the Jews highly
mortified and exasperated their enemies, who asserted, that the Christian had been bribed to give an
evidence in their favour. In another city many of the
nation were put to death for the pretended offence.*

A. D. 1349.] Soon after, a fresh insurrection
against the Jews broke out in Toledo, and their
terror and desperation on this occasion baffles all
description. One of them, perceiving the Zealots
breaking into the house in order to massacre all they
found, in a phrenzy of rage and despair killed his
relations who had taken refuge with him, and then
destroyed himself in order to avoid falling into the
hands of his enemies.†

A. D. 1396.] In the reign of Henry III. of
Castile, Martin, archdeacon of Astigi, by vehemently preaching against the Jews through the
streets of Seville and Cordova, exasperated the
populace to such a degree, that they massacred
them in both places. The persecution spread to
Toledo, Valencia, and Barcelona, where some were
plundered, others murdered, while the most artful
professed Christianity in order to escape such acts of
violence. The populous synagogues of Seville and
Cordova became almost deserted. These wretched
fugitives, who had fled to Andalusia and other provinces, were put to death by the inhabitants. King
John, the son and successor of Henry, treated the
Jews with equal cruelty. During his reign, many
perished by being deprived of the necessaries of life,
and those who survived were compelled to wear a
disgraceful mark of distinction.‡

* Basnage, p. 665.   † Basnage, p. 667.   ‡ Ibid.

..The situation of the Jews in Arragon was not much more eligible than that of·their brethren in Castile. ·That kingdom was,involved in civil,and intestine wars, which could· only;be supported by large·imposts. The heaviest taxes were levied upon a people who had been so long,the miserable objects of oppression. ~But though:they, were exposed to continual vexations and persecutions, several learned men, during·the fourteenth century, appeared among those in Spain. In particular, two physicians* of the Castilian king acquired·great celebrity., One of these famous men,,named Meir Algudes, was chief of· all the synagogues ·in Spain.~ He translated Aristotle's ,Ethics, and flourished till the year 1405.†

,,A. D. 1412.] At the commencement of the fifteenth century, the antipope Benedict; XIII. who was! then: in Arragon, distinguished himself by·his zeal·for the conversion of. the Jews. To effect·this purpose, ,he summoned the most celebrated rabbies in Spain to attend a·conference which he appointed for religious,discussions between them and the Christians.· Jerome de Sancta Fide,,who had deserted the synagogue and embraced Christianity, persuaded the pope to take this step, by assuring him that he could convince his countrymen, by passages out of the Talmud, that Jesus Christ was the Messiah. This convert was not only the chief promoter, but the principal conductor of the dispute. Rabbi Vidal

---

* The learned Dr. Friend in his History of Medicine asserts, that the Jews were the princes of that science in Europe .during the middle ages.—*Gregoire*, p. 218.

† Basnage, p. 680.

was chosen to defend the Jewish religion. The
Jews at this time expressed unusual respect for the
pope, who entertained them with politeness, and
defrayed their expences.* But they treated Jerome
with great asperity, their minds being exceedingly
embittered against him, both for deserting the synagogue, and involving them in a dispute from which
they apprehended fatal consequences.†

The tenour and result of this famous conference
is variously related by Christian and Jewish historians. The latter, however, confess that they
bribed several bishops to persuade Benedict to break
off the dispute, from an apprehension that it would
exasperate their enemies against them. But the
pope insisted upon Jerome's performing his engagement; and four or five thousand Jews were converted upon reading his relation of the conference,
which he presented to this pontiff. The high
celebrity of this performance induced Joseph Albo,‡
a Spanish rabbi, to compile his articles of faith, in
order to confirm the wavering minds of his brethren.
He pretended, that a belief of the future coming of
the Messiah was not necessary to salvation; and
censured Maimonides, without naming him, for
having made this an essential part of his creed. He

* They, it is said, even carried their impious flattery so far as to
apply to him the words of David's petition to God; " Shew us thy
mercy, O Lord, and grant us thy salvation."—*Basnage*, p. 680.

† Basnage, p 680. Modern Univer. Hist. vol xiii.

‡ This rabbi, finding the arguments which were adduced to prove
that the Messiah was come made a great impression upon the Jews,
maintained, that a belief of his coming was not an essential article
of faith, and wished to have it expunged from the creed of Maimonides.—*Basnage*, p. 344

reduced the fundamental dogmas of the Jewish faith to three, viz. the existence of God, the law of Moses, and future rewards and punishments.*

A. D. 1413.] The following year Benedict XIII. published his constitution against the Talmud, and the usury of the Jews. But, as he was deposed soon after, all his ordinances were revoked; and it does not appear that his plans were followed by Martin of Florence his successor.

A. D. 1413.] Vincent Ferrier, who has been canonized for his miracles and zeal for converting the Jews, appeared at this time. The Christians compute, that the number whom he induced to abandon their religion amounted to twenty-five thousand. According to the Jewish accounts still more deserted the synagogues. But whatever was their number, it appears that the greatest part of them renounced their former religion, merely to avoid severe and cruel treatment. They secretly circumcised their children, observed the passover, and neglected none of the Jewish rites and ceremonies.†

The dissimulation of the pretended converts did not long pass unnoticed by the clergy, who acquainted Ferdinand, the Spanish monarch, and the pope Sixtus IV. with their conduct. Exasperated

---

* Addison's Present State of the Jews, p. 17.

† Basnage, p. 689. Modern Universal History, vol. xiii. p. 347. —A small number of Jews were, however, esteemed sincere converts; among whom Solomon, the son of Levi, was included. Having read a work of Thomas Aquinas, he embraced Christianity, and took the name of Paul of Burgos. Soon after his baptism he was raised to the bishopric of that city, which was his native place, and afterwards to the patriarchate of Aquileia. He left a son who succeeded him in the bishopric, and wrote a history of Spain.—*Basnage*, p. 690.

at the affront offered to the Christian religion, the
tribunal of the inquisition* was directed to pay close
attention to the behaviour of these delinquents ; and
all Christian princes were exhorted to assist in
bringing them to condign punishment. This decree, which was published in most parts of Spain,
filled the Jews with such consternation, that seventeen thousand immediately returned to the church,
and submitted themselves to whatever censure or
penance should be inflicted. Two thousand of this
miserable people, part of whom confessed that Jesus
Christ was the true Messiah, were put to death.
Many were sentenced to a long imprisonment, and,
after regaining their liberty, were ordered to wear
two red crosses on their upper garments, in acknowledgment that they had deserved the flames.
Nor were the sacred repositories of the dead spared ;
human bodies were disinterred and burned ; their
property was confiscated, and their children were
declared incapable of succeeding to the possessions
of their parents. Notwithstanding the watchfulness
of the inquisition, many found means to emigrate ;
others were more careful to conceal their dissimu-

---

* The court of the inquisition was introduced into Spain in the
fifteenth century by Ferdinand and Isabella ; and was principally
intended to prevent the relapse of the Jews and Moors, who had
been, or pretended to be, converted to the faith of the church of
Rome. Torquemade, a Dominican, confessor to queen Isabella, pretended that the dissimulation of the Jews would greatly injure the
cause of religion The queen listened with respectful deference to
her confessor, and at length gained over the king to consent to the
establishment of this barbarous tribunal. Its jurisdiction extended
over all who in their practice or opinions differed from the established
church.—*Watson's History of the Reign of Philip II.* vol. ii.
p. 134, 135.

lation ; and some endeavoured to be better instructed previously to their professing Christianity.*

A. D. 1445.] The populace still continued to oppress and insult this unhappy people, and attributed all the public calamities to the obstinacy of the recusant, or the hypocrisy of the conforming Jews. At this time an insurrection of the inhabitants of Toledo took place, on account of a pretended infringement on their privileges. The resentment of a mutinous people was principally levelled against the Jews, whose houses they plundered, and murdered all who opposed them. After the tumult subsided, laws were enacted which excluded the new converts from all offices of trust and honour.

The Spanish clergy, however, took them under their protection. The dean of the cathedral church in the city particularly exerted all his eloquence in their favour, and endeavoured to interest the feelings of the people by representing, that many illustrious families, who had intermarried† with the converted Jews, would be deprived of all their employments by the execution of these laws. All his efforts would have proved ineffectual, had not pope Nicolas I. published a bull, by which he excommunicated all who were for excluding the Jewish or Pagan proselytes from any civil or ecclesiastical preferment. This decree of the sovereign pontiff

* Basnage, p. 691. Modern Univer. Hist.

† A number of the Grandees, who had nothing left but their titles, had married into Jewish families in order to repair the losses they had sustained by their prodigality.—*Voltaire's Works,* vol. iii. p. 33.

was so displeasing to the Spanish nation, that he
was obliged to issue a second bull to confirm it; and
Mariana is almost the only Spanish writer who has
given it a place in his history.*

A. D. 1492.] Soon after Ferdinand and Isabella
had completed their reduction of the Moors, they
issued an edict, commanding the Jews either to
embrace Christianity, or quit the kingdom in four
months. The people were at the same time prohibited, under the severest penalties, from affording
provisions or any other assistance to those who should
be found in Spain after this period. Their attachment to the law of Moses was superior to every other
consideration; and the Spanish historians affirm,
that eight hundred thousand persons abandoned
the kingdom pursuant to this decree. The Jewish
writers make the number two hundred thousand
families; which, reckoning only five to each family,
must have amounted to a million of souls.†

The reputation which the celebrated rabbi Isaac
Abarbanel enjoyed at court, could not prevent his
being included among the exiles.‡ He was born at
Lisbon, 1437, of an ancient family, who boasted
a lineal descent from king David.§ His parents took

---

* Mariana's History of Spain. Basnage, p. 691.   † Ibid.

‡ Rabbi Isaac Karo was another learned exile. He retired first to
Portugal, and thence to Jerusalem. He lived a perfect recluse in this
city, and devoted himself to study. He composed a Commentary on
the Pentateuch, partly cabbalistical and partly literal.—*Modern
Universal History.*

§ He founded his pretensions on the testimony of Isaac Aben Geath,
who says in one of his commentaries on the scriptures, that at the
time of the destruction of the first temple, two families of the race
of David went into Spain; one of whom settled at Lucena, the other
at Seville; and that from the latter Abarbanel was descended. After

great care of his education, and, as he possessed distinguished abilities, he made a rapid progress in the sciences, especially sacred literature. But his ambition to figure at court induced him to turn his chief attention to politics, finance, and commerce.

During the reign of Alphonso V. king of Portugal, he was chosen one of his privy council, and 'filled his station with dignity and splendour till the death of this monarch. But being discarded in the reign of his successor, who hated the Jews, he fled to Castile. He was graciously received by Ferdinand and Isabella, and advanced to preferments, which he enjoyed until his countrymen were expelled from Spain. He exerted himself to the utmost to save himself and his nation from this fatal stroke. But finding all his efforts useless, he embarked for Naples, and arrived there with his family in 1493. Being educated a courtier, he ingratiated himself with Ferdinand, king of Naples; and both that sovereign and Alphonso his successor protected and employed him. He died at Venice, 1508, in the seventy-first year of his age, and was interred at Padua. Several of the Venetian nobles, and all the Jews, attended his funeral. He published many learned works,* particularly a commentary on Exodus, Deuteronomy, Kings, Isaiah, Jeremiah, and other books of the Old Testament.†

---

the example of his father he assumed the title of Don, the usual custom among the nobles of Spain.—*Boissi Dissertations Critiques pour servir a l'histoire des Juifs.*

* Basnage. p. 692 De Rossie's Hebrew Biography.

† He applied himself to study with indefatigable ardour, and was held in such high estimation among the Jews, that some did not hesitate to pronounce him superior to Maimonides. They agree, that

The sufferings of the Jewish emigrants who embarked for other countries were inexpressible and almost inconceivable. Some of the vessels took fire; and the miserable objects of oppression perished in the flames. Others were so heavily laden that they sunk; and many were drowned. Great numbers were shipwrecked on foreign coasts; and perished with cold and hunger. One of the Spanish pilots formed the resolution of murdering all the Jews in his vessel, in order, as he pretended, to revenge the death of Christ, whom their ancestors had crucified. They represented to him that Christ, " who died for the redemption of mankind, did not desire the death but the salvation of the sinner." The sailor in consequence of this pathetic remonstrance gave up the design of murdering them; but caused them to be stripped naked, and set down on the next shore, where part of them perished with hunger; others were destroyed by lions who came out of a neighbouring cavern. The remainder were saved by the humanity of a master of a vessel, who took them in upon seeing their miserable condition.*

The pestilence also destroyed many of these unfortunate exiles; and, to complete their calamities, those who reached the city of Fez in Africa, were refused admittance by the merciless inhabitants, and died for want of the necessaries of life. When those who sailed for Italy arrived at Genoa, they found the city afflicted by a famine, which had greatly raised

---

to a mind clear and penetrating he added a lively and fertile imagination, which was exhibited in his easy and copious elocution.—*Dissertations Critiques, &c.*

* Basnage, p. 693.

the price of provisions. The inhabitants, seeing them macerated by sufferings, and destitute of money to purchase food, met them with the cross in one hand and bread in the other ; and refused to give sustenance to any who would not previously consent to adore the cross. Many of this wretched people, who had the courage to abandon their country and riches for their religion, were unable to resist this second temptation.*

The tyrannical manner, in which the bigotry and avarice of king Ferdinand had induced him to treat the Jews, was highly condemned by all judicious Christians. This unhappy race, upon the first notice of their intended expulsion, had found means to elude the vigilant rapacity of the monarch, and convey the richest of their effects into the countries where they intended to retire. In consequence of which, the wealth acquired by their expulsion was not so considerable as the king expected. The Spanish nobility complained that their cities and towns were disinhabited. The senate of Venice and the parliament of Paris expressed their astonishment at the banishment of a nation, whose address in pecuniary negociation was so useful to the public.†
Though pope Alexander VI. dignified the Spanish monarch with the title of *Catholic,* yet he readily received the exiles into his own dominions, and treated them with great kindness and humanity.‡

---

* Basnage, p 692.

† The expulsion of the Jews gave a violent check to the commerce of Spain, which was almost entirely in their hands.—*Bigland's View of the World.*

‡ Basnage, p. 693.

Many of the Jews sought a nearer asylum in Portugal. John II.* the sovereign of that kingdom, had formerly sent some of this nation† to make discoveries on the coasts of the Red Sea; and they brought him exact and faithful accounts. They had assisted the Portuguese adventurers in the discovery of the East Indies. Notwithstanding these important services, the king consented to receive them only on condition that each one should pay him eight golden ducats, and quit his dominions at a limited time, or forfeit his liberty. On his part he engaged, when the time fixed for their departure arrived, to furnish vessels to transport them to any place where they chose to retire. The king was desirous of fulfilling his engagement; but his orders were disregarded, and the fugitives, who were about to leave Portugal, were treated in such a barbarous manner by the seamen, that many chose to remain in the kingdom and be sold as slaves, rather than expose themselves to the perils and hardships of a new voyage.‡

Emanuel, his successor, appeared at first to commiserate their sufferings, and restored to them their liberty. Their peace, however, was of short duration; and the king reluctantly sacrificed them to an alliance which he contracted with the daughter of Ferdinand and Isabella. The queen having declared, that " she would not acknowledge a son-in-law who permitted the enemies of God to remain in

---

* In the reign of John I. the Jews had their synagogues and rabbies in Portugal.

† Murphy's Travels in Portugal, p. 223.

‡ Basnage, p. 694. Murphy's Travels in Portugal, p. 224.

his dominions," he issued an edict which expelled them from Portugal, and fixed a day on which those who remained should be deprived of their liberty.

When the appointed time arrived, the king was greatly affected with the idea of expelling such multitudes of people; and resolved at least to effect the conversion of their children. He had engaged that ships should be provided for their emigration at three principal ports; but he issued a proclamation forbidding them to embark any where but at Lisbon. When they arrived at this city, he ordered all the children under fourteen years of age to be forcibly taken from their parents, in order to be educated in the Christian faith. The execution of this barbarous command was attended with the most affecting circumstances. Many of the wretched parents, in a phrenzy of rage and despair, first killed their children, and then destroyed themselves. The king had invented so many delays to retard the departure of these unfortunate exiles, that many remained in the kingdom, and were sold as slaves. Overwhelmed with these complicated afflictions, at length they consented to assume the mask of Christianity, and recovered their liberty and children. The sincerity of these pretended converts was, however, greatly suspected, and the least discovery of their predilection for the Mosaic religion exposed them to the cruelties of the merciless inquisition.*

* Murphy's Travels in Portugal, p. 699.

CHAPTER XIX.

The Jews in Germany are accused of various crimes.—They endeavour to hinder the conversion of, a young man of their nation at Frankfort.—Part of the city is burned, and a number of Jews destroyed.—Accusation against those of Haguenau.—They are massacred at Bavaria and Bern.—Of several learned rabbies.—The Jews flourish at Lithuania in the thirteenth century.—Decrees enacted against them in the council of Vienna.—A regulation made at Augsburg respecting the oaths to be administered to them.—Disputes between the Rabbinists' and Caraites.—Raind Fleisch excites the people in various parts of Germany, to massacre the Jews.—They are protected by the bishop of Spires.—They are murdered by the Flagellants.—Persecution against them on pretence of their poisoning the rivers.—Cruelties practised against those of Bohemia.—They are accused again of poisoning the rivers, and banished the empire. —They are persecuted in various parts during the thirteenth century.

A. D. 1222.] THE Jews have been more frequently accused of enormous crimes in Germany than in any other part of Europe. When the Persians and Tartars made incursions into this country, they were charged with favouring and assisting these enterprizes, in hopes of being delivered from the persecutions which they suffered from the Christians. They were, probably, more justly accused the same year of opposing the conversion of a young man of their nation at Frankfort who was desirous of receiving baptism.* The people were incensed at this opposition, and arms were seized on both sides. Several Christians lost their lives; and about one hundred and eighty Jews perished by the sword, or the fire they had kindled. One half of the city was consumed; and the most prudent among them were

* Basnage, p. 682.

induced to profess Christianity, to avoid being sacrificed to the resentment of the multitude.*

A. D. 1241.] The Jews in Germany were frequently accused of murdering Christian children at their passover. The first instance which occurs was at Haguenau in Lower Alsatia, where three of them were found dead in a Jewish house. Complaint was made to the emperor Frederic II. who, not being inclined to believe the report, coldly replied, " that since the children were dead, they must be buried." This instance of his incredulity exasperated the people ; but as they were unable to prove the alleged crime, the Jews, upon paying a considerable sum, obtained a favourable judgment from the emperor.†

A. D. 1286.] About this time those of Munich in Bavaria suffered a severe calamity. An old woman having confessed that she sold them a child, whom they murdered, the people, without waiting the event of a trial, put to death all of this miserable race whom they could find. The town officers, after attempting in vain to suppress the tumult, advised the Jews to retire into their synagogue, which was a strong stone building. They complied ; but notwithstanding great efforts were made by the duke and the officers to appease and disperse the multitude, they were all burned and destroyed in it.‡ An accusation of a similar nature was brought

---

* The fervour of the Jews is singularly inclined to fanaticism ; and they are highly incensed when one of their members abjures his religion This is in consequence of a principle imputed to Maimonides, that those who abandon Judaism ought to be persecuted to hell. —*Gregoire*, p. 84.

† Basnage, p. 683.   ‡ Ibid.

against those of Wurtzburg and Bern, where they were massacred in the same manner.

Notwithstanding these persecutions, the Jews in Germany boast of the learned rabbies who appeared in the thirteenth century, particularly Baruc and Eliezer de Germeciman, both of whom were famous cabbalists ; and the latter wrote a celebrated treatise, called, " The Mantle of the Lord." Meir de Rottemburgh was also distinguished for his learning, and became the judge and chief doctor of his German brethren.*

The Jews flourished in Lithuania during the thirteenth century. King Boleslaus granted them liberty of conscience and other privileges, which they preserved under his successors. Their prosperity excited the envy of the populace, who endeavoured to disturb their peace, and blast their reputation. It was observed in the council of Vienna, which was convened in 1267, that they were become so numerous and powerful that the income of the clergy was considerably diminished. It was, therefore, ordained that they should reimburse them, in proportion to what they might have considered themselves entitled, had their families been Christian. The council also enacted, that they should be compelled to demolish the new and superb synagogues which they had erected, and be contented with their former places of worship. These decrees, however, proved abortive ; for the German princes and nobles protected those who refused to obey ; and even obliged their officers to afford shelter to the unhappy victims who implored their assistance.

* Basnage, p. 684.

The clergy were, therefore, necessitated to pursue more violent measures, and excommunicated all who favoured and defended the Jews.*

A new regulation was made at Augsburg upon observing that they did not consider it a crime to violate their oaths. Previously to this time they had been compelled to swear by the saints, by the blessed Mary, or even by the Son of God. But, as they made no scruple to violate these oaths, they were obliged to swear by the name of God, and the law of Moses. Yet they supposed even these solemn engagements were annulled on the great day of expiation; and could, therefore, be of force for only one year. It is also said, that a number of their casuists authorize deception, equivocation, mental restriction, and hypocrisy.† According to a concession of the Talmud, it is lawful to dissemble for the sake of peace.‡

A. D. 1285.] About this time the disputes between the Rabbinists§ and Caraites were conducted with great violence. Aaron Cohen, a rabbi of great learning, who was the head of the latter sect, wrote a treatise to expose the absurdities of the Talmud. He explained their articles of faith, and styled his work, " The Tree of Life," because he supposed a belief of their dogmas necessary in order to attain eternal salvation. Though he acknowledged a resurrection, he confined it only to the true believers of the house of Israel. But notwithstanding his attempt to lessen the attachment which the Caraites

* Basnage, p. 684.   Modern Univer. Hist. vol. xiii. p. 337.
† Gregoire, p. 81.   ‡ Modern Univer. Hist. vol xiii p. 338.
§ The Rabbinists are modern Pharisees.

began to discover to tradition, rabbi Nissi, another famous doctor of this sect, was obliged at the earnest request of his pupils, to explain the Misna. Even Aaron was at length induced to give an allegorical explication of several passages of scripture. But though this relaxation in the tenets of their opponents gratified the Rabbinists,* the hatred between the two sects continued with unabated violence.†

A. D. 1264.] During the contest between Adolphus of Nassau and Albert of Austria, each of whom had been elected emperor, a fanatical peasant, named Raind Fleisch, taking advantage of the wars which raged in Germany, commenced an itinerant preacher in the Upper Palatinate, Franconia, and other provinces. He pretended that God had sent him to exterminate the Jews ; and, in order to exasperate the people against them, asserted that they had stolen a consecrated host. The credulous multitude, without further enquiry, immediately seized upon those in Nuremberg, Rottemberg, and several other towns in Franconia and Bavaria, and put them to death. Others chose rather to destroy themselves, with their wives, children, and effects, than to be thrown into the flames by their enemies. Albert would gladly have suppressed this barbarous massacre ; but he was afraid that Raind Fleisch, who was regarded as a messenger from God, would

---

* Basnage, p. 685
† The hatred between these sects is carried so far, that the Rabbinists assert, that if a Caraite and a Christian happen to be in danger of drowning together, they ought to make a bridge of the body of the Caraite, in order to save the Christian.—*Gregoire*, p 86.

persuade the people to favour and join his, competitor. The persecution was at length stopped, and the city of Nuremberg laid under a heavy fine, besides being half consumed by the fire which the miserable Jews had set to their houses.*

A. D. 1339.] The council, which pope Clement V. convened at Vienna against the Templars, condemned the usury of the Jews, and decreed that those who favoured them should be considered as heretics. This edict involved them in vexatious lawsuits and other misfortunes. They were, however, in some measure, relieved by Menicho, bishop of Spires, who forbade them to be molested on that account, in his dominions; and alleged, that the law could not concern them, seeing the church does not judge those that are without. A few years after, Lewis I. king of Hungary, banished them from all his dominions.†

A. D. 1349.] The Flagellants, who arose in the fourteenth century, and derived their name from the cruel scourges which they inflicted upon their own persons, supposed that murdering the enemies of Christ would render their penance more acceptable.‡ Accordingly they plundered and burnt the Jews at Spires, Strasburg, and Thuringen But, after committing some outrages at

---

* Basnage, p. 685. Modern Univer. Hist. vol. xiii. p. 340.

† Basnage, p. 686.

‡ It has been asserted, that before these fanatics began their penance, they read their commission with an audible voice, which was comprised in a letter sent to them by the Almighty himself, and delivered to them by an angel, with express command to scourge themselves and massacre the Jews —*Picart's Religious Ceremonies of the Jews*, p. 172.

T

Frankfort, they agreed to an accommodation.   A
Jew named Cicogne, whose family was numerous in
that city, being dissatisfied with the compromise,
threw fire into the town house, which consumed the
building, and all the records preserved in it.   The
flames spread to the cathedral, which was reduced
to ashes.   This crime was severely punished; for
not only the incendiary, but all his brethren in
Frankfort, a few excepted who retired into Bohemia, were put to death.*

In the course of the same year the Jews were
accused of poisoning the rivers, wells, and reservoirs of water.   They were suspected of this crime
upon no other foundation, than that they had
escaped the common mortality which took place in
most parts of Europe.   A suspicion being sufficient
to condemn them, a new massacre ensued in several
provinces of Germany, in which some were burned,
and others cruelly slaughtered.   Those of Metz,
however, resolved to defend themselves; and having
seized about two hundred unarmed Christians, put
them to death in a barbarous manner.   The incensed populace collected, furiously attacked, and
killed twelve thousand Jews.   They next set fire to
their houses, which spread and raged so vehemently,
that the great bell and glass in the cathedral church
were melted down.   The persecution of this miserable people extended over all Germany.   In the
imperial cities all their houses were demolished, and
castles and towers built with the materials.†

Robert, the reigning count Palatine, and his
ministers, endeavoured in vain to suppress the

---

* Basnage, p. 686   † Ibid

tumult and afford an asylum to an injured race, whose innocence was acknowledged by honest men. But they were opposed by some of the nobility; and the populace accused them of accepting bribes to defend the enemies of Christ. All the Jewish inhabitants of Ulm, together with their property and effects, were burned ; their wretched brethren who survived in those parts were without friends or a place of refuge, the princes not daring, at so critical a time, to interpose in their behalf.

At Lithuania, however, they met with more equitable treatment. Casimire the Great, being enamoured with a beautiful Jewess, named Esther, had, at her request, granted them several considerable privileges.*

A. D. 1391.] Those Jews who had fled for refuge to Bohemia, were not better treated than their brethren in Germany. Winceslaus,† the emperor and king of Bohemia, equally discharged the cities and nobility from the debts they owed to these miserable objects of persecution. The people, therefore, considering them abandoned by, that prince, attacked them at Gotha, and a terrible carnage ensued. The Jews of Spires, without distinction of age or sex, were all put to death, except a few children, who were hurried to the font to be baptized. As a pretence for this cruelty, they were accused of insulting a priest as he was carrying the sacrament to a sick person. The citizens of Prague,

---

* Basnage, p. 686

† This prince, having rendered himself odious to his people by his intemperance and other vices, sought to regain their favour by his severity to the Jews.

irritated at seeing them celebrate their passover,
chose that time to burn their synagogue, and those
who there engaged in devotional exercises. This
inhuman deed was executed without any opposition,
and not one of them escaped.* · .

Soon after, they were again accused of poisoning
the rivers and springs, and punished for this pretended crime. The persecution was not confined to
Germany, but extended to Italy, Provence, and
other parts. The Jewish historians assert, that the
emperor was convinced of their innocence, and
represented to his council, that it was impossible for
them to be guilty of this offence, as the rivers and
springs, which have a free and unrestrained course,
cannot be contaminated by poison. But the people
were so highly exasperated against this miserable
race, that, in order to preserve them from more
dreadful calamities, the emperor was under the necessity of issuing an edict, enjoining them to depart
the country, or receive baptism. [A. D. 1400.]
The Jews assert, that few at this time were induced
to apostatize, or, as they expressed it, " to forsake
the glory of their God."†

Great numbers of the Jews had settled in Thu-
ringia and Misnia. But, at the commencement of
the fifteenth century, the landgraves exacted vast
sums for affording them an asylum. Upon their
refusal to pay an enormous tax, they were arrested
and imprisoned, and obliged to give up a large part
of their wealth in order to regain their liberty.‡

---

* Basnage, p. 687.
† Modern Universal History, vol. xiii. p. 343.
‡ Basnage p. 687

A. D. 1434.] About this period, the council of Basil commanded the prelates, in all the places where there were Jews, to appoint learned divines to preach to them, and obliged them, under the severest penalties, to attend the sermons. At the same time, the Christians were prohibited from having any social intercourse with them, or employing them as servants, nurses, farmers, or physicians. They were not permitted to reside in houses near any church, or in the inside of any city. This degraded people were also compelled to wear a particular habit; and condemned to lose all the sums they lent on sacred books, crosses, and the ornaments of churches.*

Twenty years after, Lewis X. duke of Bavaria, banished them from his dominions, without regarding his own interest, or the remonstrances of his friends. He also confiscated all their effects, and erected public edifices in the places where they had inhabited.†

A. D. 1492.] The princes of Mecklenburgh also treated this wretched people with extreme rigour. They were accused of offering an indignity to a consecrated host, which they purchased of a priest; for this crime thirty Jews, together with the priest, were put to a cruel death. Seven years after, [A. D. 1499.] those of Nuremburg, who were numerous and affluent, were banished from the city. The citizens charged them with various offences, in order to palliate their severity. But the principal cause appears to have been their wealth, and

---

* Jortin's Remarks on Ecclesiastical History.
† Basnage, p. 729.

the usurious practices to which they were addicted *

Their expulsion was probably accelerated by the
appearance of an impostor, named David Leimlein.
Though he had not the temerity to declare himself
the Messiah, he confidently affirmed, that the
mighty conqueror would appear in 1500. He styled
himself chief of the army of Israel, and went to
Lisbon and persuaded a young convert to return to
Judaism, and act in concert with him. He gave
him the name of Solomon Malcho, and exhorted
him to diligently read the rabbinical writings. His
pupil made such a rapid progress in his studies,
that the Italian Jews affirmed his sermons were
dictated by some angel. Not contented with preaching, he compiled several curious treatises, which
increased his reputation. Meantime David distinguished himself by his long fasting, being sometimes six days without taking any food, and thus
attracted public notice and admiration. The credulous Jews were hence induced to demolish their
ovens, expecting the following year to eat unleavened bread in Jerusalem. While they were
preparing for the voyage, David, perceiving that he
had set too short a time for their pretended deliverance, declared, that "the sins of the nation
had retarded the coming of the Messiah." This
caused the infatuated people to appoint a solemn
fast, in order to appease the anger of God, and
hasten the appearance of their long expected deliverer.†

At length, Malcho, who declared himself the

* Basnage, p 729.   † Ibid.

precursor of the Messiah, was so imprudent as to
desire an audience of Charles V. then at Mantua.
He was admitted ; but that monarch caused him to
be arrested and put to a cruel death.*

* Leimlein was sent prisoner to Spain, and died there a few days
after his confinement. Yet such was the infatuation of the Italian
Jews, that a long time elapsed before they would believe but that he
was still alive in this kingdom.—*Modern Universal History*, vol. xiii.
p. 393.

CHAPTER XX.

The Jews are protected by the Roman pontiffs during the thirteenth and fourteenth centuries.—They are numerous in Naples.—They are massacred in Trani.—They build a magnificent synagogue in Bologna in the fifteenth century.—The Jews are persecuted by pope John III.—Massacre of those in Trent.—Alexander VI. favours and protects the Jews.—Those refugees, who seek an asylum in Naples, are persecuted by the inquisitors.—Paul III. is partial to the Jewish nation.

WHILE the other European nations oppressed and persecuted the wretched fugitives of Israel, the Roman pontiffs, with a small exception, treated them with lenity, defended them against their persecutors, and often checked the mistaken zeal of those who sought to convert them by force.* Instances of their kindness and humanity towards the Jewish nation occur in various parts of the foregoing history. As early as the seventh century they were protected by pope Gregory the Great. In the eleventh, Alexander II. condemned the persecuting spirit of king Ferdinand, and endeavoured to defend them against the rage of the Crusaders. At a later period, Gregory IX. a zealous promoter of the holy war, observing that the Crusaders in many places began their expedition with massacres of the Jews, not only loudly reprehended them, but took all proper methods for preventing such barbarity. He also interposed in their favour when the inhabitants of Haguenau accused them of murdering Christian children. He wrote a letter to Lewis IX. to stop the persecution which was raised

* Butler's Horæ Biblicæ, p. 88.

against them during the reign of that monarch. Two other letters of his, addressed to all Christians, pass a severe censure upon those, who, under the cloak of religion, concealed their avarice in order to harass the Jews; and he there enjoined them to imitate the example of his predecessors, who had declared themselves their defenders. Many of the nation were indebted for their lives to his toleration, not only in his own dominions, but in England, France, and Spain. In 1247, Innocent IV. wrote to vindicate them from the crimes* which were laid to their charge; and said, that they were more miserable under Christian princes, than their ancestors had been under Pharaoh."†

In Naples the Jewish people were become numerous and affluent, particularly in the capital and the city of Trani. The king, in order to reward them for some important services, treated them with great indulgence, and at his death recommended them to the States. But these, instead of allowing them the full enjoyment of their religion, endeavoured to effect their conversion. The Jews, apprehending a persecution, offered to embrace Christianity upon condition of being permitted to marry into the richest and noblest families in the kingdom. To their great surprise these terms were accepted, and they were obliged to accede to their own proposal. Those, however, who could not

---

* The edicts of so many pontiffs to destroy the effects of the calumnies against the Jews render it highly probable, that these reports were not founded on sufficient evidence.—*Note to Mosheim's History*, vol. vi. p 220.

† Basnage, p 668. Butler's Horæ Biblicæ, p. 88.

form advantageous connexions, soon relapsed into
Judaism. A monk of Trani, resolved to punish
them for their dissimulation ; and, to effect this
purpose, concealed a cross in a heap of earth, and
charged a Jew of the city with the fact. Exasperated at this supposed crime, the people rose, and a
massacre immediately followed. The tumult extended to Naples, where the Jews would have been
put to death had not the nobility interposed, and
concealed the most wealthy, and consequently the
most obnoxious, in their houses. Pope Alexander
the Fourth also sent to Naples to exert his authority
in their favour.*

Clement V. who at the commencement of the
fourteenth century had removed the papal seat to
Avignon, exerted himself to save the Jews from
the persecution of the shepherds. He excommunicated them ; but the anathemas of the church made
little impression on that furious people. This
pontiff not only protected the Jews, but afforded
them the means of instruction, and ordered that
every university should have professors to teach
Hebrew, and men whose education rendered them
capable of disputing with and convincing the Jews
of their errors.†

John XXII. his successor, was for pursuing a
different method; and supposed the most probable
way of effecting their conversion was to burn all the
copies of the Talmud. Several of the bishops
having asserted, that they had seen some of this
nation ridiculing the Catholics as they carried the
cross in procession, the pope was prevailed upon to

* Basnage, p. 669.   † Ibid.

issue an edict which expelled them from all the territories of the church. In order to avoid the impending evil, they applied to Robert, king of
Naples and Sicily, who, being a friend and favourite
of the pontiff, persuaded him, upon their presenting
him with a large sum of money, to revoke his edict.

Clement VI. treated the Jews with singular kindness and humanity. When they were put to death
in various parts of the kingdom upon pretence of
poisoning the rivers, he exerted himself to the
utmost to suppress the popular fury. He also
preserved them from the cruelty of the inquisition,
which raged with unrelenting fury against the Albigenses. Under his protection they even maintained
a friendly correspondence with some of the members
of this bloody tribunal. They presented Emeric,
who compiled the directory of the inquisition, a
Bible that they pretended was written by Ezra,
which the Dominicans have preserved with great
veneration. While they were massacred without
mercy in every part of Europe, Avignon became
their asylum; and Clement VI. their friend and
protector, omitted nothing that could tend to soften
the lot of the persecuted, and disarm the fury of
their persecutors.*

A. D. 1394.] The Jews were numerous and
powerful at Bologna during the fourteenth century.
They had there built the most magnificent synagogue in Italy, and established an academy. Boni-
face IX. did not oppose their erecting this synagogue, which, by its size and beauty, excited the
attention and admiration of travellers.

* Basnage, p. 670. Gregoire, p. 8.

A. D. 1412.] Though the Jews were generally favoured and protected by the popes, yet, at the commencement of the fifteenth century, John the Twenty-third issued several edicts against them. He not only raised a persecution in his own dominions, but encouraged and stimulated the Spanish government to massacre this unhappy people. Soon, after, however, Nicolas II. being raised to the pontificate, treated them with great indulgence. He preserved those in his own dominions from the inquisition; and sent letters into Spain to prevent their being obliged to abjure their own religion.* .

A. D. 1472.] They had not long enjoyed the patronage of this pontiff before a new persecution was raised against them. Sextus IV. had been prevailed upon to canonize one Simon, who, as was pretended, had been murdered two hundred years before by the Jews in Trent. The public hatred, being thus revived, the populace, in the bishopric of Trent and in the city of Venice, plundered and massacred the circumcised. The doge and senate were obliged to interpose their authority to suppress the slaughter; but the magistrates of Trent, being less equitable, expelled the Jews from the city.

A. D. 1492.] After the Catholics in Spain and Portugal had banished the Jews, the Italians received them with open arms. Pope Alexander VI. not only relieved the wants of the unhappy fugitives, but enjoined their brethren at Rome, who had treated them with great neglect, to afford them every assistance in their power for establishing themselves in his dominions He allowed them the

* Basnage, p. 721.

same privileges as their brethren had formerly enjoyed ; and endeavoured to procure them the free
and unrestrained exercise of their religion in all the
other states of Italy.*

It is said, that when the Portuguese exiles came
to Italy, the university of Jews at Rome offered the
pope a thousand ducats on condition of his refusing
those of Spain permission to settle in his territories.
But Alexander rejected their offer with disdain, and
reproved them for their barbarity towards their
brethren. He also decreed, that they should be
banished from his dominions, and the Spanish Jews
received in their place ; and they were obliged to
pay a vast sum before they could obtain a revocation
of this order.†

The favourable disposition of pope Alexander
towards the Jewish nation, induced many of them
from various parts to seek an asylum in his territories. Among others, whom the pontiff's kindness
invited to Rome, was the learned rabbi Jochanan, a
German, who had been settled at Constantinople,
and who was celebrated for his knowledge in the
mysteries of the cabbala.‡

Part of the Spanish and Portuguese exiles sought
an asylum in Naples. But they were exposed to
the unrelenting cruelty of the inquisitors in that
kingdom, and suffered such terrible oppressions,
that the people rebelled. The viceroy was induced
to expel them, in order to be delivered from the

* Basnage, p. 722.
† This curious fact is handed down to posterity by Jewish writers.
Rossi's Hebrew Biography.
‡ Basnage, p. 722.

tyranny of these merciless men. He alleged, that
" as the ancient inhabitants were sound in the faith,
there was not any farther need of this bloody tribunal." Charles V. soon after [A. D. 1534.] authorized his viceroy's conduct, by refusing to tolerate
them either in Naples or Sicily. This severity,
however, did not deter one Ricci, a converted Jew,
from dedicating to that monarch a celebrated treatise on what he styled " Celestial Agriculture." He
was a physician in Germany and a profound cabbalist, who attempted to prove the mysteries of Christianity from that science.*

A. D. 1539.] Paul III. was so indulgent to the
Jews, and they became so numerous and powerful
during his pontificate, that cardinal Sadolet inveighed against him on account of his partial
fondness for an unbelieving race. He asserted,
that this pontiff was kinder to them than to the
Christians ; and that none could be raised to civil or
ecclesiastical dignities but through their favour and
interest ; while at the same time he persecuted the
Protestants. Though the cardinal's remonstrance
did not produce all the effect that was desired, yet
it caused a redress of the most flagrant abuses.
They were, however, sometimes persecuted in
Rome ; yet, it must be admitted, that there is no
country in the world in which less Jewish blood has
been spilled, and in which the rites of humanity
have been more respected with regard to their
nation, than in the ecclesiastical state.†

A learned writer has thus accounted for the kind-

* Basnage, p. 723.
† Basnage. p 722   Letters of certain Jews to Voltaire, p. 41.

ness of the Roman pontiffs to the Jews. " The court of Rome excelled all other courts in policy, craft, and worldly wisdom. It saw the folly of expelling and distressing the Jews; it knew the use that was to be made of an industrious people, skilful in commerce, and in the management of the revenues ; who had no particular dislike to papal authority, and no disposition to assist heretics, schismatics, or reformers, and had not credit sufficient to make proselytes to their own religion."*

The persecution of the Jews during the middle ages, which has been related in the five preceding chapters, exhibits in such a striking manner the exact accomplishment of the famous prophecy of Moses, Deut xxviii. that this chapter appears to be a correct miniature picture of the leading features in their history, drawn by the pencil of inspiration. The reflecting and devout must feel an augmented veneration for the sacred scriptures, while they turn their attention to the complete agreement of the prophecies, and the events which fulfil them ; and scepticism and infidelity be confounded by seeing the history of succeeding ages so accurately delineated, and contemplating, in the fate of this suffering people, a " striking phenomenon, incomprehensible to human reason."

Among other awful denunciations against the Jewish nation, which we have seen fully accomplished in the course of this history, Moses declares, " Thou shalt only be oppressed and spoiled evermore." Numerous instances occur of the cruel oppressions and pillages this devoted race have suffered

* Jortin's Remarks on Ecclesiastical History, vol. ii.

in England, France, Germany, and Spain. In the
east, as well as in Europe, they have been continually subjected to heavy fines and impositions. How
often in different countries have they been forced to
redeem their lives by vast sums extorted from them !
Did sovereigns want pecuniary assistance to carry
on their wars, the Jews were compelled to give up
their riches. A massacre was generally the prelude
to a plunder, as we have seen in various parts of
Europe. When banished from England in the
reign of Edward I. their estates, which were confiscated, brought immense sums to the crown. When
Philip Augustus expelled them from France, he
confiscated their estates ; yet he soon after recalled
this oppressed people in order to fleece them again.
They have " every where paid for liberty to exist,
and have scarcely obtained that of breathing an
impure air."

The great lawgiver of the Hebrew nation also
declares, " Thy sons and thy daughters shall be
taken from thee, and given to another people."
How exactly has this prophecy been fulfilled in
several countries, especially in Spain and Portugal.
In the former of these kingdoms the council of
Toledo decreed, that the children of the Jews should
be taken from them, and educated in the Christian
faith ; in the latter, when this miserable people were
expelled, all under fourteen years of age were forcibly detained, in order to be baptized. In the
frenzy and despair of the wretched parents at
parting with their children, we contemplate the
accomplishment of another prophetic denunciation :
" Thou shalt be mad for the sight of thine eyes,

which thou shalt see." "Accordingly we find that some of them, driven to madness, put a period to their own lives; and others, sacrificing nature to their religion, destroyed their tender offspring. Instances of their madness and desperation frequently occur in the preceding chapters—in England, when the Jews in York Castle killed themselves, their wives, and children; in France, when they were assaulted by the shepherds, and destroyed their children; in Spain, when a number perished by suicide at the insurrection of Toledo; and in Germany, when persecuted for the pretended crime of stealing a consecrated host, they destroyed themselves, their wives, children, and effects.

After mentioning the oppression and barbarous cruelty the Jews were compelled to endure, and the madness consequent upon their extreme sufferings, Moses declares, "Thou shalt become an astonishment, a proverb, and a by-word among all nations, whither the Lord shall lead thee." How exactly has this prophecy been fulfilled upon this unhappy race, who have been consigned to infamy ever since their dispersion! "Is not the pretended avarice, usury, and hard-heartedness of a Jew become proverbial?"* In various countries of the east, as well as in Europe, they have been subjected to invidious, humiliating, and disgraceful distinctions, and condemned to wear exteriorly the badges of their abject state; and every where exposed to the insults of the vilest populace. They have been treated as of a different species; and in several parts of

* See David Levi's Defence of the Old Testament in a series of letters to Thomas Paine.

L

Europe, subjected to the same toil with those
animals which by their religious principles they
abhor.*   Pagans, Christians, and Mahometans
have agreed in abusing, vilifying, and persecuting
the Jews.

The sacred writer proceeds in delineating, the
horrid outline of their miseries, and declares, ",The
Lord will make thy plagues wonderful, even, great
plagues, and of long continuance.". The calamities
they have endured were indeed the greatest which
the world ever witnessed. Ever since the destruction of Jerusalem they have been, outcasts from
society, subsisting amidst contempt and persecution.
For near eighteen centuries, the nations of the
earth have been treading under foot the remains of
Israel. What nation ever suffered so much, and
yet continued so long? The chief diversity in
their condition has arisen from the various kinds of
miseries to which they have been subjected. In
Christendom they have been despised, calumniated,
oppressed, banished, executed, and burned. The
tyranny exercised against them has been as capricious as it was cruel. In France they have been at
one time compelled to assume the mask of Christianity to save themselves from a cruel death; at
another epoch the estates of those who renounced
Judaism were confiscated. At one period, they
have been banished through superstition; at another, recalled through avarice. An animated writer
of their own nation has observed, " It seems as if
they were allowed to survive the destruction of their
country, only to see the most odious and calumnious

* Gregoire on the Reformation of the Jews, p. 52.

imputations laid to their charge, to stand as the constant object of the grossest and most shocking injustice, as a mark for the insulting finger of scorn, as a sport to the most inveterate hatred. It seems as if their doom was incessantly to suit all the dark and bloody purposes, which can be suggested by human malignity, supported by ignorance and fanaticism."*

* M. Michael Berr's Appeal to the Justice of Kings and Nations, published at Strasburg, 1801.

CHAPTER XXI.

State of the Jews in the east.—They suffer from the invasion of the Tartars.—Those in the Grecian empire enjoy an interval of tranquillity.—Of their state in Media and Persia.—Agreement made between Shah Abbas I. and the Jews in the latter of those kingdoms. —A general massacre of them takes place during the reign of Shah Abbas II.—Of those in Schiraz and other parts of Persia.—Of the learned men in the academy of Sapheta.—Dissimulation of a pretended convert to Christianity.—State of the nation in the Ottoman empire.

THE number and power of the eastern Jews were greatly diminished in the thirteenth century. Nasser Ledinillah, caliph of Bagdat, being a zealous Mahometan, and extremely avaricious, became jealous of a people who exerted their abilities with success in the acquisition of wealth, and who received every pretended Messiah with alacrity and joy. He therefore soon raised a persecution against them, and compelled them all to adopt the Mahometan religion, or leave the Babylonian territories. Some departed into different parts, while others dissembled in order to avoid exile.*

Palestine was greatly depopulated by the wars which raged between the Christians and Saracens, and the government of the cities was frequently changed The Jews, however, had still synagogues and learned rabbies in their native country. Moses Nachmanides, one of the greatest cabbalistical writers which the age produced, left Gironna, the place of his birth, retired to Judea, and erected a synagogue. On account of his profound know-

* Basnage, p. 655.

ledge of the law, he was styled the *father of wisdom ;* and a sermon he preached before the king of Castile, " on the excellence of the law," rendered him equally famous for his eloquence. His writings are various, but chiefly of the cabbalistical kind.*

During the thirteenth century several learned rabbies appeared in other parts of the east. In particular Aaron Cohen, a Caraite, who practised physic at Constantinople, 1294. He was the author of a commentary on the Pentateuch and other parts of scripture, and a work styled the " Perfection of Beauty." Aaron the son of Eliab, another Caraite, appeared about fifty years after. He attacked Aben Ezra, and other traditionalists, with great energy and force of argument, in a work entitled, " The Crown of the Law," which is a literal comment on the Pentateuch.†

A. D. 1291.] The Jews in the vicinity of Babylon, and in other parts of the east, suffered greatly from the invasion of the Tartars ; but at length they enjoyed an interval of tranquillity under Jehan Argun, by means of a Jewish physician named Saadeddoulat, whom that prince raised to the office of his chief minister. Being learned and of polished manners, he acquired great influence at court ; and exerted himself to the utmost to promote the welfare of his brethren, who derived important advantages from his interposition in their favour. Their prosperity, however, was soon interrupted by the death of this monarch ; and the Jewish

* Basnage, p. 655. Modern Universal History, vol. xiii. p 339.
† Biographical Dictionary, vol. i. p. 2.

physician, who had exasperated the Mahometans by
his partiality to his nation, was charged with having
poisoned his benefactor, and on the accusation con-
demned-to suffer death. The populace soon after
massacred vast numbers of his countrymen, in order
to revenge the real or pretended injuries they had
suffered from them during the life of Argun.* '

It is probable, that the Jews in the Grecian
empire were generally allowed the exercise of their
religion during the fourteenth and fifteenth centuries; for the Greek writers of those periods
severely reproach the Latins for compelling them to
be baptized and assume the mask of Christianity.† '

A. D. 1500.] During the wars and rapid conquests of Tamerlane, the Jews in Media and Persia
were not only attenuated and impoverished, but
their academies, learning, and learned men, had
totally disappeared. They had scarcely recovered
from these disasters when they were involved in new
calamities. They were numerous in Media when
Ishmael Sophi, chief of the family of the Persian
kings, commenced his conquests; and, astonished
at his rapid and wonderful success, they began to
consider him as the true Messiah. In this opinion
they were confirmed by his declaring himself a
prophet sent by God to reform the Mahometan
religion. But Ishmael exhibited a peculiar aversion
to the Jews, despised their flattery, rejected their
homage, and treated them with greater severity
than any of his subjects.‡

At the commencement of the reign of Shah

---

* Basnage, p. 659. Modern Universal History, vol. xiii.
† Basnage, p. 658.   ‡ Ibid.

Abbas, the kingdom of Persia was greatly depopulated. This monarch was hence induced to
confer important privileges on all strangers, who
would settle in the kingdom. Multitudes of people
repaired from the neighbouring parts, in particular
vast numbers of Jews. Their dexterity in pecuniary negociations, and success in engrossing the
commerce of the country, having excited the envy
and jealousy of the other inhabitants, they complained to the king. This monarch was apprehensive, that severity to them would deter others
from settling in and induce foreigners to retire from
his dominions. But having found a fortunate
pretence for persecuting them by the authority of
the Koran, he resolved to compel them to embrace
Mahometanism, or suffer death. The Mufti humanely interposed, and prevented the execution of
his cruel design. It was resolved, however, to
summon the principal Jewish doctors before the
Sophi's tribunal.*

Shah Abbas strictly examined them respecting the
abolition of their sacrifices, and other ceremonies at
the appearance of Jesus Christ, whom Mahomet
had succeeded. The rabbies, astonished at those
interrogatories, declared that they expected a Messiah, and could not receive him whom their ancestors
had crucified. Abbas was exasperated at this
answer, since the Koran mentions Christ with veneration. "Why will you not believe in Christ,"
says he, "since I believe in him?" He afterwards
asked them, "What they thought of Mahomet?"
This demand intimidated and confounded them, and

* Basnage, p. 697.

sensible of the danger of discovering their opinion of the impostor, they answered, that " Moses was the great prophet, and the only one whom they ought to follow; but that they did not absolutely reject Mahomet, because he was the son of Abraham by Ishmael." They then had recourse to prayers and entreaties for mercy; and to protestations, that their object in settling in Persia was to serve the king with fidelity and zeal.*

Abbas severely reproved them for adducing their expectation of a Messiah, as an excuse for their obstinate incredulity. " But," said he, " to remove this vain pretence, fix a time for his appearance, I will tolerate you till the accomplishment of this period. Yet, if the Messiah, who has delayed his coming for so many ages, deceive you once more, it is just you should embrace the Mahometan faith, or be deprived of your property, your children, and lives." He allowed them some time to prepare an answer. After mature deliberation they informed the king, that their great deliverer would appear in seventy years from the day on which they had been summoned before his tribunal. Their object was to elude the threatened punishment, expecting that neither the monarch nor themselves could survive till this period was terminated. Abbas, who was extremely avaricious, extorted vast sums for granting an oppressed people this interval of tranquillity. He engaged, it is said, on his part, that if the Messiah appeared within seventy years, all Persia was to profess Judaism. If not, the Jews were to embrace the Mahometan religion, or consent to

* Basnage, p. 697. Modern Universal History.

their utter destruction in all the Sophi's dominions.
After the agreement was registered and signed by
both parties, they were taxed at two millions of
gold.* Many years elapsed after the death of Abbas
before this contract was discovered, during which
the Persians were disturbed by continual wars with
the Turks. Amurat IV. who in 1638 subdued
Bagdat, found great numbers of Jews in that city;
but though he violated his engagement, and massacred the Persians, he spared the Israelites, under
the idea that they might render him essential
service.†

A. D. 1666.] It is related, that Shah Abbas II.
who enjoyed a peaceable reign, in searching the
registers of the palace found the treaty which his
predecessor had made with the Jews. A great
council was convened on this occasion, in which
it was unanimously resolved, that this wretched
people should be exterminated without delay.
Accordingly an order was issued to Persians and
strangers, to massacre them without regard of
sex, age, or condition. Those only were excepted
who should profess the Mahometan religion. This
persecution commenced at Ispahan, the capital of
the kingdom, extended with equal severity to the
several provinces inhabited by wealthy Jews, and
for three years they were pursued with fury, and

* Basnage disputes the truth of the account of Shah Abbas's entering into this agreement with the Jews, though related by many
historians. It is, however, agreed by all, that they were violently
persecuted by this monarch, as well as by Shah Abbas II.—*Basnage's
History*, p. 698.

† Basnage, p. 698.

massacred without intermission or pity. A few,
however, found means to escape into the Turkish
dominions, others into India, and many preserved
their lives by abjuring their religion.* It was,
however, at length observed, that the pretended
converts secretly practised the Jewish rites, and the
king, finding that compulsory measures could not
effect a change in their minds, permitted them to
retain their former religious principles. They were
obliged annually to pay a large sum of money to the
sovereign, and to wear a disgraceful badge of distinction †

The Jews were numerous at Schiraz, where the
Persians had a more famous academy than at Ispahan. They pretended to be descended from the
tribe of Levi. A still larger number resided at Lar,
the metropolis of one of the Persian provinces, and
had a quarter assigned them between the city and
castle. They extended themselves on the coast of
Ormus, in order to procure some part of the Indian
trade, which was once conducted by their brethren,
who were formerly numerous in those parts.‡

A. D. 1638.] Bagdat, once the residence of the
princes of the captivity, was much reduced after it

* Modern Universal History, vol. xiii. p. 369.
† Basnage, p. 699. Gregoire, p 16.
‡ After the king of Portugal expelled the Jews from his kingdom,
he suffered them to live at Goa and other places, and exercise their
religion. But in 1639 they were deluded by a pretended Messiah,
whose fame extended to Portugal. Some of the Jewish converts in
that kingdom, elated with the prospect of a deliverer, betrayed their
secret attachment to the religion of their ancestors. Upon which
the inquisition compelled all in the eastern parts, who were subject to
the king of Portugal, either to suffer exile or profess Christianity.—
Modern Univer. Hist. vol. xiii p. 365.

was taken by Amurat IV. A large proportion of the inhabitants were Jews, who possessed a synagogue, and enjoyed the unrestrained exercise of their religion. They were, however, hated and despised by the Persians.*

The Jewish historians inform us, that those of their nation in Armenia were charged with having killed a Christian; and the murder being confessed by the accused, many of this miserable people were crucified, and others burned. Three days after, the Christian appeared; the accusation was discovered to have been invented through malice, and the confession extorted by torture. Complaint being made to Solomon II. the Armenian magistrates were forbidden to take cognizance of similar criminal cases in future, and they were ordered to bring them before the tribunal of the sultan.†

The Jews, since their dispersion, have never been numerous in Palestine, but have seen their ancient and beloved country successively possessed by Pagans, Christians, and Turks. It has indeed been frequently visited by Jewish, as well as Christian devotees. But few have fixed their abodes in a province, where they found it difficult to acquire wealth, and even procure a tolerable subsistence.

Sapheta in Galilee was the most populous and celebrated city which the Jews possessed in Palestine. Those who inhabited it were treated with more kindness than in any other part of the Ottoman empire. They have had many learned rabbies and professors, who have presided in the academy in

* Basnage, p. 699.　† Gregoire, p. 18. Basnage, p. 703.

this city, to which they sent their children to be instructed in the Hebrew language ; for it was their
opinion, that it could no where else be taught with
equal purity. This academy succeeded that of
Tiberias, and acquired a similar reputation.*

The most celebrated cabbalist who has appeared
since Simeon Jochaides, taught. in. this seat of
learning. He was born at Cordova in Spain, hence
he acquired the name of Moses Cordova. He left
a cabbalistical work, entitled " The Garden of
Pomegranates."†

Dominic of Jerusalem taught for a considerable
time in the same academy. After he had completed
his studies and lectures on the Talmud, he applied
himself to the theory and practice of medicine, and
acquired such celebrity, that the sultan invited him
to Constantinople to be his physician. At length,
he embraced the Christian religion, and afterwards
translated the New Testament into Hebrew, and at
the same time answered some objections of the rabbies against Stephen's martyrdom.‡

But those who have been most celebrated in the
academy were, the learned Moses Trani and Joseph
Karo, who presided in it about the middle of the
sixteenth century. The former was a native of
Trani, and taught with such success, that he was
styled by his brethren, " the light of Israel," " the
Sinaite of Mount Sinai, and the rooter up of
Mountains," because he solved the difficulties in the

---

* It appears that this academy was not erected till after the twelfth
century, since Benjamin de Tudela does not mention it in his
travels.

† Basnage, p. 783   Modern Univer. Hist. vol. xiii. p. 395.

‡ Basnage, p. 703

law. He wrote a body of Jewish laws, in which he distinguished between those which were written by Moses, those which have been transmitted by oral tradition, and those which are only founded on the decisions of the doctors. Joseph Karo was a native of Spain, from whence he retired into Galilee. He wrote so well on the rights of the Jewish nation, that he was styled "the prodigy of the world."*

Besides the abovementioned doctors who were foreigners, there were other celebrated rabbies, who were born and educated at Sapheta;† among whom Moses Alsheh and Samuel Ozida were eminently distinguished. The former acquired great reputation by his eloquent sermons and his learned commentaries upon some parts of the law. All the titles of his works are metaphorical. One is called ".The Rose of Sharon," and others have similar titles. Ozida was also a celebrated preacher, and wrote a commentary on the Lamentations of Jeremiah, which he called ". The Bread of Tears."

The number of Israelites in Jerusalem was much smaller than in Sapheta. In 1665, an instance of profound dissimulation took place in this city. A Jew, who was induced from interested motives to desert the synagogue, so eminently distinguished himself among the Christians, that they promoted

---

* Basnage, p. 700

† The famous Judah Jona was born at Sapheta; but after he completed his studies, he travelled to Amsterdam, and from thence to Hamburg, and the Jews in this city chose him for their judge. Soon after he removed to Poland, and embraced the Christian religion. He at length settled at Rome, where he taught the Hebrew language to Bartolocci, an Italian monk, and the author of the " Bibliotheca Rabbinica," a learned work in four folio volumes. Judah died in 1668.—*Modern Univer. Hist.*

him successively to all the orders of the clergy, and
at length exalted him to the dignity of patriarch of
Jerusalem. Being a man of boundless ambition,
he repaired to Constantinople to obtain that see,
which was vacant. He was there seized with a dangerous distemper, and perceiving death approaching,
he called many Grecian bishops and a large number
of his Hebrew brethren, to whom he solemnly
declared, that " he had always believed the Jewish
religion, and renounced the bishopric of Jerusalem
to die in his old profession." Those who heard
him lay aside the mask of Christianity were filled
with astonishment and consternation.*

The Jews have long been numerous in other
parts of the Ottoman empire, particularly at Constantinople ; they inhabited a suburb in Galata,
which was called the Jewry in the time of the Crusaders. Though hated and despised by the Turks,
they rendered themselves so useful by their skill in
pecuniary transactions, that they carried on the
greatest part of the commerce of the country, and
Christians as well as Turks employed a Jewish
broker in all their negociations. Among other privileges they obtained that of selling wine ; and it
was supposed that which they prepared was of the
purest kind, because they are prohibited by their
law from making any mixture.†

Michsez, a Jew, was accused of having persuaded Selim II. to attempt the conquest of Cyprus.
In consequence of which, after the reduction of the
island, his nation obtained greater privileges than

---

* Basnage, p. 701. Modern Universal Hist. vol. xiii. p. 373.
† Basnage p. 718. Gregoire, p. 184.

the Christians, and became numerous and affluent. The sultan made choice of a Jew named Solomon Rophe, to negotiate a peace with the republic of Venice, and soon after granted them the privilege of establishing a printing-office at Constantinople and Salonichi. By this means copies of the law, which had become scarce in the east, were universally dispersed; and, in consequence of their being more assiduously studied, several eminent rabbies and heads of synagogues left the place of their birth to settle in these cities.*

In particular, Solomon, the son of Japhe, came from Germany to reside in Constantinople, where he explained the Jerusalem Talmud, and printed a comment on the Pentateuch, and several other works. Rabbi Gedaliah, another learned doctor, who boasted that he was descended from king David, left Lisbon to settle in that metropolis as a physician, and teach the laws and ceremonies of his nation. He was appointed head of the synagogue, and assiduously laboured to reconcile the Caraites and Talmudists. But both parties proved so obstinate, that his labours were ineffectual. He, however, derived the advantage of publishing several other works, as well as his own treatise of *Seven Eyes,* alluding to the vision of Zechariah.†

Many of the Jews settled at Lepanto, Corinth, and other cities in Greece. But, in consequence of the desolate state of the country, and the heavy taxes which they were compelled to pay to the Porte, they have been generally in indigent circumstances. Their condition was more eligible at Thessalonica

---

* Basnage, p. 719.   † Ibid.

(now Salonichi) where they have been settled ever
since the time of St. Paul. They for ages have
possessed a considerable academy, and in later times
a printing-office has been established. In this city
Moses Abelda published several of his works, the
most celebrated of which were, his mystical exposition of the Pentateuch, and a moral treatise on
the miseries of human life, called the " Vale of
Tears." The design of this performance was to
comfort his nation under their calamitous dispersion.
Joseph, the son of Sen, also published a treatise
" on the use of the Gemara" in this city. The
famous impostor Zabathai Tzevi chose Salonichi as
the theatre whereon to act his part, imagining, that,
if he could impose on the doctors in this academy,
it would be easy to delude his more ignorant
brethren. An account of his success among his
infatuated nation will be given in the following
chapter.

CHAPTER XXII.

The Jews frequently duped by impostors.—An account of Zabathai Tzevi, a false Messiah.—Of his precursor Nathan Levi.—Of his success in different cities.—He, repairs to Constantinople, and is imprisoned by the sultan's orders.—Of the great attention which was paid him in prison.—He is summoned to appear before the sultan, and professes the Mahometan religion.

IN the foregoing chapters we have seen the Jews during sixteen centuries obstinately persisting in rejecting the true Messiah, and frequently duped by impostors who assumed this character. This infatuation continued unabated, notwithstanding the repeated disappointments which often involved this miserable people in terrible calamities.

A. D. 1666.] The Jewish nation entertained sanguine expectations that some wonderful event would take place during this year, and false reports were eagerly circulated. It was said, 'that great multitudes marched from unknown parts' to the remote desarts of Arabia, and were supposed to be the ten tribes of Israel who have been dispersed for many ages; that a ship was arrived in the north part of Scotland with sails and cordage of silk; that the mariners spoke nothing but Hebrew, and that on the sails was this motto, " The twelve tribes of Israel." These accounts excited the enthusiasm of the credulous people, and prepared their minds to receive an impostor.*

At this period Zabathai Tzevi proclaimed himself

* According to the predictions of some Christian writers, who commented upon the Apocalypse, some wonderful event was to take place in 1666 respecting the Jews.—*Turkish History*, p. 174.

the Messiah and deliverer of Israel, to whom he
promised a glorious kingdom of prosperity and
peace. This famous, or rather infamous impostor,
was born at Aleppo, of mean and obscure parents.
But, as he early discovered a taste for learning, he
made great proficiency in that kind of literature
which was taught by his nation. As soon as he
came from school he began to preach in the streets
and fields, even before the Turks; and though ridi-
culed by them, he had the address to gain a number
of disciples by whom he was greatly admired. He
studied the prophecies so assiduously, in order to
apply them to himself, that it was supposed his intellect was deranged. He imagined, or pretended
to fancy, that he could ascend above the clouds, as
Isaiah had foretold; and upbraided his disciples
with their blindness, because they would not acknowledge they had seen him in the air. He also
pretended to perform other miracles by the power of
the name Jehovah. Upon which account some of
the most intelligent Jews summoned him to appear
before the synagogues and condemned him to death.
But, as they could not prevail upon any to execute
the sentence, they contented themselves with banishing the impostor.

He passed over to Salonichi, and, as the Jews
were numerous in this city, he supposed it a proper
theatre on which to act his part. But being expelled from thence, as well as from Athens, and
several other Greek towns, he retired to Alexandria,
where he acquired great celebrity. After travelling
into the Morea and Tripoli he arrived at Gaza, and
there preached repentance, and faith in himself so

effectually, that the Jews gave up business* and applied themselves wholly to devotion and alms. But in order to render his character more agreeable to the predictions of the prophets, it was necessary that he should be ushered in by a precursor. For this purpose he made choice of a Jew of great reputation at Gaza, named Nathan Levi, whom he easily persuaded to act this part. The time was favourable, for, according to the cabbalistical interpretation of Daniel, the Messiah was to appear in or about the year 1675.†

Zabathai Tzevi and his precursor travelled to Jerusalem. Levi, after his arrival, assembled the Jews, and abolished the fast which was to be celebrated in the month of June following, because mourning was improper at the joyful period of the Messiah's appearance. He then declared Tzevi was their long expected deliverer, and specified the time for the conquest and ruin of the Grand Seignor. Part of the nation believed in the impostor; but the most sensible men among them clearly perceived, that the intended insurrection would cause their destruction in the Ottoman empire. They, therefore, anathematized and condemned him to death, alleging that he neither possessed the characteristics of the Messiah, nor Levi those of his precursor.

Being obliged to quit Jerusalem, he came to Smyrna, and from thence to Constantinople, where

* These were prohibited from conducting business, under the penalty of excommunication. They expected that after their Messiah had subdued the nations they should gain possession of all the wealth of unbelievers.—*Turkish History,* vol. ii. p. 176.

† Basnage, p. 702. Turkish History, p. 175.

he expected to gain numerous disciples. But the
Jews in this city had previously received letters from
twenty-five rabbies, who had excommunicated him,
in which they pronounced him "an impious wretch,"
and declared, "that the person who killed him
would render an acceptable service to God, and save
many souls." This induced Tzevi to return to
Smyrna, where he received four ambassadors sent
by his precursor to acknowledge him as the Messiah.
As Levi was a man of eminence among his brethren,
this embassy greatly increased the followers of the
impostor, and even imposed upon part of the
learned rabbies. The multitude, dazzled by his
affected humility, frequent washings, diligent and
early attendance at the synagogues, and more especially by his pathetic sermons, acknowledged, him
for their Messiah and king, and brought him magnificent presents to support his dignity.*

In, the mean time Levi was employed in persuading his nation in different parts, that Tzevi was
their long-expected deliverer, who was about to subvert the Ottoman empire. He asserted that, after
being concealed nine months, this mighty conqueror
would appear in glory, mounted upon a celestial
lion ; and that a superb temple would descend from
heaven, in which sacrifices were continually to be
offered. While Levi was at Damascus, he wrote to
Tzevi, and thus began his letter, "To the king,
our king, lord of lords, who redeems our captivity,
the man elevated to the height of all sublimity, the
Messias of the God of Jacob, the celestial lion,
Zabathai Tzevi."

* Basnage, p. 703   Turkish History, vol ii.

At this period, the Jews in all the Turkish dominions entertained great expectations of glorious times. They were devout and penitent, prayed, fasted, and inflicted severe penances upon themselves. Business was neglected, superfluities were sold, and the poor provided for by immense contributions.*

The Jewish doctors at Smyrna convened again to consult upon an affair which daily became more important. The most judicious among them, not finding the character of the Messiah in Tzevi, condemned him to death. But the impostor's party being far the most numerous, he caused them to assemble in the great synagogue in this city, celebrated a new feast, repeatedly pronounced the name Jehovah, and altered the Jewish liturgy. His audience acknowledged his authority, and supposed they beheld something divine in his person. A third sentence of death pronounced by the rabbies did not intimidate him, because he was convinced none would presume to execute it. He repaired, however, to the cadi, whom his friends had found means to gain, and put himself under his protection.

Some of the credulous multitude affirmed, that fire proceeded from his mouth when he addressed the cadi, that a pillar of fire had terrified the Turkish governor, and deterred him from putting Tzevi to death. The multitude conducted him from the cadi's presence in triumph, singing these words from Psalm cxviii. 16, " The right hand of the Lord is exalted," &c.†

* Basnage, p. 701   † Basnage, p. 702. Turkish History.

The next step taken by the impostor was to cause
a throne to be erected for himself and his queen,
from which he addressed his subjects. He composed a new summary of belief, which the people
were obliged to receive with implicit faith, as
coming from the hand of their Messiah. Some,
who had the temerity to oppose it, were compelled
to save themselves by flight. Many who had been
incredulous now professed to believe in him to
whom they applied the prophecies of the Old Testament. When he had attained this height of
authority, he ordered the Jews, who were in the
habit of praying for the grand seignor in their synagogues, to erase his name from their liturgy, and
substitute his own. He styled himself, " King of
the kings of Israel," and Joseph his brother,
" King of the kings of Judah;" he also elected
princes to govern his brethren in their march to the
holy land, and to administer justice to them after
they obtained the possession of their beloved
country. At length, he declared he was called of
God to visit Constantinople, where he had a great
work to perform ; and accordingly embarked in a
small vessel for this city, while many of his disciples
followed him by land. The sultan, being informed
of his arrival, despatched orders to his vizier to apprehend and confine him in prison.*

This event, instead of discouraging, strengthened the faith of the Jews ; for they recollected
that Levi had predicted, that the Messiah was to be
concealed nine months. They maintained that the
sultan had not power to put him to death. The

* Basnage, p. 702.

criminal; upon his examination, asserted that his
nation had compelled him to assume the title of
king. This answer induced the vizier to treat him
with great mildness, and permit the Jews to visit
him in prison. Those of Constantinople were as
infatuated as their brethren in Smyrna. They
forbade commerce, and refused to pay their debts.
Some English merchants not knowing how to recover what was owing to them, from the Jews,
took this occasion to visit Tzevi, and make their
complaints to him against his subjects ; upon which
he wrote to them as follows :

" To you of the nation of the Jews, who expect
the appearance of the Messiah, and the salvation of
Israel, peace without end. Whereas we are informed that you are indebted to several of the
English nation, it seemeth right unto us to order
you to make satisfaction for your just debts, which
if you refuse to do, be it known, that you are not
to enter with us into our joys and dominions."*

Tzevi remained a prisoner in Constantinople two
months. The grand vizier, who was preparing to
go to Candia, did not think it safe to leave him in
the city during his absence, he therefore removed
him to the Dardanelles. This the Jews supposed
a new miracle ; and asserted, that the sultan had
not power to put him to death. Having bribed the
governor, great numbers repaired to the castle
where he was confined, not only those who were
near, but from Poland, Germany, Leghorn, Venice,
and other places.† They brought Tzevi rich pre-

* Basnage, p. 702.

† Even the Portuguese Jews at Amsterdam composed a form of
prayer to be made use of by those who went to Adrianople to visit
the pretended Messiah.—*Modern Univer. Hist.* vol. xiii. p. 370.

sents, and received in return his blessings and promises of advancement. The Turks raised the price of provisions upon those who visited their pretended Messiah, and the profit induced them to connive at the attention which was paid him.

The impostor, during his confinement; commanded the Jews to celebrate his birth day with feasting, illuminations, and music; and abolished the solemn fast which had been observed on that day on account of the destruction of their temple. He despatched ambassadors to various parts to proclaim him the Messiah, and publish the miracles which he pretended to have performed. He enjoined his nation to acknowledge the love of God in giving them consolation by the birth of their king and Messiah.*

In the height of Tzevi's success, Nehemiah Cohen, a Polish Jew, came to visit him in his confinement. He was a man of great learning in the cabbala and eastern languages. It is said, that he, in his conference with the impostor, maintained, that according to the scriptures there ought to be a twofold Messiah; one the son of Ephraim, a poor and despised teacher of the law, the other the son of David, and a mighty conqueror. Nehemiah was contented to be the former, and leave the dignity and glory of the latter to Tzevi. But he accused him of too great forwardness and presumption in assuming the character of the son of David previously to the appearance of the son of Ephraim. Tzevi, exasperated at this reproof, excluded Cohen from any share in the transaction. Upon which the latter went to Adrianople, and informed the mi-

* Turkish History, vol. ii. p. 177.

nisters of state; that the impostor was a dangerous
person, who sought to subvert the Turkish government. The grand seignor, at the request of his
principal officers, summoned him to appear in his
presence, and commanded him to be set as a mark for
his archers, to prove whether he was invulnerable.[*]

In order to avoid the impending trial Tzevi renounced all his vain-glorious pretensions, and confessed that he was only an ordinary Jew. The
sultan informed him, that his treason and other
crimes could only be expiated by embracing the
Mahometan faith; and that if he refused, the stake
was prepared to impale him. The impious wretch
replied, that "he had long earnestly desired to own
himself a convert; and he felt himself highly honoured in making this glorious profession of the
true faith in the presence of his sultan."[†]

The news of Tzevi's having embraced the Mahometan religion soon spread through the Turkish
dominions. His deluded followers were filled with
consternation, grief, and shame, and exposed to the
contempt and derision of their enemies. Several of
the Jews still continued to use, in their public
worship, the forms prescribed by this Mahometan
Messiah; which obliged the principal men of that
nation in Constantinople to send to Smyrna, and
forbid this practice upon penalty of excommunication.[‡]

During these transactions, the Jews, in more
remote parts, instead of attending to commerce,
wrote letters to their brethren, filled with accounts

* Basnage, p. 702. Turkish History, vol. ii. p 181.
† Basnage, p. 703. ‡ Ibid.

of the wonderful works performed by Tzevi their
Messiah.   They reported, that when the grand
seignor sent messengers to apprehend him, he
caused them all to be struck dead ; but upon being
requested, recalled them to life.   They added, that
though the prison in which Zabathai was confined was fastened with strong iron locks, he was
seen to walk the streets with numerous attendants,
and that his chains were converted into gold, which
he gave to his followers.   The Jews of Italy sent
legates to Smyrna to inquire into the truth of these
reports; who, upon their arrival, were mortified and
astonished at the intelligence, that their pretended
Messiah had embraced the Mahometan faith.   But
the brother of Tzevi attempted to persuade them
that it was only his apparition which appeared in a
Turkish habit; that he had been translated to heaven,
and that God would again send him down to earth at
a proper season.   He added, that Nathan his precursor, who had wrought many miracles, would soon
arrive at Smyrna, reveal hidden things, and confirm
their faith.   But this pretended Elias was not suffered to visit the city, and though the legates saw
him in another place, they received no satisfaction.*

Tzevi passed the remainder of his days at the
Turkish court.   He became a learned and zealous
Mahometan under the instructions of Vanni Effendi,
preacher to the seraglio, to whom he was a most do-
cile pupil.   Still, however, he continued to profess
himself a deliverer of the Jews ; but being extremely
cautious to avoid giving offence to the Turks, he
declared. " that unless his brethren would imitate

* Basnage, p. 104. Turkish History.

his example, in renouncing the imperfect elements of the Mosaical law, he never should be able to prevail with God to restore them to the holy land." This induced many Jews to repair to Constantinople from Bagdat, Jerusalem, and other remote parts; and in the presence of the grand seignor, they voluntarily professed themselves proselytes to the Mahometan religion. By this means the impious impostor ingratiated himself with the Turks, and retained his influence over large numbers of his infatuated nation. Tzevi was, however, finally, beheaded by order of the sultan Mahomet.*

After the death of Tzevi, Daniel Israel, a Jew, who had dwelt at Smyrna six or seven years, undertook to persuade the Hebrew nation, that Zabathai was yet alive and concealed, and that he would re-appear after the space of forty-five years.† Some prodigies which he pretended to perform astonished many of the Jews, and induced them to credit his assertions. His supposed miracles excited the admiration of the credulous people; and he was not only followed by the populace, but he even imposed upon several eminent rabbies. In particular Abraham Michael, and Raphael Cordoso, a physician who was famous among the Jews in Candia, openly declared for him. However, part of the learned men opposed Daniel Israel, and declared him to be an impostor. In consequence of their remonstrances, the cadi expelled him from the city, and imposed a fine upon his adherents. Cordoso, who

---

* Basnage, p. 702

† Daniel Israel attempted to support this assertion, by a false interpretation of the prophecy of Daniel xii. 11, 12.

maintained the impostor, was killed by his son-in-law; and his death blasted all the hopes of the Jews, and unveiled the deception.* The murderer fled into a Turkish mosque, and was converted to Mahometanism; but we are not told what became of Daniel Israel.

The denomination of Zabathaites is given to the followers of Zabathai Tzevi. The sect formed by this impostor survived him; and he actually has yet at Salonichi partizans, who outwardly professing Mahometanism, observe in secret the Judaic rites, marry among themselves, and live in the same quarter of the city without communicating with the Musselmans except for the purpose of commerce, and in the mosques. They never enter the syna-gogues, nor make known their schism. Hence it appears, that " the Turks pardon a secret observ-ance of another religion in favour of a public pro-fession of their own."·

Zabathai Tzevi had many adherents among the Jews of England, Holland, Germany, and Poland, who have continued in small numbers to our days.†

One of the Jews, named Jonathan, born at Cra-cow in 1690, and who in 1750 was elected grand rabbin of the three towns of Hamburg, Altona, and Wansbeck, was accused of being a follower of Zabathai Tzevi, which occasioned a very ani-mated dispute, and produced many pamphlets.

* Many of the infatuated Jews not only believed that Zabathai was living, and would re-appear, but even celebrated the day of his birth with great rejoicings, crying, " Long live sultan Tzevi."— *Basnage*, p. 756.

† Gregoire's Histoire des Sectes Religieuses. Tome ii. p. 509. Published at Paris, 1810

CHAPTER XXIII.

Of the Jews in Ethiopia.—The conformity which subsists between
their religion and that of the Christians in that country.—Of the
Falasha in Abyssinia.—Of the Jews in Egypt and other parts of
Africa.—Of their state in Morocco.—Tyrannical conduct of the
emperors of that kingdom.—They are numerous at Fez, and
several learned Jews have appeared among them.

THE Jews have enjoyed more tranquillity in
Ethiopia than in most other countries, on account
of the conformity which subsisted between their religion and customs, and those of the Christian inhabitants, who are circumcised, abstain from swine's
flesh, and observe Saturday for their sabbath.
Their kings boast of having descended from the
Jewish monarchs, and bear for their arms a lion
holding a cross with this motto, "The Lion of
Judah has conquered."*

The Jewish hierarchy is still retained by the
Falasha in Abyssinia, who claim their descent from
a colony of Jews in the time of Solomon. About
the Christian era, they elected one Phinehas to be
their king, and from him their present sovereigns
pretend to be lineally descended. This family is
called by the Abyssinians Ben Israel, to distinguish
them from the house of Solomon, from whom the
sovereigns of the country derive their origin. About
the year 960, the Falasha attempted to seize the
throne of Abyssinia, and the wars with the nation
were long and distressing. At last they were so
weakened as to be obliged to leave the flat country
of Dembea and retire to the craggy mountains of

* Basnage, p 714.

Samen, where they maintained their independence.
Their capital is still called the Jews' rock.* In 1600
they were reduced to the brink of ruin; and
Gideon and Judith, their king and queen, were both
slain in battle. Since that time they have paid
taxes to the state, but are allowed to enjoy their
own government. When Mr. Bruce† was there,
about 1771, they were estimated to amount to an
hundred thousand effective men. Their king and
queen were then called Gideon and Judith; and
these names seem to be preferred for the royal
family. According to the accounts of the Falasha
their sovereigns are of the tribe of Judah.‡

Their Old Testament is in the Geez language,
written by Abyssinian Christians and sold to them.
No dispute has ever existed about the text of scripture. They have no table of various readings; no
Talmud, Targum, or Cabbala; no fringes or
ribbands upon their garments, nor any scribe.
They have lost their Hebrew, and only speak the
language their ancestors learned in the country
where they settled. They acknowledge candidly,
that they have no Hebrew nor Samaritan copies,
and that they trust wholly to the translation. They
say the prophecy of Enoch is the first book of
scripture they ever received, after which they place
the book of Job. They maintained that the sceptre
has never departed from Judah; and apply the pro-

---

* Bruce's Travels, vol ii chap. vi. p. 114.

† Mr Bruce observes, " that he did not spare the utmost pains in
inquiring into the history of this curious people, and that he lived in
habits of intimacy and friendship with several of the most learned
among them."—*Bruce*, vol. ii. p. 406

‡ Bruce's Travels, vol. ii

phecy of the gathering of the Gentiles to the future
appearance of the Messiah.

The Falasha have no knowledge of the New
Testament but from conversation they imagine it
very absurd to suppose the Messiah is already come,
who they appear to think is to be a temporal prince,
prophet, priest, and conqueror.* The Jewish law
is in full force among this people, and all the Levitical observances, purifications, atonements, absti-
nences, and sacrifices.

The Jews for many ages have found an asylum in
Egypt; they were, however, in 1524, near the
precipice of destruction, Achmet, governor of Egypt,
having revolted against Solomon II. At the commencement of the rebellion, the soldiers plundered
their houses ; and Achmet imposed a tax upon them
of two hundred talents. They, however, pleaded
insolvency, and paid only fifteen talents into the
treasury. The governor, exasperated at this refusal, commanded all the Israelites in the kingdom
to be arrested and imprisoned. This order was
annulled by a conspiracy against Achmet, in consequence of which he was put to death ; and the Jews
celebrated a feast in memory of their deliverance.†

The liberty which this people have since enjoyed
in Egypt, has rendered them numerous and powerful, particularly at Cairo, where they possessed thirty
synagogues.‡ They have long farmed all the customs in that city, and have acquired influence and
reputation by this employment. The bashaw of
Cairo every two years lets out the custom-house for

* Bruce's Travels. vol ii. p. 413.   † Basnage, p 716.
‡ Pocock's Description of the East, vol. i. p. 177.

the benefit of the grand seignor. He adjudges it
to the best bidder, and it commonly falls to the lot
of the Jews, because they have the art of gaining
his favour either by presents or intrigues. The
greater part of the Jews in Cairo are Pharisees or
Talmudists. There are, however, a number of
Caraites, who have a synagogue of their own. One
proof of the consequence which the Hebrew nation
enjoy under the aristocracy of Cairo is, that the
offices of the customs are shut upon their sabbath,
and no goods can pass upon that day although belonging to Mahometans and Christians.*

The Jews are also numerous in other parts of
Africa, and are the principal traders in the inland
provinces. Some of them were so affluent, that
Muley Archey, king of Taphilet, by seizing the
property of a rich Jew, was thereby enabled to
achieve the conquest of the province of Quiriana,
and to dispossess his brother of the kingdom of
Morocco and Fez. To recompence the people for
this act of oppression to an individual, he allowed
them to enjoy their former privileges, and appointed
Joshua Ben Hamosheth prince of that nation. His
brother Ishmael, who succeeded him, was a still
greater benefactor to the Jewish people. As an
acknowledgment for the services he had received
from Joseph de Toledo, he not only made him one
of the principal officers of his household, but constituted him his envoy to the different courts of
Europe; and in 1684 he concluded the peace with
the United Provinces.†

* Niebuhr's Travels, vol. i. p. 102. Published 1792.
† Basnage, p. 717. Modern Univer. Hist. vol. xiii. p. 383.

The Jews had been a long time settled at Oran, and were entrusted with some of the most honourable and lucrative offices in the city. Yet, notwithstanding the ill treatment they had received from the Spanish government, they, being it is said bribed, by cardinal Ximenes,* betrayed the town to the Spanish soldiers. This, and other signal services, did not, however, preserve them from being expelled from the city in 1669; but it is not known on what pretence they were banished. In the province of Suz, they were also numerous and flourishing ; in the capital of that principality they had a superb synagogue, which was served by several priests and officers. They had their judges and interpreters of the law, who were maintained at the expense of their brethren, who supported themselves by labour and commerce.†

The Jews have been‡ and still are very nume-

* The cardinal was a great persecutor of the Jewish nation, and, it is said, that he used his influence to persuade queen Isabella to expel them from Spain.

† Basnage, p. 717.

‡ It appears that the Hebrew nation were settled in Morocco as early as the year 1062; for the Jewish rabbi Samuel, who lived at the close of the eleventh century, received his surname from that city, where he resided. Samuel, having passed into Spain, had conferences with the Christians, who succeeded in convincing him of the truth of their religion. Before his conversion was completed, he addressed a letter to rabbi Isaac, a Jew in the same kingdom, in which he says, " I would fain learn of thee, out of the testimonies of the law and the prophets, and other scriptures, Why the Jews are thus smitten in this captivity wherein we are? which may be properly called, the perpetual anger of God, because it hath no end ; for it is now above a thousand years since we were carried captive by Titus. And yet our fathers, who worshipped idols, killed the prophets, and cast the law behind their back, were punished only with a seventy years' captivity, and then brought home again. But now there is no end of our

Y

rous in all parts of Morocco; after they were
expelled from Spain and Portugal, multitudes sought
an asylum in this empire. They are not confined
to towns, but have spread over the face of the
whole country.

" They are not only tributary in these parts, but
upon every small disgust, in danger of being expelled; and can never promise themselves any
permanent settlement or security. Though this
unhappy people, in almost every place where they
have resided, have been treated with cruelty and
contempt; yet in no part of the world have they
suffered more severe and undeserved oppressions
than in Barbary, where the whole country depends
upon their industry and ingenuity, and could
scarcely subsist without their assistance.*

The lowest classes among the Moors imagine
they have a right to oppress and insult the Jews,
who suffer the greatest ill treatment with a patience
they have acquired by being daily abused. They
have not courage to defend themselves, because the
Koran and judge are always in favour of the Mahometans. Their superior knowledge and address
give them, however, many advantages over the
Moors; and their skill in pecuniary negociations
enables them to act as agents and brokers. More
industrious as well as better informed than the Mahometans, they are employed by the emperor in
farming the customs, coining the money, and in

calamities, nor do the prophets promise any."—*Dissertations pour
servir a l'histoire des Juifs. Gisborne on the Christian religion.*

  * Lancelot Addison's Present State of the Jews. Lempriere's
Tour to Morocco.

conducting his intercourse with foreign merchants, and his negociations with foreign powers.* Thus employed, they have great opportunities for benefitting and injuring the state; and they have sufficient art to enrich themselves by every resource in their power; and find means to console themselves for the indignities they are obliged to suffer.

The Jews, in most parts of the empire, live separate from the Moors, and, though oppressed in other respects, are allowed the exercise of their religion. Many of them, however, in order to avoid the arbitrary treatment to which they are continually exposed, have professed the Mahometan religion. Upon their renouncing Judaism they are admitted to all the privileges of the Moors.

There are great numbers of Jews in the mountains of Morocco,† who are engaged in laborious employments, to which the other inhabitants are averse. This, however, does not deter others from attempting to raise themselves to eminent stations at court. One of their nation, named Pacheco, was sent ambassador to the United Provinces. He died at the Hague, 1604, and was interred with great pomp. Some time after, in the same century, two Jews were residents in Holland, from the courts of Portugal and Spain.‡

A. D. 1660.] The Jewish synagogues having been demolished in the kingdom of Fez, Muley Mahomet, when he ascended the throne, not only

* Chenier's Present State of Morocco, vol. i. p. 157.

† It has been computed that there are nearly four hundred thousand Jews in Morocco, Fez, and Algiers.—*Dissertations Critiques.*

‡ Basnage, p. 717. Gregoire, p. 201.

caused them to be rebuilt, but made one of that
nation his high treasurer and prime minister. This
people, however, have frequently suffered from the
tyranny and caprice of the arbitrary sovereigns of
Morocco. Sidi Mahomet, the emperor, having
imposed a heavy tax on his son Muley Ali, commanded him to ráise the sum required, on the
Jewish community, "who, not being, as he said,
in the road to salvation, merited no indulgence."
The prince offered his father the revenues of his
government, but earnestly entreated him not to
oppress the Jews, and add to wretchedness, which
was already too great.*

A. D. 1672.] Muley Ishmael, ingenious in
finding pretences for plundering his subjects, assembled the Jews, and thus addressed them :
" Dogs as you are, I have sent for you to oblige
you to turn Mahometans. I have long been amused
with an idle tale respecting the coming of the Messiah. For my part, I believe he is come already;
therefore, if you do not fix the precise time in
which he is to appear, I will leave you neither property nor life ; I will be trifled with no longer."

The Jews, terrified and astonished at this address,
represented the punctuality with which they had paid
the enormous taxes imposed upon them. After
they had, at their request, obtained a week to
prepare an answer, they collected a large sum of
money to present to the emperor, and informed him
that their doctors had concluded, that the Messiah
would appear in thirty years. " Yes," replied Ishmael, taking the money, " I understand you, dogs

* Chenier's Present State of Morocco, vol. i. p. 159.

and deceivers as you are; you think to hush my immediate wrath, in the hope that I shall not then be alive; but I will live to show the world that you are impostors, and punish you as you deserve."[*]

The Jews were more numerous in Fez than in any city in Barbary. A traveller, who visited this country in 1619, reckoned eighty thousand in this province, some of whom were very affluent and powerful. They have guards at the entrance of their quarter to enable them to carry on commerce, without being molested; and are permitted to exercise their religion.[†] But though they have a chief of their own nation, they are exposed to all kinds of oppressions from the Mahometans.

The Jews have schools at Fez, where they study the law and Talmud. This city has produced a number of learned rabbies, who have acquired celebrity by their writings. Among others, Judah Ching, Isaac Ben Jacob, Aaron Ben Chaim, and Solomon Ben Melech.

No where in Barbary was the Hebrew nation less molested than in Algiers about the year 1804. At that time a rebellion took place in the neighbourhood of that city, and the Jews were unjustly accused of the crime. The traitors were, in fact, persons intimately connected with the Dey himself, but as some of them had borrowed money of a Jewish merchant,

[*] Chenier, vol. i. p. 150.

[†] Dissertations pour servir a l'histoire des Juifs.—At Fez a day is appointed for the Jews to pay their tribute in public, and as soon as each has put down his share he receives a blow with a stick on the feet, and after making a profound bow retires amidst the insults of the populace.—*Gregoire*, p. 50.

the Jews, though not concerned in the rebellion,
were charged with treason, and cruelly racked and
tortured. Several hundreds lost their lives from
being suspended by long ropes, and hooked nails,
on the outside of the tower walls. Others were
punished by burning; some by stripes; and the
greater part, by confiscation of their property, were
reduced to a state of poverty. This extreme cruelty induced great numbers to leave Algiers and
establish themselves in other parts of Barbary, particularly at Tunis. Many of the more religious
among them, considering the persecution as a
warning from heaven to leave distant countries,
*resorted to Palestine and to the neighbourhood of
Jerusalem, as if the time of their restoration was
at hand.* There are still, however, about nine
thousand Jews at Algiers, who have eight public
synagogues; but many of the privileges which they
enjoyed before the year 1804, they no longer possess. The Jews of Algiers are allowed three wives
at a time, whom they may repudiate at pleasure.
They are, to a considerable extent, subject to a
person of their own nation, whose decisions are
despotic, and who is elected by the Dey himself.
The present chief of the Jews in that city is
Mr. Jacob Crav Bacri.*

Even in the heart of Africa this wretched people
meet their predicted fate. At Sansanding, eight
hundred miles eastward from the Atlantic, a recent
traveller discovered some of the descendants of
Israel. " These Jews," he observes, " in dress
and appearance very much resemble the Arabs.

* Jewish Expositor, February, 1817, p. 76—78.

But though they so far conform to the religion of Mahomet, as to recite public prayers from the Koran, they are but little respected by the negroes ; and even the Moors themselves allowed, that though I was a Christian, I was a better man than a Jew." The full import of these words will be best understood by those who have learned from Mr. Park's previous accounts, the extreme degree of contemptuous malignity to which the Moors in that part of Africa push their hatred of the Christians.*

* Park's Travels into the Interior of Africa, 1790, p. 204, 205.

CHAPTER XXIV.

Of the Jews in Germany.—The bishop of Cologne expels them from his diocese.—Victor a Carbe, abjures the Jewish religion, and writes against his nation.—Another deserter of the synagogue, attempts to persuade the emperor to order the Jewish books to be burnt.—His plan defeated by Reuchlin.—Of the effects of the reformation upon the state of the Jews.—Of their situation in Mersburg, Bohemia, and Hungary.—A false Messiah appears in Germany in the seventeenth century.

IN the three last chapters an account has been given of the Jews in Asia and Africa during three centuries. It is now time to turn to those of Europe, where their sufferings in the middle ages have been already briefly related.

At the commencement of the sixteenth century, the bishop of Cologne expelled the Jews from his diocese. Victor a Carbe, who had renounced Judaism to obtain preferment in the clerical line, wrote a vehement invective against his brethren, and highly applauded the prelate for having, as he styled it, "plucked the tares from the Lord's field." He advised the Christians not to dispute with his brethren, but to compel them to abjure their religion by coercive measures.

A few years after, another convert, named Pfepfercorn, attempted to persuade the emperor Maximilian that all the Jewish books ought to be burned, because they were replete with fables, false accounts, and blasphemies against Christ. Some time before he had written upon the Jews celebrating the passover, and charged them with being apostates from the Old, as well as enemies to

the New Testament. In another publication he painted in the strongest colours the usury of his nation, and their malice against the Christians.*

Pfepfercorn's conversion and zeal were, however, much suspected, and he was accused of having formed the design of seizing the Jewish books, in order to oblige his countrymen to redeem them at an extravagant price.† But he had the address to engage so many learned divines to favour his plan, that the emperor was inclined to grant his request. As the affair had obtained great publicity, he wished previously to hear what could be said on both sides the question. Reuchlin, a man well versed in Hebrew and other literature, strenuously opposed the burning of the Jewish books in general, and maintained that those only ought to be destroyed, which contained blasphemies against Christ.‡ He also pointed out the impossibility of suppressing books by an imperial decree which were dispersed in all parts of the world, and might easily be reprinted in other places.

The moderation of Reuchlin exposed him to severe persecutions from his bigoted opponents. The affair was finally left by an appeal to the pope. Hochstrat, an inquisitor, and a man fully qualified for that cruel office, repaired to Rome, supported with remonstrances from several princes to bias, with money to bribe, and menaces to intimidate.

* Basnage, p. 730.

† Pfepfercorn, being arrested upon some suspicion, made a full confession of his hypocrisy and iniquitous conduct.

‡ He consented to the burning of two Jewish works called Nizzachou and Toldos Jeschu.—*Basnage*, p. 731.

He even threatened the pope with rejecting his
authority, and separating from the church, unless
Reuchlin, and the Jews he defended, were condemned. But all his efforts were vain, and he was
obliged to return mortified and disgraced. The
victory which his opponent had gained exposed
him to the enmity of the monkish party. But he
informed them, that "he was persuaded that
Martin Luther, who then began to make a figure
in Germany, would find them so much employment,
that they would permit him to end his days in
peace."*

The progress of the reformation in Germany
proved a powerful stimulus to mental exertion.
The protestant divines, more conversant with the
learned languages than the monks and clergy in
past ages, studied the writings of the rabbies in
order to confute them upon their own principles.
The Roman Catholic clergy paid more attention to
the languages than formerly, and pursued the same
method. Hence the Jewish publications were not
only spared, but perused more than ever. The
impulse was given to the European republic of
letters; and even the Jews, awakened by the general activity, published several grammars and
lexicons in the Hebrew language, and exerted
themselves in defending their religion against their
learned opponents.

A. D. 1547.] The reformation, in a great measure, freed the Jews from the persecutions to which
they were continually exposed in the middle ages,†

* Basnage, p. 733. Villers on the Reformation, p. 107.
† David Levi observes; "Thanks be to God and the reformation

founded upon the charges of crucifying Christian children, and profaning consecrated wafers. They, however, entertained an extreme aversion to Luther, because he deterred some Christian princes from receiving them into their dominions.

It was determined by the theological and Lutheran faculties of Wirtemberg and Rostock, that a Christian when sick cannot call in the assistance of a Jewish physician, because they employ magical remedies ; and since the curse of heaven has been pronounced against this people, they ought not to cure the Christians, who are the children of God.*

The disputes between the Christians and Jews gave rise to a new sect among the latter, who were styled in contempt, Demi-Jews. Seidelius, one of these doctors, appeared in Transylvania, and maintained that the Messiah regarded only the Jewish nation, to whom he had been peculiarly promised in the same manner as the land of Canaan. He asserted, that the Pagan world had no more share in the former, than in the latter ; and that the whole of religion is contained in the decalogue, and written in the hearts of men. Seidelius, not being able to gain converts in Silesia, his native country, removed to Poland, and there acquired a number of followers.†

The Jews at Mersburg, who pretended to have been there settled ever since the destruction of Jerusalem, were banished from the city and diocese by the

we now enjoy several privileges and immunities in the several states in which we are settled, which our ancestors were strangers to since their dispersion "—*Levi's Letters to Priestley*, p. 19.

* Gregoire on the Reformation of the Jews, p. 46.

† Basnage, p. 733.

bishop Adolphus early in the sixteenth century.' In 1559, the emperor Ferdinand I. not only protected this oppressed people, but allowed them the privilege of having princes of the captivity in Germany, and ordered that a rabbi of Worms should be preferred before any of his nation! Among the chiefs, the rabbi Jakock, a native of Worms,* was eminently distinguished for his learning. He left four sons, who all discharged important offices, and were highly celebrated by their countrymen.†

The Jews in Bohemia, ever since the tenth century, have been generally treated with more indulgence than in most other countries, on account of some important services which they rendered the Christians against the banditti. They had built a superb synagogue, and erected an academy at Prague, over which the celebrated rabbi Falk presided.‡ But in 1580, a conflagration having destroyed some part of the kingdom, they were accused of being accessaries to it, and were condemned. Those who escaped a cruel death were

---

* The Jews in Germany boasted, that their ancestors entered the country before the destruction of their second temple. Those of Worms pretended to have given good proof to the emperor and the states of the empire, that their 'ancestors had no concern in our Saviour's crucifixion, and that from time immemorial they had been settled in this city, which is the reason they have obtained privileges of which others are deprived. With this view they have inserted in the Toldos Jeschu the extract of a letter, which they pretend the sanhedrim of Worms wrote to the king of Judea, to dissuade him from putting Jesus Christ to death. Mr. Basnage supposes, that the author of the Toldos Jeschu was a member of the synagogue of Worms —*Basnage*, p. 505. *Dissertations Critiques, &c.*

† Ibid. p. 784.

‡ This rabbi introduced the Christian method of disputing, but he soon found it disgusted his brethren.

expelled the kingdom. But, the incendiaries being discovered before the end of 'the' year, the Jews were recalled, and again settled in the country.*

Several Jewish doctors have appeared in Bohe-mia, whose abilities and erudition have been highly celebrated by their brethren. Leo of Prague flourished in 1553, and was chief of the Moravian academies, and judge of his nation in that country. He wrote a number of learned works, one of which is styled "The Redemption and Eternity of Israel." In this production he assures his brethren, that the Messiah will certainly appear, and settle them in a state of permanent prosperity.†

The Jewish historian, David Gantz, was a native Prague; and in that city he composed his work, entitled " The Stem of David." This publication is a chronology from the creation to the year 1292 of the Christian era. He gave it this title either because it was his first work, or to remind his suffering nation of the branch, David or Messiah, who was to redeem them from captivity, and to induce them to pray more fervently for his appearance.‡

The Jews in Hungary had greatly decreased towards the conclusion of the sixteenth century, at which period the emperor Rodolphus imposed an enormous tax upon them. He judged that they would be unable to pay the sum required, and he might find a pretence to compel them to quit his

---

* Basnage, p. 735.

† A late author observes, that David Gantz's Tzemack David, or stem of David, though a meagre chronicle, is perhaps the best history written by a Jew since the time of Josephus.—*Adams' Religious World Displayed*, vol i. p 8

‡ Basnage, p. 736.

dominions. Those of Moravia suffered a severe persecution in 1574, and many were put to a cruel death before their friends were able to afford them assistance. Those of Franconia were accused of setting fire to several houses in the town of Bamberg, and were plundered of their effects. Notwithstanding these misfortunes they obtained liberty to settle in the duke of Brunswick's territories at the end of the sixteenth century.*

Several learned rabbies appeared in Germany during the seventeenth century ; among others a famous cabbalist, named Nathan de Spira, from Spire, the place of his birth. He published a work styled the "Good of the Land," in order to celebrate the country of Palestine ; and also a cabbalistical commentary on some verses of Deuteronomy, in which he pretended to find and resolve the deepest mysteries.†

One of the most famous doctors which Germany produced in this century was Isaac Loria, author of a metaphysical introduction to the cabbala. In this work he examines the reasons which induced God to create the world. He also published several other learned treatises. Towards the conclusion of his life he retired to Palestine, and was buried at Sapheta in Upper Galilee.

A. D. 1682.] At this period rabbi Mordecai, a German Jew, who had acquired great celebrity among his brethren for his learning and austere manner of life, pretended to be the Messiah. Many of the German and Italian Jews were seduced by the impostor, and acknowledged his divine

* Basnage, p. 736.   † Ibid. p. 737.

mission. It was not long, however, before they were sensible of the folly of their blind credulity; and the false Messiah was obliged to provide for his own safety by flight.*

* Jortin's Remarks, vol. ii. p. 306.

CHAPTER XXV.

State of the Jews in Poland.—They obtain extensive privileges from Casimire the Great.—They are also highly favoured by John Sobieski.—Of the literary Jews in Poland.—Prosperous condition of the nation at Hamburg —Of those in Hungary.—A large council of Jews are said to have convened on the plains of Ageda in this country.—Prosperous state of the Jews at Vienna.—Of their condition in other cities in Germany.—An account of several learned Jews, who, in the seventeenth century, were converted to the Christian religion.

A. D. 1333.] THE flourishing state of the Jews in Poland, under Casimire the Great, has been mentioned in a preceding chapter; in consequence of the extensive privileges which this monarch's affection for Esther, a beautiful Jewess, induced him to grant them, they, in a manner, engrossed all the commerce in the country, and thus acquired power and affluence. The prosperous state of their affairs in this kingdom was not, however, wholly owing to the king's edicts in their favour, but may in part be attributed to their own industry, the indolence of the higher classes of society, and the oppressed state of the peasants.*

The religious zeal which caused the reformation to be banished from Poland was so capricious, as to allow the Jews an entire liberty of conscience. They not only possessed superb synagogues and academies, but were owners of land, and had at Cracow a court of judicature, which was permitted to judge of criminal, as well as civil concerns. But,

* Basnage, p. 735. Coxe's Travels to Poland, vol. i. p. 143.

notwithstanding their privileges,' they sometimes
suffered from popular tumults.*.

Under John Sobieski the Hebrew nation were so
highly favoured, that his administration was invidi-
ously styled a Jewish junto. He farmed to them
the royal demesnes, and reposed such confidence in
them as raised general discontent among the nobility. After his death an ancient law of Sigismund
the First was revived, and inserted in the Pacta
Conventa of Augustus II. that no Jew, or person of
low birth, should be capable of farming the royal
revenues. Since that period they have enjoyed
their privileges rather by connivance than by legal
sanction.†

Poland has long been the principal seat of literary Jews, and the place where they have been
accustomed to send their children to study the
Talmud and rites of their religion. In the sixteenth century a celebrated rabbi named Iserdes
taught at Cracow, and collected, a vast number of
disciples, who repaired from all parts to attend his
lectures. He expounded the law during twenty
years.‡

In 1658, a Jew in the kingdom of Poland, named
John Solomon, professed the Christian religion.
He had been bound for one of his brethren, and
committed to prison ; and, as he obtained his liberty
by abjuring his former belief, his conversion was at
first greatly suspected. He, however, after his

* Basnage, p. 735.
† Coxe's Travels, 1784, vol. i. p. 144. Burnet's Present State of
Poland, 1807.
‡ Basnage, p. 735.

7

baptism, wrote thirty-seven demonstrations in order
to prove that the Messiah was come, and was a
divine person, distinct from God the Father.

Hamburg has been styled the "lesser Jerusalem,"
on account of the multitudes of Jews who have
long inhabited the city and carried on commerce.
Some of this people acquired wealth, and others
distinguished themselves by their knowledge in
various sciences, particularly that of physic. In
this city a learned rabbi, named Esdras Edgardus,
having embraced the Christian religion in 1690, assiduously laboured to convert his brethren, and his
efforts were in various instances crowned with
remarkable success.*

The emperor Ferdinand III. granted the Jews
great privileges at Prague on account of their eminent services in defending the city, when it was besieged by the Swedes in 1641. Rabbi Jehudah Leo
compiled a history of the transaction, in which he
highly extolled the fidelity and bravery of his
brethren on this occasion ; but more especially their
piety in assembling in their synagogues to offer
prayers for their success ; and appeared to ascribe
the preservation of the city to their petitions and
merit.†

In Hungary the Jews enjoyed the privilege of
farming the revenues till Ferdinand II. deprived
them of it by an edict in 1630. They notwithstanding found means to elude this decree, since

* Bishop Kidder, who corresponded with him, says, that " he has
been an instrument of converting more Jews, including many rabbins,
than have perhaps ever been converted by any one person in the world
since the age of miracles."

† Modern Universal History, vol. xiii. p. 426.

Ferdinand, III. was obliged to issue a new edict, which condemned those to the loss of their places, who admitted this people to any of them. Still, however, they retained their employment till the emperor repeatedly sent commissioners to expel them, the last of which arrived in 1655.[*]

Notwithstanding these oppressions, this kingdom, if accounts are to be credited, soon became the scene of a memorable event. It is related, that, in the year 1650, the Jews, wearied and perplexed by the miseries of a captivity protracted through sixteen centuries, resolved to hold a national council for the complete investigation of the great question; whether *the Messiah was already come.* The plain of Ageda, about thirty leagues from Buda, was selected for the assembly. This place was chosen on account of the war between the Turks and king of Hungary, both parties having given the nation permission to convene in this part of the country. Three hundred of the most eminent rabbies, and a vast multitude of other Jews, assisted at the council; and Zechariah, of the tribe of Levi, was chosen their president and speaker.[†]

[*] Modern Universal History, vol. xiii. p. 427.

[†] A narrative of the great council of Jews on the plains of Ageda in Hungary was published in the " Phœnix, or a collection of scarce and valuable papers, in 1707." An account of this assembly is also inserted in the thirteenth volume of the Modern Universal History; the authors of this work refer to Bret's narrative in the Phœnix, but mention no other authority. This part of the Universal History is supposed to have been written by Psalmanazar, and, as he was a person of great learning, and very conversant in Hebrew literature, and probably lived much with the Jews, his mentioning of it is a circumstance in favour of its credibility. It is also considered as authentic by Dr. Owen, in his " Essay on Image Worship ;" and by Mr.

After the assembly had excluded all who could not
prove themselves of Jewish origin, the president
thus proposed the following question : " We have
convened in this place to examine whether the Messiah is really come, or whether we must still expect
his appearance?" Some professed themselves inclined to believe that he had already come, since the
calamities which their nation had suffered during a
series of ages could not be owing to their idolatry,
a crime which they had carefully avoided since their
return from the Babylonian captivity. But the
majority of the council agreed, that the Messiah
had not appeared, and that his delay was owing to
their sins and impenitence.[*]

They next debated in what manner their long
expected deliverer would manifest himself; and readily agreed, that he would appear as a mighty conqueror, and deliver them from all foreign dominion.
After the session had continued six days, a learned
rabbi, named Abraham, strenuously urged upon the
council the necessity and propriety of strictly
examining into the pretensions of the Christian
Messiah, Jesus of Nazareth. The Pharisees, who
overruled the assembly, answered, that he could
not be that distinguished personage, because he

Richards of Oxford, and lately by Mr. Whitaker in his " Dissertation
on Prophecy." It is mentioned in Dr. Jortin's Remarks on Ecclesiastical History, second volume, and second edition, and in other
learned works. On the other hand, the narrative is pronounced
fabulous by Menasses Ben Israel, and his authority has the greater
weight, because, at the very time of the publication in question, he
was negociating with Cromwell for the return of his brethren The
English Jews also treat the account of this council as fabulous, and
Basnage does not mention it in his history.—*Butler's Horæ Biblicæ.*

   [*] Modern Universal Hist. vol. xiii. p. 429, 430.

appeared in a humble and despised state ; but the Messiah was to manifest, himself in a· glorious and triumphant manner. Abraham, who was dissatisfied with the Pharisaic reasoning, strongly insisted upon Christ's miracles, and asked by what power he could perform them? Zebedee, one of the chiefs of this sect, answered, that " he wrought them by the magic art." , Abraham replied, that " no magic art could give sight, hearing, and speech to those who were born, blind, deaf, or dumb."*

It appears, that, in consequence of the remonstrances of this learned rabbi, some Christian priests were admitted, and asked to explain the nature and grounds of their, faith. These priests were Roman Catholics, who, not contented to prove that Jesus Christ was the Messiah, began to extol the worship, ceremonies, and authority of their church. The council, highly irritated, exclaimed, in a tumultuous manner, " *No Christ ! No God-man ! ·No intercession, of saints ! No worship of images ! No prayers to the virgin Mary !*" They also rent their clothes, and cast dust upon their heads, crying, " Blasphemy ! blasphemy !" In this ·manner they broke up the assembly, and refused to receive any further information respecting Christ.†

The assembly met again only to agree upon another council, which was to be held three years after in Syria. It is said, that some of the Jewish doctors acknowledged that what had passed had rendered them wavering and unsettled in their former belief; and that they expressed a desire to

* Modern Univer. Hist. vol. xiii. p. 431.　　　† Ibid.

converse with some protestant divines. But ,the
presence of so many monks deterred them, and
made them apprehend some tragical conclusion to
the assembly.*

A. D. 1660.] About this period the Jews had
acquired such an ascendency at Vienna, that rabbi
Zechariah obtained permission to erect a superb
synagogue and academy, in order to revive religion
and learning among his brethren. He endowed the
latter with a sufficient pension to support twenty-
four rabbies, who were to read lectures on the
Talmud day and night. It was always to be open,
and the doctors alternately to relieve each other.
The academy, however, was scarcely completed
before the emperor expelled them from the capital,
and converted their synagogue into a church. After
the death of the empress, in 1673, who had super-
stitiously attributed a misfortune which she suffered
to the toleration of the Jews, they were recalled,
and admitted to several high offices and titles of
honour. But the populace, who envied the opulence they acquired under the government, used
the most unjustifiable measures to deprive them of
their wealth.†

The emperor found a new subject of complaint
against the Jews, because, while he was engaged
in a war with the Turks, they assisted the Mahometans in maintaining the siege of Buda, and distinguished themselves by their valour. But though
their conduct was highly resented in Germany and
Italy, yet, as they were subjects of the Ottoman

* Modern Univer. Hist. vol. xiii. p. 222.
† Modern Univer. Hist. vol. xiii. p. 431.

empire, they could not justly be condemned for their fidelity to their sovereign.*

. During the seventeenth century the Jews were numerous and flourishing in the provinces of Servia, Croatia, Moldavia, Valencia, &c. as well as in most of the large cities in the empire. They were, however, expelled from Nuremburg, but settled in most towns in the vicinity, and possessed a synagogue at Pfurt. They were only permitted to enter the city with a guide, who was obliged to remain with them till the time of their departure. Formerly they had a synagogue and academy at Augsburg, and their rabbies and pupils were supported by the rich merchants of the place. But they have since been expelled, and obliged to purchase the liberty of entering the city at the price of a florin for every hour they remained in it † .

The Jews of Worms were charged by one of their brethren, who had renounced the religion of his ancestors, with having the name of Jehovah inscribed on the top of their synagogue, from a superstitious notion that it would be an effectual mean of preserving the edifice. But the French convinced them of the vanity of this idea, when they took the city and demolished the building.‡

The Jews were so numerous in Frankfort, during the seventeenth and eighteenth centuries, that they were computed to have amounted to thirty thousand. But they were often plundered, exposed to all manner of ridicule, and employed in the most servile offices. A late traveller asserts, that "they were confined to live in one street, which was long,

* Basnage, p. 736.　　† Ibid.　　‡ Ibid. p. 737.

spacious, and irregular, while their houses were separated back and front from the other citizens by an high wall. Every evening, about ten or eleven, both ends of the street were shut up, and no Jew, without special permission, suffered to quit his prison during the time of divine service among the Christians.

The intolerable hardships which this persecuted people endured in former times would have been abolished ; but the rich Jews, finding the assistance of their poor brethren highly beneficial to them in carrying on commerce, made pressing remonstrances against any change, even though it would be advantageous to themselves."*

The Jews in Prague were so numerous in the seventeenth century as to fill a third part of the city. But, though allowed a toleration, they were hated and despised by the Christians ; and remained poor and miserable, often exposed to insults, and obliged to submit to the most degrading employments.† Their condition was more favourable in the following century ; for a late traveller asserts, that in 1780 there were nine or ten thousand of the Israelites in the city. They were remarkably industrious, and in almost every inn there is a Jew who performs the business of a servant. They are allowed entire liberty of conscience, and have artists and mechanics of their own religion, who reside in the part of the town appropriated to them, which is called the Jews' city ‡

Several learned Jews in Poland and Germany, have, at different periods, been converted to Christi-

---

* Stolberg's Travels, vol ii p 366.   † Basnage, p 736.
‡ Riesbeck's Travels, vol. i p 421.

anity. Mordecai-Ben-Moses, a native of Germany, had distinguished himself by his zeal in writing against the New Testament. But after diligently studying, and carefully comparing it with the Old, he became sensible of his error, renounced Judaism, and, in 1701, was baptized. After his conversion he published several valuable works.

Aaron Margalitha, a learned rabbi in Poland, embraced the Christian religion, and was baptized in Leyden. He was afterwards appointed, professor of Jewish antiquities in the university of Frankfort, where he published, in 1706, a treatise on the sufferings of Christ.*

Johannes Christlicl Hielbronner of Cracow, in Poland, was baptized in 1709. He wrote a treatise, in the German language, on the fifty-third of Isaiah;† and declared in his preface to the work, that this chapter was the principal mean of inducing him to embrace the Christian religion. This performance was published in 1710. Five years after, he published at Dresden, a small work concerning Jesus Christ, the true Messiah, and Son of God; with an appendix, showing what are the characteristics of the Messiah expected by his unconverted brethren. In 1718 he published another work at Hamburg, in answer to the Jewish exceptions against the genealogy of our Saviour recorded in the Gospels.‡

* Chapman's Eusebius, p. 331—334.
† It has been observed, that the Jews, in their selection of passages from the prophets to be read on their sabbaths and festivals, omit those which speak most clearly of our Saviour. For instance, it is said, that the fifty-second and fifty-fourth chapters of Isaiah are appointed, and the fifty-third passed over.
‡ Chapman's Eusebius, p. 545.

Ernestus Maximilian Borg was also convinced of the truth of Christianity by reading the fifty-third chapter of Isaiah, and baptized at Wratislaw. In the year 1722, he published an extraordinary work with this title, " The Christian Doctrine built upon Moses and the Prophets." Another learned German Jew, named Christian Meir, was baptized at Breme. Among various other productions, in 1722, he published a tract, in order to evince, from various prophecies of the Old Testament, that Jesus Christ is the true Messiah.*

* Chapman's Eusebius, p. 545.

CHAPTER XXVI.

State of the Jews in Italy during the sixteenth century.—Julius III.
commands all the Gemaras to be burnt.—Of Joseph Tzarphanti and
Elias Levita.—Paul IV. persecutes the Jews, but is prevented from
banishing them on a false accusation.—Pius V. issues an edict
against them.—Sixtus V. treats them with more indulgence, but
Clement VIII. confirms the edict of Pius.—The Jews are tolerated
at Venice, and Hebrew books printed in that city.—Learned
Rabbies appear in Venice and other parts of Italy.—Of the Jews in
Padua.—A number of Jews from Germany establish a printing
office in Soncini.—Of those in Turin.—They are favoured and
protected by pope Innocent XI. who attempts to convert them to
the Christian religion.—They are numerous in the ecclesiastical
state in the eighteenth century.—Charles, king of Naples, issues
an edict in their favour.

A. D. 1554.] IN a foregoing chapter* we have
seen the Jews in general favoured and protected by
the Roman pontiffs ; but in Italy as well as in other
countries, they have experienced various vicissitudes.
Julius III. being of opinion that the interpretations
of the Gemara had a dangerous tendency, commanded all the copies of the work throughout Italy
to be burnt. †

Under this pontificate Joseph Tzarphanti, a celebrated rabbi, embraced the Christian religion. He
was born in France, but, upon finding Jewish
learning in a more flourishing state at Rome, he
removed to this city and expounded the Talmud.
After his conversion he wrote a friendly letter to the
Jews, in which he proved, that the Messiah had
really appeared. Soon after he was appointed to
preach to his unconverted brethren, and to the new

* See Chap. XX.   † Basnage, p. 735.

proselytes. But his deserting the synagogue had rendered him so odious to the former, that, upon their remonstrance to cardinal Sirlet, the employment was taken from him. He wrote afterwards a treatise, styled, " The Confusion of the Jews," in order to prove, that all the mysteries of Christianity are found in the Old Testament.*

Among the learned Jews who appeared in the sixteenth century,† Elias Levita claims the pre-eminence, and was one of the most celebrated writers which his nation ever produced. He was born in Germany, but spent the greatest part of his life in Italy. An ardent desire to acquire knowledge induced him to study with intense application ; and he was so happy as to live at a time when the learned began to recur to the original fountain of the scriptures, and revived the study of the Hebrew language. Elias, having lost all he possessed in Padua, when that city was taken and plundered, supported himself and family by teaching Hebrew. This rendered him obnoxious to his nation, who censured him with great asperity for exposing the divine oracles to the Christians by teaching them the sacred language. He, however, had the resolution to persevere in his instructions. Some have supposed that he embraced Christianity, on account of his living in habits of great friendship and intimacy with those of that religion. But, though his mind was free from that

---

* Basnage, p 723.

† In the sixteenth century, a celebrated Jewish poetess, named Deborah, flourished at Rome, and acquired celebrity by her poetic and other works about the year 1360 ; she lived till the beginning of the seventeenth century —*Modern Univer. Hist.*

· enmity against Christians which many of his brethren have exhibited, he never renounced the faith of his ancestors.*

At the age of forty he went to Rome, and there obtained the favour and protection of cardinal Egidio. He resided with his eminence thirteen years, and instructed him in the knowledge of the Hebrew language. During this period he published several learned works, and remained at Rome till the city was sacked and plundered by the high constable Bourbon. This event, having again reduced him to extreme poverty, he retired to Venice, and from thence to Germany. But, being unaccustomed to the cold of the country, he returned to Italy, and died at Venice, in 1549, in the eightieth year of his age. This great man was humane, benevolent and sincere, and the amiable traits in his character caused him to be noticed and caressed by princes, cardinals, and bishops. Among various other learned productions he composed an Hebrew grammar and rabbinic lexicon, and enjoyed the satisfaction of seeing his works in high reputation, being translated into other languages, and repeatedly published.†

In the infancy of the reformation, a celebrated Jew, named Samuel Tremellius, of Ferrara, in Italy, was converted to the Christian religion, and constantly adhered to the protestant faith. In 1554, he published a Hebrew catechism, containing the grounds and principles of Christianity. His work was prefaced with an affectionate address to his brethren, for whose benefit he composed the tract. He also, in conjunction with Franciscus Junius,

* Basnage, p. 724.   † De Rossie's Hebrew Biography.

translated into Latin from the Hebrew all the books .
of the Old Testament, as well as those of the New
from the Syriac version.*

A. D. 1555.] Paul IV. was the avowed enemy
of the Jews, and issued several severe edicts against
them. By his decrees they were compelled to sell
all their lands ; to surrender many of their books to
the flames; to wear a distinguishing dress; to nearly
forego all intercourse with Christians; and to have
that part of the city where they resided shut every
night. He also limited the number of their synagogues, and allowed them only one in each city, on
which he imposed a tribute to be employed for the
instruction of Jewish catechumens, who were
willing to embrace Christianity.†

During this pontificate they were exposed to a
still more severe persecution. Eighty female converts from Judaism pretended to be possessed, and,
upon being exorcised, accused their unbelieving
brethren with bewitching them in order to revenge
their apostacy. The credulous pontiff, who entertained an extreme aversion against the Jews, resolved to expel them. But a Jesuit dissuaded him
from his design by painting in strong colours the
absurdity of the accusation, and strenuously enforcing the duty and necessity of making a stricter
inquiry respecting the alleged crime. The pretended demoniacs, being accordingly examined by
scourging, confessed that they had been persuaded
to act this part by some courtiers, who hoped to
have enriched themselves with the plunder of this
devoted race, whether they were banished or mas-

* Chapman's Eusebius, p. 537.   † Basnage, p. 723.

sacred. Upon this discovery the courtiers were condemned to death; and the pontiff exclaimed, "I might have suffered eternal punishment for unjustly destroying the Jews, had not my good Jesuit prevented it. I will pray to God to convert them as long as I live; but I never will hate and persecute them as I have formerly done."*

A. D. 1569.] Pius V. issued an edict against the Jews, in which he accused them of falsehood, of treachery, and of ruining the ecclesiastical state by their exorbitant usury and other crimes. By this decree he expelled them from every part of his dominions except the cities of Rome and Ancona. The reasons he assigned for permitting them to remain in his capital, were, that the people might be reminded of Christ's sufferings, that a watchful eye might be kept over them, and that the sanctity of the place and example of the Christians might encourage their conversion. But it has been supposed, that his real motive was the promotion of commerce in the eastern parts, and that he might by this mean procure substantial advantage to the Holy See.

A. D. 1587.] His successor Sixtus V. frankly declared, that the profit he derived from the Jewish merchants was his principal motive for tolerating those of this nation. A certain rabbi named Meir, of French extraction, came to Rome at this time, and being a man of learning and address dedicated a book to this pontiff, and presented to him a flattering eulogy in verse, which was translated into Italian. After he had thus conciliated the protection

* Basnage, p. 723. Modern Universal Hist. vol. xiii. p. 327.

of the pope, he petitioned for the exclusive privilege of establishing a silk manufacture at Rome. Sextus not only granted his request, but revoked all the bulls and edicts of his predecessors to the contrary, though they had been confirmed with an oath strengthened with a menace of excommunication.*

A. D. 1593.] Clement VIII. confirmed in substance the bull of Pius V. which expelled the Jews from the ecclesiastical state. He, however, relaxed so far as to add Avignon to the cities of refuge, where they have been settled ever since with entire liberty to exercise their religion. The reason he assigned for this indulgence was, his ardent desire to effect their conversion.†

The Jews were tolerated in all the Venetian territories, and had merited this indulgence by eminent services which they performed in the wars against the Turks, particularly at the siege of Candia. They were numerous and flourishing in the capital. In 1511, David Bomberg came from Antwerp to Venice, and began for the first time to print Hebrew Bibles.‡ In order to render them more

* Basnage, p. 724.   † Ibid.

‡ Bomberg printed several Hebrew Bibles in folio and quarto at Venice, most of which were esteemed both by the Jews and Christians. The division of the Scriptures into chapters was invented by cardinal Hugo in 1240. The subdivision of the chapters into verses had its origin from a famous Jewish rabbi, named Mordecai Nathan, about 1445. This rabbi, in imitation of cardinal Hugo, composed a concordance to the Hebrew Bible, for the use of his brethren. But though he followed Hugo in the division of the books into chapters, he refined upon his invention, and subdivided the chapters into verses. And thus, as the Jews borrowed the division of the books of the Holy Scriptures into chapters from the Christians, the Christians borrowed that of the chapters into verses from the Jews.—*Buck's Theological Dictionary*, vol. i. p. 79.

correct he employed one hundred Jews. He also published many learned rabbinical works ; and was hence esteemed and beloved by the nation.

Several learned rabbies flourished at Venice during the sixteenth and seventeenth centuries. David, the son of Isaac de Pomis, was born in 1523. He acquired celebrity by a work, styled, "The Branch of David," and practised physic in various places with great success. At length he retired to Venice and composed a " treatise on the miseries of human life," which was an Italian commentary on the book of Ecclesiastes.*

Simeon Luzati, another famous rabbi, composed a work styled, " Socrates," in order to prove, that the greatest geniuses are inclined to err when not guided by revelation. He published besides, a treatise on the present state of his nation. Samuel Nachmias, a native of Thessalonica, also settled in this metropolis, and, with several others of his family, was baptized in 1647. According to his account he first received a favourable impression of Christianity by being present at a public dispute in Venice between two of his nation, one of whom had renounced Judaism, respecting the accomplishment of Daniel's prophecy of the seventy weeks. In this dispute Simeon Luzati, the celebrated rabbi above mentioned, was chosen arbitrator. The condition agreed upon by the disputants was, that the person who was vanquished in the argument should embrace the religion of his opponent. The contest was conducted with great spirit and ingenuity on both sides ; but the Christian reasoned from the

* Modern Universal History, vol. xiii. p. 401.

A A

Scriptures with so much energy and strength of
argument, that Luzati exclaimed, " I beseech you
to permit us to be silent, and shut up our books ;
for if we proceed to examine the prophecies any
further we shall all become Christians. It cannot
be denied, that, in the prophecy of Daniel, the
coming of the Messiah is so clearly manifested, that
the time of his appearance must be allowed to be
already past ; but whether Jesus of Nazareth be
the person I cannot determine." This speech
closed the debate; and made such a deep impression upon rabbi Samuel and his brother Joseph,
that they both formed the design of renouncing
Judaism. A few months after, upon reconsidering
the subject seriously and calmly, they embraced the
Christian religion. In 1683, Samuel published a
work in Italian, entitled, " The Way of Faith," in
order to prove to his brethren, that they were no
longer bound to observe the ceremonial law, but to
embrace the doctrines of the Gospel.*

Another celebrated rabbi, named Mordecai
Korkos, who was a native of Venice, and taught in
this city in 1687, rendered himself odious to his
nation by writing a treatise against the Cabbala.
The Jews so highly venerate this science, that they
regard every attempt to lesson its importance levelled
against the fundamentals of religion ; and their
doctors prohibited the publication of this work.†

The synagogues of Modena, as well as those of
Venice, produced several learned men, among

* Chapman's Eusebius, p. 549. In a preface to this publication
rabbi Nachmias gives the account of his conversion above related.
† Basnage, p. 795.

whom rabbi Samuel, who was its chief, distinguished himself. In 1599, he published a work in this city, styled, "The Judgments of Samuel," which is a collection of Talmudic and Rabbinic decisions. Leo de Modena was also a man of learning, but a professed enemy to the Christians. He acquired great celebrity by his writings; his "Treatise on the Ceremonies of the Jews," in particular, has been highly celebrated by the learned of all nations. He intended to have translated the Old Testament into Italian, but the inquisitors prohibited his proceeding in this work. He died at Venice in the year 1654, being almost eighty years old.*

Pesaro† was the native place of rabbi Jechiel, who went from thence to Florence; where having heard for some time the sermons of an inquisitor, he repaired to Rome in order to renounce Judaism. Pope Gregory XIII. assisted at the numerous assembly where he made his recantation. Soon after, he was baptized by this pontiff, and became a public teacher. Some of the Italian sermons which he preached against the Jews at Florence, where they were very numerous, were printed in 1585.

Jacob Tzaphalon was born at Rome 1630, and had the degree of doctor of physic conferred upon him by the university in this city. He taught at Ferrara, and is ranked among the most eminent rabbies in the 17th century. Among other learned works he composed a book of prayers and meditations, in which there is a petition for physicians

---

* Modern Universal History, vol. xiii. p. 404.

† A small ancient city in Italy.

when they visit their patients. The authors of the
Universal History observe, that " it appears this
good Jew thought it necessary to implore the
blessing of heaven before he went to prescribe to
the sick ; and did not, like the generality of those
of his profession, depend wholly upon the natural
efficacy of the medicines."*

The Jews of Padua received the title of doctors
of physic, and were authorized to practise the
healing art in all parts of the republic of Venice.
Towards the close of the 16th century there were
eight hundred of this nation at Padua, who possessed three synagogues. They had a very handsome Ghetto, or quarter assigned them, with three
gates, which were shut every night. Their in-
scription over one of the gates begins with these
words, " that the people, heirs to the kingdom of
heaven, may have no communion with those who
are disinherited." There was also an academy in
this city, of which the celebrated rabbi Meir was
president. Menakim Rabba flourished in this seminary, and composed sermons on the four seasons of
the year, which have since been published by his
son ; he died in the year 1605. Rabbi Judas
Azael was likewise a distinguished Jewish preacher ;
and rendered himself so popular by the discourses
which he delivered at Ferrara, that even the Christians attended his lectures. He was the author of a
cabbalistical work, entitled, " The Thrones of the
House of David." He died in this city 1677.†

About the same period that Bomberg set up a

* Modern Universal History, vol. xiii. p. 402.
† Basnage, p 725 Modern Universal History, vol. xiii. p. 406.

press in Venice, a number of Jews, who came from Spire in Germany, established another in Soncino, a small town in the duchy of Milan. These printers became celebrated under the name of Soncinates; and were principally engaged in publishing Hebrew books. By their exertions many manuscripts were preserved which had become scarcely legible. As they were almost the first, who had rendered their nation such an essential benefit, they acquired reputation and opulence.

The Jews have long been settled at Turin, the capital of Piedmont, by an edict which secured to them plenary liberty of conscience. They were, however, sometimes insulted by the bigoted populace; yet they enjoyed more tranquillity than in most other parts of Italy.*

A. D. 1685.] In the seventeenth century the affairs of the Jews in Italy assumed a favourable aspect. Pope Innocent XI. treated them with great kindness and indulgence. When the Venetian general Morosini returned victorious from the Morea, and brought with him a large number of Christian and Jewish captives, he gave liberty to the former, but would have retained the latter in slavery had not this pontiff used vigorous exertions to obtain their release. He also made great efforts to effect their conversion, and built seminaries and hospitals for the new converts. Gregory XIII. had previously ordered a sermon to be preached every week for their instruction. An ingenious Clergyman was chosen to prove in these discourses, that the Messiah was come, and that Jesus of Nazareth was the

* Basnage, p. 726.

Messiah. He was ordered particularly to enlarge
on the miseries the nation had suffered seventeen
hundred years.　One third of the Israelites in
Rome were obliged to be present in their turn, and
the children who had attained the age of twelve
years were ' registered among the auditors.　But
little benefit was derived from the institution, for
the Jews either absented themselves, or attended in
order to ridicule the discourses.　Pope Innocent
endeavoured to remedy this abuse.　He prohibited
the sermons* from being preached in a consecrated
church, lest it should be profaned by their indecent
behaviour, and appointed inspectors to impose
silence upon them.　But, notwithstanding all his
exertions, the Jews generally persisted in their
unbelief; and cardinal Barberini, who took an
active part in their instruction, acknowledged that
most of the pretended conversions were hypocritical
and interested.†

The Jews have long been numerous in the ecclesiastical state, where, as late as the middle of the
eighteenth century, they are said to have possessed
nearly an hundred synagogues, nine of which were

---

* This pontiff obliged the preacher to make a prayer to God, but
ordered it to be pronounced softly lest the names of Jesus and Mary
should alarm the Jews.—*Basnage*, p. 727.

† It is said, that, in order to encourage new converts, some cardinal, or great personage, was their godfather, and made them some
handsome present after baptism.　They were dressed in white satin,
and carried about the city in a fine coach, during a fortnight, to be
seen and congratulated by the spectators; after which they appeared
in a common dress, and, to prevent their apostatizing, all who were
found guilty of it were condemned to the flames.—*Modern Universal
History*, vol. xiii. p. 407.

in Rome.* They had also an academy in this city, and appeared to assume a kind of superiority over those in other parts of Italy, who consulted them in doubtful cases, and paid great deference to their decisions.†

A. D. 1740.] At this period, Charles, king of Naples, published an edict in favour of the Jews, permitting them to return, and reside in the kingdom fifty years. They were allowed to enjoy the full exercise of their religion, and settle in what parts they pleased; and those who had studied the healing art, were promoted to the degree of doctors in that science. These concessions excited great uneasiness among the zealous Catholics; yet the king pursued his measures, and many of the nation, from various parts of Italy, repaired to this kingdom. Soon, however, the licentiousness of the Jews caused laws, so honourable to those who framed them, and so consoling to the Hebrew people, to be revoked.‡

* Gisborne on the Christian Religion.
† Modern Univer. Hist. vol. xiii. p. 408.
‡ Gregoire's Essay on the Reformation of the Jews, p. 169.

CHAPTER XXVII.

The Jews apply to the emperor Charles V. for the liberty of returning to Spain.—Cardinal Ximenes persuades him to reject their request. —Of the conspiracy of the Portuguese Jews against the house of Braganza.—Vast numbers of concealed Jews remain in Spain and Portugal.—Account of Orobio, a celebrated Spanish Jew.—Of the severity of the Spanish government.—The Spanish and Portuguese Jews claim their descent from the tribe of Judah, and refuse to connect themselves by marriage with those of other nations. —A law is enacted in Portugal which prohibits the inhabitants to call any person a Jew.

THOUGH the Jews had suffered severe persecution in Spain, and towards the conclusion of the fifteenth century were cruelly expelled from this kingdom ;* yet upon the accession of Charles V. the fugitives petitioned for liberty to return. They represented to this monarch, that " they had conducted with honour the whole commerce of the nation, and were the most useful, and perhaps faithful subjects in the kingdom ; that, therefore, the confidence they reposed in his justice and goodness induced them to hope he would allow them the free exercise of their religion." On this condition they engaged to present him eight hundred thousand crowns of gold.†

Charles was at first disposed to return a favourable answer to their petition, but cardinal Ximenes exerted all his influence to dissuade the king from permitting their return. He reminded him, that Ferdinand had refused six hundred thousand crowns which the Jews offered him, for the liberty of con-

* See Chapter xviii.　　　† Basnage.

tinuing peaceably in his dominions; and asserted, that "those who rejected Christ from reigning over them, were unworthy of the protection of Christian princes." Charles, who entertained an extreme aversion*, against this people, preferred the counsel of the cardinal to the advice of his ministers, and peremptorily rejected their request.

"A. D. 1640.] After the Portuguese had freed themselves from the tyrannical government of Spain,† in the reign of Philip IV. the archbishop of Braga, who was wholly devoted to the Spanish monarch, conspired against his sovereign, the king of Portugal, and engaged a vast number of Jews‡ to assist in the design. They had long resided at Lisbon in the external profession of the Christian faith, and had lately offered the king a large sum of money if he would free them from the inquisition, and permit them to possess synagogues in Lisbon.

* Charles hated the Jews on account of their being so frequently duped by the impostors who appeared among them. One of them was so impudent as to affirm, that he was the Messiah, even in his presence, upon which he was apprehended and suffered a cruel death, 1534.—*Modern Univer. Hist.* vol. xiii. p. 392.

† After Philip II. extended his dominion over Portugal, he enacted that those of his subjects who were descended from Jews or Moors should be excluded from all ecclesiastical and civil employments. This mark of infamy, with which the new converts to Christianity were stigmatised, caused many of the wealthy Jews to emigrate to Bourdeaux, Hamburg, and other places.—*Raynal's History of the Indies,* vol. iv.

‡ Men of superior talents were formerly found among the Portuguese Jews. Duarte Nonnez, one of this nation who was banished from Portugal, his native country, in the sixteenth century, was preferred by the Catholic king to be a privy counsellor, on account of his great abilities, though all of that persuasion were formerly banished from Spain.—*Murphy's Travels in Portugal,* p. 223.

The rejection of this offer filled them with resentment and consternation, as their appearing in this petition, had exposed them to the tortures of the merciless inquisition.*

The archbishop of Braga promised them, in the name of the king of Spain, that, if they would be instrumental to his restoration, they should be allowed liberty of conscience, and be permitted to profess their religion openly without incurring any penalty. The part assigned them was to set fire to the palace, and several houses in the city and suburbs, in order that while the people were engaged in extinguishing the flames, the conspirators might fly to the palace and assassinate the king. The grand inquisitor was also engaged in this plot against the government, and this was, perhaps, the first time that the inquisition and synagogue acted in concert. The meditated revolution, however, was not effected. Baeze, a rich Jewish merchant, being put to the rack, confessed the treacherous design formed against the house of Braganza, and the intended perpetrators of the crime were severely punished.†

* Vertot's Revolutions of Portugal, p. 82.

† Though the Jews have been accused of treason, and some other instances similar to that of the conspiracy against the house of Braganza have been proved, the greater part of these accusations were, says a late author, the children of imposture; and there are other anecdotes of a contrary nature. In 1749, Malta was saved by a Jew from a formidable conspiracy. The Turkish slaves had combined to destroy the whole order of knights in the island; and every slave had taken a solemn oath to put his master to death. This treacherous design was discovered by a Jew who kept the coffee-house.—He understood the Turkish language, and having overheard discourses which he thought suspicious, went immediately and informed the grand

The Jews, finding themselves baffled in all their
legal and illegal attempts to obtain a toleration
in Spain and Portugal, continued under the specious veil of Christianity to perform the Mosaic
rites in secret.* Their aversion to a religion, which
they were compelled to profess externally, became
more implacable. The law of Moses was still
privately transmitted from father to son ; and the
vigilance of the inquisition, and murder of so many
of their brethren, which has caused them to be
more circumspect, must, at the same time, have
rendered them more bigoted. Many, who could no
longer submit to wear the mask of Christianity,
quitted their country. The greatest part of the
fugitives have settled in England and Holland, and,
among the Jews who reside in these countries,
those of Portugal have the reputation of maintaining the most respectable characters.†

Large numbers of the Israelites have, however,
remained in the dominions of Spain and Portugal,
who have availed themselves of the liberty of dissimulation permitted by the Talmud. Outwardly
good Catholics, but inwardly Jews ; they have
abounded in various ranks and professions, and
have not hesitated to fill the most sacred departments

master. The suspected persons were instantly put to the torture,
confessed the whole plot, and were executed. We also read of a Jew,
who, during the siege of Tunis by Charles V. saved the lives of
several thousand Christian slaves, whom Barbarossa intended to have
put to death.—*Gregoire on the Reformation of the Jews*, p. 41.
Brydone's Tour, p 163

* Vertot's Revolutions in Portugal.

† Southey's Letters from Spain and Portugal, vol. i. p. 112. Murphy's Travels in Portugal.

of the Romish priesthood. By pretending to an uncommon zeal for a religion which they detest, they have generally passed unobserved, if not unsuspected. Hence. it has been said, that when a house is found to be remarkably decked with images, relics, and lamps, and the owner celebrated for being the most enthusiastic devotee in the parish; there is reason to believe the family are Israelites at heart.*

These facts rest on the unquestionable authority of Jews who themselves have practised dissimulation, and are particularly recorded on the testimony of Balthasar Orobio, a celebrated Spanish Jew, who was carefully educated in the religion of his ancestors by his parents, who assumed the mask of Christianity, and outwardly conformed to the Roman Catholic worship, and abstained from the practice of Judaism in every thing except the observation of the fast of expiation. Our author was distinguished for his talents and learning; and, having studied the scholastic philosophy as it was taught in Spain, acquired such celebrity, that he was made professor of metaphysics in the university of Salamanca. But afterwards, applying himself to the study of physic, he practised the healing art at Seville with reputation and success.†

In process of time Orobio, being suspected of Judaism, was suddenly seized and thrown into the inquisition, where he suffered such exquisite

---

* Swinburn's Travels to Spain, vol. i. p. 104. Those Jews who, in Spain and Portugal, have been compelled to profess Christianity, are styled " new Christians."

† Biographical Dictionary, vol. ii. p. 343.

torments, that he began to be deranged. Sometimes he imagined that his past life was only a dream, and that the dungeon in which he was confined, was his true birth place, and would also prove the place of his death. At other times, as he had a very metaphysical turn, he first formed arguments of that kind, and then resolved them, acting thus the three different parts, of opponent, respondent, and moderator, at the same time. In this way he diverted himself from time to time, and, notwithstanding the cruel tortures which he endured, had the fortitude constantly to deny that he was a Jew. At last, after three years' confinement, the inquisitors, finding themselves baffled by his perseverance, ordered his wounds to be cured, and discharged him from the inquisition.*

As soon as Orobio obtained his liberty, he resolved to quit the Spanish dominions; and going to France was made professor of physic at Toulouse. He continued in this city some time, still outwardly professing the Roman Catholic religion. Averse, at length, to further dissimulation, he repaired to Amsterdam, where he was circumcised, took the name of Isaac, and professed Judaism. He continued to practise physic, and was highly esteemed in his profession. In Holland, he held his famous dispute with Philip Limborch, a celebrated Protestant clergyman, concerning the truth of the Christian religion.† This dispute was conducted with great moderation on both sides. But the

* Biographical Dictionary, vol. ii. p. 344.

† Limborch published a very interesting account of this conference, under the title of " Amica Collatio cum erudito Judæo."

learned divine was not able to conquer the prejudices of Orobio, who declared, at the end of the
conference, that he was of opinion, " that every
man ought to continue in the religion in which he
was educated, since it is much easier to attack the
opinions of others, than to defend our own." He
continued in Holland till the time of his death,
which took place 1687.*

The great number of the dissemblers, and their
existence even among the grandees and clergy in
Spain, Orobio attests in the strongest terms, and
relates, that many of those who assumed the mask
of Christianity, even Franciscan monks, Dominicans, and Jesuits, came annually to the synagogue
at Amsterdam to confess and expiate their dissimulation.†

A late author informs us, that a Catholic clergyman, who had recently quitted Spain, after a residence there of twelve years, spontaneously related
to him the following circumstances : " That the
Spaniards universally believe, there are among them
very great numbers of concealed Jews, chiefly
in the trading classes, and some among the clergy ;
and that the captain of a pacquet, with whom he
was windbound at Corunna, informed him, he had
met with many persons in France, South America,
and elsewhere, who had freely confessed to him they
were Jews, though they had lived long in Spain as
Catholics ; and that one of these persons had been

---

* Bio. Dict. vol. ii. p. 345.

† The Jews are said to have been numerous in the Spanish and
Portuguese monasteries and nunneries ; and that many of the priests,
inquisitors, and even bishops, are of Hebrew origin.—*Modern Universal History*, vol. xiii. p. 357.

outwardly a Catholic clergyman, and really in orders
as such."*

Even as late as the close of, the, eighteenth
century, any person believed to be a Jew, whether
he had previously appeared as a Catholic or not,
would still be seized in Spain, if discovered by the
inquisition.† The following is an extract from
a decree of the Spanish government, promulgated
against the Jews, July 22, 1800. "His majesty
ordered his ministers to deliver no passports to Jews
intending to enter Spain, whatever, might be the
motive of their journey ; and whether they be desirous or not of making any stay in the kingdom.
He enjoined the governors of the frontiers to prevent their entrance into the Spanish territories,
and to expel all who may be discovered in it. For
a long time the laws of this monarchy have forbidden all the Jews to attempt a transit, or an establishment in the dominions of his majesty ; a late
transgression calls for a rigorous reinforcement of
these laws."

The Spanish and Portuguese Jews‡ claim their
descent from the tribe of Judah ; and found these
pretensions on a supposition which prevails among
them, that many of their ancestors, removed, or

* Gisborne on the Christian Religion, p. 110.

† It is said, that in about 1755, when a terrible earthquake in
Lisbon destroyed thirty thousand of the inhabitants, the Portuguese
believed that the mercy of God might be obtained by burning some
Jews, and other heretics, in what they call the Auto da Fe, or act of
faith.—*Voltaire's Age of Lewis XIV.*

‡ It appears that the Jews have no accurate deduction of their
descent or genealogy; they suppose that they are in general of the
tribe of Judah and Benjamin, with some among them of the tribe of
Levi.—*Butler's Horæ Biblicæ,* p. 85.

were sent into Spain, at the time of the Babylonian
captivity. In consequence of this supposed superiority, they, till very lately, would not by marriage
or otherwise, incorporate with their brethren of
other nations. They had separate synagogues;
and if a Portuguese Jew, even in England or
Holland, married a German Jewess, he was immediately expelled from the synagogue, deprived of
every civil and ecclesiastical rite, and ejected from
the body of the nation. A late instance has
occurred of a Jew in Berlin, who having married
the daughter of a Portuguese physician, the parents
of the girl went in mourning, as for the death of
a relation.*

The manners of the Portuguese Jews differ from
the rest of the nation, and are more polished.
They have nothing peculiar in their dress. The
opulent among them vie with the other nations
of Europe in refinement, elegance, and show; and
differ from them in worship only.†

In Portugal, the name of a Jew is a term of such
high reproach, that the government found it necessary to enact a law, which forbade any person to
call another by that appellation. If a man who is
styled a Jew to his face stabs the offender, the law
does not condemn him; and trifling as this regulation may appear, it has produced beneficial
effects.‡

* Gregoire, who mentions this fact, informs us, that it was communicated to him by a learned German Jew.—*Essay on the Reformation of the Jews*, p. 86.

† Letters of certain Jews to Voltaire, p. 23.

‡ Southey's Letters, vol. i. p. 118. Review of the Naturalization
of the Jews, p. 52.

The Jews in Portugal remain separated from the Germans, and retain their ritual usages; but government has destroyed the obstacles which the institutions of Portugal opposed to their marriage with the Germans.*

* Gregoire's Histoire des Sectes Religieuses.

CHAPTER XXVIII.

Account of the Jews in Holland.—One of the German Jews deludes
his brethren with the promise of a Messiah.—They erect academies
and synagogues at Amsterdam.—An account of Menasses Ben Israel,
and several other learned rabbies, who flourished in Holland, during
the seventeenth century.—Of their state at a later period.

HOLLAND has long afforded the Jews a favourite asylum; and the lenity of the government,
by giving free scope to their commercial genius, has
enabled them to accumulate wealth.

Basnage, who closes his history of this people
with the seventeenth century, has asserted, that
they enjoyed more liberty in this country, and have
been more rich and flourishing there, than in any
other part of the world.* Part of the Jews emigrated from Germany, the others from Spain and
Portugal; and, on account of some difference in
their religious ceremonies, a violent animosity has
subsisted between them.†

Zeighler, a distinguished personage among the
German Jews, came to Amsterdam, in order to
delude his brethren, who were recently settled in
the city, with the hopes of a Messiah, whom he
pretended to have seen at Strasburg when he was
only fourteen years old. He affirmed him to be
lineally descended from king David, and that his
ancestors had resided a thousand years in the kingdom of Tunis, whence they passed into Grenada in
Spain, but, upon being expelled by king Ferdinand

---

* Basnage, p. 738.
† Basnage, p. 739. Modern Universal History.

the Catholic, they settled, in Germany. Zeighler asserted, that he reserved a diadem and sword to present to the Messiah, when he should be of age to assert his dignity and appear in arms. He was then to exhibit himself as a mighty conqueror, to destroy Antichrist and the Ottoman empire, and extend his dominion over the whole world. The Messiah was also to assemble a council at Constance which was to last twelve years, and decide all religious controversies. Those who gave credit to the assertions of this impostor, regretted too late their blind credulity and infatuation.

The first assembly of Jews in Amsterdam, excited great jealousy among the citizens, who supposed them to be Roman Catholics in disguise. But in searching their houses, especially those in which they performed divine worship, they found nothing but Hebrew books, and a copy of the Mosaic law. After this discovery, they were only enjoined to pray for the preservation of the city, which they readily promised.*

Soon after, they obtained permission to build their first synagogue in this city, which they called "The House of Jacob," because a rich Jew of that name was its founder. Not long after, they erected another synagogue, which they styled, "Neve Shalam," the dwelling of peace; and committed it to the care of a celebrated rabbi named Joseph Vega, who composed a history of his nation down to the destruction of Jerusalem. He was succeeded by rabbi Uziel, who incurred the resentment of his brethren, by his severe animadversions on their

* Basnage, p. 789.

conduct. This induced them to build a new synagogue called " Ben Israel," to which the dissenters
retired. This schism lasted about twenty years,
and the disputes between the two parties were conducted with great animosity. But, in 1639, these
divisions were terminated, and the three synagogues
united in one.*

The Jews of Amsterdam founded academies as
well as synagogues, and one of them, called, The
Crown of the Law, which was built in 1643, was
governed by some of the most learned men of the
nation. Their flourishing state in Holland during
the seventeenth century, was exhibited by a superb
synagogue, begun 1671, and consecrated in the
year 1673.†

Many celebrated rabbics have flourished in Holland, among whom Menasses Ben Israel was eminently distinguished. This great man was born in
Portugal 1604; but his father Joseph, being persecuted on account of his religion, retired with his
family to Holland. Menasses was instructed in the
Hebrew language by rabbi Uziel, and made such
rapid progress in this and other branches of knowledge, that after his tutor's death, he was chosen to
succeed him in the rabbinical chair at Amsterdam,
when he was only eighteen years old. At the age
of fifteen he began to preach, and his discourses at
that early period were highly applauded by his
brethren. He pursued his studies so assiduously
that, when only twenty, he published the first
part of his Conciliator‡ on the Pentateuch, in

* Basnage, p 789   † Ibid.
‡ ... when completed was divided into f ... ts, and
com ... der of the Old Tes un...

which he endeavoured to reconcile the sacred books. By this work, which he afterwards completed, he acquired the esteem and admiration of the learned, both among Jews and Christians.*

Menasses married Rachel, of the family of Abarbanel, and boasted of his connection with one of the descendants of king David.† He was celebrated by his nation for his skill in physic, as well as for his knowledge in theology. In order to improve his fortune, he established a well furnished printing office for Hebrew books, which produced many beautiful and rare editions. He afterwards visited his brother Ephraim, a rich merchant at Basil, by whose advice he engaged in commerce. The hopes of rendering important services to his nation, induced him to repair to England, under the protectorship of Cromwell, who gave him a favourable reception, and entertained him at dinner with several learned divines. He, however, soon returned to Zealand, and died at Middleburgh in 1657, aged fifty three, and was interred with great respect at the public expense.‡

Menasses was the author of various learned works, too numerous to be particularly mentioned, which were printed by his son. In some of his writings, he directly or indirectly attacked Christianity, and defended Judaism. But, being modest,

---

* Modern Universal History, vol. xiii p. 435. De Rossie's Hebrew Biography.

† Menasses adopted the tradition of Abarbanel, that two Jewish families of the race of David came to Spain, but differed from him in supposing that they did not arrive till after the ruin of the second temple.—*De Boissi's dissertations pour servir a l'histoire des Juifs.*

‡ De Rossie's Hebrew Biography.

affable, and polite, he conciliated the affection and esteem of the Christians ; and some of the greatest men of the age, as Grotius, Episcopius, and others, were his intimate friends.* His great object appears to have been to promote the welfare of his nation both by his life and writings. One of his publications is entitled " Vindicæ Judeorum," or a letter in answer to certain questions respecting the Jews, in which he exploded all the calumnies raised against his persecuted nation. In another of his productions, styled, " The Hope of Israel," he attempted to prove, that the American natives are the descendants of the ten tribes. His works were published in Hebrew, Latin, Spanish, Portuguese, and English ; and part of them in Dutch and German.

Rabbi Zacutus, an eminent Jewish physician, and friend and panegyrist of Menasses, was born at Lisbon in the year 1575. His parents, who assumed the mask of Christianity, sent him to study philosophy and medicine at Salamanca and Coimbra. After having taken his degree of doctor at Morvedro, a famous university in Spain, he practised physic at Lisbon till 1624. He acquired great celebrity by his knowledge of the healing art, and was

* Bishop Huet, a learned Roman Catholic divine, observes, " During my stay in Holland I was induced to visit Menasses Ben Israel, a very learned Jew, known to me by his reputation and his writings, for the purpose of becoming better acquainted with him, and making inquiries of him respecting several circumstances connected with the Jewish rites, and the Christian religion. His answers appeared to me acute, yet candid, and to show that he was not far distant from a knowledge of the truth, were he treated with reason and moderation, and not with that contumely and harshness commonly displayed to his nation."—*Aikin's Memoirs of the Life of Huet*, vol. i. p. 208.

distinguished for his benevolent attention to the poor. After having dissembled about thirty years he retired to Amsterdam, and died, in the profession of the religion of his ancestors, 1642. He was the author of a history of the principal physicians and various medical works.*

Joseph Athias, a Spaniard by birth, was first a teacher of the Talmud at Hamburg, but removed from thence to Amsterdam, and purchased a printing-office. In 1661, he published an elegant edition of the Hebrew Bible, which was reprinted six years after with additions, and is remarkable for being the first edition in Hebrew in which the verses are numbered. The states of Holland rewarded Athias with a present of a golden chain and medallion.†

Uriel Acosta was born in Portugal, towards the close of the sixteenth century. His parents were of the nobility, but originally descended from those Jews who had been compelled to profess the Roman Catholic religion. His father, however, was really a Christian, and carefully instilled the principles of religion into the mind of his son. It appears, by Acosta's account of his life, that he received a liberal education, and, having been instructed in various sciences, applied himself to the study of the law, and afterward had an ecclesiastical benefice. The activity and zeal he exhibited in the service of the church, his assiduity in explaining the evangelists and other parts of the sacred scriptures, his regular and exemplary conduct, procured him, at the age of twenty-five, the dignity of treasurer in a col-

* Modern Universal History, vol. xiii. p. 437. † Ibid. p. 438

legiate church.　But the anxiety of mind which he then began to feel respecting religion disturbed all his happiness.·　Being terrified with the idea of suffering eternal death,' he sought relief by conforming to all the precepts of the church, by assiduously studying the Scriptures, and consulting the creed of the confessors. But still his distress increased; and at length, being reduced to a state of despair, he experienced the most terrible mental agonies.*　⸗   ⸗ ⸗ ⸗

After Acosta had decided that he could not be saved by the religion he had imbibed in his infancy, he began to inquire into the grounds and reasons of his faith.　These inquiries rendered him more and more wavering and undecided; and his dissatisfaction with the Roman Catholic church induced him to study Jewish authors until, at length, he became a convert to the religion of his ancestors: But as he could not profess Judaism in Portugal, he gave up an honourable and profitable employment, left an elegant house which his father had built in the most delightful part of Lisbon, and embarked for Amsterdam with his mother and brothers, whom he had ventured to instruct in the principles of the Jewish religion, even when in Portugal.　Soon after their arrival in this city they became members of the synagogue, were circumcised according to custom, and he changed his name of Gabriel for that of Uriel.†

It was not long, however, before he discovered, to use his own words, " that the modern Jewish

---

* Biographical Dict. vol. i. p. 63.　Acosta's Account of his Life.
† De Rossie's Hebrew Biography.

rabbies were an obstinate and perverse race of men, strenuous advocates for the odious sect of the Pharisees and their institutions." He declared that they did not conform to the law of Moses either in their rites, or morals, and censured their conduct with the utmost asperity. The chiefs of the synagogue, however, gave him to understand, that he must exactly observe their tenets and customs ; and that his deviation from them, even in the minutest points, would expose him to excommunication. But this threat did not intimidate him ; and, having left an elegant situation in his native country purely to enjoy the liberty of professing his sentiments with freedom, he thought it would show both want of courage and piety to submit to a set of rabbies without any proper jurisdiction. He, therefore, persisted in his invectives, and was excommunicated. In consequence of this sentence, his own brothers dared not to speak to him, nor salute him when they met him in the streets.

Acosta wrote a book in his justification, wherein he endeavoured to shew, that the rites and traditions of the Pharisees were contrary to the writings of Moses ; and soon after adopted the opinion of the Sadducees. His adversaries were overjoyed at this change in his sentiments, which they foresaw would tend greatly to justify in the sight of the Christians, the proceedings of the synagogue against him. They, therefore, made application to the magistrates of Amsterdam, and represented him as a person who endeavoured to undermine the foundation both of the Jewish and Christian religions. Upon this information he was thrown into prison,

but bailed out in about ten days after. However,
all the copies of his works were seized, and he himself fined three hundred florins. Yet he was not
deterred from proceeding still 'farther in his scepticism, and, at length, he not only denied the authority of the Mosaic law, but the truth of all revealed
religion.*

After he became a deist, as his patience was exhausted by the insults and indignities to which the
avowal of his sentiments had exposed. him, he
thought it best to dissemble for the sake of peace;
and returned to the Jewish church after he had
been excommunicated fifteen years. He made a recantation of what he had written, and subscribed
every thing as they directed. It was, however,
soon discovered that he did not live after the
Hebrew manner, and that he had dissuaded two
Christians who came from London to Amsterdam
from professing Judaism. He was summoned before the grand council of the synagogue, and, upon
his refusing to make a public confession, was sentenced to a second excommunication.† After remaining seven years in a most wretched condition,
being exposed to a series of persecutions, he declared himself willing to submit to the sentence of
the synagogue. This concession was made in con-

* Acosta's Account of his Life.

† There are two degrees of excommunication among the Jews;
the lesser which only excludes a person from some particular society,
or congregation, till he repents, which he is allowed to do in thirty
days; and if he does not, then the greater is pronounced, which confiscates his property to sacred uses; and deprives him of any dealings
with or support from his nearest relations, as well as subjects him to
many other grievous penalties.—*Abendenda's Jewish Polity.*

sequence of his receiving intimations that the judges,* being satisfied with his submission, would soften the severity of the discipline. Acosta, however, found with astonishment and indignation, that the sentence pronounced against him was executed with the utmost rigour. He was compelled to enter a synagogue full of people, assembled to see his humiliation, being dressed in mourning with a black torch in his hand. After reading a recantation of his errors, and confessing that he deserved a thousand deaths, he was subjected to a severe and disgraceful corporal punishment.

Acosta was so highly exasperated at the public infamy which he suffered, that he formed the horrid resolution of putting a period to his own life ; but determined previously, to be revenged on a relation to whom he attributed the cruel treatment he had experienced. But finding himself baffled in his attempt to kill his principal enemy, and that his design was discovered, he immediately destroyed himself; (1647) leaving a manuscript† which gave an account of his life and sentiments.

Benedict Spinoza, another extraordinary Jew, was born in Amsterdam, 1632; but his father was

* It appears surprising that Acosta did not implore the protection of the magistrates of Amsterdam to guard him from the violence of his nation. But he was apprehensive that the Christians would not be more favourable to him than the Jews, and relied upon the promise which the Parnassim or administrators of the synagogue made to him, and threw himself upon their mercy.—*Boissi's Dissertations pour servir a l'histoire des Juifs.*

† The above mentioned particulars relating to the life of Acosta are taken from his piece entitled, " Exemplar Humanæ Vitæ," which contains a severe invective against the Jews, interspersed with objections against all revealed religion. It was published and refuted by Limborch.

originally a native of Portugal, and by profession
a merchant. After having learnt Latin of a scep-
tical physician, Spinoza applied himself for many
years to the study of theology, but began very early
to be dissatisfied with the Jewish religion ; and, as
his temper was naturally open, he did not attempt
to conceal his doubts from the synagogue. The
Jews, it is said, offered to tolerate his infidelity, and
even promised him a pension of one thousand dollars
per annum, if he would continue externally to practise
their ceremonies. If this proposal was really made,
and he rejected it, his refusal was owing to his dislike of hypocrisy, or rather from a fear of the
restraint it would impose upon him. He also refused
a very considerable fortune to the prejudice of the
natural heirs, and learnt the art of polishing glass
for spectacles, that he might subsist independently.*

Spinoza would probably have continued in the
synagogue some time longer, had he not been treacherously attacked and wounded by a Jew, as he was
coming from the theatre. The wound was slight;
but he believed the assassin designed to murder him.
From that time he separated from his brethren, which
was the reason of his excommunication. After leaving
the synagogue he professed to be a Christian, and
not only went himself to the Churches of the
Lutherans and Calvinists, but frequently exhorted
others to attend, and highly recommended some particular preachers. But that he was only outwardly
a Christian, appears not only from his writings, but
from many anecdotes which are preserved of his
life. The Jews, finding all their attempts against

---

* Basnage, p. 741. Encyclopedia, vol. xvii. p. 693.

·him ineffectual, accused him of apostacy and blas-
'phemy before the magistrates of Amsterdam, and he
was expelled from the city. · .; · ·   ·   · ·'. .'.,·: :

In his exile he studied mathematics and natural
philosophy. His 'nation pursued him, however,
with the grand excommunication ; but he' wrote
·a protest against the sentence, directed to the rabbies
of the synagogue. In 1664, he published " the
principles of the Cartesian philosophy, demonstrated
geometrically," with an appendix, in which' he
advanced metaphysical opinions wholly inconsistent
with the doctrine of Des Cartes. In 1670, one of
his works was printed at Amsterdam, which contained all the seeds of that atheism which was more
fully developed in his " Opera Posthuma." He,
however, lived in retirement at the Hague, with
great sobriety and decency of manners, till the year
1677, when a consumption put a period to his
life, at the age of fifty three.*

" Spinoza was a Jew by birth, a Christian
through policy, and an atheist by principle." His
attachment to certain philosophic opinions had acquired such an ascendancy over his mind, that he
secluded himself from the world, and renounced its
pleasures in order to devote himself to abstruse meditations. He was, it is said, the first who reduced
atheism into a system, and formed it into a regular
body of doctrines.†

---

* Acosta's Life, published by Limborch.

† Spinoza taught, that the whole universe is but one substance,
which is extended, infinite, and indivisible. That substance he calls
God; but labours to prove that it is corporeal, and that there is
no difference between mind and matter ; that both are attributes of
the Deity variously considered ; that the human soul is part of the

In later times many learned men have appeared among the Jews in Holland, and by a decree passed in 1769, the nation in this country acquired certain political rites. The Portuguese Jews are more numerous and affluent than the German, their manners more polished, their morals generally more correct, and they are considered as the most enlightened part of the community. They excited the industry of the other inhabitants ; and Amsterdam is much indebted to them for its flourishing condition.* There are a large number of Jews in Rotterdam, many of whom are as much distinguished for their integrity as for their industry and opulence. †

intellect of God ; that the same soul is nothing but the idea of an human body; that this idea of the body and the body itself are one and the same thing; that God could not exist, or be conceived, were the visible universe annihilated; and therefore that the visible universe is either the same substance, or at least an essential attribute and modification of that substance.—*Bayle's Dictionary.*

* Monthly Magazine, 1809.   † Carr's Tour to Holland, 1806.

CHAPTER XXIX:

The Jews remain exiled from England three hundred and fifty years.
—Cromwell resolves to attempt their return.—Menasses Ben Israel
repairs to England in order to solicit him in behalf of his brethren.
—The protector summons a convention of divines to deliberate
respecting the Jews, but is afraid of openly favouring them.—
A number of this people, however, return to England and are
tolerated.—Charles II. connives at their admission.—James II. was
inclined to favour them.—A law enacted in the reign of queen
Anne, to oblige them to provide for their children if they should
embrace Christianity.—Of Moses Marcus, a converted Jew.—A bill
is passed in the reign of George II. for their naturalization; but
soon repealed, in consequence of the popular clamour.—State of
the Jews in England since that period.

A. D. 1656.]   THE Jews had continued exiled
from England about three hundred and fifty years.
But after the English government was changed to
a republic, Holland became a respectable object of
emulation.   The advantages that country had derived from tolerating a people so skilful in pecuniary
negotiations were too obvious to escape observation;
and the policy of Oliver Cromwell induced him to
attempt to restore their industry and wealth to Great
Britain.*

The first intercourse between the protector and
the Jews was managed by one Henry Martin, upon
whose intimation a deputation of this people waited
on the English ambassador residing in that city, and
entertained him with concerts of music in the synagogue.   By his intercession they obtained per-

* Life of Cromwell.

mission from the instrument parliament * to send a public envoy to England with proposals for their admission into the kingdom. The celebrated Menasses Ben Israel, who was deservedly held in high estimation by his brethren, was chosen to conduct the negotiation.

This venerable rabbi, after his arrival in England, presented an address to Cromwell, recognizing his authority, and soliciting his protection. "For our people," said he, "presage that the monarchical government being now changed into that of a commonwealth, the ancient hatred towards them would also be converted into good will; and that the rigorous laws, if any were yet extant, made against so innocent a people, would happily be repealed." He also printed and dispersed a declaration to the commonwealth, and a treatise, containing several arguments for toleration, addressed to the justice of the principled, the prudence of the reflecting, and the prejudices of the multitude.†

Cromwell was inclined to recal the Jews; but, being apprised of the unpopularity of the measure, and desirous of conciliating the favourable opinion of the clergy, he summoned a convention of divines and other influential men to debate whether it would be advisable to readmit them to settle in the kingdom. He declared to the assembly, " that since there was a promise of the conversion of this people, and the gospel in its primitive purity was preached in Eng-

---

* A name given to a parliament convened by Cromwell, according to a form which he had prescribed in a paper styled, " the instrument of government."

† Monthly Mag and British Reg 1796. Life of Cromwell, p. 346.

land, their recal might be a mean to induce them to embrace Christianity." Dr. Goodwin and a few other ministers exerted all their eloquence in favour of re-admitting the Jews, and allowing them equal privileges with other sects. But the majority of the clergy strenuously opposed their return, and alleged, that there was danger of their seducing others to their religion; that their customs and practices would set an evil example; and that their possessing synagogues was not only an evil in itself, but a scandal to all Christian churches. The intolerant sentiments advanced in this assembly convinced the protector that the measure could not be introduced into the pulpit in such a way as to assist its popularity. He, therefore, dismissed the assembly, saying, that, " instead of elucidating, their discussions had rendered the subject more perplexing than ever."*

The project of recalling the Jews appears to have been very unpopular among the lower classes of society, and was so vehemently opposed not only by them, but by some persons of abilities and learning,† that Cromwell took leave of Menasses with a polite, but evasive answer. Some of his nation, however, ventured to return to England; but though they were permitted to reside in the kingdom,‡ and exercise their religion, and had a part of London near Aldgate assigned for their

* Monthly Magazine. Thurlow's State Papers, vol. i. p 387.

† William Prynne, who suffered for the boldness of his publications, during the reign of Charles I. was extremely zealous against permitting the Jews to return to England, and published a work in two parts on this subject.

‡ A late author has asserted, that they were permitted to return upon three express conditions; first, that they should make no proselytes; secondly, that they should bury their own dead; and,

residence, not a single act of the British legislature was passed to settle them in the country. Not even so much as a single proclamation was made in their favour, though they were ready to advance immense sums for an establishment. It is even said, that they offered to prove Cromwell the Messiah,* but that he was ashamed of the proposal, and rejected it with contempt.

About the same time that Menasses Ben Israel came to England to solicit the re-admission of his brethren, a deputation of Asiatic Jews arrived with the celebrated rabbi Jacob Ben Azabel at their head. It is asserted, that it was their object to make private inquiries in order to ascertain whether Cromwell was not their expected Messiah! These deputies, pretending other business, were several times indulged by the protector with a private audience. They offered to purchase all the Hebrew books and manuscripts belonging to the university of Cambridge, but he rejected the proposal with contempt. They afterwards, it is said, embraced an opportunity to inquire among his relations where he was born, and whether any of his ancestors in the male line could not be proved of Jewish origin. These inquiries, however, were not conducted with all the secrecy such a scheme required, and the real motive of their coming to England soon transpired at

thirdly, that they should maintain their own poor.—*Witherby's Vindication of the Jews*, p 4

* Gregoire adduces the life of Cromwell by Gregorio Leti as a proof of this fact. " We find there," says he, " an account of the deputation of the Jews to the protector, who, instead of assuming the quality of Messias, was very angry at their request."—*Gregoire's F. . . . . . R. t . . . tion of the Jews*, p. 244.

London; and, on account of the scandal they had occasioned, they were expelled the kingdom.

Soon after, another deputation, with Menasses Ben Israel again at their head, arrived in England. But still Cromwell did not dare to give them a licence to settle in the kingdom. He only connived at their admittance, and granted them a toleration.*

Charles II. gained by bribes, and indifferent to all religious professions, connived at their settlement; and, as he introduced the sale of patents of denization, their number increased. But the parliament of England has never abrogated the decree which expelled them, and they are considered as aliens in the eye of the law.† They were not permitted to purchase houses, nor practise professions which might ennoble their genius and dignify their nation.‡

James II. whose disposition to tolerate Dissenters exasperated his subjects, remitted the alien duty upon all goods exported in favour of the Jews. This was universally resented by the English merchants, who were apprehensive that the same duties would also be remitted upon imported goods. Petitions from various mercantile companies were offered against this regulation, which to the great joy of the Christian merchants, was superseded after the revolution §

During the reign of queen Anne, a bill was

* Gentleman's Magazine, 1810.   † Blackstone, vol iv. p 372.
‡ Gentleman's Magazine, 1810
§ When William, prince of Orange, was preparing to dethrone James II his father-in-law, Schwartzau, a Jew of Amsterdam, lent him above eighty thousand pounds sterling, telling him, " If you are successful, pay me; if not, I shall lose my money with pleasure."—
- Gregoire's Essay, &c. p. 42.

passed obliging the Jews to provide for their Protestant children.

It appears, that in 1723, the church of England was deeply interested in the conversion of this extraordinary people; for we find a Jewish proselyte patronized, and his work, exposing the absurdities of the Talmud, sanctioned by a primate of the day.* This convert, named Moses Marcus, was descended from a respectable family in the city of Hamburg, and born in London 1701. His parents, who resided in this city, and were in affluent circumstances, endeavoured to procure him every advantage in their power; and he was carefully instructed in Hebrew, Chaldaic, and Rabbinical learning. Being sent to Hamburg to complete his education, he formed an acquaintance with several German Protestant clergymen, with whom he conversed upon the difference between the Jewish and Christian faith. He then applied himself to studying the New Testament, and became convinced, that Jesus Christ is the true Messiah. In 1721, his father, who had been on a voyage to India, returned with immense riches, and sent for his son from Hamburg. Marcus soon informed him of the change which had taken place in his religious sentiments. His father threatened him with being totally disinherited, and even with the loss of life, if he embraced Christianity. On the other hand, he made him the most alluring and magnificent offers to induce him not to desert the synagogue. But, his faith being confirmed by further conver-

* Dr. Wilkins, Archbishop of Canterbury, to whom Marcus dedicated his work.

sation with some English divines, all these threatenings and promises were ineffectual. He was baptized in 1723, and soon after published a work, which explained his motives for embracing the Christian religion, pointed out the fulfilment of the prophecies concerning Christ, and exposed the absurdities and contradictions of the Talmud.*

A. D. 1753.] At this time, during the reign of George II. a bill was brought into parliament for naturalizing all persons professing the Jewish religion, who had resided in Britain or Ireland three years, without being absent more than three months at a time during this period. This favour was to be obtained upon application, without receiving the Lord's supper.† They were, however, to be disabled from obtaining any civil or ecclesiastical promotion. The bill was supported by petitions from a number of merchants and manufacturers, who, upon examination, appeared to be Jews, and their dependants.‡ But it has been asserted, that many respectable members of their community opposed the passing this act, from an apprehension that it had a tendency to annihilate their existence as a distinct people.§

The British ministry countenanced and encouraged the bill, and enumerated the advantages which would result to the nation from favouring the Jews. They asserted in particular, that by admit-

* Jewish Tracts.

† The church of England, in the reign of James I. obtained an act, which prevented all persons from being naturalized unless they first received the sacrament of the Lord's supper, according to its own peculiar mode of commemoration.

‡ Monthly Magazine, &c. 1796.

§ Smollet's Continuation of Hume, vol. iii.

ting them to a participation of the civil rights of
British subjects, they would contract a warm attachment to the English constitution and country, and
diminish the public burdens ; that a great portion of
the funds belonging to foreign Jews, it was our
obvious interest to induce them to follow their
property, and spend their income in the kingdom ;
and that, connected as they were with the great
bankers and monied interest in Europe, their residence in the country would, in case of future wars,
give the inhabitants a great command of capital,
and facilitate their loans. They supposed that
passing the act would encourage the most affluent of
the nation to emigrate from foreign parts to Great
Britain, increase the commerce and credit of the
kingdom, and set a laudable example of industry,
temperance, and frugality.*

On the other hand, those who opposed the
passing of the bill argued, that the peculiar rites of
the Jews were formidable obstacles to their incorpo-
ration with other nations ; and that if they were
admitted to the rank of citizens, they would engross
the whole commerce of the kingdom, gain possession of the landed estates, and dispossess the
Christian owners. They also asserted, that it
was impious to gather a people whose dispersion
was foretold in the sacred Scriptures, and who,
according to the prophecies, were to remain without
country or habitation, until they should be converted
and collected together in the land of their ancestors;
and that an attempt to incorporate them, previous
to their renouncing their religious tenets, directly

* London Mag. 1754, p. 538.

opposed the will of heaven; by endeavouring to
procure for them a civil condition while Jews,
which, it is predicted, they should not enjoy till
they became Christians.*

The lord mayor, aldermen, and commons of the
city of London, presented a petition to parliament,
which expressed their apprehension, that the bill,
if passed into a law, would tend greatly to dishonour the Christian religion, and endanger the
excellent constitution. Another petition to the
same purpose was presented to the house, subscribed
by the merchants and traders in London. But notwithstanding the general opposition, the bill passed
the ordeal of both houses, and his majesty vouch-
safed to give it the royal sanction.†

This act, which during the last session had triumphed over the most obstinate opposition, soon
became an object of national horror and execration.
Every part of the kingdom resounded with reproaches of the ministry, who had enforced such an
odious measure. It was vehemently opposed from
the pulpits,‡ by the corporations, and by the populace. In consequence of which, by the next session
of parliament, instructions were sent to almost all the
members to solicit the repeal of this obnoxious bill.§

* Smollet's Continuation of Hume.   † Ibid.

‡ Among the clergy, however, Dean Tucker took a decided part
in favour of the naturalization of the Jews, and wrote ably in defence
of this measure. The opponents of the bill, treated him with great
rudeness and virulence on this occasion. He was not only severely
attacked in pamphlets, newspapers, and magazines; but the people
of Bristol burnt his effigy dressed in canonicals, together with his
letters on behalf of naturalization.—*Public Characters,* vol. i.
p. 140.

§ London Magazine.

The British minister did not attempt to resist the torrent; but was amongst the foremost who spoke in favour of the repeal. He was answered with much force of reasoning by Thomas Potter, Esq. Sir George Lyttleton made an elegant speech in favour of toleration, in which he asserted, that " the greatest mischief which can be done to religion is to pervert it to the purposes of faction ; and that heaven and hell are not more distant, than the benevolent spirit of the Gospel, and the malignant spirit of party." The bill was, however, repealed by an act, which received the royal assent the same session. The bishops had generally appeared satisfied with the indulgence granted to the Jews, and they acquiesced also in the repeal of the bill.[*] But, though the nobility in general concurred in the expediency of the latter measure, a few among them viewed it as too great a sacrifice to the bigotry of the populace.[†]

The parliamentary leaders of the people, endeavoured, (but their attempts were successfully opposed by Mr. Pelham and Mr. Pitt,) to repeal so much of an act for naturalizing foreigners in America, as did not exclude the Jews. It has been asserted, that the spirit of intolerance was excited by those who resented the zeal and loyalty with which they were known to oppose the late rebellion. Among many instances are the following. Two Jewish merchants had some armed ships in a river, loaded with goods for foreign markets. But upon being apprized that they were wanted by the go-

---

[*] Smollet s Continuation of Hume.
[†] Belsham's History of Great Britain, vol. ii. p 386.

vernment to prevent the enemy from landing forces on the British coasts, they tendered the ships to the service of the public, without expecting any other advantage than what they should enjoy with other, subjects under the British government.*

After this attempt in favour of the Jews was defeated, their legal condition in England was not altered; but they are no longer the objects of that contempt, and of those debasing injuries, to which formerly they were perpetually subject. They are indulged in the free exercise of their religious worship, and admitted to an equal participation of every civil right, which is essential to the acquisition, or the secure enjoyment of property; and, though their religion keeps them from taking the test oaths, and consequently from public offices, they appear to be contented with the privileges they enjoy. An English Israelite, in a letter to the sanhedrim of Paris, 1808, observes, "that the liberal policy of the British government, has already conceded to them every immunity and indulgence granted to others, who are not of the established church."†

Another Jewish writer asserts, that "his brethren in England were never so well versed in foreign and domestic literature as at this time; that many among them of both sexes possess talents and infor-

* Gentleman's Magazine, p. 417.

† A late author observes, that " the change of public sentiment in England, with respect to the Jews is evident, in their now being allowed to hold lands, and in the public exhibition of their character on the stage. Shakespeare's Jew is represented as cruel and avaricious, and endowed with all the strong prejudices of his nation; "*I hate him, for he is a Christian:*" whereas Cumberland's Jew is humane and benevolent; characteristic indeed in his manners, but honest, liberal, and friendly, to persons of all denominations."— *Adam's Religious In . . . Dis . . . d,* vol. i. p. 15, published 1804

mation, and that they could not at any period boast of more learned and enlightened rabbies, than Dr. Hirschel* and Dr. Mendola."† Among the learned Jews who have appeared in England, David Levi‡ and D'Israeli§ are eminently distinguished.

The Jews in London, are divided into those of the Portuguese and German synagogue, each of which has separate regulations for its own internal government. The brokers, and most, respectable merchants among them, are chiefly of the former. But those of the German are far the most numerous, and, with the exception of a few wealthy individuals, who carry on trade with probity and honour, it is said, they are generally poor, and frequently dishonest, and that some of them conduct their fraudulent designs, by circulating counterfeit money, and by receiving, and selling stolen goods. The reproach arising from their iniquitous practices, has engaged the attention of the respectable part of both synagogues ; but attempts to remedy the evil, have generally proved ineffectual.||

* Dr. Hirschel, the presiding rabbi of the German synagogue, was born in London, 1762, at the house of his father Hirsch Levin, who was at that period chief rabbi in the city. Some time after, he removed to Berlin, and his son was called to officiate in London, 1802.

† Dr. Mendola, the presiding rabbi of the Portuguese synagogue, is a native of Leghorn.

‡ The celebrated author of the Dissertations on the Prophecies, Account of the Ceremonies of the Jews, Translation of the Pentateuch, Letters to Dr. Priestley, and other learned works.

§ M. D'Israeli, who is said to be of Jewish origin, in early life discovered a taste for polite literature, and is the author of a number of elegant poems, besides the Curiosities of Literature, Vaurien, a philosophical novel, and other works.—See *Public Characters*, 1789, vol ' p. 462.

|| Colquhoun's London Police, p. 20, 21.

The Jews in all their synagogues, on their sabbath days, and solemn festivals, exhibit their loyalty, by using a form of prayer for the prosperity of the royal family in Great Britain. And it must be considered as highly creditable to this people, that the heads of the different synagogues in London, and other distinguished men among them, have lately addressed to their brethren a strong exhortation, "to obey the laws; not to carry on any trade on the Christian sabbath ; not to keep houses of ill fame, nor to commit other irregularities, under their high censure, and forfeiture of the privileges attached to them, as belonging to their community."*

The Jews in England, contribute towards the poor's rates, equally with the other inhabitants. The Jewish population in London, and of course the number of their poor, having much increased of late years, some means for ameliorating their condition were found expedient ; and certain propositions with that view, were suggested by J. Van Oven, Esq. a learned and distinguished member of their community, in two letters addressed, in 1801, to Mr. Colquhoun, author of the Police of the Metropolis ; and the consequence has been, the erection of a Jews' hospital at Mile End, entitled, *N'vy Tsedek*, or the Charity Workhouse, which was opened in June, 1808, " for the reception and support of aged men and women, as well as the education and industrious employment of youth of both sexes " They are chiefly indebted for the accumulation of a fund which laid the foundation of

* Adam's Religious World Displayed, vol. i. p. 44.

this establishment, to the liberal and philanthropic exertions of Benjamin and Abraham Goldsmid,* Esqrs. two eminent Jewish merchants.

Different calculations have been made respecting the number of the Jews in England. According to Mr. Colquhoun they amount to twenty six thousand.† Others have supposed, that their total number does not exceed sixteen thousand. They have now five synagogues in London, viz. one called Portuguese Jews', three called German Jews', and one which is a kind of chapel of ease at Westminster, or in the Strand. Of these, the chief is the great synagogue in Dukes' Place, in and near to which street, most of the Jews in London now reside, as formerly in the Old Jewry.‡

* Both these gentlemen have recently perished by suicide. They were eminently distinguished as the lovers and patrons of literature, for the honour and promptitude of their commercial transactions, and their active benevolence, which was not confined within the boundaries of their own peculiar people. The Marine Society, the Royal Humane Society, and other charitable institutions, have publicly expressed their gratitude to them. Abraham Goldsmid, in particular, has been described by Van Oven, as " a man who is an honour to his species in general, and to his nation in particular." He was born in 1757, and early initiated into the mercantile life. This man, who was reckoned the greatest commercial character of the age in which he lived, was remarkably successful in the acquisition of wealth, and celebrated for his munificence to charitable institutions. But, after a series of prosperity, he experienced a severe reverse of fortune, which exposed him to bankruptcy; in consequence of which he became melancholy and deranged; and finally put a period to his life, Sept. 23, 1810, aged fifty three years.—*Commercial Magazine, November*, 1810.

† London Police, p. 21

‡ Adam's Religious World Displayed, vol. I. p. 72.

CHAPTER XXX.

Of an Institution formed at Halle in Germany for the conversion of the Jews.—Of the edicts of Joseph II. and his successor Leopold, in favour of the Jews.—The regulations against them in Prussia are abolished.—An account of Mendolsohn, and several other learned Jews in Berlin.—The Jews establish a literary journal in that city.—Of their efforts to improve education—They establish schools in several parts of Germany.—They are oppressed in Frankfort upon the Maine, but restored to the complete enjoyment of their civil rights in Westphalia.—They have also obtained privileges in Russia, Sweden and Denmark.

IN the preceding chapter a sketch has been given of the favourable change which has taken place in the situation of the Jews in England. The present, will contain a brief account of the measures which have been pursued to ameliorate their condition in Germany, the progress which some eminent men of their nation have made in literary pursuits, and their successful attempts to reform the mode of education.

About the year 1728, some zealous Christians in Germany, formed a plan for the conversion of the Jews to Christianity, not in the highly censurable manner in which such attempts had been made in Spain and Portugal, but in a manner consonant with the mild spirit of the Gospel. This Institution was established at Halle, principally under the management of Dr. John Henry Callenberg, and acquired the name of the Callenberg Institution. Works were printed, with a view to state to the Jews the evidences of the divine origin of the Gospel, and the importance of receiving it as

a revelation from God. The success that attended
this benevolent attempt, does not appear, however,
to have been considerable.*

Joseph II. emperor of Germany, by a memorable
edict (1781) conferred many privileges upon the
Jewish people. He granted them the right of
exercising all the arts and trades ; of following agriculture, and freely pursuing their studies at the
schools and universities.† This monarch also called
them to military services, and had a large number of
Jews enrolled among his troops. There was a benediction printed, which was given by a rabbi in
Prague to twenty-five Bohemian Jews enrolled as
common soldiers, in which he exhorted them to
conciliate, as much as possible, the practice of their
religion with their service. He gratified each of
them with a cord of silk named Zizim, and a pair
of tephilim, or a kind of leather band, to which is
attached a parchment, on which the decalogue is
inscribed. In the course of the war which was
terminated by the division of unhappy Poland,
one army had about six Jewish battalions.‡

The emperor Leopold, the successor of Joseph
the Second, granted to the Israelites dispersed
through his hereditary dominions, the privilege of
being admitted, if properly qualified and educated,
to academical degrees in the lay faculties, and also
the liberty of acting as advocates, and pleading
as such, either for their brethren, or for Christians.

---

* Jewish Repository, vol. i. p. 1.
† Coxe's History of the House of Austria, vol. iii. p 377.
‡ Gregoire's Histoire des Sectes Religieuses, tom. ii. p. 38.

In 1791, a Jew was admitted to the degree of doctor of civil law in the university of Prague.*

In the states of the king of Prussia, the Jews at a recent epoch were vexed by certain regulations. The father of a Jewish family could marry but one of his sons, rarely could he obtain permission to marry a second, and all the others were condemned to celibacy. Each Jew who took a wife, was also obliged to purchase a certain quantity of porcelain, the refuse of the royal manufactory. These regulations were abolished in 1809 ; and the Jews in the Prussian dominions, are now assimilated in many respects to the Christians.†

It is but justice to the Jews to acknowledge, that the learning and liberality of mind exhibited by several of their nation upon the continent, have probably paved the way for the steps which have been taken in their favour. Among those who have promoted the literary improvement, and raised the reputation of their brethren, Moses Mendolsohn is eminently distinguished.

This illustrious philosopher was born at Dessau, a city of Anhalt in Upper Saxony, in 1729. He received the rudiments of his education from his father, who was a Jewish school-master. In these schools, which were formed merely for the children of the Hebrews, the summit of their education terminated with an introduction to the Talmud, and the student wasted the season of youth, in studying this vast collection of fabulous legends and superstitions.‡

* Coxe's History, &c. p. 577.　　　† Gregoire's Histoire, &c.
‡ Monthly Magazine, 1798.

Mendolsohn, who possessed a vigorous and original genius, united with an ardent desire to acquire knowledge, soon selected from the mass of rabbinical writings, the superior works of Maimonides. But such was his intense application, and the irritability of his frame, that, at the early age of ten years, he was attacked with a nervous disorder of a very peculiar nature. In addition to this misfortune, he suffered all the embarrassments of poverty, being obliged to travel on foot to Berlin to find employment for subsistence. He lived in the city several years, indigent, unknown, and often destitute of the necessaries of life. This houseless wanderer was, at length, invited by a rabbi to transcribe his manuscripts; and this man initiated him into the mysteries of the theology, the jurisprudence, and the scholastic philosophy of the Jews.*

A Polish Jew named Israel Moses, who was distinguished for the freedom of his inquiries and his love of philosophy, taught him Euclid's Elements from the Hebrew version. After the premature death of his beloved friend, Dr. Kisch, a Jewish physician, supplied him with books, and devoted some part of his time to the instruction of a student, whose strength of intellect he had the discernment to perceive, and the affection to aid. Under the instruction of this valuable friend, he was soon enabled to read Locke in a Latin version.

In 1748, Mendolsohn formed an acquaintance with Dr. Samuel Gumpertz, another learned Jew, who to his professional studies added a knowledge

* Monthly Magazine, 1793.

of the mathematics, and was well- acquainted with
the modern languages.. He introduced him to a literary circle, and this intercourse enlarged his mind.
He now applied himself to the living languages,
chiefly to the English, that he might read his
favourite Locke in his own idiom. His literary
friends soon became numerous, among whom was
the celebrated Lessing,* who encouraged and assisted him in his studious labours.

In 1751, he published some philosophical dialogues; a translation of Rousseau's Essay on the
Inequality of Man; and a dissertation on the Sensation of the Beautiful. The German language
was then in a neglected and unpolished state, and
the clearness, precision, and dignity of the style of
the Hebrew philosopher was exhibited to great
advantage. He next associated himself with Lessing, Ramler, and Nicolai, in writing a journal,
composed in the form of letters, on German literature; and this work obtained great celebrity. In
1767, he published his "Phaedon, or discourse on
the immortality of the soul." This work was considered as a most curious disquisition on a subject so
abstract and sublime, and diffused the fame of Mendolsohn through literary Germany. He was styled,
"The Jewish Socrates" for the strength of his
reasoning, and "The Jewish Plato" for the ame-
nity of his diction. This work has been translated
and published in French and English. In 1794,

* A German dramatic writer who has been celebrated in his native
country. By his philosophical plays, " Nathan the Wise," and the
" Monk of Lebanon," he attempted to lessen the prejudice against
the Jews, and ameliorate their condition —*Monthly Magazine,*
1796.

he gained the prize from the Berlin academy, for his essay on the evidence of the metaphysical science.

After these publications, amidst the daily occupations of commerce, he still retired to his studies, and composed elementary books for the children of his neglected nation. To raise the degraded character of his brethren was the favourite object, which he always had in view. One of his publications, styled, "The Ritual of the Jews," was formed under the direction of the chief rabbi Hirsch Levin.*

The tranquillity of Mendolsohn's life was at length disturbed, by his publishing a work, entitled, "Jerusalem," in which he pretends, that the Jews have a law, and not a revealed religion ; that dogmas can never be revealed ; and that the only doctrine of his nation is the religion of nature. His advancing these opinions gave rise to a controversy, which agitated his feeble and sensitive frame to such a degree, that it is supposed to have occasioned his death. Zimmerman, who was personally acquainted with him, informs us, " that his nervous system was deranged, in an almost inconceivable manner."† His whole character was a too subtle composition of

---

* Monthly Magazine, 1796. In Prussia, the rabbi was *ex-officio* the chancellor of orphans, and could claim this right from the ordinary channel of the government. He was the adjudicator of disputed testimonial property, and responsible for the just performance of his office. The important charge thus devolving upon the chief rabbi in Prussia, occasioned a demand on the part of Frederick II. for the translation of the code of laws on that subject, which was effected by Hirsch Levin, father of the present presiding rabbi of the German synagogue in London, in conjunction with Mendolsohn.—*European Mag. March*, 1811.

† Zimmerman on Solitude.

genius and sensibility, and his whole life a ma-
lady. He died of an apoplexy, 1785, aged fifty
three years. It has been said of Mendolsohn, that
" he instructed his fellow citizens as a father, and
his rivals he cherished as a brother." His soft,
modest, and obliging disposition, procured him the
esteem of the superstitious and incredulous, and at
his death, he received from his nation the honours
which are usually paid to the first rabbies.

Beside the works above mentioned, he published
letters to Lavater, a version of the Pentateuch in
German for his countrymen, general principles of
the Belles lettres and fine arts, and several other
ingenious productions.

" The renown of Mendolsohn was the electric
spark which awakened the genius of the Hebrews ;
and he had for his cotemporaries and successors
distinguished men." Mark Eleazer Bloch, a Jewish
physician, who was born in Anspach and settled in
Berlin, was said to be the first naturalist of his age.
His splendid work, on fishes, and aquatic animals,
was esteemed superior to any preceding publication
on that subject. He died in the year 1800.—Solomon Maimon,* a great metaphysician, whom
some have considered more profound and philosophical than Mendolsohn, but not equal in elegance
of diction.—Mark Hertz, a professor of natural
philosophy, who had four hundred auditors of the
first rank and genius in Berlin. He spent his life in
this city, and published works on philosophy and

* Maimon was attached to the philosophy of Kant, to whom he
dedicated one of his works. He published memoirs of his life in
1792, and the following year a work on the progress of philosophy.

medicine.—Leon Gamparte, who distinguished himself by a work on literary subjects and the drama.—Ben David, president of the society of the friends of humanity at Berlin, and author of several profound works, who has endeavoured to apply algebra itself to the theory of taste in the arts.*

There has been of late a literary journal in Berlin, composed in Hebrew by several intelligent Jews, in which the reveries of the Talmud are attacked with argument and ridicule. Under a new form, with the title of Soulamith, the journal is renewed at Dessau, and published in the German language. It is edited by Mr. Frankel and Wolf, men of ability and learning ; the former of whom is counsellor of the Israelitish consistory at Cassel.

Many intelligent Jews do not approve of having separate schools, exclusively appropriated to the children of their own nation. But the prejudices of the Christians by rejecting them, or at least attaching a kind of stigma to Judaism, induced them to establish particular schools in different cities in Germany ; as in Nuremberg, Furth, . Breslau, Koningsberg, &c. They have also such schools at Berlin, Frankfort on the Maine, Dessau, and Seezen, particularly for poor children. They have been almost all established and supported by voluntary contributions. These schools, which are now in exercise, have their regulations printed with several elementary works written for their benefit.†

In 1796, a society of Jews, chiefly young men, founded some particular schools at Dessau for the

---

* Gregoire's Observations nouvelles sur les Juifs.
† ... ... Religious ... ses, tom II p 284.

children of their nation. They were obliged to encounter various obstacles ; but the protection of the government, which approved of the statutes of the school, the success attending the mode of instruction, and the applause which was acquired by their public and solemn examinations, caused the establishment to prosper. The founders, who were chargeable with the expense, had recourse to the benevolence of those in easy circumstances, and received abundant assistance, which enabled them to enlarge their plan. They have accordingly increased the number of preceptors, and are preparing a proper place for a library. The pupils, whose number amounts to about one hundred, are under the direction of Mr. Frankel,[*] who is eminently qualified to discharge the duties of his station. He was assisted by professors worthy of him; among others, by the modest Tillich, recently dead.[†]

Seezen is a town situated between Brunswick and Gottingen. Here, in 1801, by the modest name of school, a college was founded for the Jews, by the generosity of Jacobson, who has filled an high office in the service of the late duke of Brunswick, and enjoys the esteem of all ranks. He confided the direction of it to a man of learning and zeal, Schottlænder, counsellor to the landgrave of Hesse Darmstadt. In 1804, there were ten professors, though the number of students did not then amount to more

---

[*] Editor of the Soulamith, which has been mentioned. It appears from intelligence received, 1810, that the school for the children of the Jews, is in a flourishing condition. Among an hundred pupils who are taught in this school, thirty-four poor children receive instruction gratis.

[†] Gregoire's Histoire, &c. tom ii. p. 596.

than fifty ; but they are daily increasing. The arrangement of the building and the administration of the establishment may serve as models. There, as well as at Dessau, the children are distinguished by neatness, good order,' and an air of health and content. The poor are admitted, gratis, and the others pay, according to' their abilities. They are taught the Hebrew, Latin, French, and German languages ; geography,' history, oratory, natural history, mathematics, technology, &c.*

At Seezen, they add to the above the Greek language and music. It is also intended to establish a school of industry. Each student is to have a small plot of ground allotted to him, which he is to cultivate with his own hands. It is one object of the school to detach the Jews from commerce, the spirit of which is so deeply rooted among them.

In these schools, the pupils are taught the elements of such knowledge as is necessary in every station in life, the acquisition of which prepares the way for the developement of the greatest talents with which they are endowed. The pupils, when very young, are able to converse with facility in the French and Latin languages, as well as on various subjects of instruction, and solve very complicated arithmetical problems, and make mathematical demonstrations. (These details attest the capacity and diligence of the pupils, who are all Jews, and the well directed efforts of the preceptors, some of whom are Jews and some Christians, who reside together in the most perfect harmony.†

* Gregoire's Histoire des Sectes Religieuses, tom. ii. p. 386.
† Gregoire's Histoire, &c. tom. ii. p. 387.

Beside the ascetical books with which they are provided, Schottlænder has compiled for the students a collection of poems and moral precepts, selected from various authors. He has inserted the thirteen fundamental articles of the Jewish faith by Maimonides; an abridged history of the Hebrew language; the second canto of the Moysiade, an epic poem by Hartig Vezelize, a rabbi who lately died at Hamburg; and other instructive and interesting works.*

The Jews of Frankfort upon the Maine cite with applause Wolf Heidenheim, a learned orientalist from Rodelheim, a borough near the city; Lipman Buschental, a young poet; Heidelsheim, deputy from his co-religionists to the sanhedrim at Paris; and Geisenheimer, who is gone to study the method of Pestalozzi at Yverdun with one of the institutors of their Philanthropin, or school for the poor. Geisenheimer, associating music with poetry, and restoring the two arts to their true destination, has compiled for the pupils a collection of poetry. This establishment, to which the prince primate gives six hundred florins annually, prospers, and makes sensible progress.†

The Jews laboured without ceasing to obtain their political restoration to a city, where they have been for several centuries oppressed. A proverb said formerly, that at Frankfort the Catholics had the churches, the Calvinists the riches, the Lutherans the places. What then had the Jews? Outrages and persecution on the part of the Christians. Opinion stigmatized them in such

* Gregoire's Histoire, &c.   † Ibid.

a manner, that, confined in the narrow paths of
the ramparts, they dared not, under penalty of
being insulted, enter into the large alleys which
served for walks to the Christians. The Jews,
shackled in their commerce, were victims to regulations which raised a wall of separation between
them and the Christians.*

An infamous toll placed the Jews on the level of
cloven-footed animals. By the efforts of Jacobson
and Breinteinbach, between twenty and thirty
German princes have repaired this outrage done to
the human race, by abolishing these tolls. The
primate of Germany set the example, Frankfort
being part of his territories. The Jews hoped,
that under this prince all their grievances would be
redressed. But a regulation was forced from him
in 1807, which limited the number of Jews to five
hundred families. The community gives twenty
two thousand florins for the liberty of residing in
the city. Their street is a kind of Ghetto out of
which they cannot establish themselves. An Israelite in proportion to his means, pays more contributions than a Christian ; he pays for the right of
protection for himself and each of his sons. The
women, if unmarried at the age of twenty-five, are
subject to the same imposition. The Jews are
obliged to make presents to various functionaries on
new year's days, fairs, and other times, which are
to continue till the death of those who receive them.
If they establish a manufacture, or hire a farm, they
can employ only Jewish labourers. Those who are
merchants can only sell in two streets except their

* Gregoire's Histoire, &c.

own quarter, and that only, at the time of the fair; and a particular account is given of the articles which they are allowed to buy and sell.

The Jews of Westphalia were lately placed, in more favourable circumstances than those of Frankfort. A decree passed in January 1808, breaks all the barriers between the Jews and Christians. In effecting this change in the condition of the Jews, the celebrated Muller seconded the efforts of Dohm.* In these events we every where recognize Jacobson, who pursued with ardour his projects to ameliorate the character, the manners, and condition, of his co-religionists.† This eminent man, president of the Jewish consistory in Cassel, employed his wealth to accelerate the civilization of the Jews. A medal was stamped, in memory of the privileges they obtained in Westphalia.‡

* A Prussian officer who, in 1781, offered to the German public, remarks on the means of improving the civil condition of the Jews.

† Gregoire's Histoire, tom. ii. p 390.

‡ M. Jacobson, in a letter to the senator Gregoire, dated December, 1810, with a copy of which the latter had the goodness to favour the compiler of this history, observes:

"It must be confessed, thanks be given to providence! several of my establishments flourish, and afford me moments dear to my heart. The sun of light and truth dissipates many a cloud in the house of Jacob.

"Westphalia reckons already many Jewish soldiers of different grades, who fight with courage under their beneficent king, and for their new country. A part of the Israelites devote themselves much more than in past times to the arts and sciences. The youths detach themselves more and more from commerce, they apply themselves to trades, and exercise them with success.

"Since all these metamorphoses have been produced within a few years, the future presents to us an interesting prospect, such as every friend of humanity would desire.

"We see the singular phenomenon, that the military service

In other parts of Europe as well as Germany and Prussia, the Jews appear to be making improvements in literature ; and their exertions have been encouraged, and their condition ameliorated in

numbers several Israelites who have enlisted of their own accord. Others march from pure patriotism, after having furnished their substitutes, and others serve also as substitutes.

" As President of the Israelitish consistory, I labour incessantly in clearing as far as possible the chaos of our interior constitution. Some enlightened rabbies and secular members of the college, exert themselves in the same pious work. We already see the country towns adopt more simple and better regulated courses. We may also hope from that quarter for a more happy and consoling futurity.

" A new regulation relative to the synagogues puts an end to different abuses that are found in our divine service, and renders it more worthy of its object.

" Better schools, particularly religious schools, have been established in different parts of Westphalia. As for my institute at Seezen, I particularly apply myself to educate in it artizans and artists.

" I have caused to be raised in the inclosure, a temple of a beautiful style, and regular architecture. I have caused to be built in it an organ ; it is surmounted by a tower and bell.

" On the seventeenth of July, 1810, I celebrated the dedication of the Temple. The ceremony was august and solemn, notwithstanding every thing breathed in it the most open gaiety. There were present several hundreds of all religious denominations, particularly Catholic, Lutheran, and Reformed clergymen, besides the Israelites."

The inscriptions upon the new synagogue, which is styled by the Jews, " The Temple of Jacob," are as follows :

On the eastern part of the edifice :

" Blessed is he who cometh in the name of the Lord."

On the south side :

" Have we not all one father ? Are we not all children of the same Creator ?"

On the western part :

" Hearken also to a stranger, who is not of thy people Israel, but shall come from a distant country for the love of thy name."

The north portico is decorated with two hands joined together, inscribed with these words ;

" My house shall be called an house of prayer for all people."

See Dedicace du temple de Jacob, a Seezen.

several kingdoms. They were formerly excluded from Russia, but there are now probably two millions of Jews in that empire, of which number, about four hundred thousand inhabit the Russian provinces of Poland. In 1805, Alexander, emperor of Russia, published an Ukase, which, among other privileges, granted them the liberty of educating their children in any of the schools and universities in the empire ; or they were allowed to establish schools at their own expense.* In 1817, another Ukase, published by the same emperor, offered portions of land, with peculiar privileges annexed, to such Jews in his dominions, as would embrace the Christian religion.

A colony of Caraite Jews reside in a fortress in the Crimea, and enjoy the free exercise of their ancient customs and peculiar rites. These Caraites deem it an act of piety to copy the Bible, or pious commentaries upon the text, once in their lives. All their manuscript copies of the Old Testament begin with Joshua, and even the most ancient did not contain the Pentateuch. That part of the Bible was kept apart, but only in a printed version, for the use of schools. In the synagogues, with the exception of the books of Moses, every thing was in manuscript. The difference between them and the other Jews consists in a rejection of the Talmud, a disregard to every kind of traditions, to all rabbinical writings or opinions, all marginal interpolations of the text of scripture, and in a measure of their rule of faith by the pure letter of the law. They pretend to have the text of the Old

* Repertory, June 28, 1805.

Testament in its most genuine state. The character
of the Caraite Jews is directly opposite to that
which is generally attributed to their brethren, being
altogether without reproach. Their honesty is
proverbial in the Crimea; and the word of a Caraite is considered equal to a bond. Almost all of
them are engaged in trade or manufacture. They
pay great attention to the education of their children,
who are taught publicly in the synagogues.*

The Jews have also obtained privileges in Sweden.
In Denmark, where they have enjoyed sufficient
liberty, we find many distinguished characters, even
some painters. Their mode of education is daily
improving, and the exertions of Jewish parents are
seconded by the Christians ; among others, by the
celebrated Munter. In 1803, an establishment was
formed in Copenhagen, for the instruction of Jewish
youth. It is a species of free school, and well
endowed. At the end of the year 1805, the number
of pupils was forty. A public examination was
held in 1806, and it appeared that they had made
great progress in the Hebrew, French, and German
languages, in geography, and in natural history ;
and, in short, that this establishment was in a very
flourishing condition.†

---

* Dr. Clark, a late traveller, entered this fortress, and conversed
with a rabbi, who, he says, " was highly esteemed and exceedingly
well informed, and had passed a public examination with distinguished honour at Petersburg, after having been sent for expressly
by the empress Catherine."—*Clark's Travels in Russia, Tartary, and
Turkey,* p. 387.

† Transactions of the Parisian Sanhedrim, p. 124.

CHAPTER XXXI.

Of the Jews in France after their expulsion by Charles VI.—An account of those who were established at Metz.—Letters patent
granted them by Henry IV. and his son Lewis XIII.—In 1718, their
number is limited to four hundred and eighty families.—These pay
an annual tribute to the king.—A house was established for those
who professed the Christian religion.—Of the Jews in several parts
of France.—Their condition in the kingdom during the seventeeth
and eighteenth centuries.—A plan is concerted for their reformation.
—The academy of Metz offer a premium upon the subject, and
three works are crowned.—They present petitions to the Constituent Assembly soon after the French revolution.—Aud at length
obtain the rights of citizens.—Usurious practices of the Jews in the
northern departments.—Edict of Buonaparte.—An assembly of
Jewish deputies is convened at Paris.—Sketch of their answers to
the queries proposed to them.—A grand sanhedrim is convened at
Paris to give a religious sanction to the principles contained in their
answers.—They organize the Jewish worship.—Of the literary Jews
in France.—Last decree of Buonaparte concerning the Jews.

THE cruel treatment the Jews received in France
during the middle ages has been briefly related in
a preceding part of this history;* and that after
their final banishment from the kingdom by Charles
the Sixth, (in 1394) they preserved their privileges
and synagogues at Metz, a city where they were
very anciently established. About 1566, they were
expelled; but in the following year four families
obtained the right of naturalization by the interest
of Marshal Vielleville, governor of the city. In
1603, when they had increased to twenty four families, they obtained from Henry IV.† letters patent,

* See Chapter XVII:
† Mary de Medicis, wife of Henry IV. sent for Montalto, a Jew,
who was skilled in the healing art, to Paris, to be her physician, and

which gave them liberty to reside and carry on trade
in the city, according to their ancient privileges. In
1632, Lewis XIII. by new letters patent, confirmed
those of his predecessor; and, though this monarch
had, in 1615, expelled the Jews from France, they
still were permitted to reside and trade in Metz and
Bourdeaux.* In 1644, the city of Metz contained
seven hundred and ninety five of Hebrew extraction,
who, seventeen years after, obtained new letters patent, with the additional liberty of trading in all
kinds of goods. The merchants opposed the ex-
tension of their privileges; but their, attempts were
repeatedly defeated, and the parliament of Metz
inflexibly maintained the rights of the Jewish community.†

In 1718, the different bodies of merchants in Metz
united to demand of the king, that the number of
Jews should be reduced, as they were a public
charge, and that they should not be allowed to have
any other commerce but that of lawful interest. In
consequence of this request, his majesty ordained,
that the letters patent of his predecessors should be
executed according to their form and tenor, and
therefore permitted only four hundred and eighty
families to continue in the city. Even this indulgence was granted them upon condition that they
should reside in the quarter assigned them, and be

obtained from the king absolute liberty of conscience for him and his
family.—*Basnage*, p. 676.

   * The legal existence of the Jews in Bourdeaux is traced from the
year 1650. They obtained at that epoch, under the denomination of
merchants in Portugal, called " new Christians," letters patent by
which they were permitted to acquire real estates in France.

   † Gregoire on the Reformation of the Jews, p. 2n3.

prohibited, under penalty of a heavy fine, from having houses in any other part of the city. ·The disputes between them and Christians were to be referred to the judges and consuls of Metz; and there was an appeal to parliament in cases subject to it. But they were permitted to bring before the rabbies or chiefs of their community, disputes with their co-religionists respecting their police, religion, customs, ceremonies, and impositions. They paid the king an annual tribute of twenty thousand livres.*

" From time to time the Jews of both sexes have been converted at Metz ; there was even a house with some funds attached to it for those who had been baptized."

" The Jews had in Lorrain several synagogues, of which two were at Nanci. That of Luneville has been built about twenty-five years. But Alsace was the province in which they were the most numerous; they had there fifty-two synagogues, but none at Strasburg, where they had not even the right to sojourn. Since the French revolution the number of them in that city is computed from five to six thousand; other cities in France contain a small number of them, but they are more numerous in Paris than in any part of the kingdom."†

* French Encyclopedia. This tribute was paid by the Jews of Metz, and of the Messin country, under the denomination of duty of *habitation*, *protection*, and *toleration*. After they obtained the rights of citizens, these duties were suppressed and abolished, without any indemnity to the owner of and contractor for the said tribute. — *Transactions of the Sanhedrim*, p. 5.

† The paragraphs which are marked with inverted commas, are translated from a letter which the compiler was favoured with (September 1810) from M. M. Gregoire, formerly bishop of Blois, member of the conservative senate, &c.

" At Bourdeaux, Bayonne, and some neighbouring cities, there were many thousands of Spanish
and Portuguese Jews, thus named from the countries'
from which their ancestors have been expelled. They
had more extensive privileges than the German Jews,
that is, those of Alsace, Lorrain, &c."

" Avignon, formerly subject to the popes, and
Nice to the king of Sardinia, had also, and still
have colonies of Israelites, become French by the
union of the countries." The celebrated Gregoire
having been appointed member of the convention
to organize the department of the maritime Alps,
took care at Nice to secure to them the enjoyment
of the rights of citizens which the law allowed them.

" In the seventeenth and eighteenth centuries the
history of the Jews in France offers a very few
anecdotes to collect, which proves, that they were
generally tranquil during these periods, and had not
to experience those bloody catastrophes which desolated them in preceding ages. But the public
contempt was exhibited by avoiding their society,
and sometimes an ignorant populace insulted them.
In various places they were obliged to wear a dis-
tinctive mark in their dress; those of Metz had
a black mantle and a white band. This singularity
of costume made them known, and the bad effect
which it produced was to designate them in a more
special manner for insults. However, the progress
of knowledge has insensibly attenuated the prejudices against them."*

In 1767, six mercantile societies in Paris printed
a remonstrance against the admission of the Jews

* Letter from Gregoire.

among them. This virulent piece was reprinted in 1790. In 1784, the corporal toll required of them was abolished. The following year Malesherbes united with several intelligent Israelites, Furtado, Gradix, Cerf, Berr, &c.; to concert a plan for the reformation of the Jews. The academy of Metz had offered a premium on this subject.* Three works, written by Zalkind Hourwitz, a Polish Jew, M. Thiery, counsellor of Nanci, and Gregoire, who was then a member of the academy, were crowned at Metz, and gave a favourable impulse to the public opinion. That of the last named author has, in particular, obtained the most impressive publicity.†
The learned author of this excellent work has victoriously refuted the absurd calumnies at different times charged upon the Jews, pointed out the eventful causes of the vices with which they were reproached, and proved, that they were qualified for the pursuit of every profession, and of every science.‡
" Soon after the French revolution commenced, the Jews from all parts presented memorials to the Constituent Assembly, requesting admission to equal rights with the other members of the community." Among those who exerted themselves to obtain a legal improvement of their condition in France, the first assembly has numbered Mirabeau, Tonnere, and Rabaud. " The subject was discussed with animation, and finally justice triumphant granted to the children of Moses a legal existence, and the enjoyment of the rights of citizens."

* Sectes Religieuses, tom. ii. p. 392.
† Monthly Magazine, &c. 1789.
‡ Transactions of the Sanhedrim, p. 330.

The decree, however, which was passed in 1790, acknowledged as active citizens those Jews only, who, previously to 1789, had obtained letters of naturalization. In order to remove those limitations, the national assembly, in 1791, ordained, that all of the Jewish persuasion who would take the civic oath, and unite the other qualities required by the constitution to enable them to be active citizens, should be considered as such. All the Jews in France hastened to take the oath, which constituted them citizens.*

At the time of that famous decree which, in 1791, gave the Jews a country, many, in congratulating their brethren on the greatness of the boon, addressed to them instructions on the full extent of their duties, and proved the necessity of altering in their habits and manners whatever might tend to perpetuate prepossessions and prejudices against them.

A moral revolution must, however, be the result of time and experience. And, notwithstanding the improvements made by a number of intelligent Jews, the usurious practices of some in the departments in the north of France, caused several French writers to propose annulling the act, which granted them the privileges of citizens. The complaints made against the Jewish community gave rise to the decree of May 30, 1806, by which it was enacted, that " an assembly of the principal Jews shall

---

* It was on the report of Gregoire, then bishop of Blois, who had eminently distinguished himself by his exertions in favour of the Jews, that the national assembly passed the decree, which put them on a level with the rest of the citizens.—*Transactions of the Sanhedrim.* p. 390.

be convened in Paris, and that commissioners shall be appointed to make known to them the royal intentions, who shall, at the same time, collect their opinions as to the means they deem the fittest to re-establish among their brethren the exercise of mechanical arts and useful professions, in order to replace by an honest industry the shameful resources to which many of them have resorted from generation to generation these many centuries."*

It was also enacted, that " there shall be a suspension for a year from the date of the present decree of all executions of judgment and bond obligations, except so far as to prevent limitation obtained against husbandmen not traders, of the departments of La Sarre, La Roer, Mont Terrible, Upper and Lower Rhine, Rhine and Moselle, and Vosges, whenever the bonds entered into by these husbandmen are in favour of Jews."

Respecting the formation of an assembly professing the Jewish religion, it was decreed, that "they should be convened in Paris, on the fifteenth of July next; that in all the departments of the empire where there were five hundred of them, a deputy should be named, and five deputies for a thousand." They were " to be nominated by the prefects, from among the rabbies, the land-holders, and other Jews, the most distinguished for their integrity and knowledge."†

In compliance with the mandate, the Jewish deputies arrived in Paris in the July following; on the twenty-sixth of the month they assembled, and

* Transactions of the Sanhedrim, p. 105.   † Ibid. p. 106.

were met by Buonaparte's commissioners. Abraham
Furtado, a merchant from Bourdeaux, who had
acquired a distinguished reputation both, for his
talents and virtues, was chosen president. At the
second sitting, the commissioners put twelve questions to them, relating to the internal economy of
the Jewish nation, and the allegiance due by them
to the French government.*.

A declaration preceded the answers of the Jewish
deputies, which declared, in the name of all the
Frenchmen professing the religion of Moses, that
their religion makes it their duty to consider the
law of the prince as the supreme law in civil and
political matters; that, consequently, should their
religious code, or its various interpretations, contain
civil or political commands, at variance with those
of the French code, these commands, would of
course cease to influence and govern them, since
they must, above all, acknowledge and obey the
law of the prince; that in consequence of this
principle the Jews have, at all times, considered it
their duty to obey the laws of the state; and that,
since the revolution, they, like all Frenchmen, have
acknowledged no other."†

The questions proposed to the assembly of Israelites were generally answered in a manner agreeable
to Buonaparte. The epitome of their answers is
as follows: they declared in the first place, that in
all European countries they conformed to the general practice of marrying only one wife. But that,
as several individuals in some preceding ages indulged in the practice of polygamy, a synod was

* Transactions of the Sanhedrim.   † Ibid. p. 150.

convened at Worms in the eleventh century, composed of one hundred rabbies, with Guerson at their head ; and this assembly pronounced an anathema against every Jew who should in future take more than one wife. Since this prohibition, the influence of European manners has universally prevailed.*

In answer to the second query, concerning divorces, the Jewish deputies affirmed, that though they were allowed by the law of Moses, they were not valid if not previously pronounced by the French code ; that, though before they were admitted to the rights of French citizens, their religion allowed them the liberty of repudiating their wives, yet it was extremely rare to see it put in practice ; and since the revolution, that they have acknowledged no other laws on this head, but those of the empire. At the epoch, when they were admitted to the rank of citizens, the rabbies and the principal Jews appeared before the municipalities of their respective places of abode, and took an oath to conform in every thing to the laws, and to acknowledge no other rules in all civil matters. Consequently, since the Jews have begun to enter into engagements before a civil officer, no one attached to religion can repudiate his wife but by a double divorce, that pronounced by the law of the state, and that prescribed by the law of Moses ; so that in this point of view it may be justly affirmed, that the Jewish religion agrees with the civil code.†

With respect to the marriages between Jews and Christians, the assembly declared, that the pro-

* Transactions of the Sanhedrim, p. 151. † Ibid. p. 152, 153.

hibition in the Mosaic law in general, applies only
to nations in idolatry. The Talmud declares, that,
modern nations are not to be considered as such,.
since they worship, like us, the God of heaven and
earth. And accordingly there have been, at several
periods, intermarriages between Jews and Chris-,
tians, in France, in Spain, and in Germany; these
marriages were sometimes tolerated, and sometimes
forbidden by the laws of those sovereigns who had
received Jews into their dominions. Unions of
this kind are still found in France ; but the opinion,
of the rabbies is against these marriages. They,
asserted, that although the religion of Moses has
not forbidden the Jews to intermarry with nations.
not of their religion, yet as marriage, according to
the Talmud, requires religious ceremonies called
Kiduschim, with the benediction used in such cases,.
no marriage can be religiously valid unless these
ceremonies have been performed. The rabbies,
being therefore unwilling to bless marriages between
Jews and Christians, they were declared valid in
a civil, but not in a religious sense.*   .   .

In the answers of the deputies to the three questions concerning the relations and conduct of the
Jews towards Frenchmen, and the duties which they,
owed the nation since they were admitted to the,
privileges of citizens, the assembly declared, that
the descendants of Israel considered Frenchmen as,
their brethren, and not as strangers ; that the true
spirit of the law of Moses is consonant with this
mode of regarding them, since, when they formed
a settled and independent nation, their lawgiver

* Transactions of the Sanhedrim, p. 152, 153.

commanded them to love the strangers, for, says he
to the Israelites, ye were strangers in the land of
Egypt. They declare, that they are bound to love
all as their brethren who observe the precepts of the
Noachides,* whatever their religious opinions may
otherwise be ; that it is their incumbent duty to visit
their sick, bury their dead, assist their poor, and
perform every act of humanity towards them, as
well as the Israelites ; and, in short, that all the
principles of their religion, as well as gratitude for
the recent favours they have received from the
government, induce them to consider France as
their country, and Frenchmen as their brethren ;
that, consequently, the duty prescribed towards
Frenchmen not of their religion is the same as that
between Jews themselves ; and that they do not
admit of any other difference but that of worshipping
the Supreme Being, every one in his own way. At
the present time especially, when they are incorporated with the great nation, they declare, that it is
impossible for a Jew to treat a Frenchman not of his
religion in any other manner than he would treat
his Israelitish brethren, and that they consider the
duty of defending their country as equally sacred and
honourable. As a proof of this, during the last
wars French Jews have been seen fighting despe-
rately against their brethren, the subjects of countries then at war with France.†

* These precepts are, to abstain from idolatry, from blasphemy,
from adultery, and not to kill or hurt our neighbours, neither to rob,
steal, nor deceive. to eat only the flesh of animals killed, and; in
short, to observe the rules of justice; and take care that it be impar-
tially administered to all.

† Transactions of the Sanhedrim, p. 178—180—182.

In answer to the questions concerning the nomination and jurisdiction of the rabbies, it was asserted, that since the revolution, the majority of the heads of families name the rabbies whenever there is a sufficient number of Jews to maintain one, after previous inquiries into the morality and learning of the candidate. This mode of election is not, however, uniform; it varies in different places; and to this day, whatever concerns the election of rabbies is in a state of uncertainty.*

The assembly declared, that the rabbies exercise no kind of police jurisdiction among the Jews; that the qualification of rabbi is no where to be found in the law of Moses, nor did exist in the days of the first temple, but is only mentioned towards the end of those of the second; yet that after the Israelites were totally dispersed, and had formed small communities in different places, a rabbi and two other doctors constituted a kind of tribunal, called "a house of justice;" the rabbi being judge, and the other two his assessors. The attributes, however, and even the existence of these tribunals, have, to this day, always depended on the will of the governments under which the Jews have lived, and on the degree of toleration they have enjoyed. Since the revolution, these rabbinical tribunals are totally suppressed in France and Italy. The Jews, raised to the rank of citizens, have conformed in every thing to the laws of the state; and accordingly the functions of rabbies, wherever any are established, are limited to preaching morality in the temples, blessing marriages, and pronouncing

* Transactions of the Sanhedrim.

divorces. As to judicial powers they absolutely
possess none; for there is among them neither
a settled ecclesiastical hierarchy, nor any subordination in the exercise of their religious functions.
The Jewish deputies asserted, that there were no
professions which their law forbids them from exercising ; but, on the contrary, the Talmud expressly
declares, that the father who does not teach a profession to his child educates him to be a villain.'
In reply to the queries respecting usury, the
assembly asserted, that the Hebrew word which has
been improperly translated by the term *usury*
means interest of any kind, and not usurious interest. It is, say they, even impossible that it ever
could have had this acceptation ; for usury is an
expression relative to, and compared with another
and a lawful interest: and the text contains nothing
which alludes to the other term of comparison. By
usury we understand an interest above the rate fixed
by law ; and, if the law of Moses has not fixed the
rate, can it be said that the Hebrew word means an
unlawful interest?*

," The aim of the lawgiver in forbidding the
Hebrews to lend upon interest to one another was to
draw closer between them the bonds of fraternity,
to give them a lesson of reciprocal benevolence,
and to engage them to assist each other with disinterestedness. The intention of Moses was to make
of his people a nation of husbandmen for a long
time after him, and all his regulations seemed designed to divert their attention from commerce.
His prohibition must therefore be considered as

* Transactions of the Sanhedrim, p. 197.

a principle of charity, and not as a commercial
regulation. According to the Talmud it is to be
considered as made to a man in want; for in case
of a loan to a merchant, even a Jew, profit adequate to the risk should be considered as lawful.
The Mosaic law forbids all manner of interest on
loan, not only between Jews, but between a Jew,
and his countrymen, without distinction of religion.
The loan must be gratuitous when it is not intended
for commercial speculations. These humane laws,
however, were made for a people who then formed
a state, and held a rank among nations.

" If the remnants of this people, now scattered
among all nations, are attentively considered, it will
be seen that, since they have been driven from
Palestine, they no longer have had a common
country, they no longer have had to maintain among
them the primeval equality of property. Although
filled with the spirit of their legislation, they have
been sensible that the letter of the law could not
longer be obeyed when its principle was done away ;
and they have, therefore, without any scruple, lent
money on interest to trading Jews, as well as to
men of different persuasions. *

" It is an incontrovertible point according to the
Talmud, that interest, even among Israelites, is
lawful in commercial transactions, where the lender,
running some of the risk of the borrower, becomes
a sharer in his profits." This is the opinion of all
the Jewish doctors.†

The birth day of the French emperor, was observed by the Jewish deputies on August 15th,

* Transactions of the Sanhedrim, p. 200, 201.   † Ibid.

1806, as a day of thanksgiving. On this occasion the grand synagogue was superbly illuminated and ornamented.. The imperial eagle was placed above the altar; vocal and instrumental music was performed; sermons and animated orations delivered; and a collection made for the poor of all religious denominations.*

On the eighteenth of September the deputies were again convened, and assured, by a discourse read to them by one of the emperor's commissioners, of the satisfaction their answers had given his imperial majesty. At the time it was declared " to be the emperor's intention to secure to them the free exercise of their religious worship, and the full enjoyment of their political rights. But that, in return for his gracious protection, his majesty required a religious pledge for their strict adherence to the principles contained in the replies to the queries proposed to them, and that the answers of the Jewish deputies, converted into decisions by another assembly, of a nature still more dignified and religious, might find a place near the Talmud, and thus acquire, in the eyes of the Jews of all countries, and all ages, the greatest possible authority. For this purpose it was deemed requisite to convene the grand sanhedrim, which, according to ancient custom, will be composed of seventy members exclusive of the president.. The duties of this venerable assembly shall be to convert into religious doctrines the answers which have been given by the Jewish deputies, and also those which may result from the continuance of their sittings."†

* Transactions of the Sanhedrim.　　† Ibid.

The momentous event of convening a grand san-. hedrim was announced to the dispersed remnants of the descendants of Abraham, in a grateful and pathetic address to the synagogues of Europe, signed by the president and two leading members. This address was soon after answered by one of concurrence and congratulation from the Jews of Frankfort upon the Maine.*

The grand sanhedrim assembled in Paris, 1807, and the number and distinction of the spectators greatly increased the solemnity and grandeur of the scene. Numerous addresses were read, and animated orations delivered. This venerable assembly passed and agreed to various articles respecting the Mosaic worship, and sanctioned the answers previously given by the Jewish deputies. A decree was enacted, consisting of seventeen articles; establishing a synagogue and a consistory in every department which contains two thousand individuals professing the religion of Moses.

The seats of the synagogues were to be in the most populous cities ; and each of them was to be superintended by a rabbi and two elders. No one can be a member of the consistory who has addicted himself to usurious practices. Among other functions which are to be exercised by the consistory, they are to see that the rabbies do not, in public or private, give any instructions or explanations of the law, in contradiction to the answers of the assembly confirmed by the decisions of the grand sanhedrim. They are also directed to do all in their power to encourage the Israelites to follow agriculture and

* Transactions of the Sanhedrim.

useful·professions ; and to report to government the
names of those·who cannot give a` satisfactory ac-
count of their means of subsistence. The grand sanhedrim invited the Jews to acquire landed property ;
passed·a law for the condemnation of usury ;·and
declared, that·the profession of military services.was
equally incumbent upon them as upon other citizens.*

The Jews have at present in Paris a consistory
composed of three grand rabbies, &c. &c. In most
parts of France where they are found they are
making exertions to place themselves in the·rank
of citizens. Some have become farmers ;·and one
Jew in the·department of Vosges has received a
medal from the society of agriculture in Paris. Others
devote themselves to the arts and trades of every
kind ;·others to the sciences, particularly medicine
and mathematics. Recently among·the three hundred pupils in the Polytechnic school are found six
Jews. Furtado, Rodriguez, Eli-Levi, Zinstheimer,
Cologna, Bing, lately dead, Berr-Isaac-Berr and his
son Michael Berr, Zalkind Hourvitz, Einsheim,
Luzzati, Lipman-Moses, Terquem, Anschel, &c.
all of France, are distinguished by their talents and
their works. Anschel, lately become a Christian,
is professor of physic and chemistry; and Terquem
of the highest branches of mathematics in the Ly-
ceum of Mayence.†

Among the Italian Jews convoked at the sanhedrim
are also found men of distinguished talents. There
are two Jewish poets in Leghorn ; Florentini, who
shines in one kind of elegy, and Michael Bolassi,

* Nicholson's British Encyclopedia.
† Gregoire's Histoire des Sectes Religieuses, tom. ii. p. 386.

who translated from Hebrew into Italian verse a
work of rabbi Ghevirol, on the "wonders of creation."*

Notwithstanding the great improvements which
have been made by a number of literary Jews, the
French emperor appears to be dissatisfied with the
manner of life which is still pursued by some of the
nation. The last decree which was issued concerning them, in March 17, 1808, "forbids them,
indiscriminately to pursue their speculations, and
excuse themselves from honest labour. In order to
partake of the fruits of the earth in his large dominions, they must till the ground. The rich are
enjoined to purchase rural property, and to abandon
the low pursuits of sordid avarice. . This decree
also annuls all obligations for loans made by Jews
to minors without the sanction of their guardians ;
to married women without the consent of their husbands ; or to military men without the authority of
their superior officers. Bills granted by French
subjects to Jews must be demanded, unless their
holders prove that the full value was given without
fraud. All debts accumulated by interest above five
per cent. are to be reduced by the courts of law ;
if the interest growing on the capital exceed twenty
three per cent. the contract is to be declared usurious.
No Jew is to be allowed to trade without a patent,
which patent is to be granted to such individuals
only, as produce a certificate to the prefects that
they are no usurers. These regulations are to be

* Similar improvements with those in France and Italy have been
made by the Jews in Germany and Holland. See the preceding and
following chapters

continued during ten years, in the hope, that after that period there will be no differenee between the moral character of the Jews and the other citizens of the empire; if the contrary should appear, the law will still be continued in force."*

An English Israelite, in a letter addressed to the sanhedrim of Paris, highly reprimands the conduct of this assembly, and charges many of the members with having little estimation, not only for the law of Moses, but for every species of revealed religion. The author asks them, " what suffrages they have received from the Jewish societies who are not subjects of France? Have," says he, " any of our brethren of Constantinople, of Aleppo, of Bagdat, or Cochin ; or have any of our congregations, not under the dominion of France, sent deputies to join you? or have they demonstrated any approval of your proceedings? In England they would hold no communion with you either on religious or political subjects, especially as the local welfare of the country so imperiously forbids it."†

As the Jews in Holland united with those of France and sent deputies to the sanhedrim, an account of their state in that country previous to this period, and the events which gave rise to their union with France, will be given in the following chapter.

* Nicholson's British Encyclopedia, published 1809, vol. iii.
† Letter to the Sanhedrim, 1808, p. 32.

CHAPTER XXXII.

Of the Jews in Holland.—They are prohibited from the exercise of
the arts and professions.—Conduct of the Syndics.—The intelligent
Jews in Amsterdam concert a plan, and present it to government.
—They are opposed by the Syndics, and form a new community.—
Of their altercations with the Syndics.—Regulations of. the new
community.—An account of the literary Jews in Holland.—Three
deputies from the schismatical community in Holland are sent to
the grand sanhedrim at Paris, and agree to the decisions of that
assembly.

*SIXTY thousand Portuguese and German
Jews inhabit Holland. Amsterdam contains nearly
two thirds of this number. The toleration which
their ancestors found in this country was happiness,
compared with the cruelties that were exercised
towards them in other parts of the world.† Yet in
Holland as elsewhere some lucrative and honourable
employments were shut upon them, and they were
forbidden the exercise of the arts and professions.
The burgomasters of Amsterdam enacted an ecclesiastical law, by which they were placed under the
control of the Syndics. These Syndics or Parnassim, constituted absolute masters of their co-religionists, had authority to excommunicate them.
A fine of one thousand florins was the penalty
of him who dared to complain of the proceedings of
the Syndics. A sentence to be ignominiously
scourged was pronounced against him who purchased meat of any butcher but that of the commu-

---

* The whole of this chapter is an abridged translation from Gregoire's Histoire de Sectes Religieuses.

† See chapter xxviii.

nity. Whence it would appear, that the Syndics exercised imperiously the power conferred upon them by the law.

Literature has long since been advancing among the Batavian Jews, who have produced a large number of writers, many of whose names will descend with honour to posterity. The education of their children became more an object of their attention ; they began to frequent the society of the Christians, and gradually to conform to their habits. On the late entrance of the French troops into Holland, many of the Jews of Amsterdam assembled, and concerted a plan which should secure to their sect the enjoyment of certain civil advantages, and presented it to the government. But the difficulties they encountered were very considerable : for their wishes were opposed by the Syndics, who endeavoured to render their remonstrances ineffectual.

The discussions in the national assembly of Batavia, in 1796, attest these facts. At length, the privileges of the city were decreed to them by the supreme authority. Four or five were admitted into judicial, municipal, and legislative offices ; all of whom, with one exception, have become members of the schismatical synagogue which we are about to describe, and which was almost entirely composed of Germans. As soon as the law which has been mentioned was abolished, they solicited the enaction of another, but being repulsed by the Syndics, towards the end of 1796, they resolved to effect a separation, and to erect a new community, styled, *Adath Jesurum.* The Syndics, in consequence, forbade all marriage alliances with the schismatics.

F F

The Syndics instituted twenty-three suits against twenty-three members of the new community, in order to subject them to the fine of one hundred florins, by virtue 'of an article' in the law before cited, which had been repealed.' The defendants; confident 'that the' issue of the suit must be in their favour, waited the decision with impatience; and earnestly entreated that it might be pronounced by the tribunal. But the Syndics obtained a continuation of the cause, and the defendants were 'subjected to the payment of considerable sums for costs.

The new community have discarded from their liturgy, those prayers which contain imprecations against other sects.

In general, among the Jews, the ceremony of interment is performed with great precipitation; sometimes in twenty-four and sometimes even in twelve hours after the decease. This abuse, which every wise police should prevent, is 'not permitted in the new community, which prohibits the interment within forty-eight hours, unless for urgent reasons, attested by the physicians appointed to act on such occasions.

This community has never found effectual support from the intermedial governors of Holland; except the grand pensioner Schimmelpennink: But, in general, the professors of the predominant religion have succeeded in keeping the Jews and Catholics from places of trust.

Amsterdam and the Hague have witnessed societies, the express design of whose formation was, to render Jewish children more easily admissible to

the apprenticeship of trades. Yet, scarce a Christian in Amsterdam would admit them to his shop. At the. Hague, not one of .them would be received. After this, it is not surprising, that of three hundred Jewish families in this city, but four or.five individuals are artizans. , A Jew of.Amsterdam, who supported by his exertions a superannuated mother, could not, till after difficulties and delays, obtain permission to pursue the business of. a locksmith.

. A society whose views embrace all Holland, and that has published the most interesting works on various branches of popular instruction, and adopted for its motto, Pro bono publico, has, in the first article of its regulations, excluded the Jews.

The same remark applies to another society, the Felix Meritis. They too had resolved to admit only Christians; and therefore excluded Vanlann, a Jew, a physician and mechanic, and the inventor of many astronomical instruments, one of which has been named Tellurium Laniene by M. Van Swinden, who himself in the same society has read three memoirs in praise of the discovery.

This exclusion falls upon many others.; for an academy might be formed of the literary Jews that now honour Holland with their residence , among whom are Belinfante, Desolla, Cappadoce, and Asser. The catalogue would be incomplete without adding the names of the physicians at the Hague; Heyman, Polak, and Stein, professor of botany, who has published a dissertation de Hydrope— Pinto the younger, author of a work on the efficacy of the principle of oxigene in the animal body, &c. —Heilbron, physician of Amsterdam, who has been

six times crowned by the academy of sciences at
Rotterdam—Salomon, physician of Leyden, author
of various works, who could never obtain employment in that city till he joined the sect of the
Remonstrants—David, a physician, who came at
his own expense to Paris to obtain information concerning vaccination, which he first introduced into
Holland, and which has since been promoted by
societies, one at Amsterdam for the Jews, and the
other at Rotterdam for the poor—Almeida, captain
of a ship of war, who, in a naval action in 1781,
distinguished himself against the English, and received a medal of honour—Asser the elder, one
of the first counsellors of his age in maritime laws
and insurances—Lemon and Bromet, whose writings
have greatly contributed to the reformation of the
Jews in Holland. Three persons among the Israelites have been representatives of the people; the
two last mentioned, and Acosta Athias, who presided at the national assembly. At the bar of
Amsterdam are three Jewish advocates, Charles
Asser, Mendez, and Meyer. The last named was
received at the bar when only sixteen years of age,
being a pupil of professor Cras, who was acquainted
with every language in Europe. Meyer, in 1804,
published a treatise proposed by the academy of
Berlin, " Whether the moral tendency of an action
should be taken into consideration in the formation
and application of penal laws ?" The work arrived
after the decision of the academy, otherwise it
would, probably, have received the prize.

The Syndics refused the invitation to unite
with the sanhedrim of Paris without consulting the

community; part of which has protested against them. They exerted themselves to the utmost to prevent the deputation from the new community. But the government of Holland, who had manifested a desire that the Jews should be treated as the Christians, authorized the departure of three deputies from the schismatical community—Asser, jun. a counsellor; Lemon, formerly legislator and physician; and Littwak, a mathematician. They arrived at Paris, and in the name of their constituents agreed to the decisions of the grand sanhedrim.

With regard to the new community, a regulation, digested by themselves and adopted by the government, organized their consistory. Many of its members received marks of public consideration. The physician Cappadoce was named chevalier of the order of the union; Meyer, member of the institute; Asser the elder, one of the compilers of the code of commerce; and his son was nominated minister of worship, chief of the division charged with the affairs of their co-religionists.

CHAPTER XXXIII.

Of the Jews in the Ottoman empire —They are numerous in Constantinople and Salonichi.—Some particulars respecting those of
Aleppo and Palestine —Of the independent Jewish tribes in the
high lands of Hedjas in Arabia.—An account of their emigration
into China and India.

AFTER having in the preceding chapters sur-
veyed the favourable change which has taken place
in the condition of the Jews in Europe during the
eighteenth and nineteenth centuries, we follow them
to the east, where they have experienced fewer
vicissitudes. It appears, from the accounts of late
travellers, that there has been little alteration in
their fate in the eastern countries since the seventeenth century, when Basnage closed his history.
He has computed that there were, at that epoch,
one million in the grand seignior's empire, above
eighty thousand of whom resided at Constantinople
and Salonichi; and that there were thirty synagogues, and an hundred and five thousand families
in the former of these cities.*

Though the Jews in the Turkish empire are held
in detestation, and exposed to undistinguishing
contempt, they have rendered their services indis-
pensible in conducting traffic, almost every species
of which, through the supineness and indolence of
the Turks, has fallen into their hands.

It is said, " that the Jews in Constantinople are
less affluent and more ignorant than those in Europe.
A few among them are physicians, but none

* Basnage. p 718.

farmers. They are chiefly brokers, bankers, or traders, and devote themselves to every kind of traffic, even the lowest."*

The Jews in the Ottoman empire pay a heavy tax to the Porte for the right of exercising their religious worship ; and they are subject to a chief of their own nation, called Cochan Pascha, whose power over them is said to be even greater than that which the patriarch exercises over the Greek Christians.†

The Jews at Aleppo are computed at about five thousand. They possess a synagogue, in which they have a manuscript of the Old Testament, said to be very ancient. They are distinguished by the colour of their babooge, and the form of their turban ; the former of which is orange, and the latter blue. They all wear beards, even foreign Jews are obliged by the priest to submit to this custom.‡

They speak more corrupt Arabic than the Christians. Their morning salutation on the sabbath is frequently Hebrew, and extends only to a few words, none of them speaking it familiarly, though many read it. In writing Arabic they often use Hebrew letters, as they are said to do in other places with the language of the country. Their children are sent to the reading school, but seldom get beyond their psalter. Their books are chiefly supplied from Venice.

Few of them are either manufacturers or mechanics. The principal part are either merchants

---

* Olivier's Travels to the Ottoman Empire, published 1802.
† Zimmerman's Political Survey of Europe.
‡ Russell's Account of Aleppo, vol. ii.

or bankers; the others are chiefly brokers, grocers, or pedlars. The established bankers of the seraglio are Jews, and, by being employed to act in that capacity by most of the great men, they acquire an extensive influence over those who despise and contemn their religion. They are generally more sober than the Christians.

Their chief priest is called *Khakhan*, or great *Khakhan;* but the title is also extended to priests in general. They are much respected by their own people, over whom they exercise both temporal and spiritual power; but the latter is always subject to an appeal to the Turkish authority. The scriptures are read by them in Hebrew, and explained according to the traditions of former times. Their schools are kept by inferior priests.*

They so strictly observe the sabbath, that they do no business on that day, and allow no fires to be made in their houses, except in case of sickness, and even then it is generally done by a Christian servant. The poor people on such occasions are assisted by Arabian women, who cry along the streets, " Fire to sell." This is done every sabbath. On the sabbath they remain long at table, drinking wine and singing psalms, but their music does not conform to European modes.†

The Jews, more frequently than the other inhabitants of Aleppo, believe in the existence of evil spirits, and their agency in the production of epilepsy, madness, and certain other maladies. In such cases they not only call in their own rabbies, but the Mahometan scheiks to exorcise them.

Russell's Account of Aleppo, vol. ii.   † Ibid

They generally marry at an earlier age than the Turks; and chiefly form connexions with relations who are previously acquainted with each other. The nuptial feast lasts seven days, and is celebrated with music, dancing, and festivity. Both Turkish and Christian women are frequently spectators. Polygamy, being considered as scandalous, is seldom practised among them, and then only in some particular cases.*

Besides the festivals and feasts which are observed by the Jews in general, those of Aleppo keep a voluntary fast of six entire days, in which they abstain from all nourishment, even water. The two first days they attend business at the Bazar, but afterwards employ themselves at home in reading the Bible and in prayer. In the evening of the sixth day, at the end of the fast, they moisten their throat with liquids; and afterwards return by slow degrees, to the use of solid food. It is a long time before they recover their former appetite. Few, however, attempt to keep this fast; not more than twenty-five in a year. Sometimes they are obliged to renounce it before it is finished; and it is never observed by the same person more than once in his life. They have also occasional fasts for public calamities; and individuals observe private devotional fasts. From their extensive commercial connections these fasts cause a stagnation of trade at the time, and occasion great delays in the departure and march of caravans.

The Jews, except such as are under the protection of some foreign prince, are subject to a capita-

* Russell's Account of Aleppo, vol. ii.

tion levied on the able bodied men, ten crowns
a year on the rich, six on the middling, and three
on the lower classes.*

In Palestine, where the Turks and Arabs unite in
oppressing them, few comparatively are to be found.
Yet a learned inquirer, who passed some time at
Jerusalem during the spring of 1800, supposes that
the city, at that period, contained three thousand
Jews.†

* Russell's Account of Aleppo.

† Mr de Chateaubriand, a celebrated French author, who visited
Palestine in the year 1807, has given the following account of the
miserable condition of the Jews who still reside in Jerusalem.

After a striking description of the piety and humanity of the
Christian monks who constantly perform their devotions at the tomb
of our Saviour, he observes, " While the New Jerusalem is seen
shining in the midst of the desert, you may observe between Mount
Zion and the temple, another spectacle of almost equal interest ; it is
that of the remnants of another people, distinct from the rest of the
inhabitants ; a people individually the objects of universal contempt ;
who suffer the most wanton outrages without a murmur ; who endure
wounds and blows without a sigh ; who, when the sacrifice of their
life is demanded, unhesitatingly stretch forth their necks to the sabre.
If a member of the community thus cruelly proscribed and abused
happens to die, his companion buries him clandestinely during the
night in the valley of Josaphat, within the purlieus of the temple of
Solomon. Enter their habitation and you find them in the most
abject squalid misery, and for the most part occupied in reading
a mysterious book to their children, with whom again it becomes
a manual for the instruction of succeeding generations. What these
wretched outlaws from the justice and compassion of the rest of
mankind did in past ages, they do still. Six times they have
witnessed the destruction of Jerusalem, and are not yet discouraged ;
nothing can operate to divert their looks from Zion. We are surprised, no doubt, when we observe the Jews scattered over the face
of the earth, but to experience an astonishment more lively, we have
but to seek them in Jerusalem. The legitimate masters of Judea
should be seen as they are in their own land, slaves and strangers ;
they should be seen awaiting, under the most cruel and oppressive of
all despotisms, a king who is to work their deliverance. Near the

The Jews in Arabia are regarded with extreme contempt; and, as in Turkey, despised alike by Mahometans and Christians. They abound in Yemen, the region anciently known by the denomination of Arabia Felix. Yet they are not permitted to reside in cities, but dwell as in other parts of Arabia, in a separate quarter without the gates. Their quarter adjoining to Sana, the capital, contains two thousand. They carry on a great trade, and are the best artists in Arabia. One of their merchants, named Oraeki, had been during twenty-eight years, under two successive imans of Yemen, comptroller of the customs, and of the royal buildings and gardens. But in 1760, he fell into disgrace, and was imprisoned and fined fifty thousand crowns. At the same time fourteen synagogues in the Jewish quarter at Sana were demolished by order of government, together with all private houses above a certain height, beyond which none were afterwards to be raised.*

The highlands of Hedjas are possessed by a number of independent sovereign scheiks. The most numerous and the best known of these communities is that which the Jews have formed upon the mountains lying to the north east of Medina. That tract of country is called Kheibar, and the Jewish inhabitants are known in Arabia by the name of Beni Khiebar. They are governed by their own

temple, of which there does not remain " *one stone upon another,*" they still continue to dwell; and with the cross as it were planted upon their heads, and bending them to the earth, still cling to their errors, and labour under the same deplorable infatuation."—*American Review, No 1, January,* 1811.

* Niebuhr's Travels.

independent scheiks, and are divided into three
tribes. Their settlement appears to have subsisted
for more than twelve centuries ; they are surrounded
with deserts, and the natural advantages of their situation have enabled them to preserve their freedom.*

The Jews in this district do not maintain any
intercourse with their brethren in Asia, and are
therefore supposed to belong to the sect of the
Caraites, who are few in number, much dispersed, -
and detested by the sect of the Pharisees.

The Jews settled themselves in China under the
dynasty of the Han, which began in the year 206
before Christ, and ended 220 years after his birth ;
but it is not known at what part of the period they
appeared in the empire. They not only increased
in number and wealth, but were distinguished for
literature and raised to offices, being governors of
provinces, and mandarins. The principal places of
their abode were Ham-tehen, Peking, and Cai-
fong-fou. By degrees their affairs began to decline,
and many embraced the Mahometan religion. After
this change took place among the Jews in Peking
and other parts, they were only found in Cai-
fong-fou, the capital of the province of Honan,
which is an hundred and fifty leagues from Peking.
Those in this city were, at length, involved in
various calamities ; their synagogue was inundated,
in 1446, by the river Hoango. They also suffered
by fire during the administration of Ouanhi, who
reigned from 1573 to 1620 ; and another desolating
inundation took place in 1642.†

* Niebuhr s Travels.
† Brotier's Notes to Tacitus, vol. iii. p. 578.

In 1704, father Gozani, a jesuit missionary, 'had the curiosity·to investigate the state of the Jews in the empire. To effect this purpose he contracted an, acquaintance with some of their learned chiefs, who introduced him into their synagogues. ˜According to his account he succeeded so well in ingratiating himself 'with ·this people, that they even suffered him to enter into the most secret part·of their synagogue, to ·which they have no access themselves, it being reserved for the chief of the synagogues, who never approaches·it but with profound respect.* They showed him one of their volumes, or parchment rolls of the Pentateuch, written in Hebrew in fair and legible characters, and also other parts of the Old Testament, namely, Joshua, Judges, Samuel,· Kings, part of the Prophets, and some other books containing their liturgy and commentaries, written likewise in Hebrew. They acknowledged they had lost part of their sacred books, and some of their Targums, paraphrases, expositions, &c. by the overflowing of the river ʼWhamho, which had greatly damaged their roll of the Pentateuch. To remedy this misfortune they ordered twelve fair copies to be taken of it, which are still carefully preserved in the tabernacles that are placed in the synagogue.†

They informed Gozani that they divided the five books of Moses into fifty-two lessons, one for every sabbath throughout the year, which division is supposed to have been instituted by Ezra. Our author, being ignorant of the Hebrew language, was not

---

* Lettres Edifiantes, tom. ii.
† Modern Universal History, vol. viii. p 137.

able to investigate their usages in such an accurate
manner as could have been wished. But from their
blending fictitious tales with the facts recorded in
scripture, and even in the five books of Moses, he
concluded these Jews were of the Talmudic sect.
He observes, however, that this can only be determined by one versed in the scriptures, and well
acquainted with the Hebrew language.*

Their synagogue fronts the west, and when they
address their prayers to God they turn towards that
quarter. In the middle of the synagogue stands
a magnificent chair raised very high, and richly
adorned with crimson velvet, gold fringe, tassels, &c.
This they style the chair of Moses, on which every
sabbath, and on days of great solemnity, the law
and other parts of the Old Testament are read.
The synagogue is also furnished with a table of
incense, magnificent candlesticks, large candles,
a censer, perfumes, and a painting, on which the
names and titles of the emperor are superbly engraved. There were also thirteen tabernacles placed
upon tables, and surrounded with rich curtains, in
each of which the Pentateuch, or sacred roll of the
law, is shut up. Twelve of these tabernacles represent the twelve tribes of Israel, the thirteenth Moses.†

The Chinese Jews strictly observe the sabbath,
and do not kindle any fire, or dress any food on that
day. They also observe circumcision, and several
other ceremonies mentioned in the Old Testament;
in particular the passover, feast of unleavened bread,
the week of Pentecost, of tabernacles, and other

* Modern Universal History, vol viii. p. 187.
† Winterbotham's History of China, vol. i. p. 111, 112.

occasional festivals and fasts. They pray and read the law with the thaled or veil over their faces, in remembrance of Moses. They also abstain from blood, and retain the Jewish manner of killing their animals and preparing their food.

In some cases, however, they readily comply with the Chinese customs, and address the Supreme Being by the appellation which is made use of in this country; which is, "Lord of Heaven," "Creator of all things," &c. They also honour Confucius, and imitate the solemn rites which the Chinese pay to their ancestors. Contiguous to their synagogue is a large hall, in which they burn perfumes in honour of their Chimgins, or great men of their law. But instead of such pictures as are used by the Chinese, and forbidden by their religion, they have a number of censers. The largest of these, which is intended for the patriarch Abraham, stands in the centre of the hall. The next were those of Moses, Joshua, Esdras, and several other illustrious persons of both sexes. The mandarin who is over them is also entitled to have his tablet set up in the hall, inscribed with his own name, and all his titles.*

The Jews informed father Gozani, that their ancestors came from the west, from the kingdom of Judah, which Joshua conquered after they left Egypt, had crossed the Red Sea, traversed the desert, and that the number of Jews who left Egypt amounted to six hundred thousand. They also gave him to understand, that they had formerly been numerous in the empire, but were then reduced to only seven families. They form alliances with each

* Winterbotham's History.

other, and never connect themselves with the other,
inhabitants of China.

When father Gozani, spoke to them of the Mes-.
siah, promised and announced in the Holy Scriptures, they exhibited great astonishment.' But when
the missionary informed them, that the Messiah had
already appeared, and was called Jesus Christ, they
replied, that they had heard of a holy man named
Jesus, who was the son of Sirach, but that they
were entirely ignorant of the new Jesus of whom he
discoursed.* They had not any knowledge of some
of the books of the Old Testament, and had lost
others in the inundation which took place October
29, 1642.†

Dr. Buchanan, while he resided in India, was
assiduously engaged in investigating the state of the
inhabitants.‡ "The Jews," says he, "are numerous
in India, and reside in a town, about a mile distant
from Cochin, called Jews' Town. It is almost
wholly inhabited by this people, who have two
respectable synagogues. Among them are some very
intelligent men, who are not ignorant of the present
history of nations. There are also Jews here from
remote parts of Asia, so that this is the fountain of
intelligence concerning that people in the east, there

* A modern traveller observes, that "if this be really the fact,
their ancestors could not have been any part of the ten tribes who
were carried into captivity, but may rather be supposed to be among
the followers of Alexander's army, which agrees with their own
account of the time they first settled in China.—Barrow's Travels in
China, 1805.

† Modern Univer. Hist. vol. viii. p. 139.

‡ Dr. Buchanan's first tour to Cochin was in November, 1806, and
he remained in the country till February, 1807. He again visited it
in January, 1908.

India

being constant communication by ships with the Red
Sea, the Persian Gulf, and the mouth of the Indus.
The resident Jews are divided into two classes,
called the Jerusalem or White Jews, and the ancient or Black Jews. The White Jews reside
at this place. The black Jews have also a synagogue here; but the great body of that tribe inhabit
towns in the interior of that province."

This learned author thus proceeds in his interesting relation: " On my inquiry into the antiquity
of the White Jews, they first delivered to me
a narrative in the Hebrew language of their arrival
in India, which has been handed down to them
from their fathers; and then exhibited their ancient
brass plate, containing their charter and freedom of
residence, given by a king, of Malabar. The
following is the narrative of the events relating
to their first arrival.

" After the second temple was destroyed (which
may God speedily rebuild!) our fathers, dreading,
the conqueror's wrath, departed from Jerusalem,
a numerous body of men, women, priests, and
Levites, and came into this land. There were among
them men of repute for learning and wisdom; and
God gave the people favour in the sight of the king
who at that time reigned here, and he granted them
a place to dwell in, called Cranganor. He allowed
them a patriarchal jurisdiction within the district,
with certain privileges of nobility; and the royal
grant was engraved, according to the custom of
those days, on a plate of brass.* This was done

* Dr. Buchanan requested the Jews to shew him their brass plate.
Having been given by a native king, it is written of course in the

G G

in the year from the creation of the world-four-thousand two hundred and fifty, (A. D. four hundred and ninety ;) and this plate of brass we still have in possession.

"Our forefathers continued at Cranganor for, about a thousand years, and the number of heads. who governed were seventy-two. Soon after our settlement, other Jews followed us from Judea ; and among these came that man of great wisdom, rabbi Samuel, a Levite of Jerusalem, with his son,.

Malabaric language and character, and is now so old that it cannot be well understood. The Jews preserve a Hebrew translation of it which they presented to the learned author. This ancient document begins in the following manner according to the Hebrew translation: "In the peace of God the king, which has made the earth according to his pleasure. To this God I, Airvi Brahmin, have lifted up my hand, and have granted by this deed, which many hundred thousand years shall run—I, dwelling at Cranganor, have granted, in the thirty-sixth year of my reign, in the strength of power I have granted, in the strength of power I have given in inheritance to, Joseph Rabban."

Then follow the privileges of nobility, such as permission to ride on an elephant, to have a herald to go before to announce the name and dignity; to have the lamp of the day; to walk upon carpets spread upon the earth; and to have trumpets and cymbals sounded before him. King Airvi then appoints Joseph Rabban to be "chief and governor of the houses of congregation, (the synagogues) and of certain districts, and of the sojourners in them. What proves the importance of the Jews at the period when this grant was made is, that it is signed by seven kings as witnesses. There is no date in this document, further than what may be collected from the reign of the prince, and the names of the royal witnesses. Dates are not usual in old Malabaric writings. One fact is evident, that the Jews must have existed a considerable time in the country before they could have obtained such a grant. The tradition before mentioned assigns for the date of the transaction, the year of the creation 4250, which is in Jewish computation, A. D. 490. It is well known, that the famous Malabaric king, Cerani Perumal, made grants to the Jews, Christians, and Mahometans, during his reign ; but that prince flourished in the eighth or ninth century.—*Christian Researches*, p. 220, 221.

rabbi Jehuda Levita. They brought with them the silver trumpets, made use of at the time of the jubilee, which were saved when the second temple was destroyed ; and we have heard from our fathers, that there were engraven upon those trumpets the letters of the ineffable name.* There joined us also from Spain and other places, from time to time, certain tribes of Jews who had heard of our prosperity. But, at last, discord arising among ourselves, one of our chiefs called to his assistance an Indian king, who came upon us with a great army, destroyed our houses, palaces, and strong holds, dispossessed us of Cranganor, killed part of us, and carried part into captivity. By these massacres we were reduced to a small number. Some of the exiles came and dwelt at Cochin, where we have remained ever since, suffering great changes from time to time. There are amongst us some of the children of Israel, (Beni Israel) who came from the country of Ashkenaz, from Egypt, from Isoba, and other places, besides those who formerly inhabited this country.†

" The native annals of Malabar confirm the foregoing account in the principal circumstances,‡ as

* This circumstance of the Jubilee trumpets is to be found in a similar account of the Jews of Malabar, published in the " history of the works of the learned" for March, 1699. It is not necessary to suppose that these trumpets belonged to the temple, for it is well known, that in every considerable town in Judea there were jubilee trumpets.—*Buchanan's Christian Researches.*

† Buchanan's Christian Researches, p. 218—220.

‡ The above account is also confirmed in the principal circumstances by the testimony of Moses de Paiva, a Portuguese Jew of Amsterdam, who, having visited Cochin in 1686, published on his

do the Mahometan histories of the later ages, for
the Mahometans have been settled here in great
numbers since the eighth century.

"The desolation of Cranganor the Jews describe
as being like the desolation of Jerusalem in miniature. They were first received into the country
with some favour and confidence, agreeably to the
tenor of the general prophecy concerning the Jews,
for no country was to reject them ; and after they

return to Europe an account of his tour, which is now become very
rare, and contains what follows :

"In the year four thousand one hundred and thirty of the creation
of the world, after the destruction of the second temple by Titus,
seventy or eighty thousand Israelites penetrated as far as the coast of
Malabar. The king Cheram Iberimal assembled, and gave them the
city of Cranganor, with a certain extent of territory and divers privileges, which were engraven on tables of brass. These Israelites
brought two trumpets of which the Levites in the temple made use.
Cranganor having at length been taken from them, they took refuge
in Cochin.

"The Jews of Cochin," says our author, " loaded him with civilities, and gave him a number of entertainments. Though the
climate had rendered them so swarthy that they were almost mulat-
toes, they would have considered themselves dishonoured, if they
had eaten, drank, or prayed with the black or negro Jews of Malabar, because the last were descended from the slaves in the service
of the Jews at Cranganor, who were afterwards emancipated. The
negro Jews had nine synagogues, three in Cochin, and the others in
the vicinity. In the French translation of the travels of P. Paulin
de St. Barthelemy it is said they formed four hundred and sixty
families" This account is copied verbatim from the relation of
Paiva ; and the elements of which his calculation is composed give as
a total number four hundred and sixty-five. The other Jews ground
their aversion towards them on the pretence, that the Malabar Jews
have been mixed with the Canaanites and the Ishmaelites. But
though they have separate synagogues their worship is the same.
Thus we see a diversity of colour, but none of sect.—*Gregoire's
Histoire des Sectes Religieuses*, tom. ii.

had attained some, wealth, and attracted the notice of men, they are precipitated to the lowest abyss of human suffering and reproach. The recital of the sufferings of the Jews at Cranganor resembles much that of the Jews at Jerusalem, as given by Josephus."

The Black Jews retain the tradition that they arrived in India soon after the Babylonian captivity. "Their Hindoo complexion, and their very imperfect resemblance to the European Jews, indicate that they have been detached from the parent stock in Judea many ages before the Jews in the west, and that there have been intermarriages with families not Israelitish. The White Jews look upon the Black Jews as an inferior race, and not of a pure cast; which plainly demonstrates that they do not spring from a common stock in India."*

Dr. Buchanan observes, that "the Black Jews communicated to him much interesting intelligence concerning their brethren, the ancient Israelites in the east; traditional indeed in its nature, but in general illustrative of true history. They recounted the names of many other small colonies resident in Northern India, Tartary, and China, and gave him a written list of sixty-five places. He conversed with those who have lately visited many of these stations, and were about to return again. The Jews have a never ceasing communication with each other in the east. Their families indeed are generally stationary, being subject

---

* Buchanan's Researches in Asia; and Memoir of the Expediency of an Ecclesiastical Establishment in British India.

to despotic princes ; but the men move much about in a commercial capacity, and the same individual will pass through many extensive countries. So that when any thing interesting to the nation of the Jews takes place, the rumour will pass rapidly throughout all Asia."*

* Buchanan's Researches in Asia, p. 221, 222.

CHAPTER XXXIV.

Of the Jews in America.—Of their settlement in Surinam and Jamaica.—But few have settled in New England.—Of Judah Monis. —State of the Jews in New York, Philadelphia, Charleston, Virginia, and Georgia.

THE exact time in which the Jews first entered America, cannot be ascertained. But it appears, that there were some of the nation in the Spanish colonies, at the time when they were expelled the parent country by Ferdinand and Isabella.

The inhabitants of the colonies which belonged to France, in their severity to the Jews imitated the conduct of the parent country. The first article in the edict of March, 1605, enjoined the French officers to expel them from their American colonies; and commanded them to depart within three months, under the penalty of the confiscation of their goods.*

The history of the Jews in Surinam, who emigrated from Holland, has been compiled by a society of Portuguese Jews, who resided in that country. It appears from this work, that, in the year 1639, David Nasci, a Portuguese Jew and a native of Brazil, obtained permission from the West India company in Holland to form a colony in the island of Cayenne. His countrymen who accompanied him were to be allowed the full enjoyment of every civil and religious privilege, on condition that they should grant the same without reserve to all who might choose to be their fellow colonists. On the conquest of this island by the French in 1664,

* French Encyclopedia.

Nasci and his followers retired to Surinam, which then belonged to the English, who not only allowed them the free exercise of their religion, together with every civil privilege and all the immunities which the peculiar rites of their law rendered necessary, but also permitted them to erect a court of judicature in which all civil cases beneath a certain amount between individuals of their community should be determined by their agents. All these privileges were confirmed to them by the Dutch, who took possession of the settlement 1667.*

Thus secured in the enjoyment of their liberties, the Jews soon became a numerous and flourishing society. In 1689, they possessed forty plantations, and a large number of slaves. According to their account they have always been useful citizens, who were disposed to make every exertion for the welfare of the community, and have often sustained more than their share of the public burdens. They complain of having frequently suffered injustice and oppression in consequence of the arbitrary spirit of some of the governors, and the jealousy of some of their fellow colonists. However, notwithstanding these disadvantages, and the invidious partiality and contemptuous treatment which they often experienced, they increased in numbers and wealth. In 1760, no less than one hundred sugar plantations were possessed by the individuals of the community. The year 1799 appears to have been the most prosperous era of the colony.

In Paramaribo, the capital of the colony, the Dutch Calvinists, Lutherans, and Moravians, had

* Monthly Review, 1792.

their several churches and chapels ; and the Portuguese and German Jews their respective synagogues. The Roman Catholics were long exempted from the toleration so liberally extended to those of every other religious persuasion. But at length, in the year 1785, they were allowed to erect a place of public worship, towards the building of which all the inhabitants, both protestants and Jews, generously contributed. No where is the peace of society less disturbed by religious opinions than in Surinam. Persons of the most opposite persuasions, live in the most intimate connexion and unreserved friendship.

The great check to the prosperity of Surinam has arisen from the inhabitants being exposed to the invasion and depredation of the Maroons, or runaway negroes, who have formed several communities in the inaccessible parts of the woods, and are the most implacable and cruel enemies of the colonists. The Jewish militia have often signalized themselves against them, and have been of great use to the colony; one third of whom are of this nation. Under the patronage of the Germans, two societies have been instituted to improve education ; one for the cultivation of natural history ; the other for literature and moral philosophy. Jews as well as Christians may be members of these institutions.*

Malouet, the French commissioner, gives the following account of a town, or village of Jews on the river Surinam. "It is fifteen leagues," says he, "above Paramaribo, and to render our visit more interesting, the children of Israel were induced

* Monthly Review, 1792.

to pay us the honours of the New Jerusalem. For
this purpose they were at much expence, and their
attentions merit my gratitude. I became acquainted
with two Jews, whose erudition and powers are
astonishing. The one is named Joseph Barious,
and the other Isaac Nasci, The last is an extraordinary man, if we consider that he never has
been out of Surinam, where he was born; received
no aid but from his own genius; and has risen
above the errors of his sect. His knowledge of history is profound; and he has studied methodically
Arabic, Chaldean, and rabbinical Hebrew. Yet
this man, who passes eight hours every day in his
study, and has a correspondence with the most
celebrated men in Europe, employs himself as the
meanest of his countrymen, in buying and selling
old clothes. He has composed a Dictionary in the
Indian Calibi language, and thinks he finds the
themes in it to be Hebrew."*

The Jews were early settled in Jamaica, being
attracted by the gold and silver brought into circulation, and the mild disposition of the government
towards them. In the reign of William III. of
England, the council of the island addressed the
crown to expel them from the British dominions,
because they were descended from those who had
crucified our Saviour; but the king refused to
comply with their request. In these days they were
not taxed as other subjects, but obliged to raise
a certain annual tribute which the assembly varied
at pleasure. Though the government was compa-

---

* The compiler of this History was favoured with the above
account from the Rev. Mr. Bentley of Salem.

ratively mild, they suffered some oppression. At length, however, they began to make a considerable figure, and were permitted to erect synagogues and perform divine worship according to their own ritual. Their knowledge of several languages, and acquaintance with their brethren dispersed over the Spanish and other West India colonies,, contributed greatly to extend the trade and increase the wealth of the island. Though they are excluded from filling any post in the government, they are required to bear arms in the militia, and have shown themselves useful subjects on many occasions. They are not, as in many other parts, loaded with unequal and oppressive taxations, and have the privilege of purchasing landed property, and in the possession and enjoyment of it they are protected equally with other subjects.*

The tranquillity this people enjoy under the government is, however, disturbed by their own religious schisms. They are divided into two parties, one of which is called the Smouse Jews, which is an epithet of contempt. Their brethren regard them as heretics, because they have relaxed in the observance of some of their rituals, and formed alliances by marriage with Christians. They have, therefore, a distinct meeting at a private house, where they vociferate to the great disturbance of the neighbourhood.†

* Long's History of Jamaica, vol. ii. p. 293. They enjoy almost every privilege possessed by the Christian whites, excepting only the right of voting at elections, of being returned to serve in the assembly, and of holding any office of magistracy.—*Edward's History of the West Indies.*

† Long's History of Jamaica, vol. ii. p. 296. Gregoire's Histoire des Sectes Religieuses, tom. ii. p. 360.

The chief men among the Jews in Jamaica are worthy characters, who strive to gain an honest living and assist their indigent brethren. There are no common beggars of this nation, the elders having an established fund for the relief of the poor. There are among this people several very opulent planters and capital merchants; and it is said, that those in this island are not such rigid observers of the Mosaical ritual as in other countries. Being allowed the public exercise of their religion, they have erected two or more synagogues.*

The Jews have never been numerous in New England; but among those who settled in the colonies some have been distinguished for the respectability of their characters. Judah Monis, a Jewish convert to the Christian religion, was admitted a public teacher at Harvard University. He is stated to have been a native of Algiers, who probably received his education in Italy, though we know nothing of him till his arrival in this country. But after he came to Boston he seems to have been soon invited to fill the office of Hebrew instructor in the university, where he was settled March 27th, 1722. Before he could be admitted, it was rendered necessary by the statutes, that he should change his religion, which he professes to have done with perfect disinterestedness, though he continued till his death to observe the seventh day as the sabbath. From the address delivered upon the occasion by the Rev. Dr. Coleman of Boston, it may be suspected that doubts were entertained of the sincerity of his declaration. The expressions,

* Long's History.

" Is your heart right with God ?" " We cannot be content with good professions," &c. &c. shew no very strong confidence in his integrity. However, it is certain he always sustained an unblemished character, and was well contented with his condition. He married at Cambridge ; and when death deprived him at a very advanced age of the society of his wife, he resigned his office, and retired to Northborough, where he resided with her relations. He died,* in 1764, at the age of eighty-one years, forty of which he spent in his office.†

Monis bequeathed a small sum to be distributed among seven clergymen then living in the vicinity ; and left a fund, the interest of which was to be divided among ministers in indigent circumstances ; and the remainder of his estate, which was considerable, he gave to the relations of his wife. His printed works are, a discourse delivered at his baptism ; one entitled " the truth," another, " the whole truth," and a third, " nothing but the truth," and a Hebrew grammar.‡

Previous to the American revolution, while the Jews convened at their synagogue in Rhode Island, the late president Stiles commenced an acquaintance with Haijim Carigal, a rabbi who had lately arrived in the city. " Having travelled very extensively in the eastern world, and being a man of

---

* It is said, that at the time of his death he was attended by several clergymen, to whom he professed his firm belief in the Christian religion, and his assured hope of salvation by Christ. One of the divines observed to him, " Now, good father, you will go to Abraham's bosom." " No," he replied, " he was but a Jew, I will go to Christ, for he is my only hope."

† Monthly Anthology, 1810, p. 59.

‡ Whitney's History of Worcester, p. 272.

observation, learning and intelligence, his conversation was highly entertaining and instructive. He
was born at Hebron, and educated there and at
Jerusalem.   He had travelled all over the Holy,
Land, and visited many cities in Asia and Europe.
The doctor was greatly delighted with his society,
and had frequent intercourse with him for the
purpose of acquiring the pronunciation of the
Hebrew; of ascertaining the meaning of ambi-
guous expressions in the original of the Old Testament; of learning the usages of the modern Jews;
of conversing on past events relating to this extraordinary nation, as recorded in sacred history; and
of tracing its future destiny by the light of prophecy.   They cultivated a mutual friendship when
together, and corresponded in Hebrew when
apart."*

The rabbi, not long after his arrival, attended
his worship by agreement, and heard him discourse
in an affectionate manner on the past dispensations of
God's providence towards his chosen people; on his
promised design of rendering them an exalted
nation in the latter day glory of the Messiah's
kingdom; and on the duty of Christians, and of
all nations, to desire a participation in their future
glorious state.†

" So catholic was the intercourse between this
learned Jew and learned Christian, that they often
spent hours together in conversation; and the
information which the extensive travels of the Jew
enabled him to give, especially concerning the
Holy Land, was a rich entertainment to his Chris-

* Dr. Holmes's Life of President Stiles.   † Ibid

tian friend. ' The civilities of the rabbi were more than repaid. The doctor very frequently attended the worship of the synagogue at Newport, not only when rabbi Carigal officiated, but at the ordinary service before his arrival, and after his departure." ;
-. With six other rabbies of less eminence he became acquainted, and shewed them every civility, while he maintained a friendly communication with the Jews in general in Newport. Such rare and unexpected attentions from a Christian minister of distinction could not but afford peculiar gratification to a people, conscious of being a proverb and bye word among all nations. To him they accordingly paid every attention in return, and expressed peculiar pleasure in admitting him into their families, and into their synagogues.

Dr. Holmes in concluding this account judiciously remarks, that " this civility and catholicism towards the Jews is worthy of imitation. It is to be feared that Christians do not what ought to be done towards the conversion of this devoted people. While admitted into most countries for the purposes of trade and commerce, instead of being treated with that humanity and tenderness which Christianity should inspire, they are often persecuted and condemned as unworthy of notice or regard. Such treatment tends to prejudice them against our holy religion, and to establish them in their infidelity."*

A respectable rabbi† of New York has given the following account of his brethren in the United States

---

* Holmes's Life of President Stiles.
† Rev. Gershom Seixas, the presiding rabbi.

" There are about fifty families of Jews in New York, which, with a number of unmarried men, make from seventy to eighty subscribing members to the congregation *Sherith Israel,* which is incorporated by an act of the legislature of the state, empowering all religious societies to hold their property by charter, under the direction of trustees chosen annually by the communicants of the society, according to certain rules prescribed in the act.*

" The trustees have the management of all the temporalities, as is customary in other societies. They have one synagogue established conformably to the customs and forms of prayer used among the Portuguese Jews in Europe. Their public service is altogether in the Hebrew language, excepting in particular cases provided for in the constitution of the society. There were some Jewish families in the city when it was owned by the Dutch ; but the documents which are among the archives of the congregation, do not extend farther back than about one hundred and fifty years.

" Some of the Jews who settled in New York were of Portuguese, others of German extraction, besides Hollanders. There are also the descendants of those who arrived after New York became an English colony. The Jews had the right of soil under the Dutch government, and the English never attempted to deprive them of it ; on the contrary, they granted letters patent to several Jewish families in the time of queen Anne, who had arrived in London from France among the Huguenots, to settle in North America.

* See laws of New York.

" In Philadelphia there may be about thirty families of Jews. They have two synagogues, one for those who observe the Portuguese customs and forms of prayer, and the other for those who adhere to the German rules, customs, &c.; neither of them are incorporated. There may be about from eighty to one hundred men, in the whole state of Pennsylvania, who all occasionally attend the synagogues in Philadelphia.

" There is in Charleston (South Carolina) a large society incorporated, (with their laws.) They have an elegant synagogue established on the Portuguese customs, &c. They also have different institutions with appropriate funds for benevolent and charitable purposes likewise incorporated."

A more particular account of the Jews in South Carolina has been given by one of the principal members of their congregation in the capital of the state, the substance of which is as follows.

" The first emigration of the Jews to Charleston took place long before the revolution. The spirit of commerce can never be extinct in them; and their wealth increased with their numbers, which were augmented from time to time, both by marriages, and acquisitions from Europe. The present number of Jews may be estimated at about a thousand. Charleston alone contains about six or seven hundred individuals.

" The present number of Hebrews in the city are chiefly Carolinians, the descendants of German, English, and Portuguese emigrants.

" The religious rites, customs, and festivals of the Jews are all strictly observed by those of this

H H

nation in Charleston. The seats in the Jewish synagogue are often crowded with visitors of every denomination. The episcopal functions are now discharged by the Rev. Cavalho, late professor of the Hebrew language in the college of New York.

" The Jews in Charleston enjoy equal literary advantages with the other members of the community. Most of the parents being rich, the prejudice is here despised, which confines the important object of education to the tenets of religion; and the Hebrews can boast of several men of talents and learning among them. Those Jewish children who are intended for professions, receive a handsome classical education. There is now in the city an academy, where the French, Italian, Latin, and Greek languages are taught, together with other branches of learning. The Rev. Cavalho, mentioned above, also teaches the Hebrew and Spanish languages.

" The dress and habits of the Jews in Charleston do not distinguish them from the other citizens. Open and hospitable, as Carolinians generally are, they unite, with considerable industry and knowledge of commercial affairs, rather too much of that love of ease and pleasure, which climate, as well as national character, tends to nourish. Individuals, however, among those in this country, for their enterprize and judgment, have been entrusted with municipal offices; and one has held a seat with honour to himself and his constituents among the representatives of the state.

" The institutions which the Jews have established in Charleston, are chiefly religious and

charitable. They have built an elegant synagogue. They have also societies for the relief of strangers, for attending the sick, and for administering the rites of humanity and burial to the dying and the dead. The most modern institution is a society for the relief of orphans. The capital is already considerable, and it is yearly increasing. The children receive every advantage which is necessary to enable them to be well informed and honourable citizens of their country."*

In Richmond, (Virginia) there are about thirty Jewish families, who are now building a synagogue; but they are not as yet incorporated. The number of unmarried men is unknown, though there may be about an hundred scattered throughout the state, who are and will become members of the congregation. At Savannah in Georgia there are but few Jewish families, who assemble at times, and commune with each other in public prayers. The United States is, perhaps, the only place where the Jews have not suffered persecution, but have, on the contrary, been encouraged, and indulged in every right of citizens.†

The Jews in all the United States, except Massachusetts,‡ are eligible to offices of trust and honour; and some of them in the southern states are in office. They are generally commercial men, and a number of them considerable merchants.

* The above account is an abridgment of a letter written Jan. 1811, by Mr. Philip Cohen, a repectable Jewish merchant in Charleston.
† Extract of a letter from Rev. Gershom Seixas.
‡ According to the Constitution of Massachusetts, those who are chosen to fill important offices, must declare their belief of the Christian religion.

CHAPTER XXXV.

Of the rites and ceremonies of the Jews.—Of their synagogue worship.—Method of observing the sabbath.—Of their celebration of
the festivals of the new moon; the passover; days of Pentecost;
feast of trumpets; of tabernacles; and of Purim.—Of the feast at
the dedication of the temple.—Of the Jewish feasts on the great
day of expiation, on the destruction of the temple, and other
occasions.—Government and discipline of the Jewish church.

THE Jews, since the destruction of their temple,
have not offered any sacrifices ; and several religious
rites, which were enjoined upon their ancestors,
cannot be observed by the nation in modern times,
on account of their being local, and confined to the
promised land.   Such, for instance, as the offering
of the sheaf of the first fruits of barley harvest on the
morrow of the passover ; the two wave loaves made
of fine flour, which were the first of the wheat
harvest, and offered on the morning of the feast of
Pentecost ; the basket of all the first fruits of the
earth, with the offering of him who brings it ;* the
cities of refuge ;† the tythes to the priests and
Levites, and to the poor; the sabbatical year‡ for
the land to rest; and also the year of jubilee, when
there was to be a general release of lands, servants,
pledges, &c. the cleansing of the leper ; with
various other local ceremonies too numerous to be
mentioned.§

There are other directions respecting their political state and government, contained in their code

* Deuteronomy xxvi. 2.   † Numbers xxvi. 6—11.
‡ Leviticus xxv. 2, 3.
§ David Levi's Ceremonies of the Jews, p. 221.

of laws in the 21st and 23d chapters of Exodus, which concerned both their civil and criminal jurisprudence, that cannot be observed by the Jews since their dispersion. Not having any jurisdiction either civil or criminal, they are obliged to be governed by the laws and policy of the countries under which they live.*

The modern Jews, however, still adhere as closely to the Mosaic dispensation as their dispersed condition will permit them. Their religious worship consists chiefly in reading the law† and prophecies in their synagogues, together with a variety of prayers.‡ They repeat blessings and particular praises to God, not only in their prayers, but in all accidental occasions, and in almost all their actions. It is a rule among them that no day must be passed without reading a portion of the law at home, nor any affair undertaken till they have implored the divine blessing. They are strictly prohibited from all vain swearing, and pronouncing any of the names of God without necessity. They abstain from meats forbidden by the Levitical law; for which reason whatever they eat must be dressed by those of their own nation, in a manner peculiar to themselves.§

At the east end of every synagogue is an ark, or

* David Levi's Ceremonies of the Jews, p. 221.

† They divide the law into fifty-two parts, and read one of these sections every sabbath, so as to go through the whole every year.

‡ As formerly, while they enjoyed an established religion, they still have liturgies, in which are all the prescribed forms of their synagogue worship; "and those who have not time to go to the synagogue must say their prayers at home three times every day, i e. in the morning, in the afternoon, and at night."—*Levi's Ceremonies of the Jews*, p. 178.

§ Picart's Religions Ceremoni s

press, in commemoration of the ark of the covenant,
which was in the temple. Here the Pentateuch is
deposited, written on a volume or roll of parchment
with the utmost exactness, and wrapped up in silk
curiously embroidered. When the Jews say their
prayers in the morning they put on a talith or vail
over their other clothes, and a robe with fringes at
the four corners, with tassels, called Tzitzith ; and
also the Tephilin or Phylacteries.*

All the rites, precepts, and ceremonies of the
Jews, which are not contained in the Pentateuch,
are founded upon and derive their authority from
the Talmud. There is, however, some variation
in their customs and ceremonies, and in the liturgies
which the nation have made use of at different
times, and in various countries. The German,
Polish, and Russian Jews follow the same ritual.
But the Spanish and Portuguese have another,
which still varies from that of the Italian and Levan-
tine Jews, those of Jerusalem, China, and some
other places. But in the principal points of belief
and observance they all agree.†

* " It is an article of faith among us," says David Levi, " that
every Jew must every morning, during the time of reading the Shema,
and saying the nineteen prayers at least, have on the Phylacteries,
because it is a sign of our acknowledging the Almighty to be the
Creator of all things, and that he has power to do as he pleases ; and
therefore on the sabbath, and other festivals, we do not put on the
Phylacteries, because the duly observing of them is a sufficient sign
of itself, as expressed in Exodus xxxi. 12."—*Ceremonies of the Jews*,
p. 190.

† Ockley's translation of Leo Modena's Ceremonies of the Jews,
p 4 There are three divisions or classes of modern Jews, who are
variously denominated from the countries where the arrangements of
their liturgies took place, and are known by the designations of
German, Portuguese, and Avignon, or Italian Jews.

In the synagogue worship, the Cohen or priest leads the devotional exercises by chanting prayers; but laymen are admitted to read the book of the law to the people; the precedence is, however, given to the priest. After prayers, the rabbies frequently deliver a sermon; but their discourses are not composed in Hebrew, which few of the Jews at present perfectly understand, but in the language of the country where they reside. The passages of scripture and sentences from the doctors are, however, quoted in the Hebrew, and explained.*

The Jews venerate the sabbath above all other festivals, and observe it with the utmost strictness on account of its being enjoined in various parts of scripture, particularly in the decalogue. On this day they are forbidden to kindle or extinguish any fire; the food is, therefore, prepared on Friday. They are also prohibited from discoursing on any kind of business,† from carrying any burden, from riding on horseback, in a carriage, going by water, or walking above a mile from the city or place where they reside, or playing upon any musical instrument.‡ They are likewise forbidden to inter their dead, or mourn, or fast on the sabbath; but are sometimes permitted to circumcise a child, be-

---

* Levi's Ceremonies of the Jews.

† David Levi's Ceremonies of the Jews, p. 7, 8—17. The rabbies have reduced the several works forbidden on the sabbath under thirty-nine heads, and enumerated the species under these generals.

‡ Vocal music is very common in their synagogues, but instrumental music is seldom used; yet not because it is deemed improper, for the synagogue in Prague had an organ; but because it cannot be performed on the sabbath or holidays.—*Adam's Religious World Displayed.*

cause that ceremony must oe performed exactly on the eighth day.

The sabbath begins on Friday, an hour before sun-set both summer and winter, for they suppose the day commences from the preceding evening, according to Genesis i. 5. and " the evening and the morning were the first day." As soon as the time arrives they leave all manner of work, and, having cleansed and decorated themselves in honour of the holy day, repair to the evening service. The women are bound- to light a lamp with seven cotton wicks, in remembrance of the days of the week, saying, " Blessed art thou, O Lord, our God ! king of the universe, who has sanctified us with his commandments, and commanded us to light the lamp of the sabbath." The reason why this ceremony is invariably assigned to the women is, that as their original mother, by her crime in eating the forbidden fruit, first extinguished the lamp of righteousness, they are to make an atonement for that sin by rekindling it, in lighting the lamp of the sabbath.*

They then spread a clean cloth upon their table, and set two loaves of bread upon it, baked on Friday, and covered with a napkin, in memory of the manna which fell with dew under and above it, yet descended not (for on the Friday they had a double portion) on the sabbath. When they are placed at table, the master of the family takes a cup of wine repeating the three first verses in the 2nd chapter of Genesis, and after giving God thanks, and enjoining them to observe the sabbath,

* Levi's Ceremonies, &c.

he blesses the wine, drinks, and gives some to the rest of the family. He then blesses and distributes the bread. They repeat the usual grace after supper, with the addition of making mention of the sabbath.*

In the morning they repair to the synagogue later than usual on the week days, where, after the accustomed prayers, besides others which are appropriate to the day, they read a lesson from the law, and afterwards a corresponding portion from the prophets.† When the reading is concluded they pray for the peace and prosperity of the government under which they live, in observance of the direction in Jeremiah xxix. 7. Then the law is put into the ark. They then pray that God would be pleased to deliver them from captivity, and bring them to the holy land, where they should be able to perform the offerings of the sabbath according to the law. After some other prayers the morning service is concluded.

The religious rites observed at dinner are similar to those used at supper. They frequently have sermons either in the morning or afternoon, the subject of which is taken from the lesson read that day in the Pentateuch. They make three meals on the sabbath, one on Friday evening and two the

---

* David Levi's Ceremonies, &c.

† The custom of reading portions from the prophets on the sabbath has obtained since the time of Antiochus Epiphanes. He having prohibited the Jews from reading the law, they substituted passages from the prophets. When the law was restored by the Maccabees, they retained this custom in remembrance of their severe affliction and great deliverance, and it is observed at this day.—*Note to David Levi's Translation of the Pentateuch,* vol. i.

next day in honour of the festival. On this holy
day they beseech God to be merciful, and grant
them an inheritance in that day, which is all sabbath,
and eternal rest.* In the evening, as soon as the
stars appear, they suppose the sabbath is ended,
and that it is lawful to do any work after they have
attended the evening prayers at the synagogue.

The Jewish year is either civil, or ecclesiastical.
The civil year commences in the month Tishri, or
September. The Jews have a tradition that the
world was created on the first day of this month,
and from this epoch they compute the age of the
world, and make use of this date in all their civil
acts, The ecclesiastical year commences about the
vernal equinox, in the month Nisan, which answers
to part of March and April. All the religious rites
and ceremonies are regulated by the ecclesiastical
year.† On the first of every month they celebrate
the feast of the new moon, praying God to restore
them to the holy city, and erect the temple at Jerusalem, where they could render the offering for the
feast according to the law, Numbers xxviii. 11.‡

On the fourteenth day of the month Nisan, the
celebration of the passover commences, and imme-

* Meaning the kingdom of the Messiah ; for they suppose that the
world is to continue six thousand years, (according to the six days of
the creation) and the seventh to be that of the Messiah. It is that
which is here alluded to, as being the day which is all an entire sabbath —*David Levi's Ceremonies of the Jews*, p. 206.

† The Jews call the seventh month of the civil, the first of the
ecclesiastical year, because at the departure of the children of Israel
from Egypt, it is enjoined, that " this month shall be unto them the
beginning of months, and the first month in the year."—Exodus
xii. 2.

‡ David Levi's Ceremonies of the Jews.

diately after the feast of unleavened bread; the whole includes eight days. On the evening preceding the festival, the first born of every family observes a fast, in remembrance of God's mercy in protecting the nation. During the whole of this feast the Jews are obliged to eat only unleavened bread,* and refrain from servile labour. The two first and two last days are kept as strictly as the sabbath, only they permit fires to be kindled, and prepare food. As they cannot now offer the paschal sacrifice, the passover cakes are placed on the table with some bitter herbs, and they eat a piece of unleavened bread instead of the paschal lamb. The festival concludes with psalms and thanksgivings to God for their great deliverance, and petitions, that he would put a period to their captivity and bring them to Jerusalem.

The feast of Pentecost commences seven weeks after the passover, hence it is called the feast of weeks. It is also styled in scripture, the day of the first fruits, because on that day they offered the first of their fruits in the temple. At present this festival is observed two days, during which time all servile labour is prohibited. As it was instituted to recall the remembrance of the law's being given at Sinai, that part of scripture, which declares the delivery of the decalogue, is solemnly read in the synagogue, and all those passages from the prophets which correspond with the subject. They generally have a sermon delivered in praise of the law. Their prayers are suitable to the occasion, con-

---

* They begin the passover with carefully searching the house, and removing every thing which has had leaven in it.

cluding with petitions for their deliverance from
captivity, and for the welfare of the government
under which they dwell.*

The feast of trumpets is observed on the first and
second of Tishri, or September, the seventh of the
ecclesiastical and first of the civil year; hence the
first of this month is called new year's day. On
this festival, besides a portion from the law and
prophets, part of the two first chapters of the first
of Samuel are read. They then pray for the protection of the government under which they reside,
and blow the trumpet, which is made of a ram's
horn,† saying, "Blessed be thou, O Lord, our God!
king of the universe, who has sanctified us with his
commandments, and commanded us to hear the
sound of the trumpet." After this ceremony, they
repeat with a loud voice the following verse,
"Happy are the people who hear the joyful sound,
they shall walk, O Lord, in the light of thy countenance."

On the morning of the second day they repair to
the synagogue, and repeat nearly the same prayers
as on the preceding day. They then read the 22nd
chapter of Genesis, which gives an account of
Abraham's offering his son Isaac, and God's blessing
him and his seed for ever. For, according to their
received tradition, that great event took place on
that day. They, therefore, beseech the Almighty
through the merits of this memorable event to bless

---

* David Levi's Ceremonies, &c. p. 78.

† The trumpet is made of a ram's horn in remembrance of Abraham's seeing a ram caught by the horns in a thicket, which he took
and offered for a burnt offering to the Lord, instead of his son.—
Genesis xxii 12—13.

them. After reading the law and prophets, they blow the trumpet, and pray as usual, that God would gather them from their dispersion, and conduct them to Jerusalem.[*]

The Feast of Tabernacles is observed on the fifteenth of the month Tishri, and lasts nine days. Each person at the commencement of the festival, erects an arbour,[†] which is covered with green boughs, and decked with a variety of ornaments in remembrance of their miraculous preservation in the wilderness. The two first and two last days are kept with great solemnity; but the intermediate time is not observed with equal strictness. On the first day they take branches of palm, myrtle, willow, and citron bound together, and go round the altar, or pulpit,[‡] singing psalms, because formerly they used to perform this ceremony in the temple.

The Jews chiefly reside in their respective tabernacles during the feast, both night and day, if the weather will permit. At every meal, during seven days, they are obliged to repeat the following grace: " Blessed art thou, O Lord, our God, king of the universe, who hast sanctified us with his commandments, and commanded us to dwell in tabernacles." During the feast they beseech the Lord to be merciful, and erect for them the tabernacle of David which is fallen; and portions of the law and prophets are read in their synagogues.[§]

On the seventh day of the festival, they take

[*] David Levi's Ceremonies of the Jews, p. 100.

[†] Levit. xxiii. 39.

[‡] In the midst or at the upper end of the synagogues, there is a kind of altar or pulpit.

[§] David Levi's Ceremonies of the Jews, p. 125.

seven of the laws from out of the ark and carry them to the altar, and those who are possessed of the palm branch, &c. with the reader at their head, go seven times round the altar, in remembrance of the sabbatical years, singing the 29th Psalm. On the evening of this day the feast of solemn assembly commences, which being a time of rejoicing, they assemble and entertain their friends; but are strictly enjoined not to do any servile labour. They read passages from the law and prophets, and entreat the Lord to be propitious to them, and deliver them from captivity. On the ninth day they repeat several prayers in honour of the law, and bless God for his mercy and goodness in giving it to them by his servant Moses, and read that part of scripture which makes mention of his death. After going to the synagogue in the evening, and saying the usual prayers, the festival is concluded.[*]

On the fourteenth of, Adar, or March, the Jews celebrate the feast of Purim, in commemoration of their deliverance from the destruction designed by Haman. This festival is observed two days, and derives its name from Esther ix. " Therefore they called these days Purim." Previous to the feast, a solemn fast is observed in remembrance of Esther's fasting. The whole book of Esther written on parchment is repeatedly read during the feast, and as often as the name of Haman[†] is mentioned it is

[*] David Levi's Ceremonies of the Jews, p 125.

[†] In some places the reading is concluded with curses upon Haman and his wife, and blessings upon Esther and Mordecai. They had a custom in some countries of erecting a gibbet, and hanging up a man in effigy to represent Haman's punishment. But this custom has been for a considerable time disused, because it was insinuated, in

customary for the children (who have little wooden hammers) to knock against the wall, as a memorial that they should endeavour to destroy the race of Amalek. Part of the first day is spent in feasting and rejoicing, sending presents to each other, giving liberally to the poor, in visiting their friends, and entertaining them by all kinds of diversions.

, The Jews, at the present day, observe many festivals which were not appointed by Moses. In particular they celebrate the dedication of the altar, which was instituted by the Maccabees, in remembrance of the victory they obtained over Antiochus Epiphanes. This tyrant, having profaned the temple, reduced them to the necessity of cleansing and dedicating it anew. The festival is observed in a splendid manner, and lasts eight days ; and is appointed to be kept by lighting lamps. The reason they assign for this ceremony is, that, after they had purified and dedicated the temple, there was only enough of pure oil left to burn one night, which miraculously lasted eight nights, till they were able to obtain a fresh supply.

The great day of expiation is observed by the Jews, though they have no high priest to officiate, nor temple wherein to offer the sacrifice. Before the fast commences, they think it a duty incumbent upon them to ask pardon of those they have offended ; to make restitution to those whom they have defrauded of any property ; to forgive those who have offended them ; and, in short, to do every

the dark ages, that they did it in contempt of Christ.—*Basnage,* p. 453.

thing which may serve to' evince the sincerity of their repentance.* This great fast is observed on the tenth day of the month Tishri, or September. In the preceding evening† they repair to the synagogue, where they remain saying prayers upwards of three hours; and when they return from the synagogue they may not taste any kind of sustenance; and are even prohibited from taking one drop of water. 'They are also forbidden to do any kind of labour, even to kindle a fire, and observe this day as strictly as the sabbath.

At six in the morning they attend the synagogue, and offer those prayers and supplications for the pardon of their sins, which are peculiar to the occasion. In the course of the service, various portions of scripture are read, particularly part of Leviticus xxvi. Numbers xxix. and Isaiah lvii. They mention in their prayers the additional sacrifice of the day, and entreat God to rebuild their sanctuary, to gather their dispersions among the Gentiles, and conduct them to Jerusalem, where they may offer the sacrifice of atonement, agreeably to the Mosaic law. In the afternoon service, besides portions from the law and prophets, the greatest part of the book of Jonah is read in the synagogues. They beseech God to be propitious, and forgive their sins.

---

* Maimonides affirms that the goat Azael expiated both great and small sins which were repented of, and that repentance, supplying the place of sacrifice, has at present the same effect, provided it is accompanied with renunciation of sin.—*Basnage,* p. 450.

† All the commanded ordinary fasts of the Jews begin in the evening, and they neither eat nor drink till they can see the stars the following evening

The fast continues from morning to night,* for up-wards of twelve hours, without intermission.

In Awb, which answers to July or August, in the fifth month of the ecclesiastical year, the Jews observe a strict fast, occasioned by the destruction of the first temple by Nebuchadnezzar. On this day also the second temple was burnt by the Romans. During this fast they not only abstain from all food, but do not even taste a drop of water. In the evening they go to the synagogue, and, after their usual prayers, the book of Jeremiah is read in a low mournful voice. In the morning they attend the synagogue early, and read a portion of the law, and part of the 8th and 9th chapters of Jeremiah. They go to the synagogue again in the afternoon, and read passages from the law and the prophets suitable to the occasion. All their prayers on this day tend to remind them of their captivity; and the destruction of their temple, which deprived them of offering the daily sacrifice by which an atonement was made for their sins.†

Besides the public fasts, which the Jews are com-manded to observe, there are some others peculiar to the nation in different countries. The German Jews for instance, both after the passover, and the feast of tabernacles, keep three fasts, viz. on Monday, Tuesday, and the following Monday. The reason assigned for this practice is, that they might, during the preceding feasts,‡ have committed

---

* Some remain in the synagogue all night, to say prayers and penitential psalms.

† David Levi's Ceremonies of the Jews.

‡ This custom appears to be founded upon the practice of Job, who offered sacrifices for his children after they had feasted, for fear they should have sinned against God.—*Job* i. 4, 5.

some offence against God. They fast also on the vigil of the new year, and some on that of every new month. Several other fasts and festivals have been instituted, but not generally received, and are not observed at present.*

The Jewish church is, at present, governed by a presiding rabbi in the city or town where they may be settled, who attaches to himself two other rabbies, and these three combined form a kind of tribunal in sacred or religious cases, and frequently determine private disputes. This tribunal is termed Beth Din, or the house of justice. As the priesthood is at present totally abrogated, having ceased with the temple, the term high priest is an exploded one, no presiding rabbi now exercising the functions of this pontiff, which were only applicable to the temple. Hence the choice of rabbi is not confined to the tribe of Levi; although that tribe be the only one that they conceive can now be at all distinguished. Its members are all at present considered as laymen. They have notwithstanding some trifling distinctions paid them in the synagogue service; for those among them that are descended from the priests, who are called Cohen, or in the plural Cohenim, perform the benediction, and are called first to the law. They also personate the priest in the ceremony of redeeming the first born, and have some other complimentary precedencies paid them. The Levites, i. e. those who are descendants from the singers in the temple, are second in rank, and are called next to the law, and wash the hands of the Cohenim before they go to the benediction, &c. With all this the rabbi has

* Leo Modena's Customs, &c. of the Jews, p. 137.

nothing to do, unless he be of this tribe. The ministry of a presiding rabbi, elected for that purpose from the general mass of learned rabbies in the congregation, whose head he is, consists of nothing more than that, as a spiritual director, he solves questions which arise in the ceremonial observances; occasionally preaches, marries, super-intends divorces, and the ceremony of throwing the shoe, called Chalitza,* &c. He is generally allowed a competent salary, which, together with per-quisites, renders it unnecessary for him to engage in any secular business, nor is it thought honour-able; although it is said, that, in a few instances, some presiding rabbies in Germany and Italy, have been engaged in trade, through the medium of some intervening friend.†

Other rabbies may follow any worldly occupation, as the title of rabbi is merely honorary, and does not confer any priestly ordination, or sacred cha-racter.‡

* Marriage, in all regular societies, is always performed by the presiding rabbi, or by some one deputed by him: but a marriage so-lemnized with the due ceremonies by any other orthodox Jew is valid. The ceremony of throwing the shoe takes place when a Jew refuses to marry his brother's widow, and is grounded on Deuter-onomy xxv. 9.

† Adam's Religious World Displayed, (published 1809,) vol. i. p. 48, 49.

‡ Ibid.

CHAPTER XXXVI.

Of the religious tenets of the Jews.—Articles of faith which were drawn up by Maimonides in the eleventh century.—Explanation of their belief respecting several articles.—Prevalence of infidelity among them.—Of the ancient sects which remain at present among the Jews.

THE religious tenets maintained by the modern Jews coincide with the confession of faith which the celebrated Maimonides drew up at the close of the eleventh century, which is as follows :

1st. " I believe, with a true and perfect faith, that God is the Creator, (whose name be blessed) governor and maker of all creatures, and that he has wrought all things, worketh, and shall work for ever.

2nd. " I believe, with perfect faith, that the Creator, (whose name be blessed) is *one ;* and that such a unity as is in him can be found in none other, and that he alone has been our God, is, and for ever shall be.

3d. " I believe, with perfect faith, that the Creator, (whose name be blessed) is not corporeal, nor to be comprehended with any bodily properties ; and that there is no bodily essence which can be likened unto him.

4th. " I believe, with perfect faith, the Creator, (whose name be blessed) to be the first and last, and that nothing was before him, and he shall abide the last for ever.

5th. " I believe, with a perfect faith, that the Cre-

ator, (whose name be blessed) is to be worshipped, and none else.

6th. " I believe, with perfect faith, that all the words of the prophets are true.

7th. " I believe, with perfect faith, that the prophecies of Moses our master, (may he rest in peace) are true ; that he was the father and chief of all wise men who lived before him, or ever shall live after him.

8th. " I believe, with perfect faith, that all the law, which at this day is found in our hands, was delivered by God himself to our master Moses, (God's peace be with him.)

9th. " I believe, with a perfect faith, that the same law is never to be changed, nor any other to be given us of God, (whose name be blessed for ever.)

10th. " I believe, with a perfect faith, that God, (whose name be blessed) understandeth all the thoughts and words of men, as it is written in the prophets, " He fashioneth their hearts alike, he understandeth all their works."

11th. I believe, with a perfect faith, that God will recompence good to those who keep his commandments, and will punish those who transgress them.

12th. " I believe, with a perfect faith, that the Messiah is yet to come ; and though he retard his coming, yet will I wait for him till he appears.

13th. " I believe, with a perfect faith, that the dead shall be restored to life when it shall seem fit to God the Creator, (whose name be blessed, and memory celebrated, world without end.　Amen.)"*

* Butler's Horæ Biblicæ, p. 95.

The Jews consider the unity of God as one of
the most essential of the above articles. "The
Christians and Jews," says Basnage, "separate at
the second step in religion, for after they have
united in the adoration of one God, absolutely
perfect, they find immediately after the abyss of the
trinity,* which entirely separates them." The
Jewish nation, ever since their dispersion, have
been vehemently opposed to the Christian doctrine
of the trinity, which, they suppose, destroys the
unity of the Supreme Being.

The twelfth article of the creed of Maimonides,
or the expectation of the promised Messiah, is the
leading tenet and distinguishing feature in the religion of the modern Jews. Infatuated, however, with
the idea of a temporal Messiah and Deliverer, who
is to subdue the world, and reinstate them in their
own land, the Jews still wait for his appearance.
But they have fixed neither the place whence, nor
the time when he is to come, for though many have
endeavoured to calculate upon the seventy weeks of
Daniel, they discourage all attempts this way,† and
deem them improper, since a miscalculation may

* Some learned Christian writers, however, find the doctrine of the
trinity in the Jewish Cabbala, and suppose, that the three principal
Sephiræ are meant for the three persons in one essence, and the other
seven, the seven spirits, or seven orders of angels that stand before
God. But Basnage, who assiduously applied himself to studying the
history and opinions of the Jews, supposes, that all the ten Sephiræ
are alike to be considered as the attributes of God, and explodes the
idea of finding the doctrine of the trinity in the Cabbala.—*Maurice's
Indian Antiquities*, vol. iv. p. 454. *Horæ Solitariæ*, vol. i. p. 358,
and *Basnage's History of the Jews*, p. 200.

† The rabbies have denounced the most dreadful anathemas against
all who shall attempt to calculate the time of the Messiah's appearance.

tend to shake the faith of the ignorant; and Maimonides had an eye to this in the composition of this same article, "and although he retard his coming," &c.

Finding it difficult to evade the force of those texts in Isaiah, &c. which speak of a suffering Messiah, some have had recourse to the idea of two Messiahs, who are to succeed each other, one Ben Joseph of the tribe of Ephraim, in a state of humiliation and suffering; the other, Ben David, of the tribe of Judah, in a state of glory, magnificence, and power. This, however, is said not to be a settled belief, but an opinion exhibited in a book of Medrash, or commentary. And yet something very like it seems to have been the tenet of the rabbies; for Abarbanel observes, that "although when they first go up from the captivity, they will "appoint themselves one head," (Hosea i. 11.) who he says is the person called by the Rabbins,* Messiah Ben Joseph, as he will be slain in battle; Israel will then seek David their king, a rod from the stem of Jesse, whom God will make choice of for to reign over them."†

As to the character and mission of their Messiah, "he is to be of the tribe of Judah, the lineal de-

---

* Rabbies is the modern title, but when we are speaking of the ancient Mishnical and Talmudical doctors, the term rabbins is then more properly used.—*Adam's Religious World Displayed.*

† (Abarbanel on Hosea iii. 5.) Mr. Levi says, that "this opinion of the rabbins, concerning the death of this personage, was what gave rise to the Christian system of a suffering Messiah, as the prophecies of the Old Testament do not inculcate any such principle whatever." —*Dissertation on the Prophecies,* p. 100, *quoted in Adam's Religious World Displayed.*

scendant of David, and called by his name. He is
to be endowed with the spirit of prophecy, and his
special mission is to restore the dispersed sheep of
Israel, plant them safely in their own land, and
subdue their enemies, and thereby bring the whole
world to the knowledge of the one true God."

His coming and their restoration have not yet
taken place, " because they are still unworthy of
being redeemed, and have not repented, or have
not yet received the full measure of their punishment." At the same time they insist that their redemption is not conditional, but will take place at
the appointed time, though they should not repent ;
that God will not restore and redeem them for any
merit of theirs, (for there will doubtless, even then,
be many wicked and unbelieving among them) but
for his name sake, " for the sake of the few righteous, and also in consideration of what they will be
after their redemption, when they will all be good
and righteous.* Those therefore, who are righteous
in captivity, will happily attain to the redemption.
But those that are wicked will be destroyed in the
wars and troubles which will take place before their
final restoration."†

They believe, that " Judea will finally be the
seat of those wars which will precede their redemp-

---

* "They will," says a celebrated Jewish writer, " no more follow
their irregular desires, and their cupidity, for the great and stupendous miracles, that will then be performed in their sight, will make
such a lasting impression on them, as entirely to destroy their evil
imagination, and incline them to all good; so that they will then be
in the same state that Adam was in before his fall." Thus David Levi
interprets Ezekiel xxxvi. 26

† Adam's Religious World Displayed.

tion, and that after due vengeance is taken on the nations for the cruelties exercised on the people of God, during this long and deplorable captivity, they will terminate in the complete subjection of all nations to the power of the Messiah, and in the introduction of universal peace and happiness that shall never more be interrupted.*

" Although they profess to know nothing certain, as to the real place of abode, or the present state of the ten tribes, yet they believe, that they are lost only in name, and that they shall be restored together with Judah and Benjamin, and likewise that all those Jews that have embraced Christianity or Mahommedism, shall then return to the religion of their fathers ; that their nation thus restored and united shall never again go into captivity, nor ever be subjected to any power ; but on the contrary they suppose, that all the nations of the world shall thenceforward be under their dominion. Judea will then become fruitful as formerly, Jerusalem will be built on its ancient ground plot, and the real descendants† of the priests and Levites will be reinstated into their respective offices, although they may have been forced to apostatize. Then likewise will be restored the spirit of prophecy, the ark and

---

* Adam's Religious World Displayed, vol. i. p. 22.

† Should it be asked, how it shall be known that they are thus descended ? Mr. Levi answers, " By means of the spirit of prophecy, which will then be restored to the nation ; for then the tribe of Levi will be distinguished in a particular manner, as the prophet Malachi said, chapter iii. 3."—*Dissertations on the Prophecies*, vol. ii. p. 87.

It is generally admitted, that the distinction of tribes is lost, yet some Jews seem to be of opinion, that the tribe of Levi can be now in some measure distinguished, however incorrect such distinction may prove to be intrinsically.—*Adam's Religious World Displayed.*

cherubim, fire from heaven, &c. the same as their fathers enjoyed in the tabernacle in the wilderness, and in Solomon's temple. And, in fine, then will idolatry "wholly cease in the earth, and all men acknowledge the unity of God and his kingdom, agreeable to what Zechariah said, chap. xiv. 9."* Such are the expectations of the Jews in regard to the Messiah and his kingdom, which they still avow to be not of a spiritual, but of a temporal nature."

The Jews believe that two great ends are to be effected by the resurrection, the one particular, and the other general. Accordingly David Levi observes, "that which is particular is for his brethren; and the other which is general, is for them and all the other nations."†

Several other doctrines are maintained by the Jews, which are not contained in the thirteen ar-

---

* Levi's Dissertation on the Prophecies, vol. iii. p. 228, quoted in Adam's Religious World Displayed, vol. i. p. 24. According to this author, " All those that shall be restored shall serve God together in unity; for then there shall be no separation of the tribes, no division of the kingdom, and no calves in Dan and Bethel; and on account of the great and stupendous miracles which will then be wrought by God for the deliverance of the nation, all nations will sanctify him as a great and holy God."—*Levi's Dissertations, &c.*

† " The first great end," says David Levi, " which I call a particular one, as it is for the Jewish nation only, is to effect, that those who have been persecuted and slain, during this long and dreadful captivity, for adhering to the true faith, may enjoy the salvation of the Lord, according to what the prophet says, (Isaiah xxvi. 19, and lxvi. 10.) The second great end, which I call a general one, because it affects all mankind, whether Jews, Gentiles, or Christians, is to bring all nations to the knowledge of the true God, and to effect that the firm belief of his unity may be so unalterably fixed in their hearts, as that they may attain the end for which they were created, to honour and glorify God, as the prophet observes, Isaiah xliii. 7." *Levi's Dissertations, &c.*

ticles. The rabbies acknowledged, that there is in man a fund of corruption ; and the Talmud speaks of original sin thus : " We ought not to be surprized that the sin of Adam and Eve was so deeply engraven, and that it was sealed as it were with the king's signet, that it might be thereby transmitted to all their posterity ; it was because all things were finished the day that Adam was created, and he was the perfection and consummation of the world, so that when he sinned, all the world sinned with him. We partake of his sin, and share in the punishment of it, but not in the sins of his descendants."*

The rabbies teach, that the evils in which men were involved by sin will be removed by the Messiah. They do not, however, entertain the idea that this illustrious personage will make an atonement for sin ; this they suppose is done by the fulfilling of the law, and circumcision.†

The Jews maintain, that the souls of the righteous enjoy the beatific vision of God in paradise,‡ and that the souls of the wicked are tormented in hell with fire and other punishments. They suppose, that the sufferings of the most atrocious criminals are of eternal duration, while others

---

* Fleury's Ancient Israelites, p. 341.

† Basnage, p. 371. They pray God to remember unto them the merits of their ancestors, Abraham, Isaac, Jacob, and Moses.—Levi's Ceremonies, &c. p. 78—115.

‡ One party of Jews, with Maimonides at their head, suppose that the souls of the righteous after death are to inhabit the garden of Eden till the appearance of the Messiah, at which epoch their souls are to be united to their bodies, and enjoy the delights prepared for them by the Messiah during a thousand years. This opinion is supported by Menasses Ben Israel and Abarbanel.—Basnage, p. 391.

remain only for a limited time in purgatory, which does not differ from hell with respect to the place, but to the duration. They pray for the souls of the dead, and imagine that many are delivered from purgatory on the great day of expiation.

They suppose that no Jew, unless. guilty of heresy or certain crimes specified by the rabbies, shall continue in purgatory above a year ; and that there are but few who suffer eternal punishment. Maimonides, Abarbanel, and other celebrated Jewish writers maintain the annihilation of the wicked. Others suppose, that the sufferings of hell have the power of purifying souls and expiating sin.*

Some eminent Jewish writers assert, that it is a mistake to suppose that their nation are intolerant. "They hold indeed, that all men are obliged to observe what are called the Noachides, or seven precepts of the sons of Noah ; but it is the unanimous opinion of their rabbies, that the Sinaite covenant, or law of Moses, is obligatory on those of their nation only." They say, " It was a covenant between God and the Jews, that they therefore are bound to the observance of it ; but that it is not binding to the rest of mankind ; for if they do but keep the law of nature, that is, the precepts of the Noachides, they maintain that they thereby perform all that God requires of them, and will certainly by this service render themselves acceptable to him, and be partakers of eternal life."†

---

* Basnage, p 390. Picart's Religious Ceremonies of the Jews.

† Levi's Letters to Dr. Priestley, p. 16, 17, and Maimonides on Repentance, chap. iii. quoted in Adam's Religious World Displayed.

Mr. Schott, director of the institute at Seezen, pronounced a discourse at the dedication of the temple in that place, July 17th, 1810,

It appears from authentic accounts, that many Jews at the present day have imbibed the principles of infidelity,* and no longer receive the writings of the Old Testament as divinely inspired, or expect the coming of the Messiah. A modern author, who has deeply investigated their history, and is well versed in their opinions, observes, that " many of the Israelites are disgusted with the follies of the Talmud; but not distinguishing between the absurd tales which good sense reproves, and the truths which enlightened reason reveres, they have involved the absurdities of the rabbins and the revelation from heaven in one common proscription."†

" The spirit of infidelity is exhibited among the Jews of Leghorn, of Holland, and Germany, and especially of Berlin,‡ where the greatest part do not attend the synagogues."

in which he declares, " Our religion is not the only one which conducts to eternal happiness ; those who profess another are neither heretics, nor reprobates. We are far from entertaining this horrid idea."—*Dedicace du Temple de Jacob*

* The learned author, whose authority is so frequently referred to in this work, observes, that " indifference to religion has passed as a contagion from the Christians to the Jews," and gives a recent instance, " in the 21st of Brumaire, an 11, when the assassins attempted to despoil the temples, those Israelites in the street of the Boucheries of Paris offered the spoils of their temple to the convention, ruled by the faction called *la Montagne*, saying to them, the Israelites always receive good from the wise laws emanating from the mountain. Others have imitated the scandal of pretended Christians, and thrown their sacred books on a pile, as a light for impiety.—*Gregoire's Histoire des Sectes Religieuses*, tom. ii. p. 398.

† Gregoire's Histoire, &c.

‡ In 1798, a large number of Jews in this city, heads of families of respectable character, subscribed and published a letter to Dr. Teller, provost of the upper consistory, (the department which has the superintendence of ecclesiastical affairs) in which they declare, that being

This statement is confirmed by a distinguished Jewish writer ; David Levi complains, that there are two different parties in the nation who slight the prophecies which speak of their future restoration, and ridicule the idea of a Messiah coming to redeem them. The one consists of such as call themselves philosophers, enlightened men, who, says he, " are perfect deists,* not believing a syllable of revelation,

convin'ed the laws of Moses are no longer binding upon them, as not being adapted to their circumstances at this day, they are willing and ready to become Christians as far as relates to the moral doctrines of Christianity, provided they shall not be required to believe the miraculous part of the Christian creed, and above all, the divinity of Jesus Christ; and provided they may be admitted to enjoy all the rights and privileges enjoyed by the members of the established religion.

They ask Dr. Teller's advice on this plan, and whether he thinks it practicable ? This gentleman has published an answer, in which he informs them, that they do well to believe as much of Christianity as they can, and that if they cannot in conscience believe more, they do well to profess it ; but as to the question whether their fragment of faith ought to entitle them to share the civil and political privileges enjoyed exclusively by entire Christians, it is not in his province, but belongs to the civil authority of the country to decide.

Mr. de Luc, a celebrated chemist and theologian, has published a letter to these Jews, in which he boldly advances to meet them on the ground Dr. Teller eludes ; he tells them that " far from scrupling points of Christian doctrine, they ought not even to abandon the standard of Moses ; that the history of the earth and its present appearance are the strongest of all possible testimonies to the truth of the Mosaic history, and that if they would only take the pains to be better natural philosophers, they will not be so ready to renounce their faith as Jews." There have been numerous pamphlets more written and published upon this subject, which made, as the French term it, a great sensation in the north of Germany.—*Letters from an American resident abroad on various topics of foreign literature,* published in the Port Folio, 1801, *Monthly Magazine,* vol. x. 1800, *and Gregoire's Histoire des Sectes Religieuses,* tom. ii.

* Levi's Dissertations on the Prophecies, vol. ii. Mr. Levi seems to view it as one reason why infidelity gains so much ground among

and not ascribing our sufferings to the immediate providence of God, but to a concatenation of causes in a political light." The other party are such, as either through the length of the captivity, or the easy circumstances that they are in, and the splendid and voluptuous manner in which they live, neither look for nor desire a restoration."*

The same author remarks, that " both these parties, nevertheless, adhere to the body of the nation, and outwardly conform to the Jewish rites ; they thus remain Jews ; are denominated God's people, the same as the true believers of the nation ; and in like manner bear God's covenant in the flesh." " Even those of the nation that have not the least spark of religion in them, would yet be highly offended at being called Christians, Gentiles, or apostates."†

An ancient Jewish writer numbers among the children of Israel four sects, viz. the rabbinists,

his nation, that " many wish not to be shackled with the burden of the ceremonial law."

* Dr. Adam Clarke informs us, that a Jewish rabbi, a man of extensive information and considerable learning, lately observed to him, " that as Moses had to do with a grossly ignorant, stupid, and headstrong people, he was obliged to have recourse to a pious fraud, and pretend that the laws he gave them were delivered to him by the Creator of all things, and that the time was not far distant when all the civilized world would be of one religion, that is, deism. When our author expressed his surprise at hearing a Jew talk thus, and asked him if any of his brethren were of the same mind, he answered, " Yes, every intelligent Jew in Europe, who reflects upon the subject, entertains the same sentiments."—*Clarke's Translation of Fleury's Ancient Israelites, English edition.*

† " This," says Mr. Adam, " is no doubt wonderful, and may be adduced as a proof of the truth of prophecy, and that the Jews are held together by an invisible and Almighty hand."—*Religious World Displayed,* vol. i. p. 25.

the Caraites, the Samaritans, and the disciples of
Anan ; but the account which he gives of the last,
contains no particulars ; they appear to hold the
middle rank between the Caraites and Talmudists.*

The Rabbinists, or modern Pharisees, form the
bulk of this nation. The two branches of Portuguese and German Jews are of this denomination,
which includes all who admit traditions, &c. They,
however, differ in practice from the ancient Pharisees, as they are far from affecting such an extraordinary sanctity.†

The Caraites reject the Talmudic traditions, and
for that reason they are detested by those who admit
them. In the last age a Caraite was at Frankfort
on the Maine, and narrowly escaped being assassinated by the Jews of that city. A few of this denomination may be found in Turkey, in Europe,
in cidevant Poland, and in the Ukraine, where they
cultivate the land. There is a very ancient and
interesting body of Caraites, in a fortress called
Dschoufait Kale, near Bahchisaray in the Crimea,
who possess and often use a translation of the Old
Testament in Jagatai Tartar. An approximate
calculation, made about the middle of the seventeenth century, gives only four thousand four hundred and thirty for their total number.

The sect of the Sadducees have made but little
figure since the destruction of Jerusalem. A few
indeed are said still to subsist in Africa, and some
other places ; but they are rarely found, at least
there are but few that declare themselves of these

* Gregoire's Histoire des Sectes Religieuses, tom. ii. p. 308.

† Picart's Religious Ceremonies.

opinions, and they are held by the other Jews as heretics.

A brief account of the ancient Samaritans, whose history is closely connected with that of the Jews, has been inserted in the introduction to this work. A sketch of the history of this singular people in later periods, and a detail of the religious tenets which are maintained by them at the present day, will be given in the following chapter.

CHAPTER XXXVII.

An account of the Samaritans.—After the destruction of Samaria,
the principal place of their residence has been Naplouse, the
ancient Sichem.—Their history was investigated by Joseph Scaliger, by Ludolph, and Huntington, and in the present century by
the Senator Gregoire.—Recent account which was received from
the Samaritans respecting their condition, belief, and customs.

*THE Samaritans were scattered in small num-
bers over several countries of the east ; they had
synagogues at Cairo, in Damascus, Jaffa, Gaza,
Ascalon, and Cesarea.   But after the destruction of
Samaria, their chief place has always been Naples,
or Naplouse, the ancient Sichem, the birth place of
Justin Martyr, at some distance from Samaria, with
which it has been improperly confounded by Her-
belot, founded no doubt on the testimony of Stephen
of Byzance, while he might have kept to that of
St. Jerome, who lived in Palestine.   Maundrell, and
with him all the modern geographers, place Naplouse or Sichem between the Ebal, or Mount of
Curses, and the Gerizim, or Mount of Blessings,
which is held sacred by the Samaritans.   They
pretend, that Gerizim is understood in that passage
of Deuteronomy, which enjoins all males to present
themselves three times a year before the Lord.

Benjamin of Tudela asserts, that he found only
one hundred Samaritans, poor and miserable, at
Sichem, where they continued to offer sacrifices.

* The whole of the account of the Samaritans is translated from
a late work of the senator Gregoire's, entitled, Histoire des Sectes
Religieuses.

This author is discredited ; but his account is confirmed by those travellers who followed him. Beau-
veau pretends,.that the whole number of Samaritans
at Naplouse, when he visited the city,, did not
exceed one hundred and fifty individuals.

The Chronicles of the Samaritans report, that, in
the time of Adrian, they placed the figure of
a pigeon on the summit of Gerizim, which made
itself heard when a Samaritan came to pray on this
mountain; and that on this pretext, the Jews
accused them of worshipping a dove.

Joseph Scaliger, having written to the Samaritans
of Cairo and Naplouse, received, in the year 1590,
an answer in Hebrew, which the learned Sylvester ·
de Sacy translated into Latin from the autographs
deposited in the national library, and which have
been inserted in a journal of biblical and oriental
literature. " We are ignorant," say they to Joseph
Sullami, which is the name they give to Scaliger,
" what is thy faith ? thou declarest that from thy
youth thou hast loved our law ; we cannot transmit
to thee, by the hands of the uncircumcised, the
copy which thou demandest. Send us two worthy,
pious, prudent, and learned men, if thou wouldst
know our law ; send us also alms for the treasury of
Israel." On the part of their high priest, they
demand a present of stuffs for sacerdotal vestments.
They consider themselves of the tribe of Joseph by
Ephraim, and boast of having a grand pontiff of
the race of Phinehas, son of Eleazar, son of Aaron.
He is, according to them, the two hundred and
twentieth from Aaron ; like him he has a son named

Phinehas, and these pontiffs never leave the inside of
the temple. The Samaritans offer sacrifices ; they
give the shoulder and some, other parts to the priest.
They celebrate seven feasts ; they are monogamists,
and practise the legal ablutions. They reproach
the Jews with not observing continency ; with
going out of the city and lighting fires on the
sabbath, and not obliging children to fast on the
days prescribed by the law until they are · seven
years old, whilst among the Samaritans they except
from this obligation only children at the breast.

A Jew of Palestine, being at Frankfort on the
Maine, in 1684, Ludolph sent by him a letter to
the Samaritans. He received answers, which are
inserted by Morin in his Antiquitates Ecclesiæ
Orientalis. The last reply, which was made in
1689, did not reach him till 1691. They asked
whether there were any Samaritans in his country ?
We have here, say they, a small number, who are
very poor. They thanked him for the present of
money which he had sent them, and requested new
assistance to repair their holy place.

Ludolph, who inherited from Scaliger an ardent
desire of renewing the correspondence with the
Samaritans, wrote once more on the subject to
Robert Huntington. This man, who was born in
1636, and died in 1701, was agent of the English
factory at Aleppo. While travelling in Palestine,
he visited Naplouse, where he found thirty Samaritan families, the remains of the Cutheans. There
are, he asserts, perhaps as many at Gaza. It
appears by a letter which they wrote to Joseph

Scaliger, that there were some of them at Cairo ; but Huntington found there only one poor old man and his wife.

The Samaritans at Naplouse, says Huntington, call themselves the only Hebrews and Israelites. They despise, hate, and fly from the Jews for fear of being contaminated by them. They religiously regard the sabbath. A young Samaritan to whom it was proposed to come to England, and who desired to make the voyage, dared not undertake it, because it would have been necessary to have sailed on the sabbath. They have two calendars, the Hegira, and the Grecian computation. They appear not to have any determinate ideas respecting the Messiah, though, in their Chronicle, like to Josephus, they make honourable mention of the Saviour. In their little obscure synagogue Huntington found two copies of their law, which appeared to be about five hundred years old. They asserted to him, that the original of one of these was written by Abisha, the grandson of Aaron, and that this fact is mentioned at the end of the work. Huntington, having proved to them the falsity of this assertion, they persisted in saying, that the last leaves had been unfortunately torn off formerly.

These Samaritans, whom he had occasion to visit twice in an interval of five years, were at Naplouse, at Joppa, and Gaza, scribes to the Pacha and his agents for levying imposts, like the Cophts in Egypt, and the Jews in different parts of the Ottoman empire ; they were habited as decently as their extreme misery would permit. They de-

manded of Huntington if there were any Hebrews
in his country, he replied affirmatively, and added,
that in England they were called Jews. But as he
informed them he read Samaritan with facility, they
pretended that a Samaritan alone could have taught
him, and that the Hebrews in England were their
brothers. "It is not true," says Huntington, "that
I persuaded them that they had brethren in my
country ; I supported the contrary opinion, but
they would not believe me."

In this persuasion, the Samaritans, in 1672, sent
to him at Jerusalem a copy of their law for their
brethren in Great Britain, with a letter in the
Hebrew language, (Samaritan characters) written
by Merchib-Ben-Jacob, the most distinguished personage among them ; it is written from Naplouse,
near to Gerizim, the habitation of God, and addressed to their brethren in the city of England.
They demand of them if they are Samaritans, if
they believe in the holy mountain Gerizim ; they
solicit presents, as both Jews and Christians had
sent presents to their holy places.

Huntington enclosed and transmitted the whole to
Thomas Marshal, a learned Oxonian, who replied,
and kept up a correspondence with them until the
time of his death, which happened in 1685. Marshal spoke of the disobedience of the first man,
which had rendered us all children of Belial, and
brought death and a malediction upon all his descendants. He questioned them concerning the
Shiloh, recalled to their remembrance the promise
of a deliverer, and insensibly led them to recognize
Jesus Christ. On the other side, the Samaritans

exhibited their doctrines, declaring that they had no images, repelled the charge of idolatry, and the accusation of adoring a dove, (an article which they never could forget) and requested alms. Their letters were translated into German by Schnurrer, professor of Tubingen. The care with which they have preserved the Samaritan Pentateuch attests its authenticity. Huntington here acknowledges the hand of divine providence in preserving this further proof of religion, and additional argument against incredulity, before the extinction of this feeble colony. Huntington believed that this epoch was at no great distance; but the following details prove, that he was deceived in this particular.

While Gregoire, bishop and senator, was occupied with his researches concerning the Hebrew nation, upon finding nothing in modern history respecting the Samaritans, since their letters to Joseph Scaliger, Huntington, Marshal, and Ludolph, and an age having elapsed since the latest of these accounts have been received, he, being eager to collect information, digested a series of questions, which the minister of foreign relations had the kindness to transmit to the French consuls at St. Jean d' Acre, Tripoli, Syria, and Aleppo. Their responses, which arrived in 1808, attest a zeal at once enlightened and courteous.

"The Samaritans," (said the consul of St. Jean d' Acre) "persist in believing that the English Jews are of their sect. They live in the most abject poverty. Those whose condition is most tolerable are in the service of the chief of the country. This employment just affords them bread. The

others endeavour to gain it by industry; they inhabit deserted old houses in a bad quarter of Naplouse.

" The desk on which they place the holy scriptures
is surmounted by the figure of a bird, which they
call *Achima*, a word peculiar to their sect. When
they invoke the Supreme Being, they do not say
Adonai, like others, but *Achima*. From this they
are supposed to adore the divinity, under the
symbol of this bird which has the form of a dove.

" If they are forced in their employment to touch
a stranger, or his garment, they purify themselves
as soon as possible. They marry only among themselves. The dead are considered impure; they
cause them to be buried by the Turks and Christians. The men have the manners of the wretched
of all countries, being intemperate. A few of their
women have disordered manners, but without publicity.

" At their passover they go annually upon Gerizim to offer a sheep for a sacrifice. Formerly
each family, at least the most considerable, sacrificed a sheep and a lamb; but their means being
straitened, they content themselves at present with
a general offering."

The reply of the consul of Tripoli proves that
the taste for ancient literature is hereditary to the
family of Guys. He examined the accusation
levelled by the Jews against the Samaritans relating
to their pretended adoration of a dove, and saw in
it only a commemorative symbol of the bird which
brought to Noah the sign of peace. He was led to
examine an accusation too visibly marked by calumny

not to induce scepticism, because it had been often
repeated to him by a Jewish rabbi of Tripoli, who
called the Samaritans Cutheans, a name which they
abominated. This rabbi exhibited the measure of
his charity by praising the harshness with which
the Sarrat, (a Jew) who accompanies the Pacha of
Damascus in his annual tour through Palestine in
order to levy contributions, treated the unhappy
Samaritans.

The consul of Aleppo observes, that the Samaritans inhabit a distinct part of Naplouse, which
bears their name. This quarter is a large khan,
composed of ten or twelve houses communicating
with each other, in one of which is a synagogue
containing two or three chambers. In the largest
of these is a level space on which they place their
Bible, concealed by a curtain, which the kakhan
alone has a right to draw. The whole assembly
rise at the sight of the Bible, on which is sculptured
the image of a dove.

The first day of the passover the Samaritans celebrate at midnight the feast of the sacrifice. The
kakhan kills a sheep in the synagogue. They then
light a fire in the place prepared for the purpose.
The whole victim is roasted, and divided among the
assistants, who eat it in the synagogue.

The Samaritans, like the Jews of the east, eat
only of the flesh of animals killed by one of their
own sect, and with certain formalities. They are
separated from the Jews, Turks, and Christians,
and form no alliances with them. They are poor
and inconsiderable ; many of them keep shop, and
live by petty commerce.

There are among them some Serafs, (brokers)
particularly the Seraf-el-Beled, or Seraf of the
governor.   The Turks in Naplouse leave them in
quiet ; Gezar Pacha, however, would have molested
them, but they escaped by pretending they were
Jews.   The Samaritans speak Arabic and corrupt
Hebrew.

To this information the consul of Aleppo, wishing
to add some more particulars, transmitted directly to
the Samaritans of Naplouse, the questions of Gregoire amplified, and obtained from the chief of
their synagogue an answer in Arabic, which was
translated into French* by Corances, jun.

" To Mr. Corances, senior consul of France at
Aleppo.

" We have received your kind letter in which you
propose thirty questions concerning the religious
doctrines of the Samaritan nation.   You demand
a circumstantial reply, and we will grant your
request.

" We beseech you to continue the correspondence, for your letter gave us extreme pleasure.

" You desire to know in what places the Samaritans are now found ?   You will find an answer to
this question among the others ; but we desire you
to examine the letter which you have received from
Paris, and see if any mention is there made of those
who are at Genoa, for we have received two letters
from them which inform us, that our nation is much
more scattered over Europe than Turkey, and
that their number amounts to one hundred and

* The 21st article will appear undoubtedly very obscure, and even
unintelligible.

twenty-seven thousand, nine hundred and sixty souls. Do us the favour to enquire of the senator Gregoire, whether he has any knowledge of these Samaritans; and request him to establish through your medium, a correspondence with them, with us, and with those who are in Russia.

" The 14th of July according to the Grecian calendar ; the year 6246 of the Hebrew era, since Adam ; the year 3256, since the departure of the Israelites from Egypt; Tuesday 3d of Jumaelhi, 1223, (of the Hegira.)

" Signed Salame Kahenm Kahenm, of the Sama-ritan nation at Naplouse.

" P. S. We request a speedy reply."

" I Salame, Son of Tobias, Levite, priest at Sichem, praise the Lord. Amen.

" Article 1st. There are no Samaritans to be found in our eastern countries excepting at Naplouse and Jaffa; but it is now a hundred-years since we received letters from Genoa, brought by a European, who was going to Jerusalem, and had 'a Hebrew Bible, written in a character similar to ours.

" Art. 2d. It is now a hundred years since there have been any Samaritans in Egypt.

" Art. 3d. The Samaritans at Jaffa and Naplouse amount to two hundred persons, men, women, and children.

" Art. 4th. They consist of about thirty families, and dwell in the quarter of Rhadera, which was named by our lord Jacob, the king of the Sama-ritans, and where he resided, as is written in our holy Bible.

" Art. 5th. The origin of the Samaritans is de-

rived from the true Israelites. We are really descended from our lord Jacob, called Israel, from whom sprang the twelve tribes, who entered into Egypt, amounting to seventy persons, and went out again by the number of six hundred thousand. After the miracles performed by their minister in Egypt, and in the desert by our lord Moses, son of Amram ; and who entered into the land of Canaan, where we, the descendants of the first settlers, still continue, after all the migrations which have happened to us. We are of the tribe of Joseph, son of our lord Jacob the Israelite.

"Art. 6th. This is the difference between the Jews and ourselves ; the law is one, and consists of six hundred and thirteen precepts according to both. The only difference between us concerns the purification, which we observe, but which they cannot, because they are no longer masters of Jerusalem.

" Art. 7th. Their law is exactly the same as ours from the beginning to the end, but we pronounce it differently from them.

" Art. 8th. Our law is written in the true Hebrew language, the same which was found written on the tables of precious stone containing the ten commandments given by God to Moses. Some rabbies from Jerusalem, having examined the writing of our law, acknowledged it for the ancient Assyrian, handed down on the tables of precious stone.

" From this we shall never deviate, and conformably to the word of God, " neither add nor diminish."

" Art. 9th. There is then no difference between our law, and that of the Jews, except in the characters.

" Art. 10th. The adoration of the golden image of a turtle dove is the greatest disobedience to the law ; for God has said in the ten commandments, " I am the Lord thy God, thou shalt have no other God but me ; make not to thyself any graven image, nor the likeness of any thing which is in heaven, or earth, nor in the waters under the earth, for I the Lord am a jealous God."

" After these prohibitions how can we adore the image of a dove ?

" Art. 11th. Our worship is that of God alone, as it is written in our law, " Adore the Lord thy God."

" Art. 12th. As to what regards other animals, and golden birds, far, very far, be it from us to worship them, God forbid, that we should act contrary to our law ! God has said, " Thou shalt not make gods of silver and gold."

" How can we adore a dove or any other animal when God has so strictly forbidden us ? We worship God alone, the eternal being, who has no beginning or end. We know that God created birds, men, brutes, and all things.

" God says in his law, God is your God, the God of gods, the most excellent, the powerful, the great, the majestic, who makes no distinction of persons, and cannot be tempted by presents.

" God also says, each Israelite ought to repeat the law of God at all times, on entering the house, on the way, in lying down, in rising up. It should be always in his hands, between his eyes, and on the door of his house. For this is the sacred

precept there meant, " Hear, O Israel, God is our
God, he is one, &c."

" After all these prohibitions, how can we adore
images of gold in an apartment, and pervert the
worship of the true God to that of a turtle dove, or
other animals wrought by men's hands ? .

" God says again, Thou shalt fear and adore the
Lord thy God, and continue in his religion ; thou
shalt swear by him.   How then can we worship
images, and forget his commands ? There are many
similar precepts.   God is our God, and we adore
him at all times.

" Art. 13th. The sacrifice of sheep and lambs is
the foundation of our law, and at the epoch of the
tabernacle established by Moses, there were in the
interior of it many altars for sacrifice, each for
a certain era.   One was an altar of expiatory
sacrifice, the other for peace offerings.   Moses
ordained, that every day the chief of the tribes of
Israel should offer a sacrifice morning and evening.
This took place while the tabernacle stood.   After
the end of the time of grace, and the destruction of
the tabernacle, our chief priests, of the family of
Aaron, ordered us in place of the sacrifices, to
make a prayer for a testimony of our fear of God,
and to solicit from him pardon and indulgence.

" Art. 14th. The feast of the passover, which
God commanded all Israel to observe, is in a fixed
and invariable time, which is the first month of the
year, as it is said, This is a law for all ages, on the
first month, the fifteenth day, at the setting of the
sun, it is to be observed in the chosen place, which is

Mount Gerizim. We eat it at midnight, according to the rites prescribed by the law, and that once a year.

. " Art. 15th. We offer, our victims with the rites which are commanded, as it is said, " You shall take a lamb of the first year, without blemish, from the goats or from the sheep, and keep it until the fourteenth day of the month; you shall roast it in the fire, and eat it in haste rejoicing." This sacrifice is accompanied by other ceremonies, too long to be detailed.

" Art. 16th. These sacrifices ought to be offered on Mount Gerizim ; but for the last twenty years we have made them in the city, as we cannot now repair to the mountain.

" Art. 17th. We offer our sacrifices in the open air, because God said to our lord Moses, 'Say to Pharaoh, Let us go three days' journey (from the city) and sacrifice to the Lord our God.

" It was at first commanded that these sacrifices should be offered in the country. After the entrance of the people of Israel into Canaan, Mount Gerizim was chosen for this purpose, as God has declared in his law. The sacrifice of the passover must not be made in any of the inhabited places which the Lord has given you, but only in the spot which God has designated for this purpose. This place is the mountain above mentioned ; this renders it evident, that it can be offered but once a year. Those who are not present at this solemnity ought to celebrate it in the second month.

" Art 18th. To the question when, and why sacrifices have ceased ? we reply ; that God forbid

that we should omit them, while it is in our power
to perform them; but only for twenty years past,
instead of Mount Gerizim, we offer them in the
city, because it is comprised in the chosen place.
Therefore we exactly observe the prescribed rites.

"Art. 19th. We have a Levite priest of the race
of Levi, but no Iman, or grand pontiff. In this
country, we have had no priests of Aaron for one
hundred and fifty years past.

"Art. 20th. The grand pontiff is called in the
law in Hebrew Hakchem Haggadol, and in Arabic
illustrious chief, (raies et djalil). His functions, and
those of all the tribe of Levi, are prescribed by the
law. He may take the tithe of our sacrifices and
property; he is to judge according to what is
written in the law. He has also other privileges
which would be too long to detail.

"Art. 21st. You inquire whether the Samaritans
are divided into different classes, and what are these
divisions? There exists among us some known and
observed divisions. These are the engagements
which God entered into with our fathers Abraham,
Isaac, and Jacob, and before these with Noah, and
also with Phinehas, by which he established him
Pontiff. We have likewise the divisions of heaven,
and three engagements with Moses; and the Hebrew
sea, which appears in the eclipses of the sun and
moon, and the conjunctions by which we know on
what day of the week the first of the month commences. We also know by this means the day of
the feast which we celebrate, and on what day of
the week it will take place. We have many other
divisions; but these are all whose names it is neces-

sary to mention. Such are the divisions among us.

" Art. 22d. There are no Caraites among us, nor have we any intercourse with this sect.

" Art. 23d. The Khassams, called Rabbinists in France, a sect which, you say, is found in Egypt, are totally unknown to us. There are none in our country ; we have no relation with them ; we know not what is said of them, nor have we ever even heard their names pronounced.

" Art. 24th. We are separated from all nations, even the Jewish ; we have houses and temples apart. We have already said, that the character of our writing differs from theirs ; we add, that they do not read the former, nor we the latter. Such is the difference which exists between them and us.

" There are besides some articles of their law which they cannot observe out of Jerusalem.

" Art. 25th. Our customs in our houses are, to adore and praise God at all times, to observe the rules of the law, and to abstain from every usage which is contrary to the words of God in the law. " Do not cause evil to enter into your houses ;" the meaning of which is, not to admit any worship but that of God.

" We do not therefore admit any images ; our sole occupation is to read the law during our whole life.

" As to the relations between parents and children, husbands and wives : the father is obliged to teach his offspring the rules of justice, and to teach them to read. They are bound to honour their father and mother, as is enjoined in the decalogue.

L L

" We cannot marry, but conformably to the rules, and in the degrees permitted by the law.

" Art. 26th. Our dress is different from that of all other nations. We always wear a turban ; but on sabbaths and festivals, when we go to the temple, we dress wholly in white.

" Art. 27th. Our population was scattered over Egypt, Damascus, Ascalon, and Cesarea. But six hundred years have elapsed, since these were carried away by the Franks, and are now found in their country. This is the cause of our diminished population. We have been reduced by the migrations which have taken place in past ages, according to the will of God.

" Art. 28th. Our usages are, the observation of the commandments concerning holy days, and the sabbaths ; the observation of the degrees permitted and prohibited in marriage. The prayers which were ordained by God, and enjoined by the priests of Aaron, in place of the daily sacrifices which were abolished after the destruction of the tabernacle of Moses. Since that epoch, prayers were instituted for every festival, with particular ceremonies. There are three prayers for the sabbath, and each holy day has appropriate ones, as the prayers peculiar to the passover ; the feast of seven days, when we eat unleavened bread ; the pilgrimage to Mount Gerizim ; the feast of Pentecost, which is observed a certain number of days, and is terminated by a solemn festival in which we present ourselves before God. At that time we do not sleep, and employ ourselves without ceasing, day and night, in reading the law, and praising God. The fifteenth

is the feast of tabernacles, which has its own appropriate ceremonies, and we are also to appear before God.

" Finally, the twenty-second is the festival of the closing of all the holy days, with ceremonies conformable to the orders of our high priests. All the above mentioned festivals are performed according to the commands of God.

" Art. 29th. By an express order, given by God to Abraham, we observe circumcision, which is performed on the eighth day at sun-rise, and we observe all the ceremonies commanded on that occasion ; we, cannot alter or disobey a single article.

" Art. 30th. We say our prayers turned towards. Mount Gerizim, which is the house of God, and of his angels, and where the Deity exhibits his majesty, and the place for the sacrifices, enjoined in the law. Our faces are therefore turned towards this place during prayer. According to the order of our pontiffs, prayers are now substituted for the sacrifices of sheep, which were offered morning and evening.

" The 15th of July, according to the Greeks, in the year 1808, of Jesus Christ."

The learned author to whom we are indebted for this recent account of the Samaritans observes, " that during one hundred and nineteen years the communication between this sect and the Europeans had entirely ceased. The answer which I obtained to my queries, preserves a traditional chain of documents concerning them. Conformably to the promise which they exacted, I wrote to undeceive them respecting the opinion they had formed, that persons

of their sect were to be found in Russia and Genoa.
They are not known in any part of Europe, and
every circumstance concurs to induce us to believe,
that those of Jaffa and Naplouse are the only Samaritans in existence.   What they say of the transmigration of their brethren, who were carried to
Europe by the Franks, appears to be totally destitute of proof.   My researches into the history of
the Crusades has afforded me no information to
confirm their assertion.

  " Under the name of the Palestine Association,
a society has recently been formed in England, the
object of whose labours is every thing relating to the
holy land, and the adjacent countries.   The amiable
and learned Hamilton of the academy of Calcutta is
the president.   The barriers interposed by war and
politics between different parts of the globe deprives
me of the means of corresponding with him ; but if
some happy circumstance should place this account
before his eyes, he will find in it the expression of my
esteem, and my desire that he and his worthy coad-
jutors should second my researches concerning the
Samaritans."

CHAPTER XXXVIII.

An account of the Chasidim.—Of a Society of Jews in Podolia.—Of the followers of Zabathai Tzevi.

AFTER having in the two preceding chapters given an account of the ancient Jewish sects, notice will be taken of those which appeared in the last century, and continue to exist at the present time.*

The following details concerning the sect of the Chasidim are extracted from notice published in 1799, at Frankfort on the Oder, by Israel Loebel, second rabbin from Novogroduk in Lithuania. This account was reprinted in 1807, in the Sulamith, an interesting journal published at Dessau, by Frankel and Wolf, which has for its object the diffusion of useful knowledge among the Jews, and their co-religionists. The following account is an abridgment from Loebel's own words.

A rabbi, named Israel, rendered himself very famous at Miedzyvorz, in the Ukraine, between the years 1760 and 1765. He was an ambitious man, who, being destitute of Talmudic knowledge, and not able to gain reputation by his learning, sought other means to acquire influence, and became an exorcist. My spirit, said he, frequently detaches itself from my body to explore the novelties of the intellectual world ; it reveals to me whatever passes there, and averts many evils with which the world of spirits threatens our earth.

* This chapter is translated from Gregoire's Histoire des Sectes Religieuses, tom. ii. p. 337, &c.

In order to realize his designs, Israel assumed the mask of exemplary piety, and joined to his name that of Balschem, or possessor of the name of God. The propensity of ignorant, and credulous men towards the occult sciences procured him, in less than ten years, more than ten thousand followers, whom he called Chasidim: This name designated those men, who not content to follow the ritual laws of Moses, laboured to unite themselves more intimately to the Deity by their sanctity. But it was soon discovered, that the connexion between rabbi Israel and his disciples did not conduce to the end he had announced, and that their intentions and their actions were hostile to the principles of piety and morality. It was this which induced the Talmudist Elias, grand rabbin in Wilna, in concert with the elders of the synagogue of Brod, to write a work against the new sect, in order to prove, that it was injurious to the Jewish religion, and to the state. Elias, being near his death, enjoined all who visited him, to proclaim, that whoever loved God and man, ought carefully to shun all communication with the Chasidim, who, under the mantle of hypocrisy, concealed the most profound immorality.

The artful Israel Balschem, seeing it was necessary to strengthen his party to oppose the orthodox, exerted himself to gain the most opulent people, and published a work, which is the code of his doctrine, and which contains abominable principles. He prohibits his adherents, under the most severe spiritual penalties, to cultivate their minds. Those who possess information ought to suppress it; for it is dangerous, said he, to permit reason to interfere in

matters of religion. He is not willing that those who pray to God should melt into tears; for the father beholds with more pleasure his children cheerful and happy, than discontented and sorrowful.

Israel Loebel, the writer of this narrative, observes, that " these ideas are contrary to the Jewish law; for Moses commands us to study the laws of religion and the state. For why should God have given us reason, if we do not apply it to enlarge our religious knowledge? Is it not our special destiny on earth to endeavour to approach the divinity? The successors of Moses in the dignity of prophets have thought and taught like him.

" If prayer is not accompanied with a fervent elevation of the heart to God, what is it, but an assemblage of insignificant words? Are not the tears shed in prayer often signs of true devotion? Do not the Talmudists teach, that in order to increase it, it is necessary to pray slowly, and without clamour? Many of our nation, indeed, maintain that a large part of the ceremonies joined to prayer are superfluous; yet they serve to strengthen our recollection."

The following is a specimen of the maxims of this sect :—If any one has committed, or wishes to commit sin, he can promise himself absolution from his leader, without subjecting himself to a change of conduct, and leading a regular life. This detestable principle, especially among those who have received but little instruction, increased the number of Balschem's partizans to such a degree, that they amounted to forty thousand at the time of his death,

which took place fifteen years after the sect was
founded. .   .

At that time, his plan, both interior and exterior,
assumed a new form. To a single leader they substituted many directors, who, to defend their doctrine,
printed various works, after having published two
posthumous ones attributed to their founder. . : .

One of these productions, called Kesser Schemtow
appeared at Korstchik and Zulkiew, in two parts.
In the first part, he gives to his followers a general
absolution for the sins which they have committed,
and shall commit, on condition that they educate
their sons Talmudists. He asserted, that his soul,
being transported in an extacy to heaven, the
archangel Michael, the protector of the Jews, declared to him, that on this condition every sinner
should not only obtain remission, but even a reward
for his crimes. In the second part, he invites his
adherents to pray to Abraham, the father of the
Jews, who has conducted so many of his unhappy
race to the true belief, and who has preserved it in
the souls of many disposed to quit it. He condemns
all connection between their children and those who
do not belong to the Hebrew nation, especially his
sect.

The second posthumous work of Balschem, under
the title Likute Amomir, has been printed at Lemburg, and in the two other cities before mentioned.
He teaches, that in order to be united to the divinity
it is necessary to commit sin upon sin ; and that the
more horrible they are, the more agreeable are they
to him. For God being the first in the scale of

beings, and the greatest sinner being in the last grade, there is between them a species of contiguity by representing to ourselves, that the scale is of a circular form.

Baer Medsersitz, rabbin of Kortschik, and one of the directors of this sect, has commented upon the principles of the founder in a work in which he proscribes every exercise of virtue. But the most abominable book, entitled Noam Hamelech, has for its author Melech, another of the directors, and grand rabbin of Lezanst. Balschem had granted a general absolution upon conditions which could not always be performed. Melech goes much further; he teaches, that each of the directors can absolve the greatest crimes, past and future, if one of the directors wishes to commit them ; and, at the same time, encourages men to abandon themselves to vicious practices, by assuring the guilty, that, having no terrestrial power to fear, they will controul nature by their prayers, provided, however, that the sect will remain faithful to their engagements. In this work he prohibits the use of medicine to the sick, seeing that he who can give them eternal life, may at his pleasure prolong their temporal life.

From these specimens, drawn from the books of this sect, we see how pernicious it is to the state, and apprehend, that it must have found many adversaries. But the Hebrew works published against these sectarians, are less of the polemic kind, than exhortations to preserve themselves from the contagious principles of the Chasidim. In combating them in this manner they hoped to restore the lost sheep to the fold of Israel. Unhappily these expec-

tations have failed, and while we render justice to
the talents and integrity of the authors, we regret
that most of them, having their residence out of
the country ravaged by the sect, attain their knowledge only from the relation of others.

When I, says Loebel, was rabbin at Moholyw,
I had an opportunity to look about me and observe
the progress of this sect, which obliged me to make
exertions to preserve the community committed to
my care from these pernicious sentiments. The
Chasidim, having circumvented by their art, and
entrapped in their errors, my only brother, an
intelligent, and in other respects a good young
man, I wrote many letters to him to open his eyes,
by the contrast between his actual immorality, and
the estimable conduct he had before maintained.
I wrote also to the principal director of this sect,
the famous rabbin Solomon Witeyst, and proved to
him his errors by invincible arguments, with a menace
of combating him publicly, if I could not recover
my brother. My letters were unsuccessful, as was
also a journey I made with the same views. But
my journey having procured me an opportunity of
disputing with the director, as I thought our conference would be interesting to many people, I printed
it in Hebrew at Warsaw, under the title of Bituach.
Emboldened by the success of this pamphlet, I published, in the same city, my work Kiwroth Hataywa,
which is a severe, but impartial criticism upon the
writings of the Chasidim. It obtained the flattering
approbation of the wise Talmudists, whether national or foreigners. I am now about to give
a succinct account of my conference with the rabbin

Solomon Witeyst, who being very urgent to see me, began the debate by addressing me in this despotic manner.

Solomon Witeyst. Who has ordered you to attack us? Are you more wise than many others, who have failed in the enterprize? If you have any thing to object to us, at least it was not necessary to divulge it to discredit our nation, already too much humbled.

Israel Loebel. It is necessary to correct our erring brethren. I might turn the question against you, for you know it is not permitted to any individual, ecclesiastical or civil, to found or patronize a new sect. It is said in holy writ, the laws are binding upon your descendants. Jeremiah says, Has any man ever changed his God and his faith? Why from the commencement of your sect have you affected a clandestine progress? If you only aspire to the title of separatists, live as a considerable part of our nation, who, though they do not strictly follow the Talmud, at least do not hate those who reject their opinions; but you abhor all who are not of your sect. As to what you say respecting the contempt which oppresses our nation, let us discuss this article. The Christians no longer revenge the death of Jesus Christ upon the descendants of the Jews. They do not believe that the Jews should be obliged to detest all who are not of their religion. They do not believe that our religion is contrary to morality and the state. Let us hope that from henceforth they will respect all the rites of humanity.

They reproach the Jews with their dishonesty.

But many of the Christians will not see that this
accusation is only a pretence invented by hatred
against our nation. They have left us no other
profession than traffic, in which deception is more
easily remarked than in any other calling. They
have extremely restricted the faculty of commerce
granted to the Jews, and they are loaded with
taxes. But it is known that very honest merchants
are found among them; and that there are some
very dishonest Christian merchants. The Christians do not hate the Jews as such; and, in exposing your maxims as contrary to religion and the
state, I have done no injury to our nation. I think
we ought to free ourselves from contempt by re-
vealing the crimes of our co-religionists.

 Solomon Witeyst. All that you allege is without
foundation; it is an attempt to oppress our sect.
But you will fall into the pit which you have dug for
us

 Israel Loebel. I abhor the maxims of your
sect; for all your books contain invitations to liber-
tinism. In that which is entitled, Kesser Schemtow,
do we not read, that " sins committed upon certain
conditions will be rewarded." The nocturnal revels
are, according to your system, the means of salvation. You intimidate the simple by false prophecies;
you forbid the sick to consult a physician; and,
levying a contribution on credulity and misfortune,
you take money from the unhappy, and persuade
them you can avert from them the wrath of heaven.
By your dishonesty and rapine you have made
thousands of men to perish; you have caused divorces, and given trouble to society, &c. &c.

This frank declaration irritated my adversary so much the more, as he saw that I was acquainted with the intrigues of the directors ; and, from that moment, he swore implacable vengeance against me.

Encouraged by the good cause which I had defended, in 1797 I set out to visit the countries where this sect had the most adherents, and unmasked the hypocrites, who usurped the reputation of saints. In my journey I carried two hundred and fifty copies of my two works. In the course of my travels I had the satisfaction of recovering a few of the sectarians into the right path by my sermons. On my arrival at Cracow, I applied to the administration called the Revision, or Revision office, to examine my writings, that I might obtain a certificate of approbation, which was granted me. I then directed my way to Lemburg, to continue every where my exhortations. But upon my arrival at Stsechow, where the sect were powerful, they imputed to me the project of endeavouring to bring evils upon my co-religionists, and reproached me with having introduced books from the Prussian territories into the country subject to Austria. In consequence of this denunciation they came in the night to seize my works ; but I obtained restitution by showing to the regency of this city the certificate which I had obtained at Cracow.

I arrived at last at Lemburg in September, 1798 ; and dreading new oppressions, I confined myself in my first sermons to treat of moral subjects, without making mention of the sect. But soon after, two emissaries arrived from the cantons through which

I had passed, who pointed me out to the rabbins of
Lemburg as an enemy to the Chasidim. They
repeated their accusations against me, and robbed
me of my certificate of approbation, which the
governor of the city caused to be restored to me;
I returned to Cracow, where they showed me a decree
from the chancery of Gallicia, sitting at Vienna,
which commanded the seizure of my books, until
a new order, considering that some members of the
sect of pious Jews, (die fromen juden) had made
remonstrances against them.

I perceived then the necessity of a journey to
Vienna; and, in Jan. 1799, I presented my petition
to the emperor, with a copy of my pamphlets, and
supplicated him to order them to be translated by the
rabbies of Moravia and Hungary. The consequence
of my request was, that the Chasidim were prohibited from assembling in public, under severe penalties, in Austrian and Russian Poland.

Many chiefs of this sect emigrated into other
parts. They established themselves in another part
of Poland, especially at Grodzisk, at Bielsk, and at
Strikow.

The learned author of the work,* from which the
above account is translated, observes, "Thus ends
the narrative of Israel Loebel. He promises the
public further details of what he can collect concerning the Chasidim, who are a most abominable
sect, if all the facts which have been mentioned
against them are true. Many of them have, however, been contradicted by a Polish Jew, well informed and disinterested respecting the subject in

---

* Gregoire's Histoire des Sectes Religieuses, tom. ii. p. 348.

question. For example, he denies that the Chasidim
are forbidden when sick to consult physicians, and
medicine. He even cites one of the richest partizans of this sect, who had recourse to all the
succours of art to heal his daughter, and expended
more than five thousand ducats. Some of the
crimes imputed to the Chasidim are so enormous,
that they surpass credibility; and how can we judge
a cause of this kind upon the exclusive evidence of
one advocate?"*

In 1756, a small society of Jews in Podolia, being
disgusted with the Talmud, made a profession of
faith almost Christian, which is as follows : "We
believe all that God has taught and ordained in the
Old Testament. The grace of God is indispensable
in order to understand the sacred writings. The
Talmud ought to be rejected, because it contains
blasphemies against God. God is the Creator of
all that exists; God is one in essence, and triple in
person. It is possible that God became incarnate,
and submitted to human infirmities, in order to
expiate human sins. According to the prophecies,
it is certain that Jerusalem will never be rebuilt.
The Messiah promised in the scriptures is no longer
to come. God himself will abolish the malediction
pronounced on our ancestors and their posterity,
and he is the true incarnate Messiah.†

These Anti-Talmudists held assemblies at Lan-
koron in Podolia, for the purpose of reading the
Bible, and performing other religious exercises.
They were accused by the Talmudists of giving

* Gregoire's Histoire des Sectes Religieuses, tom. ii. p. 348.
† Gregoire's Histoire des Sectes Religieuses, tom. ii.

themselves up to dissipation, and being associated with the sect of Zabathai Tzevi,* under the direction of a Jew from the frontiers of Turkey. The accused proved that these imputations were false; and as they were incessantly insulted by the more numerous Talmudists, who caused them to be excommunicated and proscribed, they demanded an official safeguard from the bishop of Caminiek; when they were declared innocent, their enemies were condemned to pay them a fine, and also to give one hundred and fifty-two Hungarian crowns of gold towards repairing the towers of the cathedral of Caminiek. The bishop declared himself the protector of the Anti-Talmudists, and exhorted the two parties to live in peace, and to search truth in the holy scriptures. Some time after, the Anti-Talmudists wrote to Augustus III. king of Poland, and to the primate, who answered them affectionately, and to the archbishop of Lemburg, declaring to him that they recognized Jesus Christ as the Messiah, and desired baptism.†

Towards the conclusion of the last century, there were at Prague Jews who were, or who were said to be, disciples of Zabathai Tzevi. The rabbi excommunicated them *even from the other world,* and interdicted them from entering the synagogue, from whence they were driven with great fury. The magistrate, obliged to interpose his authority, caused several of the principal persecutors to be imprisoned, and condemned them to bread and

---

* That the followers of this impostor have continued till the present time has been mentioned in chapter 22nd.

† Gregoire's Histoire des Sectes Religieuses, tom. ii. p. 312.

water for some time ; he even inflicted punishment on some children, who, in imitation of their parents, had manifested too great zeal for Judaical orthodoxy.

About sixty years since, a rabbi at Mayence was supposed to be of the sect of Zabbathai Tzevi; these suspicions were fortified by his not appearing in the synagogue on the anniversary of the destruction of the temple, which is not observed as a fast by the Zabathaites. They had watched him for some time; and seized this opportunity of ascertaining his sentiments. The Jews ran to his house, which they found shut up; they broke open his doors, and found him at table, and instantly carried him to the synagogue, covered with a napkin, where he was derided and insulted.

In 1808, a musician of the sect of Zabathai Tzevi came to Paris. He is perhaps the only one of this denomination, who has for a long time appeared in France.*

* Gregoire's Histoire des Sectes Religieuses, tom. ii. p 313.

CHAPTER XXXIX.

Of the dissimulation of many Jews who have professed the Christian
religion.—An account of several distinguished converts.—Account
of a Society formed in London for the express purpose of converting
the Jews.—Of their success.—A large extract from a speech made
by Dr. Buchanan at the first anniversary meeting of the London
Society.

NOTWITHSTANDING the long protracted
calamities the Jews have suffered since their dispersion, the most violent persecutions have never prevailed upon the general mass of this people to abjure
their religion. David Levi, speaking of those
among his brethren, who, in all ages have professed
Christianity, observes, that " they have not acted
voluntarily, but by compulsion, as in Spain and
Portugal, or from interested motives, as there, and
elsewhere ; that notwithstanding they seemed to
apostatize, and pretended to embrace Christianity,
yet in their hearts they secretly adhered to the true
faith and law of Moses ; and such are at this day
called among us, *the compelled,* because they act by
compulsion ; for, as soon as they can by any means
escape from the popish countries, they instantly
return to Judaism." " I am free to assert," says he,
" that there is scarcely an instance of a Jew ever
having embraced Christianity on the pure principles
of religion, but merely from interested motives."*

It is an acknowledged fact that there have been
multitudes of dissembling Jews, particularly in
Spain and Portugal. But still there has been,

* Levi's Dissertations, &c. vol. ii. p. 15.

doubtless, a number in every age, who have professed the Christian religion from a real conviction of its truth ; some of whom have written and preached in defence of the faith they once denied. Several instances, apparently of this kind, have been mentioned in the preceding parts of this work, to which may be added a few others at a later period.*

About the year 1762, Solomon Duitch, a learned rabbi and teacher of several synagogues in Germany, renounced Judaism. During seven years his mind had been perplexed with doubts respecting religion ; but, at length, the difficulties which had embarrassed him were removed, and he openly professed himself a disciple of Christ. After he was fully convinced of the truth and excellence of the Christian religion, he published a narrative of his conversion, and became a zealous preacher of the Gospel. He lived and died in Holland.†

In 1797, Juan Joseph Heydeck, a learned Jewish convert in Spain, published at Madrid, a work entitled, " A defence of the Christian Religion," in four volumes quarto. He was chosen professor of oriental languages in that country.‡

Mr. Lapidoth, a wealthy and respectable Jew in Holland, in early life entertained doubts respecting the Jewish religion ; and having secretly procured a New Testament, and continued his researches,

---

* In Chapman's Eusebius we have an account from Wolfius, J. Scaliger, Kidder, Bayle, &c of twenty-nine Jews of talents and credit converted to Christianity by an accurate investigation of the prophecies. Some of these have been mentioned in chapter xxv and other parts of this work.

† Christian Observer, 1809.

‡ Gregoire's Histoire, &c.

after various perplexities, he and his wife and adult
children became firmly convinced of the truth of the
Christian religion. In 1805, he and his family
were publicly baptized.*

The Missionary Society in London were engaged,
about the year 1800, in attempting the conversion of
the Jews, but without any encouraging success.
In 1809, however, a Society was formed for the
exclusive object of converting the Jews, and called
the " London Society for promoting Christianity
amongst the Jews." Lectures were accordingly
preached in order to convince the Jews that Jesus
of Nazareth was the true Messiah ; and Schools
were opened to receive the children of such Jewish
parents, as would allow them to be instructed in the
principles of Christianity. Tracts were also printed
containing evidences of the divine origin of the
Gospel. This Society was at first composed of
Christians of various denominations. At length,
however, the pecuniary affairs of the Society became
embarrassed, and other inconveniences were fore-
seen ; it was therefore agreed, in the year 1815,
that the affairs of the Society should be entrusted
to a Committee of Members of the Established
Church of England, and that it should be from that
time forward a Society regularly conducted on the
principles of that Church. It ought to be recorded
in a history of the Jews, that to the munificence of
a benevolent individual, is the Society indebted for
relief from its pecuniary difficulties. The Right
Rev. the Lords Bishops of St. David's and Glou-
cester, are Patrons of this Institution, and Sir

* Evangelical Magazine, 1806.

Thomas Baring, Bart. President. Divine worship
is regularly performed at an Episcopal Chapel, at
which the Jewish children in the schools attend.
Tracts continue to be printed at the Society's office,
for the purpose of distribution amongst the Jews.

A monthly publication, styled, "The Jewish
Expositor and Friend of Israel," issues from the
press; where works in defence of Christianity, in
answer to rabbi Crooll, have been also published, by
the Rev. T. Scott, and William Cuninghame, Esq.

At the first Anniversary of the Society (in 1810)
the Rev. Dr. Buchanan gave a most interesting
account of the state of the Jews in India, and the.
nation of the Affghans, supposed by the late Sir
William Jones to be descended from the ten tribes.
The greatest part of this speech is as follows, given
in the learned author's own words.*

" During my residence in the east, my mind was
much occupied with the present state and circumstances of the Jews. I visited them in different
provinces, examined their books, and discoursed
with them on the subject of the prophecies; and
I found that no where do they despair of being
restored to Jerusalem ; no where do they despair of
beholding their Messiah. It is with great satisfaction then, that, on my return to England, I contemplate the establishment of your Society. It is,
indeed, with much surprise I behold three hundred
gentlemen assembled on the present occasion, under
the patronage of noblemen of our country, to
promote this noble design. The sudden elevation
of your institution, and the interest which it has

* Edinburgh Christian Instructor, 1810, vol. i. p. 205.

almost instantaneously created in the public mind, are sure prognostics of its perpetuity. It is one of those institutions, which, like the Bible Society, needs only to be proposed, to recommend itself to the minds of men, by its perfect reasonableness and propriety ; and 1 may add, by the divine obligation it involves. I entertain a confident hope, that this Society, or some institution analogous to it, will be perpetual in the church of Christ ; and that it will endure, to use an oriental expression, as long as sun and moon endure ; or, at least, as long as there is a Jew in the world, who is not a Christian. .

" There is a measure I would propose to the consideration of your Society, which I think will contribute to its celebrity and success. I would suggest to you to open a correspondence with the Jews in the east. .

" Perhaps it may not be known to some, that, by the events of the late war in India, a colony of Jews have become subjects to Great Britain. This is the colony of the White and Black Jews of Cochin. The number is calculated to be about sixteen thousand. I am informed, that the number of Jews in the United Kingdom is not computed to be greater than fourteen thousand. So that our Jewish subjects in the east are yet more numerous than those in the west ; and they are equally entitled to the regard and attention of your Society.

" I visited Cochin soon after the conquest of the province. The Jews received me hospitably, and permitted me to examine their libraries and their synagogues ; and they presented to me many valuable manuscripts which are deposited in the library

of the university of Cambridge. One of these is a roll of the Pentateuch, on goats' skins dyed red; one of the most ancient perhaps which the east can produce. The White Jews live on the sea coast, and have commerce with foreign nations; the Black Jews live chiefly in the interior of the country. The Hindoos call them Israeli; they call themselves Beni-Israel, and not Jews; for their ancestors did not belong to Judah, but to the kingdom of Israel. They consider themselves to be descended from those tribes which were carried away at the first captivity. In some parts of the east, the Beni-Israel never heard of the second temple; they never heard of the Christian account of the coming of the Messiah. Some of them possess only the Pentateuch, the Psalms, and Book of Job; others have no portion of scripture left. But their countenance, and their observance of the sabbath, and of peculiar rites, demonstrate that they are Jews. The White Jews of Cochin despise the Black Jews, as being of an inferior cast, and do not approve of intermarriages with them, because they do not belong to the second temple. Both among White and Black Jews I found that there was a general impression that there would soon be a rumour of wars, and a commotion among the peoples on their account. The White Jews expect a second Cyrus from the West, who shall build their temple the third and last time.*

* Dr. Buchanan, in his Researches in Asia, observes, "I have had many interesting conferences with the Jews on the subject of their present state; and have been much struck with two circumstances; their constant reference to the desolation of Jerusalem, and their confident hope that it will be one day rebuilt The desolation of the

" You may address the Jews of Cochin with
great advantage on the subject of the Christian
religion ; for they have the evidence of the Syrian
Christians before them. These ancient Christians
live in the vicinity, and are your witnesses. At one
place in the interior of the country, which I visited,
there is a Jewish synagogue and a Christian church
in the same Hindoo village. They stand opposite
to each other, as it were the law and the gospel;
bearing testimony to the truth, in the presence of
the heathen world.

" I was informed, that many years ago one of
the Jews translated the New Testament into Hebrew
for the purpose of confuting it, and of repelling
the arguments of his neighbours, the Syrian Christians. The manuscript fell into my hands, and is
now in the library of the university of Cambridge.

holy city is ever present to the minds of the Jews, when the subject is
concerning themselves as a nation ; for though without a king, and
without a country, they constantly speak of the unity of their nation.
Distance of time and place seems to have no effect in obliterating the
remembrance of the desolation. I often thought of the verse in the
Psalms, "If I forget thee, O Jerusalem, let my right hand forget her
cunning." They speak of Palestine as being close at hand, and
easily accessible. It is become an ordinance of their rabbins in some
places, that, when a man builds a new house, he shall leave a small
part of it unfinished, as an emblem of ruin, and write on it these
words, Zecher Lachorchan, i. e. in memory of desolation.

" Their hopes of rebuilding the walls of Jerusalem, the third and
last time, under the auspices of the Messiah, or of a second Cyrus,
before his coming, are always expressed with great confidence. They
have a general impression, that the period of their liberation from
the heathen is not very remote ; and they consider the present com-
motions in the earth as gradually loosening their bonds. ' It is,' say
they, ' a sure sign of our approaching restoration, that in almost all
countries there is a general relaxation of the persecutions against us.' "
—*Researches in Asia*, p. 226.

It is in' his own hand writing, with the first interlineations and erasures; and will be of great use in preparing a version of the New Testament in the Hebrew language. It appears to be a faithful translation as far as it has been examined; but about the end, when he came to the epistles of St. Paul, he seems to have lost his temper, being moved perhaps by the acute arguments of the learned Benjamite, as he calls the apostle; and he has written here and there a note of execration on his memory. But behold the providence of God! The translator became himself a convert to Christianity. His own works subdued his unbelief. "In the lion he found sweetness;" and he lived and died in the faith of Christ. And now it is a common superstition among the vulgar in that place, that if any Jew should write the whole of the New Testament with his own hand, he will become a Christian by the influence of the evil spirit.

"This event occurred in the south of India; but a conversion no less remarkable took place, some time afterwards, in the north. Jacob Levi, a Jew from Smyrna, travelled over land to Calcutta, and heard the Gospel from one of the Lutheran preachers, belonging to the Society for promoting Christian knowledge, and became a convert to the truth. He delivered a testimony to the Jews, Hindoos, Mahomedans, and Christians; for he was acquainted with various languages, and spoke eloquently, like Apollos. But his course was short. He was ordained, like many witnesses of the Christian faith, to abide but for a moment. These solitary instances of the power of the Gospel seem to occur, in almost

every nation, previous to the general illumination. The conversion of Jacob Levi is recorded in the proceedings of the Society, in Bartlett's Buildings, London.

" But there is another body of Jews, not a colony, but a kingdom of Jews, to which this Society may also address itself; and that is the ten tribes; for the ten tribes, so long lost, have, at length, been found. It has been sufficiently ascertained by the investigation of the learned in India, that the Affghan and Pyran nations consist of the descendants of the Jewish tribes of the first dispersion.

" When I was in the south of India, I asked the Black Jews where their brethren, the great body of the ten tribes, were to be found? They answered promptly, that they were to be found in the north, in the regions adjacent to Chaldea, the very country whither they were first carried into captivity. On my return to Calcutta, I prosecuted the inquiry, under the advantages which my superintendance of the College of Fort William afforded me. Sir William Jones* had recorded it as his opinion, that the Affghans were Jews; and referred to various autho-

* This great man strongly recommended an inquiry into the language, literature, and history of the Affghans. " We learn," says he, " from Esdras, that the ten tribes, after a wandering journey, came to a country called Arsareth, where we may suppose they settled. Now the best Persian historians affirm, that the Affghans are descended from the Jews; and they have among themselves traditions of the same import. It is even asserted, that their families are distinguished by the names of Jewish tribes, though since their conversion to Islamism they have studiously concealed their origin. The language they use has a manifest resemblance to the Chaldaic, and a considerable district under their dominions is called Hazareth, which might easily have been changed into Arsareth."—*Asiatic Researches*, vol ii p. 7, and *Works of Sir William Jones*, vol i p. 23'

rities. A further investigation confirmed the judgment of this illustrious scholar. There were Affghan Jews in Calcutta at the time: one of my own servants was an Affghan. The Affghans are generally reputed by us to be Mahomedans. I asked my servant if he was a Mahomedan ? " No," said he, " I am a Mahomedan Jew." I plainly discerned in his countenance the features of the London Jew. The general account of the Affghans is this ; that their ancestors were Jews ; that their common histories record the names of David, Saul, and other kings of Israel ; that the Mahomedans came upon them with an invading army; and said unto them, We are Jews as well as you ; we observe circumcision, and keep the sabbath ; let us incorporate our nations, and be one people, and unite against the infidels,—that they made a show of yielding to Mahomedanism (as the Jews of Spain and Portugal pretended to yield to Christianity); but in process of time the ascendancy of the new religion corrupted their ancient institutions ; their sacred books began to diminish in number ; and it came to pass at last, that in many places they could be only recognized to be Jews by their countenance, by tradition, by peculiar rites, and the observance of the sabbath ; which are the only marks which distinguish some of the Beni-Israel of the south of India. Let us therefore address the ten tribes, and receive them in the state in which, by the providence of God, they are to be found. Some of the Jews of London are as ignorant, and as little entitled to the name, as the Affghans of India.

" But there is a third body of Jews to whom you

ought to write ; I mean the Samaritan Jews. They
are not far from the shores of the Mediterranean,
and are easily accessible. They possess only the
Pentateuch. They are few in number, and will
receive with much deference, any communication
which you will be pleased to make to them, relating
to their religion, and to the present state of the
Jewish nation.

"Let letters then be addressed to these three
bodies of Israelites ; not in the name of Christians,
but in the name of the converted Jews, who compose
a part of this Society : but not in the rabbinical
Hebrew, (for there are upwards of twenty dialects
of rabbinical, or commercial Hebrew in the world)
but in the Hebrew of the Old Testament, which all
understand ; let them be informed of the great events
that have taken place in the west, namely, that
Jews have become Christians ; that the Christians
are sending forth preachers to teach all nations ; that
the Messiah is surely come ; and that the signs of
the times encourage the belief, that Israel is about
to be restored in a spiritual sense."

The doctor expresses his surprise, that "the
Society have not as yet obtained a version of the
New Testament in the Hebrew language for the
use of the Jews. How strange," says he, " it
appears, that, during a period of eighteen hundred
years, the Christians should never have given the
Jews the New Testament in their own language!
By a kind of infatuation, they have reprobated the
unbelief of the Jews, and have never at the same
time told them what they ought to believe."*

* Since this important suggestion from Dr. Buchanan a translation

Dr. Buchanan concludes with observing, that "the chief difficulties which this Society will probably meet with, will be from the opposing Jews at home. But when they see that your converts mul- tiply, and when they hear that you are writing to other nations, regardless of their ignorance and opposition at home ; when they learn that you have discovered the ten tribes; that you have sent to them the New Testament in the holy language ; that you are discussing with them the subjects of the prophecies; and that converted Jews are going forth as " ambassadors in light ships, to carry the tidings of gladness to a nation scattered and peeled, terrible from their beginning hitherto," (Isaiah xviii.) the hostile Jews will be alarmed, their spirits will sink within them, and they will begin to think, that a great day in Zion is indeed at hand.

" Every time you meet here, in this public manner, in the presence of the Israelites, your cause acquires strength. Every time that these annual sermons are preached, and the voice of prayer and supplication for the outcasts of Israel ascends to heaven, it is like the blasts of the rams' horns before the wall of Jericho ; and so the enemy will soon begin to consider it ; and I doubt not that before you have encompassed the wall seven times, an impression will be made."*

of the New Testament into Biblical Hebrew has been completed by the Society, and the whole of the first edition has been circulated amongst the Jews at home and abroad, who have generally received it with a readiness and candour which is truly encouraging.

* For a further account of the proceedings and success of the London Society our readers are referred to their two last Reports, to the Jewish Expositor for the two last years, and to "A Letter, addressed

to the Right Rev. the Lord Bishop of St. David's, dated Moscow,
February 1818, by the Rev. Lewis Way, of Stansted Park, Sussex,"
who, in company with the Rev. Nehemiah Solomon, a converted Jew,
recently ordained to the ministry in the church of England, has travelled from Holland to Russia, and from thence to the Crimea, for the
sole purpose of ascertaining the present state of the Jews, and of dis-
tributing the Hebrew Testament amongst them.

All the publications of the London Society are to be had at their
house, No 10, Wardrobe Place, Doctors' Commons.

CHAPTER XL.

General character of the Jews, moral and literary.—Of the number of
this people now existing.—Concluding Reflections.

THE Jews, notwithstanding the calamities they
have so long endured, still look down upon all
nations, and continue to claim the partial kindness
and protection of heaven. The miracles, performed
in favour of the first Hebrews, inspired their
descendants with a contempt for those nations which
the Deity never honoured in the same manner.
They are more elated with the advantages granted
to their ancestors, than humiliated by the calamities
which they have endured since their dispersion.[*]

We may number among the most striking traits
which designate the Jewish character, the wonderful
uniformity of views that appear to have influenced
the actions of this extraordinary people through the
course of so many ages.[†] The Rabbinists, which
form the bulk of the nation in different countries,
agree in their dogmas, rites, and religious habits;
because no religion establishes such an uniformity
in doctrine as the Mosaic, which, joined to the traditions of the doctors, regulates with the utmost
minuteness every thing which respects life. These
people, wherever dispersed, have carried with them
their language and religion, and abandoned none of
the customs but those which they could not preserve.
Even climate has had scarcely any effect upon them,

---

[*] Basnage, p 748   Gregoire on the Reformation of the Jews,
p. 37.

[†] Essay on the Commercial Character of the Jews, p. 5.

because their manner of life counteracts and weakens its influence. Difference of periods and countries has, therefore, strengthened their character, instead of altering its original traits.*

The Jews, since their final expulsion from Palestine, have universally attached themselves to traffic for a subsistence. Being generally prohibited from acquiring and cultivating land, and interdicted from following trades and professions, the objects of their industry have been limited, and they compelled to confine themselves to commerce. The political state of the European powers in the middle ages furnished them with many, and even lawful means, of enriching themselves. Buying and selling were occupations confined exclusively to them ; and they conducted the whole retail trade in Europe,* espe-

* The author of the Letters of certain Jews to Voltaire asserts, that " the Jews, being dispersed in different nations, have assumed their character. A Portuguese Jew of Bourdeaux," says he, " and a German Jew of Metz, appear both to be absolutely different."— But the learned author, from whose work on the Reformation of the Jews the above remarks are extracted, observes, " I allow this may be the case in some shades ; the usual consequence of disparity of fortune, poverty and opulence, luxury and misery.—But by searching historical documents we shall find, that, unless in the above respects, the Jewish nation has ever been the most like itself at all times, both in belief and usages.

" These people, however," says our author, " have been modified by their dispersion ; but this modification extends only to two objects, their obstinate attachment to their belief, which they abandoned with so much facility in ancient times, and that spirit of avarice which seems to be their ruling passion." Commerce has introduced a remarkable change in their morals. But even commerce, which tends to efface national characters, and to render them perfectly alike, has scarcely made any impression on those of the Hebrew people.—*Gregoire on the Reformation of the Jews*, p. 34—36.

* It has been adduced in proof of this assertion, that the Jews have only applied themselves to commerce since their dispersion ; that

cially in Germany. They improved the opportunities afforded them of acquiring wealth; and their opulence having awakened the avarice and jealousy of their enemies, interest conspired with superstition to endeavour their destruction. Being continually persecuted and stript of their riches, they found it essential to their existence to oppose oppression by fraud. These acquired habits were continued from age to age, and all the energy of their minds directed to the pursu't f gain. In consequence of which their usurious practices increased the public hatred, and excited fresh persecutions.

" It would, however," says a celebrated author, " be highly unjust to imagine, that the whole Hebrew nation are a people destitute of principles and good morals. We find a number of striking exceptions among the Jews of Portugal, Italy, France, and above all Holland, where, for two centuries, not one of them has been condemned to death ; among the Jews of Germany, Amsterdam, Berlin, and even in Lorrain ; among those in the English colonies, where many of them, by their good conduct, have attracted the notice of government; and if we attend to the general prejudice entertained against them, we must allow, that the Jews who meet with esteem are undoubtedly worthy of it."*

while in Palestine there never was a people more attached to agriculture. The sacred history speaks of the trading fleets of Solomon, but no others can be mentioned: the genius of that great prince created them; and we find they were not continued by any of his successors. Among the Hebrews there was always very little circulation, and little barter; their law appears to have been almost directly contrary to the spirit of commerce.—*Gregoire on the Reformation of the Jews,* p. 106.

* Gregoire on the Reformation of the Jews, p. 40.

Another late author remarks, that " the Jews on many accounts are entitled to a very high degree of esteem, from their general character and deportment. Their charities to the poor of their own communion are immense; and their peculiar isolated situation through the world, in the midst of strangers, has drawn the bonds of affection towards one another more close. Their care to adjust their differences in civil concerns amicably among themselves is edifying; and let it not be forgotten, that, if on any account they are justly censurable, our unworthy treatment of them may have forced them into the very acts which we condemn."*

In the midst of their calamities and depression, the Jews have all along paid some attention to their language and religion; but dispersed as they are, and without a country of their own, they cannot be expected to have such national establishments. as universities; yet in almost every considerable town on the continent, where they reside in any great numbers, schools† are formed under the auspices of their presiding or dominant rabbies, who confer titles on their scholars, or on others who deserve them. They appear to have two degrees, analogous

---

* Adam's Religious World Displayed, vol. i. p. 80.

† They formerly established the celebrated academies of Jafna, Tiberias, Jerusalem, Lydda, Cesarea, Sephora in Galilee, Pheruty, Bitterah near Shibour, Sora, Nahardea, Pundebita, Lunel, Alexandria, and at a later period those of Sapheta, Thessalonica, Prague, Fez, Cracow, Rome, Bologna, Vienna, and Augsburg. In the present century, since their condition is ameliorated, we find them establishing schools in Germany, and other places; and making great improvements in literature. The following are their most distinguished academies in the present day; viz. Salonichi, Fez, Padua, Amsterdam, Rome.

to, and most probably taken from the usages at universities; the one rabbi, nearly equivalent to A. B. and the other Morenu Rab, answering to doctor. These appear to be of modern institution, and to have commenced about the year 1420; previous to which the latter term is not found; and the distinction is supposed to have become necessary, in order to prevent the irregular conducting of marriages and divorces, which every one presumed to do, in consequence of the title of rabbi, although not sufficiently informed, or qualified for the office. The origin of these schools was evidently the sanhedrim in the temple; by whose determination the laws were explained, and all the Mosaic institutions were reduced to minute and actual practice. The form, period, and manner of all ceremonies and observances were by them established, and handed down to successive sanhedrims, who, as intricate circumstances and questions arose, gradually enlarged the code, and provided for both extraordinary and ordinary situations.*

An ingenious author, who is said to be of Jewish origin,† has, however, observed, that " the entire system of Hebrew education is inimical to the progress of the human mind. Dark and stationary in ignorance, or bewildered with intricate super-

* Adam's Religious World Displayed, vol i. p. 57.

† M. Berr Isaac Berr, a celebrated literary Jew, in a letter addressed to his brethren, 1791, observes, " we have been in a manner compelled to abandon the pursuit of all moral and physical sciences, of all sciences in short, which tend to the improvement of the mind, in order to devote ourselves entirely to commerce, to be enabled to gather as much money as would ensure protection, and satisfy the rapacity of our persecutors —*Transactions of the Sanhedrim of Paris*, p. 14.

stition, their modes of life are little favourable to
forming a taste for the productions of nature and
art; and the sole occupation permitted them, the
art of acquiring wealth, extinguishes their bolder
and prominent passions.* Men of learning among
the Jews are obliged to encounter numerous obstacles; and their most malignant and powerful
enemies are found among their domestic associates.
If a literary Christian is matured at thirty, a literary
Jew can scarcely be matured at forty. They have,
therefore, addicted themselves to those studies which
have little connexion with the manners of men.
They have had severe metaphysicians, and industrious
naturalists; and have excelled in the practice of
medicine. But in polite letters they have had few
literary characters of eminence. Sensible that they
do not at present bear chains under tyrants, they
feel grateful that they exist under men; but the
energies of glory die in inertion, and honour is
strangled by the silken cord of commerce."

The Hebrew nation are at present scattered over
the face of the habitable globe. They are numerous in some parts of Asia, particularly the
Turkish dominions. Various countries in Africa
contain a large number, as Egypt and Ethiopia;
and it is computed, that there are four hundred
thousand in Morocco, Algiers, and Fez.† They
are said to be more numerous in Poland than any
part of Europe; and have been estimated at seven

---

* D'Israeli's Vaurien, or Sketches of the Times, vol. ii. p. 245—
250.

* Boissi's Dissertations Critiques, &c.

hundred thousand.* It is calculated that there are about one hundred thousand Jews in France and Italy,† Their number in Westphalia is estimated at eighteen thousand.

The Jewish population in the world is computed to be three millions, one of which resides in the Turkish empire, in Europe and Asia; three hundred thousand in Persia, China, India, and Tartary; and one million seven hundred thousand in the rest of Europe, Africa, and America.‡

The history of the Jews exhibits a melancholy picture of human wretchedness and depravity. On one hand we contemplate the lineal descendants of the chosen people of God, forfeiting their inestimable privileges by rejecting the glory of Israel, and involving themselves in the most terrible calamities; condemned to behold the destruction of their city and temple; expelled their native country; dispersed through the world; by turns persecuted by Pagans, Christians, and Mahometans; continually duped by impostors, yet still rejecting the true Messiah.

On the other hand, we see the Christian world enveloped in darkness and ignorance; and the

---

* Gregoire's Histoire, &c. The Marquis de Salvo in his Travels in 1806, observes, that "without the Israelites the stranger in Lithuania would find it impossible to travel, or even exist; it seemed as if the government itself, the lands, productions, houses, all, in short, were in their possession."

† Transactions of the Sanhedrim.

‡ This is the calculation made by Basnage, when he concluded his history. But Gregoire has observed, that since that epoch they have experienced no great revolution by war, and we may increase this number by one half, which will give four millions five hundred thousand persons."—*Essay on the Reformation of the Jews,* p. 67..

professed disciples of the benevolent Redeemer
violating the fundamental precepts of the Gospel;
assuming a shew of piety as a mask for avarice, and
a pretence for pillaging an unhappy people. If
from the west we turn to the east, we shudder over
similar scenes of horror; wherever the Mahometan
banner is erected, contempt and misery await the
Jews. In short, their history exhibits all the wild
fury of fanaticism; the stern cruelty of avarice;
a succession of massacres; a repetition of plunders;
shade without light; a dreary wilderness, unen-
livened with one spot of verdure.*

Still, however, in traversing the desert, a wonderful object arrests our attention, and the feelings
of indignation and compassion are suspended by
astonishment while we contemplate the "bush
burning with fire, and not consumed,"—a helpless
race of men, whom all nations have endeavoured to
exterminate, subsisting during ages of unrelenting
persecution; and though dispersed in all nations,
still in all countries preserving their own customs
and religious rites; connected with each other by

* Such has been the state of the Jews for a series of ages. But
in the last and present century their condition has been greatly ameliorated in various parts of Europe. "Christians," says Dr. Buchanan,
" in all countries begin to consider, that the *indignation against the
holy people* is nearly accomplished. Many events declare it. The
indignation of man is relaxing. The prophecies have been fulfilled
regarding it. The great crime at Calvary has been punished by all
nations: and we now hear the words of the prophet addressing us,
" Comfort ye, comfort ye my people, saith your God; speak ye comfortably to Jerusalem, and cry unto her, that her warfare is accomplished. that her iniquity is pardoned," Isaiah xl. i. This is the
divine command. And behold, Christians begin now, for the first
time, " to speak comfortably to Jerusalem."—*Buchanan's Researches
in Asia.* p. 210.

a community of sentiments, of antipathies, and pursuits, yet separated by a wonderful destination from the general mass of mankind.

The preservation of the Jews as a distinct people, is an event unparalleled in the annals of history. To use the animated language of a modern writer*, of their own nation, " Braving all kinds of torments, the pangs of death, the still more terrible, pangs of life, we have withstood the impetuous torrent of time, sweeping indiscriminately in its course, nations, religions, and countries. What is become of those celebrated empires whose very name still excites our admiration by the ideas of splendid greatness, attached to them, and whose power embraced the whole surface of the known globe? They are only remembered as monuments of the vanity of human greatness. Rome and Greece are no more ; their descendants, mixed with other nations, have lost even the traces of their origin ; while a population of a few millions of men, so often subjugated, stands the test of thirty revolving centuries, and the fiery ordeal of fifteen centuries of persecution. We still preserve laws which were given to us in the first days of the world, in the infancy of nature. The last followers of a religion which had embraced the universe have disappeared these fifteen centuries, and our temples are still

* M. Michael Berr's "Appeal to the Justice of Kings and Nations," written and published at Strasburg in 1801, and cited in the Transactions of the Parisian Sanhedrim. This learned author is counsellor-at law, member of several academies, and deputy for the department of la Seine. He still continues to exert all his talents in defence of the rights and interests of the Jews, whom he proved, in the above work, entitled to the benevolence of all sovereigns.

standing. We alone have been spared by the undis-
criminating hand of time, like a column left standing
amidst the wreck of worlds, and the ruins of nature.
The history of this people connects present times
with the first ages of the world, by the testimony it
bears of the existence of those early periods. It
begins at the cradle of mankind, and its remnants
are likely to be preserved to the very day of universal
destruction.",

"The Jews," says a late Christian author, "are
a living and continual miracle, continuing to subsist
as a distinct and peculiar race for upwards of three
thousand years, and even in the midst of other
nations; flowing forward in a full and continued
stream, like the waters of the Rhone, without
mixing with the waves of the expansive lake through
which the passage lies to the ocean of eternity."*

The preservation of this extraordinary people
during their calamitous dispersion exhibits the faith-
fulness of the Deity in fulfilling his gracious promise,
that, "when they are in the land of their enemies, he
will not cast them away, nor destroy them utterly,"†
and, "I am with thee, saith the Lord, to save thee;
though I make a full end of all the nations whither
I have scattered thee, yet I will not make a full end
of thee, but will correct thee in measure,"‡ &c.
The care of Divine Providence is wonderfully displayed in saving the outcasts of Israel from utter
extermination, while groaning under the most furious
intolerance.§

---

* Adam's Religious World Displayed, vol. i. p. 16.
† Leviticus xxxiii. 44.   ‡ Jeremiah xxx 11.
§ " We ought above all," says a Jewish writer, " to return our

Though, from the destruction of Jerusalem to the sixteenth century, there are few countries in which they have not been successively banished, recalled, and again expelled; yet they have never been banished from one country without finding an asylum in another.

The exemption of the Jews from the common fate of nations, affords a striking proof of the truth of the sacred scriptures. They are, as was foretold, dispersed over the habitable globe, being themselves the depositories of those oracles in which their own unbelief and consequent sufferings are clearly predicted. " Had the Jews," says Pascal, " been all converted, we should have had none but suspected witnesses; had they been all destroyed, we should have had no witnesses at all." The exact accomplishment of our Saviour's prediction respecting the destruction of their city and temple, and the calamities they have endured since their dispersion, have furnished every age with the strongest arguments for the truth of the Christian religion. One of the great designs of their being preserved and continued a distinct people appears to be, that their singular destiny might confirm the divine authority of the Gospel, which they reject; and that they might strengthen the faith of others in those sacred truths, to which they refuse to yield their own assent.

The future conversion of the Jews has been the subject of various works published in Europe in the last, and especially since the commencement of the

thanks to Providence, who has not suffered that the aged tree should be torn up by the roots, though it has often permitted that its branches should severely suffer."

present century.* Many pious and learned men
have supposed that they will not only be converted
to the Christian religion, but restored to Palestine,
and placed in a state more splendid and glorious than
ever. In support of this opinion it is argued, that
they never have received that abundance of temporal
and spiritual blessings, which.it was predicted they
should enjoy after their return from captivity;—that
the promises relate to the twelve tribes,.as well'as
those of Judah and Benjamin ;—that a double
return is predicted by several prophets ;. and that
those who lived after the Babylonian captivity have
foretold their restoration in similar terms with those
who preceded them. The concurring testimony,
which arises from the state of the Jews in the world,
and the expectation they entertain of being restored
to their own land, have also been adduced in support
of this opinion.†

The prophecies, however, which are alleged in
order to prove the return of the Hebrew nation to
Palestine, can only be completely explained by the
events which accomplish them. " Over the Jews as
well as us revelation extends its majestic veil."

* Dr. Hartley, Dr. Priestley, and others, have written in defence
of the restoration of the Jews to their native country. At a later
period Mr. Faber has published a work on this subject, in which he
adduces various passages from the prophets, with a view to show,
that after a period of the most terrible political convulsions which the
world ever witnessed, the Jews will be restored to Palestine, partly in
a converted, and partly in an unconverted state; that the ten tribes
will be afterwards converted and restored, and with the tribe of Judah
united under one head, the king Messiah, and reign with him a thousand years in high pre-eminence among the nations of the earth.
Then modern Judaism and Popery, Paganism and Mahometanism,
will be exchanged for the pure and undefiled religion of the Gospel.

† Hartley's Observations on Man, vol. iii. p. 373.

But while the operations of Divine Providence are rapidly unfolding the volume of predictions, the sacred page has already clearly opened a source of consolation to those who are anxiously waiting for the redemption of Israel. An inspired apostle has assured us, that the Jews, " the natural branches of the Olive Tree,"* though now broken off by unbelief, will " be grafted in again," and participate with the Gentiles in the blessings resulting from faith in Jesus the Messiah. Persuaded then of this, on the ground of Divine Revelation, and commiserating a people who have been, during so many ages, exiles from their own land, and exposed, as this history has fully shewn, to numberless calamities attendant on banishment, the Christian reader cannot surely close this volume more suitably than with a resolution to pray frequently and fervently for their promised conversion, and with a generous desire to enrol his own name amongst those of the subscribers to the " London Society for promoting Christianity amongst the Jews ;"—a Society whose views are pure, disinterested, and extensive ; and whose efforts, it seems highly probable, the God of Abraham, Isaac, and Jacob, will in the present age honour, as the means of bringing descendants of those illustrious patriarchs, to the acknowledgment of the "truth as it is in Jesus," and " the obedience of faith."

* See Romans xi. 24.

APPENDIX.

THE ten tribes who were carried captive by the king of Assyria have been lost for more than two thousand years. Various conjectures have been formed, both by Jews and Christians, respecting the place of their residence;* some of which shall be briefly mentioned.

Menasses Ben Israel, in a work, styled, " The Hope of Israel," has attempted to prove, that the American natives were the descendants of the ten tribes. This opinion has been adopted by some Christian writers, particularly by James Adair, Esq. a trader with the Indians, and resident in the country for forty years. He was a most careful observer of their whole economy, both public and private, and had the best opportunity of knowing it, without much danger of deception. In a work, entitled, " The History of the American Indians," he concludes his observations on their origin and descent as follows : " From the most exact observations I could make in the long time I traded among the Indian Americans, I was forced to believe them lineally descended from the Israelites, either while they were a maritime power, or soon after the general captivity ; the last, however, is the most probable. Had the nine tribes and a half of Israel, which were carried off by Shalmaneser, king of Assyria, and settled in Media, continued there long, it is very probable, by intermarrying with the natives, and from their natural fickleness and proneness to idolatry and the force of example, that they would have adopted and bowed before the gods of the,

---

* For far more satisfactory observations, than this Appendix furnishes, respecting the places of residence of the descendants of the ten tribes, see Dr. Buchanan's Christian Researches.

Medes and Assyrians, and have carried them along with them; but there is not a trace of this idolatry among the Indians." Hence he argues, that the ten tribes, who were the forefathers of the Americans, soon advanced eastward from Assyria, and reached their settlements in the new continent before the destruction of the first temple.*

In order to prove that the American Indians are descended from the ten tribes, Mr. Adair adduces various arguments; a sketch of his mode of reasoning is as follows:

1st. All the Israelites were divided into tribes, and had chiefs over them, so the Indians divide themselves; each tribe forms a little community within the nation. As the nation hath its particular symbol, so each tribe hath the badge from which it is denominated. The sachem of each tribe is a necessary party in conveyances and treaties, to which he affixes the mark of his tribe. If we go from nation to nation among them, we shall not find one, who doth not lineally distinguish himself by his respective family. The genealogical names, which they assume, are derived either from the names of those animals whereof the cherubim are said in revelation to be compounded, or from such creatures as are most similar to them. The Indians, however, bear no religious respect to the animals from whence they derive their name; on the contrary, they kill them when opportunity serves. When we consider that these savages have been above twenty centuries without the use of letters to carry down their traditions, it cannot reasonably be expected, that they should still retain the identical names of their primogenial tribes; their principal customs corresponding with those of the Israelites sufficiently clears the subject. Besides, as hath been hinted, they call some of their tribes by the names of the cherubinical figures that were carried on the four principal standards of Israel.

2nd. By a strict permanent divine precept, the Hebrew

* Adair's History of the American Indians.

nation were ordered to worship at Jerusalem, Jehovah, the true and living God, who, by the Indians, is styled Yohewah. The ancient heathens, it is well known, worshipped a plurality of gods, as various as the countries they inhabited ; and as numerous with some as the days of the year. But the Indian Americans pay their religious devoir to the " great beneficent, supreme, holy spirit of fire," who resides, (as they think) above the clouds, and on earth also with unpolluted people. He is with them the sole author of all animated and vegetable nature. They do not pay the least perceivable worship to any image, or to dead persons, neither to the celestial luminaries, nor evil spirits, nor any created being whatsoever.[*]

3d. Agreeably to the theocracy, or divine government of Israel, the Indians think the Deity to be the immediate head of their state. All the nations of Indians are exceedingly intoxicated with religious pride, and have an inexpressible contempt of the white people. They used to call us in their war orations, the accursed people. But they flatter themselves with the name of the beloved people, because their supposed ancestors, as they affirm, were under the immediate government of the Deity, who was present with them in a very peculiar manner, and directed them by prophets, while the rest of the world were aliens and outlaws to the covenant. When the old Archimagus, or any one of their Magi, is persuading the people at their religious solemnities to a strict observance of the old beloved, or divine speech, he always calls them the beloved or holy people, agreeably to the Hebrew epithet Ammi, (my people) during the theocracy of Israel. He urges them with great energy to imitate their virtuous ancestors, and flourishes upon their beloved land, which flowed with milk and honey. It is their opinion of the theocracy, or that God chose them out of all the rest of mankind, as his peculiar people, which alike animates

* Adair, p. 15.

both the White; Jew; and the Red American with that steady hatred against all the world except themselves, and renders them hated or despised by all.

4th. The Indian language and dialects appear to have the very idiom and genius of the Hebrew. Their words and sentences are expressive, concise, emphatical, sonorous, and bold ; and often both in letters and signification are synonymous with the Hebrew language.*

5th. They count time after the manner of the Hebrews. They divide the year into spring, summer, autumn, or the falling of the leaf, and winter. They number their years from any of these four periods, for they have no name for a year; and they subdivide these, and count the year by lunar months, like the Israelites, who reckoned by moons. The number and regular periods of the Indians' religious feasts is a good historical proof that they counted time by and observed a weekly sabbath long after their arrival on the American continent. They began their year at the first appearance of the first new moon of the vernal equinox, according to the ecclesiastical year of Moses.

6th. In conformity to and after the manner of the Jews, the Indian Americans have their prophets, high priests, and others of a religious order. As the Jews had a sanctum sanctorum, so have all the Indian nations. There they deposit their consecrated vessels, none of the laity daring to approach this sacred place; the Indian tradition says, that their ancestors were possessed of an extraordinary divine spirit, by which they foretold things future, and controuled the common course of nature, and this they transmitted to their offspring, provided they obeyed the sacred laws annexed to it. Their pontifical office descends by inheritance to their children. Mr. Adair also traces a resemblance between the dress of the Indian Archimagus, when he officiates in making the supposed holy fire for the

---

* Mr. Adair has adduced a number of examples to shew the similarity of the Hebrew and Indian languages.

yearly atonement for sin, and that of the Jewish high priest.*

7th. The ceremonies of the Indians in their religious worship are more after the Mosaic Institution than of Pagan imitation, which could not be if the majority of the old nation were of heathenish descent. They are utter strangers to all the gestures practised by Pagans in their religious rites. According to Mr. Adair, the American Indians have, like the Hebrews, a sacred ark, in which are kept various holy vessels. " It is," says he, " worthy of notice that they never place the ark on the ground, nor sit on the bare earth while they are carrying it against the enemy. On hilly ground where stones are plenty they place it on them; but in level land upon short logs, always resting themselves on the same materials. They have also as strong a faith of the power and holiness of their ark, as ever the Israelites retained of theirs. The Indian ark is deemed so sacred and dangerous to touch, either by their own sanctified warriors or the spoiling enemy, that neither of them 'dare meddle with it on any account. It is not to be handled by any, except the chieftain and his waiter, under penalty of incurring great evil; nor would the most inveterate enemy dare to touch it. The leader virtually acts the part of a priest of war, pro tempore, in imitation of the Israelites fighting under the divine military banner.†

8th. The Israelites had cities of refuge for those who killed a person unawares. In like manner each of the Indian nations have either a house or town of refuge, which is a sure asylum to protect a manslayer or the unfortunate captive if they once enter into it. In every Indian nation there are several peaceable towns, called old beloved, ancient holy, and white towns, which appear to have been formerly towns of refuge.

9th. Mr. Adair proceeds to point out the resemblance between the festivals, fasts, and religious rites of the Hebrews, and those of the American Indians. He ob-

* Adair, p. 81.   † Adair, p. 162.

serves, that before the latter go to war, they have many
preparatory sacrifices of purification and fasting. He
points out the similarity in their daily sacrifice; their
ablutions and anointings; their abstinence from unclean
things; their marriages, divorces, and punishment for
adultery; their several punishments; their burial of the
dead; their mourning for the deceased, and various other
particulars. He then proceeds to adduce his last argument for the origin of the Indian Americans, from their
own traditions, from the accounts of our English authors,
and from the testimonies which the Spanish writers have
given concerning the primitive inhabitants of Peru and
Mexico.

INDEX.

A

thirteenth century till they were expelled from the empire, 269—278; their condition during the same periods more tolerable in Italy, though they were sometimes persecuted, 280—286; exact accomplishment of prophecy in their fate during the middle ages, 287—291; account of those in the east from the thirteenth cen. tury to 1665, 292—304; of Zabathai Tzevi, a false Messiah who appeared 1666, 305—316; account of their number and condition in various parts of Africa, 317—327. Of those in Germany, in the sixteenth and seventeenth centuries, 328—335; their flourishing state in Poland under John Sobieski in the seventeenth century, 337; particulars respecting them in various parts of Germany and Poland, 337—346; account of those in Italy from the sixteenth to the eighteenth century, 347—359; they attempt in vain to obtain a settlement and a toleration in Spain and Portugal, and assume the mask of Christianity, 360—367. Of their settlement in Holland, and the learned men who appeared among them in the seventeenth century, 370—382; of their return to England in the seventeenth century, 385; their state in the kingdom from that period to the nineteenth century, 386—396. Favourable change in their condition in Germany and other countries during the eighteenth and nineteenth centuries, 397—412. Account of those in France from their establishment in Metz to the nineteenth century, 413—431; in Holland, in the eighteenth and nineteenth centuries, 432—437; of their state in the Turkish dominions, and other countries in Asia in the eighteenth and nineteenth centuries, 438—454; of those in various parts of America, 455—467; of their synagogue worship, religious rites and ceremonies, 468—483. Account of their religious tenets, and of the sects which still exist among them, 484—497. Of the dissimulation of many of this people who have professed Christianity; and of the efforts which are now used in England to effect their conversion, 530—533. Of their character, moral and literary, 544—548; of their number, 549. Concluding reflections, 549—555.

ADVERTISEMENT.

THE following " History of the Jews," by Mrs.
Hannah Adams of America, is now printed in
England, with that Lady's kind permission, at the
expense and for the benefit of the " London
Society for promoting Christianity amongst the
Jews;" and the hope is warmly cherished, that
when British Christians shall have been made more
fully acquainted, through the medium of this publication, with the calamities which have befallen
the Jews since their last dispersion, such sympathy
will be excited, as to stimulate them to co-operate
zealously with the above Society, in its benevolent
endeavours to impart the knowledge of the crucified
Jesus, the true Messiah, to that long oppressed
nation, whose past sufferings, present degradation,
and future glory, are equally foretold by the
prophets of the Old Testament, and the apostles
of the New. It is proper to remark, that a few
alterations were deemed expedient, in the present
edition.

THE

HISTORY OF THE JEWS,

FROM THE

DESTRUCTION OF JERUSALEM

TO THE

PRESENT TIME.

———◆———

BY HANNAH ADAMS,

OF BOSTON, AMERICA.

" And the Lord shall scatter thee among all people from the one
end of the earth even unto the other;—and among these nations
shalt thou find no ease, neither shall the sole of thy foot have rest."
Deut. xxviii. 64, 65.

London:

Printed by A. MACINTOSH, Brick Lane, Spitalfields:
SOLD AT THE LONDON SOCIETY HOUSE,
10, WARDROBE PLACE, DOCTORS' COMMONS;
AND BY OGLES, DUNCAN, AND COCHRAN, PATERNOSTER ROW;
SEELEY, FLEET STREET; AND HATCHARD, PICCADILLY.

1818.

Page

FINIS.

MACINTOSH, Printer, London Society's Office, Spitalfields, London.